French

Without the Fuss

Want to take your French further?

Living Language® makes it easy with a wide range of programs that will suit your particular needs.

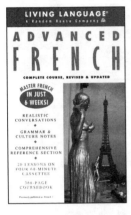

ADVANCED FRENCH

ISBN: 0-609-60486-4 • $29.95 / C$42.00

The perfect follow-up to *French Without the Fuss*—*Advanced French* will help you master the art of French conversation. The program teaches advanced vocabulary, idiomatic expressions, and grammar while introducing you to the finer points of French culture. There are 20 lessons on four 60-minute cassettes, plus a 352-page coursebook.

Also available in Spanish. Coursebooks are also sold separately for $6.95 / C$9.50.

SKILL BUILDER: FRENCH VERBS

ISBN: 0-609-60443-0 • $29.95 / C$42.00

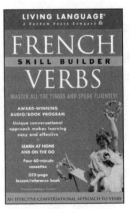

An award-winning program that will help you master verbs—the key to fluency. This is not just a book full of verb charts, but a program that teaches you how to USE verbs. There's also a handy grammar summary for easy reference. There are 40 lessons on four 60-minute cassettes, plus a 352-page coursebook.

Also available in Spanish, Italian, and German.
Coursebooks are also sold separately for $6.95 / C$9.50.

THE FEARLESS INTERNATIONAL FOODIE CONQUERS THE CUISINE OF FRANCE, ITALY, SPAIN & LATIN AMERICA

ISBN: 0-609-81113-4 • $11.00 / C$17.00

The ultimate guide to help you conquer the fine art of international dining, whether abroad or in your own neighborhood! Each section begins with an overview of the cuisine followed by typical ingredients and dishes, from appetizers through desserts. There is an easy-to-follow pronunciation key, loads of fascinating culture notes, and a helpful glossary on spices, sauces, and more!

Also available: *The Fearless International Foodie Conquers Pan-Asian Cuisine*

AVAILABLE AT YOUR LOCAL BOOKSTORE OR BY CALLING 1-800-726-0600

For a complete list of Living Language titles, please visit our Web site at
www.livinglanguage.com

French

Without the Fuss

BY

Jenny Barriol

LIVING LANGUAGE®
A Random House Company

AUTHOR'S ACKNOWLEDGMENT

*To Zvjezdana Vrzić, editor of this book, all my thankfulness
for her work and help to bring this book to completion,
and to everyone else who contributed to it.*

Published by Living Language, A Random House Company, New York, New York.
Living Language is a member of the Random House Information Group.

Random House, Inc. New York, Toronto, London, Sydney, Auckland

www.livinglanguage.com

Living Language and colophon are registered trademarks of Random House, Inc.

Manufactured in the United States of America.

Layout and graphics by Barbara M. Bachman

Illustrations by Norman Bendell

ISBN 0-609-81061-8

10 9 8 7 6 5 4 3 2

First Edition

PUBLISHER'S ACKNOWLEDGMENT

Thanks to the Living Language team: Lisa Alpert, Elizabeth Bennett, Sophie Chin, Denise DeGennaro, Pat Ehresmann, Fernando Galeano, Mary Lee, Suzanne McQuade, Lisa Montebello, Marina Padakis, Erik Riesenberg, Linda Schmidt, Helen Tang, and Christopher Warnasch. Special thanks to the dedicated reviewers, Evelyne Pommateau Tessler and Christine Boucher.

CONTENTS

WHAT'S GOING ON IN THE DIALOGUES	WHAT WORDS YOU'LL LEARN	WHAT STRUCTURES YOU'LL KNOW

WHAT'S GOING ON IN THE DIALOGUES	WHAT WORDS YOU'LL LEARN	WHAT STRUCTURES YOU'LL KNOW

WHAT'S GOING ON IN THE DIALOGUES	WHAT WORDS YOU'LL LEARN	WHAT STRUCTURES YOU'LL KNOW

WHAT'S GOING ON IN THE DIALOGUES	WHAT WORDS YOU'LL LEARN	WHAT STRUCTURES YOU'LL KNOW

WHAT'S GOING ON IN THE DIALOGUES	WHAT WORDS YOU'LL LEARN	WHAT STRUCTURES YOU'LL KNOW

Lesson 14: PRÉVERT'S SONG • 249

What to Buy? A guy looks for the right jazz CD for his girlfriend *At the Concert* A group of friends enjoy some good music	• **It's music to my ears:** Let's talk about music and the French *chanson* • **Let's celebrate!:** Talking about events in life worth celebrating • **Give them some applause!:** Going to a concert	• **What will be, will be:** The future tense of some irregular verbs • **I could have been somebody:** Using *somebody* and *nobody* in French • **I scream, you scream:** More irregular verbs—*offrir* (to offer) and its look-alikes • **It's worth the effort:** Using the expressions *cela vaut* (it's worth) and *il vaut mieux* (it's better)

Lesson 15: "THE AMERICAS" HOTEL • 271

A Charming Hotel A couple checks in at the hotel . . . *Finally, Some Quiet!* . . . and has a "quiet" breakfast on the terrace	• **Closed for vacation:** Learning the French you'll need in hotels and on vacation • **Head and shoulders . . . :** Names for body parts	• **I scream, you scream:** The irregular verbs *paraître* (to seem), *connaître* (to know), and *mettre* (to put, to place) • **The way we were:** A new tense to talk about how things used to be • **To whom it may concern:** Putting sentences together using relative pronouns • **Strut your stuff!** (review)

xiii

CONTENTS

WELCOME!

So you want to learn some *français*? But you don't want to do it by just memorizing long verb charts or ever-handy stock phrases like "Jeeves, please serve the mutton to the ambassador at eight." If that's the case, then you've come to the right place! *Bienvenue!* Welcome!

French Without the Fuss will help you learn as quickly and easily as possible, and the best part is—you'll have fun along the way. You'll have a chance to hear real talk, the kind you might actually hear on the street and not just read in textbooks. And you won't need a crash course in grammar jargon before you start. We've tried to make this book as accessible and user-friendly as possible. Of course, this doesn't mean you'll just wake up one morning fluent in French. The bad news is: you **will** have to do some studying, but the good news is: it **won't** be dry and boring. That, you can count on.

So, what's *French Without the Fuss* all about? Well, you'll start off with an introduction to the sounds of the language. French is fairly easy that way—what you see is pretty much what you get, so you should be able to start speaking right off the bat. Then we really get down to business with 15 lessons and an hour-long audio CD to give you plenty of listening and speaking practice. There are appendices, too, for quick reference if you get stuck, and a two-way glossary where you can look up any word in the book.

To make things easy, all the lessons have the same structure, and it's not just any structure—it's been scientifically designed to help you learn most effectively. Yes, we have the technology! Here's the basic layout of each lesson:

COMING UP...
Get a brief overview of what you'll learn in the lesson.

LOOKING AHEAD
Get ready to listen to the lesson's dialogues and get some advance tips to help you follow along.

LET'S WARM UP
Think ahead about the topic of the lesson and learn a few new words so you can get more out of the dialogues.

HEAR...SAY
Listen to a dialogue, try to understand as much as you can, then **read along** and **learn to speak** by repeating the phrases from the audio CD.

HOW'S THAT AGAIN?
Make sure you got the gist of the dialogue.

WORKSHOP
Discover the secrets of the French language; learn about its words and structure.

WORDS TO LIVE BY
Stock up on new words and phrases and get to use them, too.

THE NITTY-GRITTY
Overcome your fear of grammar with simple explanations and plenty of practice.

TAKE IT FOR A SPIN
Practice makes perfect! Try out all the good stuff you've just learned.

LET'S PUT IT IN WRITING
Read all about it! Texts taken from real life help you learn to maneuver through the written word.

TAKE IT UP A NOTCH
Challenge yourself with additional practice that'll really make you think!

STRUT YOUR STUFF!
Put it all together and review what you've learned with more practice.

CRIB NOTES
Get answers to all your questions, and check the translations of the dialogues.

But that's not all! You'll also get loads of good stuff that will spice up your learning, teach you **how** best to learn a new language, what pitfalls to avoid, and tell you about the culture and customs of the place. All at no extra cost!

TAKE A TIP FROM ME!
Be smart and get the most out of your efforts—you'll get shortcuts, memory tricks, and tips on how to study.

HEADS UP!
Watch for the pitfalls and common mistakes typically made by new learners!

THE FINE PRINT
Get ambitious and learn more about grammar or vocabulary.

WORD ON THE STREET
Talk like a real French person: learn common expressions, idioms, and even slang terms, so you won't sound like an out-of-date textbook.

DID YOU KNOW?
Get in the know by learning about France and the francophone world, its culture and the everyday life of its people. A great place to start not just talking like a French person, but feeling like one, too.

So, that's it! You're ready to start. Good luck, or as the French would say . . . . *Bonne chance!*

BEFORE WE BEGIN...

Before we start, let's talk a little bit about language learning in general. The first thing you need to know is: **You know more than you think!** You don't believe me? Check out some of these words: *avenue, boutique, culture, parent, guide, moment, possible, radio, client.* So? What's the big deal, right? You already know English! Well, as it turns out, this means that you also already know some French because these words are spelled exactly the same and have the same meaning in both languages. They're just pronounced a little differently. And then, to make things **really** easy (despite the adamant disapproval of French purists), French has simply borrowed some words from English. Just look: *baby-sitter, steak, bridge, budget, chewing-gum, cool, e-mail, fast-food, fax, film, Internet, job, lobby, manager, marketing, parking, rock, scooter, shopping, week-end,* and the list goes on.

To be fair, the borrowing works both ways, and we seem to have been much more liberal about adopting words from other languages. Did you know that more than 50 percent of English words take their roots from Romance languages (the family of languages French belongs to)? Absolutely! In fact, the word *absolutely* is a perfect example: in French, it's *absolument.* See? They look pretty similar, don't they? And there are many more words that look only a little different in the two languages, words you should be able to recognize pretty easily. See for yourself:

acteur	actor
adresse	address
appartement	apartment
banane	banana
banque	bank
bicyclette	bicycle
centre	center
cinéma	cinema
favori / favorite	favorite
langue; langage	language
littérature	literature
mariage	marriage
masque	mask
musée	museum
photographe	photographer
ridicule	ridiculous

sexe	sex
signe	sign
titre	title
universel	universal

But French and English don't just have word roots in common. They also share identical or similar word endings. Take a look:

SOME WORD ENDINGS FRENCH AND ENGLISH HAVE IN COMMON

FRENCH	ENGLISH	AS IN . . .
-ion		*conversation* = conversation
-ent		*différent* = different
-i / able		*possible* = possible
-ie	-y	*harmonie* = harmony
-sel	-sal	*universel* = universal
-que	-c(al)	*pratique* = practical
-eur	-or / -er	*acteur* = actor
-ice / -esse	-ess	*actrice* = actress
-cien	-cian	*musicien* = musician

If you're feeling confident now, just wait! There's a lot more to *communication* than just words and grammar. It's amazing how much you can glean from a conversation just by looking at facial expressions and body language. Try this sometime: watch a movie or a sitcom and mute the sound. You'll be surprised by how much you'll be in tune with what's going on even without hearing a single word spoken.

And there's also *la culture* (You guessed it!). Communication happens in context, and the more you know about the daily life of French speakers and their rich history, the more easily you'll be able to read between the lines, get the point, and get your own message across. Don't worry, you're not on your own here either—there'll be plenty of cultural tidbits and information to help you impress (or fool!) even the most discerning locals.

Okay, now that your head is probably bigger than your doorway and you're wondering why you need to study another language in the first place, let's get serious for a moment. The truth is (you might want to sit down for this) that despite how much you already know, you still have to learn and study. That's the bad news . . . unless you're a little on the nerdy side, like me, and you actually get excited when you hear words like "learn" and "study." The good news is that, throughout this book, I'll be there to guide you, as if I were sitting next to you . . . well . . . almost. In any case, I'll be there to help, not just by telling you **what** you need to learn but also by giving you some tips on **how** to do it best and most easily.

Take a Tip from Me!

Here comes my first tip: pace yourself. Try to come up with a work schedule and set goals. Ideally, you should spend a little bit of time on your French every day—sometimes 30 minutes a day will go a lot further than two hours in one sitting. But if you can't manage to find time every day, don't despair. Just try to work regularly and grab a free moment here and there to remind yourself of what you've learned.

Take advantage of your free time—go on the Web and look for Web sites in French, see movies in French (with subtitles is fine), listen to French music, flip through French papers and magazines, etc. Many musicians, actors, filmmakers, painters, and writers from French-speaking countries are mentioned in this book. Check them out! Do anything you like, but do it *en français*! The goal is to get as great and as varied an exposure to the language as possible. Words and expressions have a way of creeping into your memory. The most important thing is to have fun. As I said, French is a lot more than just a language. Francophone cultures are diverse and vibrant . . . and very easy to fall in love with. I'm hoping that's exactly what happens to you. Once it does, the words will come easily . . . .

Take a Tip from Me!

Enough talking . . . . Are you ready? Let's go! *Allons-y!* Let's talk about French pronunciation.

SOUNDING IT OUT IN FRENCH

ABC's

English and French share the same alphabet, even if the pronunciation of the letters is a little different:

THE FRENCH ALPHABET			
a	[ah]	n	[ehn]
b	[beh]	o	[oh]
c	[seh]	p	[peh]
d	[deh]	q	[kü]
e	[uh]	r	[ehr]
f	[ehf]	s	[ehss]
g	[zheh]	t	[teh]
h	[ash]	u	[ü], very sharp
i	[ee]	v	[veh]
j	[zhee]	w	[doo-bluhveh]
k	[kah]	x	[eeks]
l	[ehl]	y	[eegrehk]
m	[ehm]	z	[zehd]

Now that we have the alphabet out of the way, let's spend some time on individual sounds. French spelling is not phonetic, but neither is English, so it shouldn't come as a shock. With a bit of practice and study, you will easily be able to guess the pronunciation of a word. There are rules that will help you out . . . if rules scare you, don't panic! The pronunciation of the words used in this book is indicated in the Glossary, and in the lessons, too, for particularly tricky words. Also, remember that you can always refer back to this section on pronunciation, whenever you need help.

Take a Tip from Me!

When you first begin to speak, do some warmup exercises to loosen your mouth. Say all of the vowels in order (a–e–i–o–u), going from one vowel right into the next, and stretching your mouth as much as possible on each sound. Do this *loudly!* Stand in front of a mirror and watch your mouth as you make each sound. When you're speaking, try to imitate a French speaker—try to feel the language, its melodic intonation. Exaggerate the sounds a little, even, wave your arms around (although you should be careful if you do this in front of native French speakers, as they might think you're making fun of them). Yes, it'll probably feel silly, but silly can be fun, and it will help you loosen up and get over the embarrassment of speaking—aaaaaaaaack!!!—a foreign language! Also, try to get as much listening exercise as you can. I can't stress the importance of listening enough. Hearing the sounds pronounced by a native speaker will help you develop an ear for the language, which will in turn improve the way you speak. Slowly you'll be able to tell if something "just sounds right" or not, and that's your goal.

Take a Tip from Me!

OOHS AND AAHS: FRENCH VOWEL SOUNDS

Basic Vowel Sounds

French (like English) has many vowels and some of them do not exist at all in English. I will simplify things for you and give you approximate pronunciations for their sounds and the most common spellings. Note that this is only a guide; for best pronunciation, there are only three words: listen, listen, and listen.

FRENCH VOWEL SOUNDS		
LETTER	PRONOUNCED AS...	AS IN...
a, à, â	ah (as in f*a*ther)	*chat* (shah), "cat"; *à* (ah), "to"; *pâte* (paht), "dough"
é, er, ez, et	eh (as in b*e*d), but with very tight lips	*été* (eh-teh), "summer"; *aller* (ah-leh), "to go"; *allez* (ah-leh), "Go!"; *ballet* (bah-leh), "ballet" [Be careful not to pronounce the *eh* sound as (eh-ee) at the end of the word.]

LETTER	PRONOUNCED AS...	AS IN...
e + a final pronounced consonant, è, ei, ai, aî	eh (as in _bed_), very relaxed lips	_belle_ (behl), "beautiful"; _père_ (pehr), "father"; _veine_ (vehn), "vein"; _faire_ (fehr), "to do"
e (at the end of the word or without an accent)	uh (as in _above_)	_le_ (luh), "the"; _lever_ (luh-veh), "to lift"
eu, oeu	uh (as in _fur_), but keep your lips very rounded	_feu_ (fuh), "fire"; _coeur_ (kuhr), "heart" [Pronounced with tight lips when no other sound follows (_feu_), but with relaxed lips when other sound / s follow (_coeur_).]
i	ee (as in _beet_)	_ici_ (ee-see), "here"
o, au, eau, ô	oh (as in _caught_)	_mot_ (moh), "word"; _mode_ (mohd), "fashion"; _auteur_ (oh-tuhr), "author"; _eau_ (oh), "water"; _hôtel_ (oh-tehl), "hotel"
ou	oo (as in _tool_)	_fou_ (foo), "crazy"
u	ü (no equivalent), keep your lips rounded as you pronounce _ee_	_tu_ (tü), "you"

Okay, so now that we have our *oohs* and *ahs* in order, what happens when you have two vowels in a row? You get vowel combinations, where the two vowels flow naturally one into the other, as when you say *Oy, vey!*, for instance. Here they are:

FRENCH VOWEL COMBINATIONS		
LETTER	PRONOUNCED AS...	AS IN...
ey, eille,	ehy (as in _hey!_)	_seyant_ (seh-yah[n]), "becoming"; _bouteille_ (boo-tehy), "bottle"
ie	yeh (as in _yes_)	_hier_ (yehr), "yesterday"
oeil	uhy (no equivalent)	_oeil_ (uhy), "eye"
ille	eey (no equivalent)	_fille_ (feey), "girl; daughter"
oi	wah (as in _choir_)	_moi_ (mwah), "me"
oui	(w)ooee (no equivalent)	_Louis_ (l^wooee), "Louis"
oy	wah + y (no equivalent)	_foyer_ (fwah-yeh), "home"
ui	wee (no equivalent)	_lui_ (lwee), "him", "her", "it"

Nasal Vowel Sounds

A note is in order here on nasal vowels, especially since they are one of the most recognizable features of a French accent. In case you're wondering, they're pretty much what their name suggests: the regular vowels discussed above—*ah, eh, oh, uh*—are pronounced "nasally," i.e., the air comes out of your mouth **and** your nose while you're saying them. This happens when an "n" or "m" follows a vowel but is not pronounced fully. Instead, the preceding vowel is made to sound very nasal. There are four nasal vowels in French and they can all be found in a single (and very French!) phrase—*un bon vin blanc* (a good white wine). This is how you would pronounce this phrase: (uh^n boh^n veh^n blah^n). Each time the "n" is not fully pronounced; rather the vowel that precedes it is pronounced "through the nose." Let's look at more examples:

FRENCH NASAL VOWEL SOUNDS		
LETTER	PRONOUNCED AS...	AS IN...
an, en / em	ah^n	*France* (frah^{n}s), "France"; *entrer* (ah^n-treh), "enter"; *emmener* (ah^n-muh-neh), "to take along"
in / im, ain / aim, ein / eim, ien, oin	eh^n	*vin* (veh^n), "wine"; *vain* (veh^n), "vain"; *faim* (feh^n), "hunger"; *sein* (seh^n), "bosom"; *rien* (ryeh^n), "nothing"; *loin* (lweh^n), "far"
on / om, ion	oh^n	*bon* (boh^n), "good"; *tomber* (toh^n-beh), "to fall"; *station* (stah-syoh^n), "station; stop"
un / um	uh^n	*un* (uh^n), "one; a"; *parfum* (pahr-fuh^n), "perfume"

Nasal vowels can be spelled with either an "n" or an "m" following the vowel. This does not make any difference for pronunciation. I will continue marking each nasal vowel throughout the book with a superscript ^{n} after the vowel.

Accents

You may have noticed that certain vowels have accents on them. Let's take a look at what they mean.

FRENCH ACCENTS		
VOWEL	PRONOUNCED AS...	AS IN...
e (without an accent, can be pronounced in three different ways)	—*uh*	*le* (luh), "the"; *lever* (luh-veh), "to lift"
	—short *eh* (followed by silent "r", "z", "t")	*met* (meh), "dish"; *aller* (ah-leh), "to go";
	—silent (at the end of a word)	*signe* (seeny), "sign"
é	closed, tight lips, long *eh* (almost like "ay" but cut off)	*été* (eh-teh), "summer"
è, ê	open, relaxed lips, short *eh*	*scène* (sehn), "scene"; *forêt* (foh-reh), "forest"

There is a little trick that may help you remember when to use "ê." Usually, when a word has an "s" before a "t" in English, as in *forest*, it will have "ê" before "t" in French, as in *forêt*, with the same meaning. You might want to think of the accent as a reminder that there's an "s" missing after the vowel.

There is usually no difference in pronunciation between "a," "à" and "â": it's always *ah*, and the presence of the accent is simply a spelling convention.

PSSST: FRENCH CONSONANT SOUNDS

The good news about consonants is that most of them sound just like they do in English: a "b" is a *b*, and a "d" is a *d*. Other letters that are pronounced the same in French as in English are: "f", "k," "l," "m," "n," "p," "s," "t," "v," and "z." *Pas de problème!* No problem! But here, too, there are a few important rules to remember.

Don't Forget to Gargle! Zee French "R" Is Guttural

In order to pronounce an "r" in French, you need to raise the back of your tongue towards your tonsils, as if you were gargling. Take a look at these French words and let's see how well you can "gargle" the "r":

radio	(rah-dee-oh)	radio
rapide	(rah-peed)	rapid
rare	(rahr)	rare
retour	(ruh-toor)	return
réalité	(reh-ah-lee-teh)	reality

Some Letters Do Double Duty

A few letters are pronounced differently, depending on the letter that follows. The letters "c" and "g" have a hard and soft pronunciation:

- "C" is pronounced *k*, like the "c" in "car," when it comes before "a," "o," and "u" (or another consonant), as in *cave* (kahv). It's pronounced *s*, like the "c" in "cent," when it comes before "e," "i," or "y," as in *cinéma* (see-neh-mah). In words where "c" comes before "a," "o," or "u" (or another consonant), but it still has the "soft" pronunciation, it's written "ç," as in *français* (frahn-seh).
- "G" is pronounced *g*, like the g in "gold," when it comes before "a," "o," or "u," as in *gâteau* (gah-toh). [When "g" is followed by "u," the "u" itself is not pronounced, as in *guerre* (gehr).] It's pronounced *zh*, like the "s" in "mea<u>s</u>ure," when it comes before "e," "i," or "y," as in *âge* (ahzh).

Let's practice:

cave	(kahv)	wine cellar
combien?	(koh^n-byeh^n)	how much?
curieux	(kü-ryuh)	curious
cette	(seht)	this
ciel	(syehl)	sky

cycle	(seekl)	cycle
clé	(kleh)	key
garer	(gah-reh)	to park
golfe	(gohlf)	gulf
guide	(geed)	guide
globe	(glohb)	globe
géant	(zheh-ah^n)	huge
girafe	(zhee-rahf)	giraffe

- "S" is pronounced *s* when it comes at the beginning of a word or before a consonant, as in *salle* (sahl) and *disque* (deesk), but it's pronounced *z* as in "zebra" when it comes between two vowels: *maison* (meh-zohn).
- "X" is pronounced *gz*, like the "x" in "exact," as in *exact* (eh-gzahkt), unless it comes before another consonant, in which case it's pronounced *ks*, like the "x" in "excellent," as in *excellent* (eh-kseh-lahn).
- "T" is generally pronounced *t*, but in the combinations *-tion* and *-tiel*, it's pronounced *s*, as in *national* (nah-syoh-nahl).
- "LL" (double "l") is pronounced *l*, unless it comes between an "i" and an "e," in which case it's usually pronounced *y*, as in *vieille* (vyehy).

Take a Tip from Me!

If you have trouble remembering when a letter is pronounced one way, and when another, pick a word that will remind you. For example, if you're trying to remember when "c" is pronounced *s* and when it's pronounced *k*, remember *cinéma* for the soft "c" sound, and *cave* for the hard "c" sound. When you see a new word, and you're not sure how to pronounce it, just fall back on your examples!

Some Letters Sound Just Plain Different in French

- The letter "h" is always silent in French, as in *hôtel* (oh-tehl), "hotel."
- The letter "j" is pronounced *zh*, like the "s" in "mea*s*ure," as in *Jacques* (zhahk), "James" or *jour* (zhoor), "day."

Sometimes, Two Consonants Are Put Together

There are some common consonant combinations whose pronunciation you should be aware of:

LETTER	PRONOUNCED AS...	AS IN...
ph	f (as in *file*)	*photo* (foh-toh), "photo"
pt	pt (as in *warped*)	*apte* (ahpt), "capable"

LETTER	PRONOUNCED AS...	AS IN...
th	t (as in *tea*)	*thé* (teh), "tea"
ch	sh (as in *ship*)	*chaud* (shoh), "hot"
gn	ny (as in *onion*)	*gagner* (gah-nyeh), "to win"

You will also encounter "mm," "nn," "rr," or "pp." These double letters are pronounced just like single ones. While "ch" is normally pronounced as *sh*, there are some exceptions where it's pronounced as *k*, as in *orchestre* (ohr-kehs-tr), "orchestra."

Take a Tip from Me!

One of the best ways to improve your pronunciation is to hear yourself speak. University language classes require visits to the language lab where you can record yourself pronouncing assigned words or phrases and then compare your pronunciation to a native speaker's. Now, you don't have to invest thousands of dollars in a personal language lab, but you might want to consider spending a few bucks on a cassette voice recorder or a microphone for your computer. Then, as you work through the lessons, record yourself reading the dialogues in this book after you've listened to them on the CD. You can also record yourself reading individual words from this book, liner notes to a French CD, a recipe from a French cookbook, a menu you swiped from a French restaurant, or anything else you can get your hands on, as long as it's in French. Just listen to yourself speak. You'll be surprised by how easy it is for you to spot (and correct!) your typical mistakes.

Take a Tip from Me!

Okay, so now we've talked about the sounds of French, but how are these sounds combined into words? Let's take a look . . . .

WORDS, WORDS, WORDS

Connecting One Word to the Next

In speech we tend not to enunciate every word individually—that would make our speech sound very choppy and unnatural; instead we connect words. Although this is true of any language, it's also true that we are more struck by it when we listen to a foreign language. Foreign speech often sounds like a long, uninterrupted stream that's very hard to understand. Again, with time and patience, we manage to start telling words apart from one another. But, in order to sound natural, we have to use the same "connected" speech ourselves. In French, words are connected in one of two ways:

- Using apostrophe and elision

When two words meet, one ending in a vowel and the other beginning in a vowel, the last letter of the first word is dropped, and the two words are pronounced as one. The apostrophe takes the place of the dropped vowel. This is called an *élision* or elision. For example:

la + amie	**l'amie** "friend"
la + école	**l'école** "school"
je + aime	**j'aime** "I love"
ce + est	**c'est** "it's / this is . . . "
si + il te plaît	**s'il te plaît** "please"

- Bridge-making or *liaison*

Letters "t", "d", "s", "z", "x", and "p" are usually silent when found at the end of a word. (There are some exceptions to this rule, and I'll warn you when that happens.) For example:

intéressant	(ehⁿ-teh-reh-sahⁿ), "interesting"
grand	(grahⁿ), "big"
nous	(noo), "we"
Allez!	(ah-leh), "Go!"
deux	(duh), "two"
trop	(troh), "too much"

(Final consonants that are usually pronounced are: "c," "r," "f," and "l." To remember this, think of the consonants in the English word *CaReFuL.*)

Now, if the last letter of a word is one of these silent consonants and the word that follows starts with a vowel or a silent "h," the final consonant of the first word is pronounced, thus forming a bridge connecting the two words. This is called *liaison*, which means "linking." Makes sense, no? Compare:

il est + américain	(eel eh <u>t</u> ah-meh-ree-kehⁿ)	he is American
un grand ami	(uhⁿ grahⁿ <u>t</u> ah-mee)	a good friend
nous avons	(noo <u>z</u> ah-vohⁿ)	we have
Allez-y!	(ah-leh <u>z</u> ee)	Go (there)!
deux amis	(duh <u>z</u> ah-mee)	two friends
trop intéressant	(troh <u>p</u> ehⁿ-teh-reh-sahⁿ)	too interesting
		(This *liaison* is less common.)

Remember that:
- "s" and "x" are pronounced *z*
- "d" is pronounced *t*

Finally, the final letter "f," while normally pronounced, changes to the sound *v* if a word that follows starts in a vowel or a silent "h." For example:

neuf	(nuhf), "nine"
neuf heures	(nuh<u>v</u> uhr), "nine hours"

Heads Up!

The letter "h" is always silent in French, and counts as a vowel for *liaison* purposes. However, some words begin with what's called an aspirated "h," a sort of hard "h." This doesn't mean you pronounce it, only that you can't make a *liaison* with it. Unfortunately, there's no way to know when an "h" is truly silent and when it's aspirated. You'll just have to memorize the words as you come across them. Sometimes, words starting in aspirated "h" are marked with an asterisk. For example:

les hommes (leh <u>z</u> ohm), "the men"
les *héros (leh *eh-roh), "the heroes"

Heads Up!

CAN YOU HANDLE STRESS?

Word stress, that is. Sure you can . . . .If anything is really easy in French, stress is it. French words are normally stressed on the last syllable, as in *intéressant* (eh^n-teh-reh-**sah**^{n}). In speech, however, words are connected together, as we said earlier. It is the last syllable of the last word in the group that gets the stress: *Il est un homme intére**ssant**.* In other words, for stress purposes, this sentence counts as one long word.

Well, that's it on the sounds (and stress!) of French. But before I let you go, a final word of advice: Never let the fear of saying something less than perfectly (whether it be due to a pronunciation or grammar or vocabulary mistake) stop you from talking to someone. Even if you make a mistake, chances are that you will be understood, and that should be your main goal in learning any language. Think of all the people you encounter who speak English with an accent, and yet you can do business with them, discuss politics with them, get to know them. The only way to learn to speak a foreign language is to actually speak it. Painfully obvious, I know, but you'd be surprised how many people seem to lose sight of this simple fact. Don't let that be you. Now, we can move on and get down to business. *Allons-y!* Let's go! Lesson 1 awaits . . .

Bonne chance! Good luck!

French

Without the Fuss

1.

THE FIRST STEP

Le premier pas

Hello. I'm Julienne Nyollo.

COMING UP. . .

- *Hello, my name is . . .* : **How to meet and greet people in French**
- *Me, myself, and I*: **The personal pronouns**
- *To be or not to be*: **The verb** *être* **(to be) in the present tense**
- *To have and have not*: **The verb** *avoir* **(to have) in the present tense**
- *(In)definitely so*: **The** and **a / an in French**

"Le premier pas" ("The First Step") is a famous song composed and recorded in the early 1980s by the French musician Claude-Michel Schönberg. Schönberg's work has since successfully crossed the Atlantic. As a matter of fact, he's one of the creators of two popular musicals—*Miss Saigon* and *Les Misérables*.

LOOKING AHEAD

*   Are you ready? *Vous êtes prêt?*
*   I beg your pardon?

Relax! You are on your way to having an exciting and fun *expérience*, the one of learning a new language and encountering a new culture. This task may seem a bit intimidating to you right now, but I can assure you of this: you are in good hands. I, your personal teacher, will lead you every step of the way.

All you need to do is pace yourself and have fun. When you are not sure or you feel lost, just turn back the pages or take a break. After all, there is no pressure, is there?

Take a Tip from Me!

As I said in the introduction, the importance of listening to a new language as much as possible cannot be overstated. In the beginning, anewlanguagesoundslikeajumbleofsounds-andit'sveryhardtotellonewordfromanother. (Got it?) This is quite normal and it happens to everyone. Listening as much as possible will help train your ear. At first, you should just be listening for the sounds and melody of the language. Eventually, individual words will start to emerge. If you have the time, you should listen to all of the dialogues a few times before you read along.

Take a Tip from Me!

You're about to meet some of the characters (*personnages*) of this book, three men (*trois hommes*) and three women (*trois femmes*). First, they will introduce themselves (*se présenter*) and speak (*parler*) a little about themselves, and then . . . .You're on! *À vous!*

Are you ready to listen? Pop in the CD and hit "play." *Allons-y!* Let's go!

HEAR . . . SAY 1

Introductions   (Les présentations)

Luc Comte: Oui, bonjour, je suis Luc, Luc Comte. J'habite à Paris, mais je suis de Perpignan.

Jason Durand:	Ah, oui! C'est dans le sud de la France! Moi, je suis du Canada et je m'appelle Jason Durand. J'habite à Paris aussi. Et vous, Mademoiselle?
Julienne Nyollo:	Bonjour. Eh bien, je suis Julienne Nyollo. Je suis née à Douala au Cameroun. Et je suis étudiante à Paris.
Luc Comte:	C'est un très beau pays.
Julienne:	C'est vrai, Luc! Ah! Voici Paco!
Paco Rodriguez:	Salut tout le monde! Comment ça va? Moi aussi, j'habite à Paris . . .

Feel lost? No need to despair! A little patience will go a long way! If you want, you can now take a peek at the translation of the dialogue at the end of the lesson, and then listen to the dialogue again.

Now, let's see if you can answer these "difficult" questions . . . .

ACTIVITY 1: HOW'S THAT AGAIN?

You choose: Answer the questions in French (no complete sentences required here!) or in English:

a) What are the characters' names? And your name?
b) The characters all live *à Paris*. How about you (*Et vous*)?
c) Are you an *étudiant*?

Take a Tip from Me!

You may have figured this out already, but the Crib Notes section at the end of each lesson has translations of the dialogues. You're allowed to look there now to preserve sanity. You're even allowed to look at the translation before you get ready to listen to a dialogue. This is not cheating, especially in the beginning (or for as long as you want, actually), where your goal is to acquire the basic stock of French words and sentences. It's just a shortcut to making connections between English and French. (You'll know next time, right?)

Don't worry about getting every single word. What you're going for is the gist of the conversation, just like in real-life situations where there is no opportunity to stop or rewind.

Did You Know?

French is spoken around the world, and it is an official language of more than twenty-five countries. In North America, French is spoken in Canada (mostly Quebec) and in the United States (mostly northern New England and Louisiana). More people speak *français* today than ever. However, relatively speaking, the number of French speakers keeps getting smaller. The once–*langue universelle,* French, is being replaced by indigenous languages and English as the new world language.

WORKSHOP 1

THE NITTY-GRITTY

In this lesson, you're going to learn some basic elements of a French sentence: personal pronouns (equivalents of English *I, he, she, they,* and *it*), and verbs (things like *to be* or *to live*).

Let's go!

ME, MYSELF AND I: THE PERSONAL PRONOUNS

Sometimes, you just get tired of using nouns, i.e., words like *house* or *woman,* over and over again. "Who you gonna call?" The personal pronouns. They are these little (but useful) words used to replace nouns. So, instead of *John is coming,* you can say *He is coming* if you mentioned his name earlier. Here are the personal pronouns in French:

PERSONAL PRONOUNS			
SINGULAR		**PLURAL**	
je	I	*nous*	we
tu	you	*vous*	you (plural)
vous	you (formal)		
il	he	*ils* (masc.)	they*
elle	she	*elles* (fem.)	they
on	one, we		

A few comments . . .

1. *Vous* is a pronoun that has two meanings: you can use it to address a group of people or to address a single person.

   When *vous* is used to address a single person, it represents a very formal and polite usage. *Vous* is used between two people whenever there is some kind of disproportion in their relationship: a big difference in age (e.g., child-adult), status (e.g., student-teacher), or lack of familiarity among adults (e.g., at the bank, at the office, in the grocery store, etc.). Your best bet is to keep using *vous* until the other person says or proposes otherwise.

2. The pronoun *tu* is used in all other cases, basically between family and friends, among children and younger adults.

Masc. stands for "masculine" and *fem.* stands for "feminine."

The French have loosened up in this matter (or is it just another influence of America?). In the past, children used to *vouvoyer* their parents! (Stop! *Vouvoyer* just means "to say *vous*.") And vice versa . . . .Couples did likewise. In-laws still often do. However, the custom is changing and even fading away in many contexts. But don't try to use *tu* with your waiter on your next trip to France! In many situations, *tutoyer* ("to say *tu*") is still a sign of misplaced familiarity.

Did You Know?

3. *On* is an indefinite personal pronoun. "Indefinite" because it is used to refer to a person or people who are not specified, similar to "one" in English. It is also used to replace *nous* (we) in more colloquial language. For example:

   On parle français ici.

   French is spoken here. (*Lit.* * One speaks French here.)

   On habite à Paris.

   We live in Paris.

ACTIVITY 2: TAKE IT FOR A SPIN

Ready for a search? Write down all the personal pronouns you can find in the Hear . . . Say 1 section.

TO BE OR NOT TO BE: THE VERB *ÊTRE* (TO BE) IN THE PRESENT TENSE

In French, there are two helping verbs, *être* (to be) and *avoir* (to have). (Helping verbs are those verbs that can be used with other verbs to express different nuances of time or mood. In *I have eaten*, *have* is a helping verb, not the main verb.) Both are also used as main verbs, as we saw in the dialogue.

Unfortunately, *être* is an irregular verb (just like the English *to be*), so different forms are used for different persons. The good news is that this verb is extremely common and you will be hearing it a lot, which will help you memorize it.

THE PRESENT TENSE OF *ÊTRE* (TO BE)			
SINGULAR		**PLURAL**	
je suis	I am	*nous sommes*	we are
tu es	you are	*vous êtes* [voozeht]	you are
il / elle est	he / she is	*ils / elles sont*	they are

Lit. stands for "literally."

Notice that I have added the pronunciation for the form *vous êtes*. This is because this form involves a special pronunciation, due to *liaison*. Whenever the pronunciation is not completely predictable based on the rules introduced in the Getting Started in French chapter, I'll make a note of it in this way.

Now, take a look at the examples from the dialogue:

Je suis du Canada.

I am from Canada.

Je suis Jason Durand.

I am Jason Durand.

Je suis née à Douala au Cameroun.

I was born in Douala in Cameroon.

Je suis étudiante à Paris.

I am a student in Paris.

The expression *c'est* corresponds to English "this is . . ." or "it is . . ." You'll hear it (and soon enough, use it!) all the time in French. For example:

C'est Luc. Il est de Perpignan.

This is Luc. He's from Perpignan.

C'est le Canada.

This is Canada.

C'est mon amie.

It's / This is my friend.

C'est vrai.

This is true.

C'est can even be used to replace *je suis . . .*, in very colloquial French.

Moi, c'est Aziza.

My name's Aziza. (*Lit.* Me, it's Aziza.)

Instead of:

Moi, je suis Aziza.

I am Aziza.

TAKE IT FOR A SPIN

Fill in the blanks with the appropriate form of *être*.

a) *Nous _____ étudiants à Paris.*
b) *Mademoiselle, vous _____ du Canada?*
c) *Ils _____ nés à Douala.*
d) *Tu _____ ici.*
e) *Elle _____ Julienne.*
f) *Je _____ étudiante aussi.*

WORDS TO LIVE BY

HELLO, MY NAME IS . . . : HOW TO MEET AND GREET PEOPLE IN FRENCH

Ça va? (Doing alright?) You've heard how to make introductions (*les présentations*). Now, let's nail down some of the requisite vocabulary. Soon you will be able to introduce yourself, which is . . .

se présenter   to introduce oneself

But before we go on . . .

Take a Tip from Me!

One of the best ways to learn new vocabulary words is to use flash cards. Write the French word on one side and the English translation on the other. When you use your flash cards, begin with the French sides first and always say the words out loud. Try to go through them as fast as you can. You're aiming for instant recognition. Remember to shuffle your cards regularly to avoid remembering a word just because of the card that came before it. Once you have the French side down, start with the English first. You'll probably find that this is more difficult, but don't give up, because you want to be able to translate in either direction. As you work through the cards, you can begin to eliminate the ones that you recognize instantly, and focus on the ones that are more difficult. If you get stuck on a word, try to come up with an association (funny associations are good), then get rid of your crutch when you no longer need it. Pop a few of your flash cards in your pocket and go through them as you're eating lunch, waiting for the bus, or even waiting on line in the supermarket. Now, here's some material to put on those cards!

Let's go on . . .
    After saying *Bonjour!*, you can say . . .

Je m'appelle . . .   My name is . . . (Lit. I am called . . .)
Je suis . . .   I am . . .

Or, less frequently:

Mon nom est . . .   *My name is . . .*

But, first you need to learn a few *salutations* or greetings . . .

Bonjour!   *Hello!, Good morning!, Good afternoon!*
Salut!   *Hello!, Hi!, Bye!*

If you'd like to be particularly polite, follow your *Bonjour!* by . . .

Madame, Mesdames   *Madam, Ladies*
Mademoiselle, Mesdemoiselles   *Miss, Young ladies*
Monsieur, Messieurs   *Sir, Gentlemen*

Of course, we're all humans first . . .

la femme   *woman*
l'homme (*masc.*)   *man*
tout le monde   *everybody*
la personne   *person*
le personnage   *character*

There are also family and friends . . .

l'ami, l'amie   *male friend, female friend*
la famille   *family*
les parents   *parents*

And another useful expression . . .

Vous êtes d'où? / Tu es d'où?   *Where are you from?*

These questions are quite informal, but common in everyday language. You'll learn more about forming questions later.

They can answer:

Je suis de . . .   *I am from . . .*

Or:

Je suis né (*masc.*) / **née** (*fem.*) **à**   *I was born in . . .*

You can also give your nationality:

Je suis . . .

américain(e)   *American*
camerounais(e)   *Cameroonian*
canadien, canadienne   *Canadian*
espagnol(e)   *Spanish*
français(e)   *French*

We'll learn more about this in a later lesson, but let me note here that the addition of a single letter, "e," changes words a lot in French. The form without "e" is used for men (as in *un homme américain*), and the one with "e" is used for women (as in *une femme américaine*). The addition of "e" changes the pronunciation, and the final consonant, which is silent in the masculine form, is clearly pronounced in the feminine form.

américain	[ahmehreekeh^n],	**américaine**	[ahmehrikehn]
camerounais	[kamuhrooneh],	**camerounaise**	[kamuhroonehz]
canadien	[kanadyeh^n],	**canadienne**	[kanadyehn]
français	[frah^{n}seh],	**française**	[frah^{n}sehz]

Heads Up!

The Fine Print

In French, unlike in English, you should use the definite article before country names. For example:
> **le Cameroun, le Canada, l'Espagne, la France**

If the country name ends in "e," like *France,* it is feminine, i.e., it must be preceded by *la*. If the country name ends in another vowel or a consonant, like *Canada* or *Cameroun*, it is masculine, i.e., it should be preceded by *le*.

And then, there are country names that are always plural (and have an "s" at the end), like *les États-Unis d'Amérique* (the United States of America) or *les États-Unis* for short.

When talking about places of origin, remember this question:

Vous êtes d'où?	*Where are you from?*

And the answer can be . . .

J'habite à . . .	*I live in . . .*
Je suis de . . .	*I am from . . .*

Or, you can say . . .

Je travaille à . . .	*I work in . . .*

You can also specify . . .

Je suis étudiant (*masc.*) **/ étudiante** (*fem.*)	*I'm a student*

Heads Up!

Note again that adding *-e* (which is silent) to *étudiant* makes the word feminine, *étudiante*. The final "t" must be clearly pronounced when "e" is there.

In addition, did you notice that no article is necessary before *étudiant(e)*?

Heads Up!

And what you're trying to do right now is . . .

apprendre le français   *to learn French*

So, say it . . .

J'apprends le français.   *I'm learning French.*

And after a while, you will become . . .

francophone   *French-speaking*

Le français is *une belle langue* (a beautiful language). Check this irregular adjective out:

beau (*masc. sg.*),	**beaux** (*masc. pl.*)	*beautiful*
belle (*fem. sg.*),	**belles** (*fem. pl.*)	*beautiful*

Did You Know?

I promised earlier that you'll be able to recognize many words in French, because similar cognate words exist in English. English borrowed from Romance languages—and French in particular—during the period when French was the language of the English court. In this lesson, these words are: *excellent* [eh-kseh-lah^n] and *super* [sü-pehr], which is used a lot in informal, colloquial language. The only thing you need to worry about here is the difference in pronunciation.

Did You Know?

And, now let's take a look at some useful little words . . .

aussi	*as well*
avec	*with*
bien	*well; really; very*
et	*and*
mais	*but*
mon (*masc. sg.*)	*my*
ma (*fem. sg.*)	*my*
mes (*pl.*)	*my*
non	*no*
oui	*yes*

And finally, don't go to France without these very common expressions . . .

Word on the Street . . .

À toi!, À vous!	*Your turn!*
C'est vrai.	*This is true.*
(Comment) ça va?	*How's it going?*
Eh bien	*Well (you'll hear this all the time)*
Voici	*Here is . . .; This is . . .*
Voilà	*There is . . .; That is . . .*

That's all for now. But before getting back to the dialogue, show off your newly acquired knowledge . . . .

TAKE IT FOR A SPIN

Let's pretend that you are at a party. Friendly people are speaking to you . . . **in French!** Now, don't panic, this is just an activity preparing you for all those real parties you will have to attend . . . .Fill in the blanks!

Bonjour, je m' _____ Aziza Bensaïd. Et vous?
Je m'appelle _____.
Vous êtes d'où?
Je _____ des _____.
Ah! Vous _____ américain. Moi, je suis française. J' _____ à Paris.
Et là, c' _____ mon amie Florence.
Salut Florence!

LET'S PUT IT IN WRITING

Take a look at Julienne's personal info.

NOM:	**Nyollo**
PRÉNOM:	**Julienne**
NÉE À:	**Douala, Cameroun**
DATE:	**le 14 juin 1974**
RÉSIDENCE:	**22, rue du Chalet, 75010 Paris**
OCCUPATION:	**étudiante**

ACTIVITY 5: **TAKE IT FOR A SPIN**

You've got this, haven't you? Now, write your personal info next to Julienne's.

HEAR . . . SAY 2

The Introductions (Les présentations)

Jason Durand: Vous êtes d'où, Paco?
Paco Rodriguez: Je suis né à Marseille. Mes parents sont d'Andalousie, en Espagne.
Florence Fajardi: Paco est musicien!

Paco Rodriguez:	Oui, j'ai un groupe de musique du monde. Mais Florence, tu es la seule parisienne . . .
Florence Fajardi:	Non, Aziza est de Paris aussi. Aziza?
Aziza Bensaïd:	Mesdames, Messieurs, bonjour! Je suis Aziza Bensaïd.
Florence Fajardi:	Oui, nous sommes nées à Paris. On travaille ensemble à M7, la chaîne de télévision musicale. Eh! J'ai le CD de Paco, ici. C'est excellent! Voilà . . .
Aziza Bensaïd:	Tu as raison, Flo, Paco a du talent . . .

ACTIVITY 6: HOW'S THAT AGAIN?

Answer the following questions, whenever possible, in French.

  a) Who is a musician?
  b) Where do Florence and Aziza work (*travaillent*)?
  c) Who was born in Paris?
  d) *D'où est Paco?*

Did You Know?

THE FRENCH KISS

What do the French do when they greet? Among family and friends, the French don't hug . . . they kiss, and not just once! At least one *bisou* (kiss) on each cheek, sometimes even three or four altogether, according to regional tradition!

In formal situations or when they first meet someone, people shake hands and say *Enchanté(e) de faire votre connaissance!* (*Lit.* Pleased to make your acquaintance!). A short *Enchanté(e)!* [ah^n-shah^n-teh] will suffice, too.

In the past, it was considered inappropriate or rather, "unmanly" for a man to kiss a male friend or even a male family member. Things have changed . . . . It all started in show business, and has become a new custom, followed by many young men.

Indeed, in France and especially in Paris, young people love to kiss. Imagine you're meeting a group of friends at a *café*. There are about ten people, some you know, some you don't . . . . Know what? Chances are they will all expect you to kiss them, two, three, or even four times! That's forty kisses altogether! Enjoy!

Did You Know?

WORKSHOP 2

THE NITTY-GRITTY

TO HAVE AND HAVE NOT: VERB AVOIR (TO HAVE) IN THE PRESENT TENSE

Let's look at some examples used in the previous dialogue.

> **J'ai un groupe de musique.**
>
> I have a music group.
>
> **J'ai le CD de Paco.**
>
> I have Paco's CD.
>
> **Il a du talent.**
>
> He has talent.

And here are all the different forms of *avoir*:

PRESENT TENSE OF *AVOIR* (TO HAVE)			
SINGULAR		**PLURAL**	
j'ai	I have	*nous avons* [noo zah-voh^n]	we have
tu as	you have	*vous avez* [voo zah-veh]	you have
il / elle a	he / she has	*ils / elles ont* [eel zoh^n]	they have

Heads Up!

Watch the pronunciation: all plural forms have *liaison* in them, so the final "s" of the *nous*, *vous* and *ils / elles* will be pronounced as a *z* sound and smoothly connected to the verb.

While we're at it, here are a couple of useful expressions with *avoir*.

avoir raison	to be right
avoir tort	to be wrong

For example:

J'ai raison.	I am right
Tu as tort.	You are wrong.

À vous! Find the right form of *avoir* and complete the sentences below:

ai, avons, a, as, ont, avez

a)   Ils _____ un groupe d'amis.
b)   Vous _____ raison.
c)   Nous _____ un CD de Paco.
d)   J' _____ un groupe de musique.
e)   Tu _____ du talent.
f)   Il _____ tort.

True (*vrai*) or false (*faux*)? Are the following sentences correct or not? Can you fix them?

a)   Je sommes à Paris.
b)   Tu as raison.
c)   Elle sont étudiantes.
d)   Nous sommes du talent.
e)   Vous as américain.
f)   Ils ont français.

On to the next topic: In French, as in English, nouns (words like *house*, *man*, or *love*) are usually preceded by little (but important) words called articles.

(IN)DEFINITELY SO: *THE* AND *A / AN* IN FRENCH

Okay . . . .Here we are in one of the trickiest territories of the French language. We've touched on this already: *en français*, nouns are of either masculine or feminine gender. Gender is a bit like the sex of a person, but in French, even things have gender—so *table* is *la table* (feminine) and *band* is *le groupe* (masculine), although there doesn't seem to be any particular reason for this. You'll just have to memorize it!

The articles preceding nouns are useful since they tell you which gender a particular noun belongs to. Obviously, you'll have a masculine article preceding a masculine noun, and a feminine article preceding a feminine noun. Therefore, articles are very valuable. One more thing: as in English, articles are either definite or indefinite.

1. The Definite Articles

DEFINITE ARTICLES		
MASCULINE SINGULAR	*le, l'*	the
FEMININE SINGULAR	*la, l'*	the
MASCULINE AND FEMININE PLURAL	*les*	the

le musicien	(male) musician
la femme	woman
les femmes	women
les musiciens	(male) musicians

Heads Up!

Heads Up!

When a noun starts with a vowel or a silent "h" and is preceded by *le* or *la*, *élision* applies. This means (you might remember it from the Getting Started in French chapter) that the article's vowel is erased and replaced by an apostrophe—*le* and *la* become *l'*. For instance:

l'homme (← *le homme*)	the man
l'étudiant / e (← *le / la étudiant / e*)	the student

2. Indefinite Articles

INDEFINITE ARTICLES		
MASCULINE SINGULAR	*un*	a
FEMININE SINGULAR	*une*	a
MASCULINE AND FEMININE PLURAL	*des*	

Note that in contrast to English, French has an indefinite article in the plural form, *des*.

un pays [uhⁿ pehyee]	a country
un ami [uhn ami]	a friend (male)
une langue	a language
une famille	a family
des amis	friends
des musiciens	musicians

Take a Tip from Me!

Take a Tip from Me!

Learn every noun together with its article, as there is no steadfast rule to help you to determine a noun's gender in each and every case.

ACTIVITY 9: TAKE IT FOR A SPIN

Please go back to the first and the second dialogue and find and write down all the articles together with their nouns. Classify them: separate the definite articles from the indefinite articles, and then, the masculine from the feminine articles.

And now, let's look at your next bundle of new words.

One important point before going on . . .

The Fine Print

When referring to more than one item, nouns take an ending —s in French, as in English. There are some irregular plural forms, of course, and I'll let you know each time we encounter one. Unlike in English, though, this final —s is **never** pronounced. So, there is no audible difference between singular and plural for most nouns in French. For example, *homme* "man" and *hommes* "men" sound exactly the same. So, how do you know the difference between singular and plural in speech? Listen to what precedes the noun, i.e., the article. Compare: *l'homme* and *les hommes,* or *un homme* and *des hommes.*

WORDS TO LIVE BY

Earlier, you learned to say "Hello." Now, it's time to say "Goodbye."

Au revoir!	Goodbye!
À bientôt!	See you soon!
À la prochaine (fois)!	See you (next time)!

And the most colloquial and useful multi-purpose greeting . . .

Salut!	Bye!; Hi!

Our *amis* were speaking of their occupations (*les occupations*) . . .

le groupe de musique	music group
le musicien, la musicienne	musician (male, female)
la profession	profession

And of *l'art et la culture* (the art and culture) . . .

la chaîne de télévision	TV channel
le CD [sehdeh], **le compact disc**	CD
la musique	music
la musique du monde	world music
le talent	talent

And when talking about the arts, you better . . .

avoir du talent	to have talent

Some more useful little words . . .

ensemble	together
seul	only; alone
mais	but

TAKE IT FOR A SPIN

Fill in the gaps with the appropriate article.

a) Tu travailles à _____ télévision?
b) J'habite dans _____ très beau pays.
c) Florence est _____ seule parisienne. Elle est _____ amie de Paco.
d) Paco a _____ groupe de musique.
e) Et voici Julienne! Elle est _____ étudiante.
f) Bonjour, tout _____ monde!
g) Tu es de Perpignan? C'est dans _____ sud de _____ France.
h) À _____ prochaine, _____ amis!

Ready for some extra challenge? Why not take it up a notch? Do the following two activities and I'll let you go.

ACTIVITY 11: **TAKE IT UP A NOTCH**

Complete the following sentences with the appropriate form of *être* or *avoir*.

a) Je _____ Paco Rodriguez et je _____ né à Marseille.
b) Julienne et moi, nous _____ un groupe de musique.
c) Moi, je _____ Florence. Et je _____ née à Paris!
d) Aziza _____ de Paris aussi.
e) Salut tout le monde! Moi, je _____ Jason, et je _____ canadien.

ACTIVITY 12: **TAKE IT UP A NOTCH**

Now, how about translating these sentences?

a) Hi everybody, how is it going?
b) My name is Jason and I live alone in Paris.
c) Luc is in Paris, too. But he's from Perpignan.
d) My name is Julienne and I am a student.
e) See you soon!

Bravo! Great job! I'm so proud of you . . .

If you can, go back to the dialogue and read it aloud, or at least listen to it one final time, before taking a well-deserved break. *À bientôt!* (See you soon!)

And because I'm so nice, here are the answers to all your questions . . .

CRIB NOTES

HEAR...SAY 1

Luc Comte:	Yes, hello, I'm Luc, Luc Comte. I live in Paris, but I am from Perpignan.
Jason Durand:	Ah, yes. That's in the South of France! I'm from Canada and my name is Jason Durand. I live in Paris, too. And what about you, Miss?

Julienne Nyollo:	Hello. Well, I am Julienne Nyollo. I was born in Douala in Cameroon. And I am a student in Paris.
Luc Comte:	That's a very beautiful country.
Julienne Nyollo:	That's true, Luc. Hey, here is Paco!
Paco Rodriguez:	Hi, everyone! How is it going? I live in Paris, too, . . .

HEAR...SAY 2

Jason Durand:	Where are you from, Paco?
Paco Rodriguez:	I was born in Marseille. My parents are from Andalusia, in Spain.
Florence Fajardi:	Paco is a musician.
Paco Rodriguez:	Yes, I have a world music group. But Florence, you are the only Parisian . . .
Florence Fajardi:	No, Aziza is from Paris as well. Aziza?

Aziza Bensaïd:	Ladies and gentlemen, good morning! I am Aziza Bensaïd.
Florence Fajardi:	Yes, we were born in Paris. We work together at M7, the music TV channel. Hey! I have Paco's CD here. It's very good! Here . . . .
Aziza Bensaïd:	You're right, Flo. Paco is talented.

ANSWER KEY

ACTIVITY 1

a) Les noms des personnages sont: Luc Comte, Jason Durand, Julienne Nyollo, Paco Rodriguez. Je m'appelle _____. / Je suis _____. / Mon nom est _____.
b) Non, j'habite à _____.
c) Oui, je suis étudiant.

ACTIVITY 2

1st singular person: je (suis)–j'(habite)–je (suis de)–je (suis du)–je (m'appelle)–j'(habite à)–je (suis)–Je (suis née)–je (suis)–j'(habite).

ACTIVITY 3

a) Nous sommes étudiants à Paris.
b) Mademoiselle, vous êtes du Canada?
c) Ils sont nés à Douala.
d) Tu es ici.
e) Elle est Julienne.
f) Je suis étudiante aussi.

ACTIVITY 4

Bonjour, je m'appelle Aziza Bensaïd. Et vous? Je m'appelle . . . . Vous êtes d'où? Je suis des États-Unis. Ah! Vous êtes américain. Moi, je suis française. J'habite à Paris. Et là, c'est mon amie Florence. Salut Florence!

ACTIVITY 5

Nom:	(last name)
Prénom:	(first name)
Né(e) à:	(place of birth)
Date:	(date of birth)
Résidence:	(current address)
Occupation:	(occupation / profession)

ACTIVITY 6

a) Paco est musicien.
b) Florence et Aziza travaillent à M7, la chaîne de télévision musicale.
c) Florence et Aziza sont nées à Paris.
d) Paco est né à Marseille.

ACTIVITY 7

a) Ils ont un groupe d'amis.
b) Vous avez raison.
c) Nous avons un CD de Paco.
d) J'ai un groupe de musique.
e) Tu as du talent.
f) Il a tort.

ACTIVITY 8

a) FAUX—Je suis à Paris.
b) VRAI—Tu as raison.
c) FAUX—Elles sont étudiantes. *or* Elle est étudiante.
d) FAUX—Nous avons du talent.
e) FAUX—Vous êtes américain. *or* Vous êtes américains.
f) FAUX—Ils sont français.

ACTIVITY 9

a) Definite article / masculine singular: le sud–le monde–le CD
b) Definite article / feminine singular: la France–la parisienne–la chaîne de television
c) Definite article / feminine plural: les présentations
d) Indefinite article / masculine singular: un pays—un groupe de musique

ACTIVITY 10

a) Tu travailles à la télévision?
b) J'habite dans un très beau pays.
c) Florence est la seule parisienne. Elle est l'amie de Paco.

d) Paco a un groupe de musique.
e) Et voici Julienne! Elle est étudiante. (No article here, remember?)
f) Bonjour, tout le monde!
g) Tu es de Perpignan? C'est dans le sud de la France.
h) À la prochaine, les amis!

ACTIVITY 11

a) Je suis Paco Rodriguez et je suis né à Marseille.
b) Julienne et moi, nous avons un groupe de musique.
c) Moi, je suis Florence. Et je suis née à Paris!
d) Aziza est de Paris aussi.
e) Salut tout le monde! Moi, je suis jason, je suis canadien.

ACTIVITY 12

a) Salut tout le monde, comment ça va?
b) Je m'appelle / je suis Jason et j'habite seul à Paris.
c) Luc est à Paris aussi. Mais il est de Perpignan.
d) Je m'appelle / je suis Julienne et je suis étudiante.
e) À bientôt!

2.

PARIS AT NIGHT

Do you see Aunt Clarisse?

COMING UP. . .

- *Have a pleasant flight*: Talking about airports and travel
- *Just say NO!*: Using *non* (no) and *ne . . . pas* (not)
- *Living in the present*: Verbs ending in *–er* in the present tense
- *Any questions?*: Asking questions using intonation or *est-ce que*
- *I scream, you scream*: The irregular verbs *voir* (to see) and *croire* (to believe) in the present tense

"Paris at Night" is a song performed by the late actor and singer Yves Montand, featured with Marilyn Monroe in Cukor's film *Let's Make Love*. Yves Montand belonged to a famous generation of French *chansonniers* from the 1950s. He was also the favorite actor of many great French directors, including Costa Gavras and Claude Sautet.

This particular song was penned by poet Jacques Prévert.

Did You Know?

TAKING OFF FROM PARIS' ROISSY–CHARLES DE GAULLE AIRPORT

The work on a new airport started in 1966 in the middle of a farm in Roissy, north of Paris. The project was entrusted to a talented and innovative architect, Paul Andreu, who gave an almost futuristic look to the new airport. In 1974, Roissy–Charles De Gaulle Airport, or, as it is often called in French, CDG [seh-deh-zheh], was inaugurated. Since then, it has been further enlarged to become one of the world's most modern airports. A new terminal is scheduled to be ready in 2003!

Did You Know?

LOOKING AHEAD

Here you are in Lesson 2. Don't you have the feeling you've already learned a lot? Well, you have, and there is much more to come. Remember, you are not alone in this.

In this chapter, you're going to learn about the world *des aéroports*, which is useful because the airport is the first place where you will get to use your newly acquired language skills and form your first impressions about a country.

In the coming dialogues, you'll meet two young women, Jeannie *et* Florine Diop, who've just arrived in Paris from Senegal, *un pays francophone* in West Africa. This is their first *voyage en France*! But in spite of their excitement and *la belle architecture de CDG*, their first moments in France turn out to be a bit *bizarre*. They are now about to face the immigration officer.

HEAR...SAY 1

Arrived at Last! (Enfin arrivées!)

Jeannie:	Paris, Paris, nous voici!
L'agent d'immigration:	Passeports et billets d'avion.
Florine et Jeannie:	Oui, oui, bien sûr. Bonjour, Monsieur.

Florine:	Voici!
L'agent:	Vous voyagez ensemble? Et vous?
Jeannie:	Euh . . . les voici! Oui, Monsieur, nous voyageons ensemble, nous sommes cousines et . . .
L'agent:	Est-ce que vous avez une attestation de logement?
Florine:	Oui, bien sûr, Monsieur. Voici.
L'agent:	Tout est en règle, Mesdemoiselles.

Jeannie and Florine walk and walk and walk.

Jeannie:	Oh là là, c'est loin?
Florine:	Non, je ne crois pas. . . . Enfin!
Message:	Bienvenue à l'aéroport Roissy–Charles de Gaulle.
Jeannie:	Tu vois ça, Florine? Un vrai film de science fiction!
Florine:	C'est vrai. . . . C'est génial! (*Coughing.*)
Jeannie:	Et les bagages?
Florine:	Ce n'est pas là-bas? Ouh, les gens fument beaucoup ici!

With a lot of luggage, Florine and Jeannie go through customs. Then . . .

Florine:	Tu vois Tante Clarisse?
Jeannie:	Non, je ne vois pas Tata. Mais, on a beaucoup de retard!
Florine:	Tu as raison. Eh bien, on téléphone. Mais, on n'a pas d'euros . . .
Jeannie:	C'est vrai. . . . On a besoin de changer de l'argent. S'il vous plaît, Madame, Madame? Bon.
Florine:	Monsieur? Oui, bonjour, le bureau de change, s'il vous plaît?
L'homme:	Mais je ne travaille pas ici!
Jeannie:	Les gens sont bizarres ici.
Florine:	Mais non. C'mon girl, on est à Paris! (*Coughing.*)

ACTIVITY 1: HOW'S THAT AGAIN?

Yes, airports can be cold places where people rush by . . . *Enfin*, let's see how much you were able to get from this first dialogue. Do your best to answer using French, even if you use a single word to answer.

a) Are Jeannie and Florine best friends?

b) What does *l'agent d'immigration* ask for?

c) Is Jeannie and Florine's aunt at the airport?

d) Why is Florine coughing?

e) At the end of the scene, what do they ask the man for?

THE NITTY-GRITTY

JUST SAY NO!: USING *NON* (NO) AND *NE . . . PAS* (NOT)

1. You can say "no" in French by simply using the word *non* (no). For example:

Non, merci.

No, thank you.

Eh non, c'est là-bas.

Well, no, it's over there.

Non is also used to reinforce a negative sentence.

Non, je _ne_ vois _pas_ Tata.

No, I don't see Auntie.

Which brings us to the second way of saying "no":

2. To say "not" in French use *ne . . . pas*, a two-piece form you already saw in the previous example. Here are some further examples (on the right) straight from the dialogue.

On a des euros. →	**On _n'a pas_ d'euros.**
We have some euros.	We don't have any euros.
Je crois. →	**Non, je _ne_ crois _pas_.**
I think.	No, I don't think so.
Je travaille ici. →	**Mais je _ne_ travaille _pas_ ici.**
I work here.	But I don't work here.

As you can see, the two-part form *ne . . . pas* is placed around the verb: *ne* comes immediately before the verb and *pas* comes immediately after it. Together they mean "not."

Heads Up!

In the first example, you noticed that *ne* has the form of *n'*. This is another case of *élision*. When the verb starts with a vowel or a silent *h*, *ne* becomes *n'*.

Heads Up!

The Fine Print

ACTIVITY 2: TAKE IT FOR A SPIN

Make these sentences negative using *ne . . . pas.*

   a)   *Vous parlez bien français.*
   b)   *Nous habitons au Sénégal.*
   c)   *Je suis étudiant.*
   d)   *Tu as ton passeport.*
   e)   *Ils sont à l'aéroport.*
   f)   *Elle fume.*

LIVING IN THE PRESENT: VERBS ENDING IN –*ER* IN THE PRESENT TENSE

The two verbs you have studied so far, *être* and *avoir*, are irregular, that is, their *je* (*je suis*, *j'ai*) form is different from their *tu* (*tu es, tu as*) form which is different yet from their *il / elle* (*il / elle est, il / elle a*) form, and so on. But luckily, most verbs in French are regular, so once you know one verb, you can pretty much say you know all others that belong to the same group. All you need to do is to add the right endings. French verbs are divided into three regular types depending on how they end when in their *to* form or the infinitive. (The *to* form of the verb, or the infinitive, is the form of the verb you find in the dictionary.)

* —*er* verbs (e.g., *travaill<u>er</u>* "to work")
* —*ir* verbs (e.g., *fin<u>ir</u>* "to finish")
* —*re* verbs (e.g., *vend<u>re</u>* "to sell")

The present tense of the –*er* verbs is formed by taking off the ending –*er* (e.g., *travaill–er*) and adding the following endings to what is left, or the stem (e.g., *travaill–*):

For *je, tu, il / elle:* **–e, –es, –e.**
For *nous, vous, ils / elles:* **–ons, –ez, –ent.**

You already know the verbs *habiter* (to live; to inhabit) and *travailler* (to work). Here are their different forms in the present tense:

THE PRESENT TENSE OF THE VERB *TRAVAILLER* (TO WORK)

je travaille	I work	nous travaillons	we work
tu travailles	you work	vous travaillez	you work
il / elle travaille	he / she works	ils / elles travaillent	they work

L'homme ne travaille pas à l'aéroport.

The man doesn't work at the airport.

Nous travaillons ensemble à CDG.

We work together at CDG.

THE PRESENT TENSE OF THE VERB *HABITER* (TO LIVE; TO INHABIT)

j'habite	I live	nous habitons	we live
tu habites	you live	vous habitez	you live
il / elle habite	he / she lives	ils / elles habitent	they live

Les cousines habitent au Sénégal.

The cousins live in Senegal.

Tu habites à Paris?

Do you live in Paris?

The Fine Print

Notice that you can say *tu habites à Paris* or *tu habites Paris*. In the second example, the preposition *à* is omitted. Both ways are commonly used by the French.

Heads Up!

Note that the first three forms corresponding to pronouns *je, tu, il / elle* and the very last one, *ils / elles*, are all pronounced exactly the same, that is, (trah-vahy) and (ah-beet) respectively. The difference between the different personal forms exists only in writing. In other words the endings *−e, −es,* and *−ent* are not pronounced.

ACTIVITY 3: TAKE IT FOR A SPIN

Search! (*La recherche!*) Make a list of all *−er* verbs you can find in the first dialogue. Write down the different present tense forms you find there together with their subject (i.e., nouns or pronouns that precede them). And, *s'il vous plaît* (please), write down their infinitive or *–er* form, as well.

TAKE IT FOR A SPIN

It's time to apply what you've learned! Write down and read aloud all the different forms of the verb *marcher* (to walk) in the present tense.

WORDS TO LIVE BY

HAVE A PLEASANT FLIGHT: TALKING ABOUT AIRPORTS AND TRAVEL

Bienvenue à Paris!	*Welcome to Paris!*

You may need to know the following if you travel to a francophone country.

un aéroport	*airport (of course!)*
un avion	*airplane*
le billet d'avion	*plane ticket*
une hôtesse	*flight attendant (female)*
le steward	*flight attendant (male)*
le voyage	*trip; travel*
voyager	*to travel*

Once at the airport, you need to pass through passport control and luggage control. Your identity is checked by . . .

un agent d'immigration	*immigration officer*
la police d'immigration	*immigration services*

This can sometimes turn into a pretty unpleasant experience, if your papers aren't in order . . .

être en règle	*to be in order*
le passeport	*passport*

Did You Know?

Unless you are from the United States or the European Union, French immigration laws require that you carry *une attestation de logement*, a certificate of room and board, in addition to *un visa* (a visa). It's a letter attesting that you have a place to stay during your *séjour* (stay) in France.

Did You Know?

Once you have passed immigration, you can go to the luggage pick-up area. By the way, there is no specific term in French to describe the place where you pick up your luggage in the airport. You should look for a sign: *Bagages*, that is, luggage.

Then, it's customs' turn to check you out . . .

la douane	*customs*
la sortie	*exit*

Enfin! Finally! You're out. Good! Now, you can meet your friends or relatives and enjoy your stay . . .

le cousin, la cousine	*cousin (male / female)*
la famille	*family; relatives*
l'oncle (*masc.*)	*uncle*
la tante	*aunt*

After all that, you may need (*avoir besoin de*) a drink (*une boisson* or *un verre*), to call someone (*téléphoner*), or change some money (*changer de l'argent*) . . .

l'argent (*masc.*)	*money; silver*
le bureau de change	*currency exchange*
la monnaie étrangère	*foreign currency*

Be prepared! In spite of some rather scarce "No smoking" signs (*Ne pas fumer!*) at the airports, French smokers will be with you wherever you go.

fumer	*to smoke*
tousser	*to cough*

At this point, you must be tired. Never mind! For you are only a few miles away from your destination.

ACTIVITY 5: TAKE IT FOR A SPIN

Which don't belong? Cross out the words with no direct connection with airports.

la douane / habiter / la sortie / les bus / l'immigration / les hôtesses / l'oncle / Bon voyage / seul

LOOKING AHEAD

Because of the delay of their flight, Jeannie and Florine missed their Aunt Clarisse at the airport. *Les deux cousines* (the two cousins) are on their way to Paris now on their own. They decided to take *le bus*. But where is *l'arrêt de bus* (the bus stop)?

HEAR...SAY 2

This Is It, We're in Paris! (Ça y est, on est à Paris!)

Outside the airport . . .

Florine: (*Coughing.*) Tu vois les bus? Ils sont super!

Jeannie: Oh oui! Ah . . . Voilà l'arrêt pour Denfert-Rocheteau!

Florine: Denfert-Rocheteau? Tu crois?

Jeannie: Oui, c'est dans le quatorzième arrondissement. Paris, nous voici! Les bus passent souvent, je crois . . .

Florine: Enfin! J'ai soif, Jeannie. . . . Est-ce que tu . . . (*Coughing.*)

Jeannie: D'accord. J'arrive . . .

Florine: Merci, cousine. . . . Pardon, Monsieur, est-ce que c'est bien l'arrêt de bus pour Denfert-Rocheteau?

L'homme: "Rocheteau"? Hmm. . . . Rochereau, Mademoiselle, Denfert-Rochereau. Eh non, c'est là-bas. Vous voyez, le bus arrive . . .

Florine: Oh, non!

L'homme: Ah, mais oui!

Florine: Non, ce n'est pas ça. . . . Merci beaucoup, Monsieur.

Jeannie: Voilà! Mademoiselle . . . (*She gives a drink to Florine.*)

Florine: Le bus, Jeannie! Oh, trop tard! Enfin, merci, Jeannie . . .

L'homme: Mesdemoiselles, les bus passent souvent. Courage! Et bienvenue à Paris!

ACTIVITY 6: HOW'S THAT AGAIN?

Voilà! The two young women are about to discover Paris . . .

a) Are Florine and Jeannie taking the train to Paris?
b) Where are they now?
c) Where are they going?
d) What is the matter with Florine?
e) Do the buses come often?

Did You Know?

WHERE THERE'S SMOKE, THERE'S FIRE!

Or in French, *Il n'y a pas de fumée sans feu!* The French might need more than a law to change their smoking habits. In 1991, *la Loi Evin* was introduced by the National Assembly (*Assemblée Nationale*), the government body equivalent to the U.S. Congress. Since then, the law, which forbids any advertising related to tobacco and restricts (but only "restricts") smoking in public places, has received much criticism and become quite unpopular in many corners of France. Someone even declared in the National Assembly, somewhat pessimistically, that the law "may not be adaptable to French society."

Nevertheless, the introduction of the *Loi Evin* has started a long-needed debate in French society related to smoking and helped spread an awareness of its dangers.

WORKSHOP 2

THE NITTY-GRITTY

ANY QUESTIONS?: ASKING QUESTIONS USING INTONATION OR *EST-CE QUE*

There are several ways to ask a question in French, depending on the level of formality required. Let's start with the most informal—and the easiest—way. Aren't you lucky?

1. Questions Using Intonation

You can ask a question by simply modifying your intonation, just like in English. In this case, nothing in the sentence changes; instead, the intonation just goes up at the end of the sentence.

In everyday speech, this is what people do most of the time. Next time you listen to the dialogues, pay attention to the rising intonation of the questions in them.

Tu as soif?

You're thirsty?

Tu vois les bus?

You see the buses?

C'est bien l'arrêt de bus pour Denfert-Rochereau?

This is the bus stop for Denfert-Rochereau?

Vous voyagez ensemble?

You're traveling together?

C'est loin?

It's far?

2. Questions Using Est-ce Que

The phrase *est-ce que* is commonly used in French to form questions. This is the most neutral type of question, and can be used in both formal and informal situations.

All you need to do to form a question is place *est-ce que* at the beginning of the sentence.

Tu as soif. →	*Est-ce que tu as soif?*
You are thirsty.	Are you thirsty?
Tu vois Tante Clarisse. →	*Est-ce que tu vois Tante Clarisse?*
You see Aunt Clarisse.	Do you see Aunt Clarisse?
Vous voyagez ensemble. →	*Est-ce que vous voyagez ensemble?*
You are traveling together.	Are you traveling together?
C'est loin. →	*Est-ce que c'est loin?*
It's far.	Is it far?

Remember, it's as easy as: *Est-ce-que* + regular sentence + ?

ACTIVITY 7: TAKE IT FOR A SPIN

What a mess! *S'il vous plaît*, make sentences by putting the words provided in the right order. All sentences should be questions. *Ah, merci, mon ami(e)!*

a) *tu / la France / Est-ce-que / habites?*
b) *Florine / du Sénégal / Jeannie / arrivent / et?*
c) *vous / cousines / êtes / Est-ce que?*
d) *voient / Tante Clarisse / elles / Est-ce qu'?*
e) *avez / les / Vous / passeports?*
f) *C'est / de bus / pour / l'arrêt / Paris?*

Next. . . . The irregular verbs!

There are about 150 irregular verbs in the French language. C'mon . . . It's really the small minority of the French verbs! So, don't panic. You'll be fine.

I SCREAM, YOU SCREAM: THE IRREGULAR VERBS *VOIR* (TO SEE) AND *CROIRE* (TO BELIEVE) IN THE PRESENT TENSE

Let's talk about "seeing" and "believing," or *voir* (to see) and *croire* (to believe). Believe me, I'll do everything I can to help you out with irregular verbs. First and foremost, I'll introduce irregular verbs in groups sharing the same pattern.

To form the present tense of the two verbs, you drop the ending from their infinitive form (*–re* for *croire* and *–r* for *voir*), then add these present tense endings (which are also used by many other irregular verbs):

For *je, tu, il / elle:* **–s, –s, –t.**
For *nous, vous, ils / elles:* **–ons, –ez, –ent.**

Note that only the first three endings (i.e., the singular endings) are different from those used by the regular –er verbs discussed earlier. And, like before, the –s,–s, –t, and –ent endings are not pronounced.

THE PRESENT TENSE OF THE IRREGULAR VERB *CROIRE* (TO BELIEVE)	
je crois	nous croyons
tu crois	vous croyez
il / elle croit	ils / elles croient

THE PRESENT TENSE OF THE IRREGULAR VERB *VOIR* (TO SEE)	
je vois	nous voyons
tu vois	vous voyez
il / elle voit	ils / elles voient

As you can see, the only unpredictable forms are the *nous* and the *vous* forms. There, the *y* replaces the final *i* of the stem.

By the way, check out the pronunciation . . .

je vois (vwah)	I see	but	**nous voyons (vwahyoh^n)**	we believe
tu vois (vwah)	you see	but	**vous voyez (vwahyeh)**	you (all) see

Let's look at a few more examples:

Non, je ne crois pas.

No, I don't think so.

Vous voyez, c'est un vrai film de science fiction!

You see, it's like a science fiction movie!

Est-ce qu'ils voient l'arrêt de bus?

Do they see the bus stop?

Draw lines between the pronouns on the left and the corresponding verb forms on the right.

vous	voit
tu	croyons
elles	crois
nous	voyez
il	voient
je	crois

Très bien! (Very good!)

WORDS TO LIVE BY

So, you've arrived at the airport and no one is there to greet you? No problem! You can take a cab (*un taxi*), the train, or a bus . . .

un autobus, un bus	*a bus*
un arrêt de bus	*a bus stop*
le métro	*subway*
le train	*train*
passer	*to pass; to go by*

And now, for some useful little words . . .

beaucoup	*a lot, much*
couramment	*fluently*
un peu	*a little*
enfin	*at last*
souvent	*often*
trop tard	*too late*
ici et là	*here and there*
là-bas	*there*
loin	*far*
voici	*here is / are / ; there is / are*
un	*one*
deux	*two*

Word on the Street

Bon voyage!	*Have a nice trip!*
C'est génial / super!	*It's great!*
C'mon, girl!	*(Guess . . .)*
cool	*And guess again . . .*
Courage!	*Keep up! / Don't worry!*
D'accord.	*Sure. / Okay.*
merci	*thank you*
s'il vous plaît / s'il te plaît	*please (formal / informal)*

And some expressions with the auxiliary verb *avoir:*

avoir besoin de	*to need*
avoir du retard	*to be delayed*
avoir soif	*to be thirsty*
avoir faim	*to be hungry*

Did You Know?

L'Amérique has influenced the everyday life of the French and their language in many ways. Although everyday spoken French and French slang are very rich, you'll quickly notice some English words used *ici et là.* Young people especially find it very *cool* to use American English words. Besides *cool,* other common Americanisms are: *okay, bye, speed,* and *c'mon.*

Did You Know?

There are a lot of tiny words in French called interjections. They express the emotions of the speaker. Here are a few used in this chapter:

Ah!	*Used to express surprise and relief put together*
Euh!	*Used to express hesitation*
Oh!	*Used to express suprise*
Oh là là!	*"Seems like there's a problem!"*

Yes, you're almost done with this chapter, but before you close your book, are you ready for a little extra challenge?

ACTIVITY 9: TAKE IT UP A NOTCH

Put the verbs in parentheses into the appropriate present tense form.

a) *Jeannie et Florine (arriver) à Paris. Elles (être) cousines.*
b) *Florine (avoir) soif, mais elle n'(avoir) pas d'euros.*
c) *Elles (avoir besoin) de changer de l'argent au bureau de change.*

d) *Monsieur, le bureau de change? Mais, vous (voir) bien, je ne (travailler) pas ici.*

e) *Tu ne (voir) pas, c'est l'arrêt de bus pour Denfert-Rochereau!*

CRIB NOTES

Jeannie: Paris, Paris, here we are!

Immigration Officer: Passports and plane tickets . . .

Florine and Jeannie: Yes, yes, of course. Good morning, sir.

Florine: Here they are!

Immigration Officer: Are you traveling together? What about you?

Jeannie: Euh. . . . Here they are! Yes, sir, we are traveling together, we are cousins and . . .

Immigration Officer: Do you have a certificate of room and board?

Florine: Yes, sir, of course. Here it is.

Immigration Officer: Everything is in order. Ladies . . .

Jeannie and Florine walk and walk and walk.

Jeannie: Whoa. . . . Is it far?

Florine: No, I don't think so . . . At last!

Message: Welcome to Roissy–Charles de Gaulle airport.

Jeannie: Do you see that, Florine? It's like a real science fiction movie!

Florine: It's true. . . . It's great! (Coughing.)

Jeannie: And the luggage?

Florine: Isn't it over there? People smoke a lot here!

With a lot of luggage, Florine and Jeannie go through customs. Then . . .

Florine: Do you see Aunt Clarisse?

Jeannie: No, I don't see Auntie . . . . But we're really late!

Florine: You're right. Well, we should call. But we don't have any euros.

Jeannie: You're right. We need to change some money. Please, Ma'am. Oh well . . . .

Florine: Sir! Yes, hello, where is the currency exchange, please?

A man: But I don't work here!

Jeannie: People are strange here.

Florine: No. . . . C'mon, girl, we're in Paris! (Coughing.)

Outside the airport . . .

Florine: (Coughing.) Do you see the buses? They're great!

Jeannie: Oh, yeah! Ah . . . here is the bus stop for Denfert-Rocheteau.

Florine: Denfert-Rocheteau? You're sure?

Jeannie: Yes, it's in the 14th *arrondissement*. Paris, here we come! The buses come often, I think . . .

Florine: At last! I'm thirsty, Jeannie . . . . Can you . . . (Coughing.)

Jeannie: Okay, I'll be back.

Florine: Thank you, cousin! Excuse me, sir, is this the bus stop for Denfert-Rocheteau?

A man: Rocheteau? Hmm . . . . Rochereau, Miss, Denfert-Rochereau. And no, it's there. You see, the bus is arriving . . .

Florine: Oh, no!

A man: Oh, yes!

Florine: No, it's not that . . . . Thank you so much, sir.

Jeannie: Here! Miss . . . (She gives a drink to Florine.)

Florine: Jeannie, the bus! Oh, too late! Well, thank you, Jeannie . . .

A man: Ladies, the buses come often. Don't worry! And welcome to Paris!

ACTIVITY 1

a) Non, Jeannie et Florine sont cousines.

b) *L'agent d'immigration* asks for their *passeports*, *billets d'avion* and *certificats d'hébergement*.

c) Non. Tante Clarisse n'est pas là.

d) Florine is coughing because *les gens fument beaucoup*.

e) They ask for *le bureau de change*.

ACTIVITY 2

a) Vous ne parlez pas bien français.
b) Nous n'habitons pas au Sénégal.
c) Je ne suis pas étudiant.
d) Tu n'as pas ton passeport.
e) Ils ne sont pas à l'aéroport.
f) Elle ne fume pas.

ACTIVITY 3

Vous voyagez, nous voyageons (voyager); Les gens fument (fumer); On téléphone (téléphoner); changer; Je ne travaille pas (travailler).

ACTIVITY 4

Je marche, tu marches, il / elle marche; nous marchons, vous marchez, ils / elles marchent.

ACTIVITY 5

Cross out: habiter, l'oncle, seul.

ACTIVITY 6

a) Non, *Florine et Jeannie* are taking *le bus*.
b) Elles sont à l'arrêt de bus.
c) They are going to Denfert-Rochereau *dans le 14ème arrondissement*.
d) Florine coughs a lot *et elle a soif*.
e) Oui, les bus passent souvent.

ACTIVITY 7

a) Est-ce que tu habites en / la France?
b) Florine et Jeannie arrivent du Sénégal?
c) Est-ce-que vous êtes cousines?
d) Est-ce qu'elles voient Tante Clarisse?
e) Vous avez les passeports?
f) C'est l'arrêt de bus pour Paris?

ACTIVITY 8

vous voyez / tu crois / elles voient / nous croyons / il voit / je crois

ACTIVITY 9

a) Jeannie et Florine arrivent à Paris. Elles sont cousines.
b) Florine a soif, mais elle n'a pas d'euros.
c) Elles ont besoin de changer de l'argent au bureau de change.
d) Monsieur, le bureau de change? Mais, vous voyez bien, je ne travaille pas ici.
e) Tu ne vois pas, c'est l'arrêt de bus pour Denfert-Rochereau!

3.

TRAFFIC

Trafic

No need to rush; just leave on time.

COMING UP. . .

- *Stuck in traffic*: Talking about the pleasures of driving
- *Happy Anniversary!*: Shopping for a present
- *Any questions?*: Asking questions using *who?*, *what?*, *where?*, etc.
- *I scream, you scream*: The irregular verbs *vouloir* (to want) and *pouvoir* (can) in the present tense
- *I'm on my way*: The irregular verb *aller* (to go) in the present tense
- *It's going to rain*: Talking about things in the immediate future
- *The countdown*: Let's count from 1 to 29
- *Make your point!*: Using stressed pronouns

The film *Trafic* (*Traffic*) is a comedy masterpiece created in 1971 by the famous director and actor Jacques Tati (1908–1982). Jacques Tati's final film expresses his concerns about technology and modern progress, in addition to traffic jams, of course. The film is full of hilarious gags, even though the pace is typically French and somewhat slow for American tastes. Tati's views about the modern world have influenced many artists since.

LOOKING AHEAD

Here you are in Lesson 3 and eager to go on, aren't you?

This chapter is about the pleasures of driving (*to drive* is *conduire*), traffic (*trafic*), and cars (*voitures*). In the Hear . . . Say section, you will hear *deux frères et une soeur* (two brothers and a sister)—Jean-David, Lucien and Delphine. They are going to their parents' house (*maison*) in *la banlieue parisienne* (a Parisian suburb) for a traditional Sunday lunch. Lucien, the eldest brother, *conduit* (is driving). *Il a l'air en colère.* (He seems upset.) His little *soeur* is bugging him, and they're running late. To make things worse, *il pleut* (it's raining), and the traffic is dense. But, wait, haven't they forgotten something? Of course! Their parents' wedding anniversary! *Aïe!* . . . Where can they get a present on a Sunday afternoon? Let's hear about it!

HEAR ... SAY 1

The Pleasures of Driving   (Les plaisirs de conduire)

Lucien:	On va être encore en retard!
Jean-David:	Lucien, tu peux peut-être conduire plus vite . . .
Lucien:	Non, je ne crois pas, Jean-David. Tu ne vois pas la circulation?
Delphine:	Rien ne sert de courir, il faut partir à point!
Lucien:	Eh là, mademoiselle Futée! Qui est-ce qui est toujours en retard?
Delphine:	C'est lui . . . Jean-David.
Jean-David:	Lucien, là, tu peux doubler la voiture?
Lucien:	Peut-être . . .

The horn beeps . . . (On klaxonne . . .)

Lucien:	Peut-être pas!
Delphine:	Oh, les hommes au volant! Et on ne parle pas du reste. . . . Moi, je veux bien conduire mais . . .
Lucien:	Toi, un mot de plus et . . .
Delphine:	Mais, Lucien, pourquoi est-ce que tu es en colère?

parks

Lucien gets into the right lane and parks the car on the side of the road. (Lucien va sur la file de droite et gare la voiture sur le bord de la route.)

Lucien: Delphine, dehors!

Delphine: Zut! Le cadeau!

Jean-David: Un cadeau, pourquoi?

Delphine: Mais, c'est l'anniversaire de mariage des parents!

The car starts again and goes from lane to lane. (La voiture redémarre et passe de file en file.)

Jean-David: Aïe aïe aïe! On va arriver en retard et sans cadeau! Ça va barder . . .

all hell will break loose

HOW'S THAT AGAIN?

It seems that Delphine, the only girl in the family, is enjoying teasing her brothers! Look at the following statements and decide which ones are *vrais* (true) and which ones are *faux* (false). And if they're false, try and make them correct.

a)	*Jean-David conduit.*	VRAI ou FAUX
b)	*They are going to their parents.*	VRAI ou FAUX
c)	*Lucien est toujours en retard.*	VRAI ou FAUX
d)	*They forgot to get gas.*	VRAI ou FAUX
e)	*Delphine est en colère.*	VRAI ou FAUX

WORKSHOP 1

THE NITTY-GRITTY

ANY QUESTIONS?: ASKING QUESTIONS USING *WHO?*, *WHAT?*, *WHERE?*, ETC.

Some questions require a question word specifying what the question is referring to. This is what you need to do to ask such questions in French.

1. Start with a question using *est-ce que:*

   est-ce que + sentence

2. Add a question word:

   question word + est-ce que + sentence

And here are several French question words:

que? (what), *qui?* (who), *à qui?* (to whom), *où?* (where), *quand?* (when), *pourquoi?* (why), *comment?* (how), *combien?* (how many / how much)

Notice that with *qui?* (who), the phrase *est-ce-que* becomes *est-ce qui*. Here are some examples:

b **Qui est-ce qui a une idée?**

Who has an idea?

c **Qu'est-ce que vous cherchez?**

What are you looking for?

a **À qui est-ce que Delphine parle?**

Who is Delphine speaking to? (*or* To whom is Delphine speaking?)

f **Où est-ce qu'ils vont?**

Where are they going?

e **Quand est-ce qu'ils arrivent?**

When are they coming?

Comment est-ce que tu vas?

How are you doing?

d **Combien est-ce qu'ils sont?**

How many are they? (*or* How many of them are there?)

Heads Up!

Take another look at the above examples. Note the *élision*: *que* + *est-ce que* becomes *qu'est-ce que*, and *est-ce que* + *ils* becomes *est-ce qu'ils*.

Heads Up!

The Fine Print

Note that *qui?* (who) can be used alone, without *est-ce qui* after it:

Qui est-ce qui a une idée? or

Qui a une idée?

Who has an idea?

Look at the list of questions above to find the one that best fits each of the following answers:

a)   *Delphine parle à Lucien et à Jean-David.*
b)   *Delphine a une idée.*
c)   *Nous cherchons un cadeau d'anniversaire.*
d)   *Ils sont trois.*
e)   *Ils arrivent en retard.*
f)   *Ils vont chez les parents.*

I SCREAM, YOU SCREAM: THE IRREGULAR VERBS *VOULOIR* (TO WANT) AND *POUVOIR* (CAN) IN THE PRESENT TENSE

Here's a new pattern of irregular verbs: *pouvoir* (can) *and vouloir* (to want).

In the present tense, these two verbs are formed in a similar fashion.

The endings are very similar to those we used for *voir* (to see) and *croire* (to believe). The only difference is that the *je* and *tu* forms take an *–x* instead of an *–s*.

For *je, tu, il / elle:* **–x, –x, –t.**
For *nous, vous, ils / elles:* **–ons, –ez, –ent.**

THE PRESENT OF THE IRREGULAR VERB *POUVOIR* (CAN)	
je peux	*nous pouvons*
tu peux	*vous pouvez*
il / elle peut	*ils / elles peuvent*

THE PRESENT OF THE IRREGULAR VERB *VOULOIR* (TO WANT)	
je veux	*nous voulons*
tu veux	*vous voulez*
il / elle veut	*ils / elles veulent*

Once again, the *nous* and *vous* forms are the same (their stem remains unchanged) while being different from the *je, tu, il / elle,* and *ils / elles* forms. *Je, tu, il / elle,* and *ils / elles* forms are irregular: they use the stem *peu–/peuv–* and *veu–/veul–* instead of the expected *pouv–* and *voul–*. For example:

Lucien, tu peux doubler la voiture.

Lucien, you can pass the car.

Ils ne peuvent pas conduire plus vite?

They can't drive any faster?

Qu'est-ce que vous voulez?

What do you want?

Maman veut aller à Perpignan.

Mom wants to go to Perpignan.

TAKE IT FOR A SPIN

Draw lines to connect the phrases on the left with the appropriate phrases on the right to make full sentences. (Use each phrase only once.)

a) *Est-ce que je*   *conduire ma voiture.*
b) *Vous voulez*   *pouvons garer la voiture.*
c) *Les parents*   *peux aller à Paris?*
d) *Nous*   *veut aller à Perpignan.*
e) *Lucien ne peut pas*   *ne veulent pas être en retard.*
f) *Maman*   *doubler la voiture.*

I'M ON MY WAY: THE IRREGULAR VERB *ALLER* (TO GO) IN THE PRESENT TENSE

While you're at it, why not learn another one . . . the irregular verb *aller* (to go) in the present tense.

A very useful verb indeed . . . unfortunately, *aller* is in a league of its own and doesn't follow any recognizable pattern. However, as with other verbs, the stem of the verb remains intact in the *nous* and *vous* forms.

THE PRESENT TENSE OF THE IRREGULAR VERB *ALLER* (TO GO)	
je vais	*nous allons*
tu vas	*vous allez*
il / elle va	*ils / elles vont*

Here are some examples:

Les frères et la soeur vont chez les parents.

The brothers and sister are going to the parents' house.

Lucien va sur la file de droite.

Lucien gets into the right lane.

Tu ne vas pas plus vite?

You don't / can't go faster?

And let's remind ourselves of some expressions containing *aller* that you encountered before:

Comment ça va?

How's it going?

Ça va . . .

It's going all right. . .

Nous allons bien.

We are doing fine.

IT'S GOING TO RAIN: TALKING ABOUT THINGS IN THE IMMEDIATE FUTURE

Another good thing about *aller* is that it is used to form an easy and common tense—the immediate future. The immediate future is used to describe an action that is expected to happen very soon, e.g., *It's going to rain any moment* or *It's going to get dark soon.*

As a matter of fact, the *going to* form used in these English sentences is an immediate future tense that is formed just like the immediate future in French: take a present tense form of the verb *aller* (to go) and follow it by whatever verb you need in its basic, infinitive form (*to* in English, *–er, –ir* or *–re* in French). For example:

On <u>va</u> encore <u>arriver</u> en retard.

We're going to arrive late again.

Je <u>vais doubler</u> la voiture.

I'm going to pass the car.

Ils ne <u>vont</u> pas <u>habiter</u> à Paris.

They are not going to live in Paris.

ACTIVITY 4: TAKE IT FOR A SPIN

Complete the following sentences by using the appropriate present tense form of *aller* (to go). Also, identify the sentences that are in the immediate future.

a) *Delphine et Lucien _____ chez les parents.*
b) *Bien sûr, Delphine est en retard et Lucien _____ être en colère.*
c) *Est-ce que Jean-David _____ conduire?*
d) *Nous n'_____ pas arriver sans cadeau!*

e) On _____ passer sur la file de droite.

f) Les parents ne _____ pas être en colère.

WORDS TO LIVE BY

STUCK IN TRAFFIC: TALKING ABOUT THE PLEASURES OF DRIVING

In every big city, traffic is a problem, as is the pollution (*la pollution*):

la ville	city; town
la banlieue	suburb

Another problem with the word "traffic" is that in English it takes two "f"s, but in French only one—*le trafic*.

le bouchon	traffic jam
la circulation	traffic

Here are more new words related to cars and traffic:

la voiture	car
aller moins vite	to go slower
aller plus vite	to go faster
conduire	to drive
démarrer / redémarrer	to start / to start again
doubler une voiture	to pass a car, to overtake
garer	to park
klaxonner	to beep the horn
passer de file en file	to go from lane to lane

Did You Know?

If you happen to be behind the wheel (*au volant*) in France, make sure you respect *la limitation de vitesse* (the speed limit). In France, you might be surprised, the speed limit is much higher than in the United States: 50km / hour (about 30 miles / hour) when you are driving in town, 90km / hour (about 56 miles / hour) on a secondary road, 110km / hour (about 69 miles / hour) on a highway and 130km / hour (about 81 miles / hour) on an expressway.

Remember, in France, distances are calculated in *kilomètres*. For your information, 1 mile is equivalent to about 1.6 km.

Did You Know?

Back to our new words. . . . Do not confuse:

l'autoroute (fem.)	expressway
la route	road

Roads or *routes* can be of two types: *la route départementale* (small, two-lane road) or *la route nationale* (larger, national road). There are more:

la rue	*street*
le bord de la route	*side of the road*
le trottoir	*sidewalk*

Did You Know?

France is divided into 95 administrative units or *départements* and 4 additional *départements d'outre-mer* (overseas departments). The overseas departments are: *La Guadeloupe, La Guyane, La Réunion*, and *La Martinique*.

Did You Know?

Did You Know?

There is a French saying: *Rien ne sert de courir, il faut partir à point*, which literally means, "There's no point in running; you should leave on time." Good advice that our three siblings from the dialogue haven't quite absorbed yet!

By the way, this line is *la morale* (the moral of the story) from one of the many famous fables by the French poet Jean de La Fontaine (1621–1695), *Le lièvre et la tortue* (*The Hare and the Tortoise*).

La Fontaine's fables are an essential part of French culture and French kids learn many of them by heart during grade school.

Did You Know?

And now for more useful little words . . .

bon	*well; good*
peu après	*soon after*
peut-être	*maybe*
sans	*without*
sous	*under*
sur	*on*
souvent	*often*
toujours	*always*

Word on the Street

Like many *frères* (brother) and *soeurs* (sister), Lucien and Delphine often fight. In the dialogue, Lucien was upset because Delphine kept nagging him. If a similar thing happens to you, here's a useful expression you can use to describe how you feel:

être en colère	to be angry

Just say: *Je suis en colère* (I'm angry).

And you can also issue a threat by saying:

Un mot de plus et . . . !   *One more word and . . . !*

Or else, *Ça va barder!*, All hell is going to break loose!

We'd better move on . . .

ACTIVITY 5:   TAKE IT FOR A SPIN

Grab your pencil! Relate the words on the left with those on the right—the words have either similar meanings or opposite meanings. (Use the glossary when in doubt.)

la route	le frère
souvent	sous
plus	sans
sur	démarrer
garer	la rue
avec	moins
la soeur	toujours

LOOKING AHEAD

Sunday lunch is still a firm tradition in France and a time when many families gather. Until only a few years ago, almost nobody worked on Sunday and most stores would be closed *(fermés)*, which explains why our friends are having such trouble finding a present *(un cadeau)* for their parents' anniversary.

It's getting late *(il est tard)* and our friends have to solve a problem. Where will they *trouver* (find) a present for their parents' *anniversaire de mariage* on a Sunday afternoon?

ACTIVITY 6:   LET'S WARM UP

Please answer the following questions:

a) *Et vous, est-ce que vous travaillez le dimanche?*
b) *Est-ce que vous allez voir la famille?*

HEAR...SAY 2

An Original Present! (Un cadeau original!)

Jean-David:	Où aller? Le dimanche, tout est fermé.
Delphine:	Non, pas tout . . . *what are you cooking up?*
Lucien:	Qu'est-ce que tu mijotes, toi encore?
Delphine:	Vous voyez, vous ne pouvez pas vivre sans femmes!
Jean-David:	Bon, Delphine!
Delphine:	Lucien . . . tu vois la prochaine sortie. . . . Ici!
Lucien:	La station d'essence Esso?
Jean-David:	Mais on n'a pas besoin d'essence!

At the gas station store. (À la station d'essence.)

Lucien:	Qu'est-ce que vous voulez trouver ici?
Delphine:	Bonjour, Madame, nous cherchons un cadeau. . . . Un cadeau d'anniversaire de mariage . . .
La dame de la boutique:	Vous cherchez un cadeau d'anniversaire de mariage ici?
Delphine:	Oui, un cadeau très original . . .

Shortly after, they arrive at their parents' home in the Parisian suburb of Vincennes.

Lucien:	C'est absurde! Ils ne vont pas apprécier . . .
Delphine:	Mais Maman veut faire une croisière. Hmmm! J'ai faim!
Jean-David:	Moi aussi . . .
Lucien:	Une croisière sur un bateau pneumatique?!

ACTIVITY 7:   HOW'S THAT AGAIN?

Delphine, *la futée de la famille* (the family smartypants) runs her world pretty well, don't you think? Please answer these questions now.

a) Who comes up with *une idée* for the anniversary present?
   1. *un des frères*   2. *la tante*   3. *la soeur*

b) Why does Delphine suggest stopping at the gas station?
   1. *C'est la seule boutique ouverte* (open).   2. *She needs to go to the bathroom.*
   3. *So they can get gas.*

c) What do they get?
   1. *flowers*   2. *l'essence*   3. *un cadeau absurde*

d) Where do their parents live?
   1. *dans un appartement à Paris*   2. *dans une maison à Vincennes*

Did You Know?

As you might expect, Paris, like any big city, has a lot of traffic problems. In order to avoid traffic jams *(les bouchons)* and excessive levels of pollution reaching their peak during the summer months, people are encouraged to rely on *les transports en commun* (public transportation). As a bonus, riders avoid all the parking troubles, too.

And how about Paris by bike? *Paris à bicyclette*, what a wonderful idea! By the way, another common way to say *la bicyclette* in French is *le vélo*.

Did You Know?

WORKSHOP 2

THE NITTY-GRITTY

THE COUNTDOWN: LET'S COUNT FROM 1 TO 29

You might have a calculator, but you still need to know your numbers. . . . So, *voilà*, numbers in French from 1 to 29. Pay attention to the pronunciation of the numbers from 1 to 10, 20, and 21 as they are not entirely predictable.

NUMBERS FROM 1 TO 29		
1: un (eh^n)	11: onze	21: vingt et un (veh^{n}t eh uh^n)
2: deux (duh)	12: douze	22: vingt-deux
3: trois (trwah)	13: treize	23: vingt-trois
4: quatre (kahtr)	14: quatorze	24: vingt-quatre
5: cinq (seh^{n}k)	15: quinze	25: vingt-cinq
6: six (sees)	16: seize	26: vingt-six
7: sept (seht)	17: dix-sept	27: vingt-sept
8: huit (weet)	18: dix-huit	28: vingt-huit
9: neuf (nuhf)	19: dix-neuf	29: vingt-neuf
10: dix (dees)	20: vingt (veh^n)	*(More to come...)*

Notice that 21 is *vingt et un*, while all other numbers just have a hyphen, eg., *dix-huit* or *vingt-deux*.

ACTIVITY 8: TAKE IT FOR A SPIN

Un, deux, trois, go! C'mon, give the solutions, *en français*, to the following math problems.

a)   4 + 13 = _____
b)   5 + 9 = _____

c) $7 + 22 =$ _____

d) $29 - 18 =$ _____

Bravo!

MAKE YOUR POINT!: USING STRESSED PRONOUNS

You can say in French:

Je veux conduire. I want to drive.

or:

Moi, je veux conduire.

The second sentence means about the same thing as the first one, except that the pronoun *je* is reinforced or emphasized by the use of *moi*, corresponding roughly to the English phrase, "(as for) me."

The stressed pronouns are used very frequently in spoken French and it is important that you know them. So, here they are:

THE STRESSED PRONOUNS			
moi	me	*nous*	us
toi	you	*vous*	you
lui	him	*eux*	them (masc.)
elle	her	*elles*	them (fem.)

By the way, what are the personal pronouns? C'mon, I'm listening . . . That's right: *je, tu, il / elle, nous, vous, ils / elles. Très bien!* And now look at some examples from the dialogue:

Moi, je veux bien conduire.

Me, I am willing to drive.

Qu'est-ce que tu mijotes encore, toi?

What are you up to again, you?

Moi, j'ai faim. Lui aussi.

Me, I'm hungry. So is he.

In addition to emphasis, the stressed pronouns are also used in the following situations:

1. In the expression *moi aussi* (so do I), *toi aussi* (so do you), *lui aussi* (so does he), *elle aussi* (so does she), etc.

2. In short answers to *qui?* (who?), when the pronoun is used by itself, without a verb:

> **Qui est-ce qui est en retard encore?—Lui!**

Who is late again?—He is!

> **Qui est-ce qui va à Vincennes?—Eux.**

Who is going to Vincennes?—They are.

> **Qui est dans la voiture?—Moi.**

Who is in the car?—I am.

3. After a preposition, such as *à* (at, in), *chez* (at someone's place), or *avec* (with).

> **Ils vont chez eux.**

They're going to their place.

> **Tu vas chez les parents avec elle.**

You're going to your parents' place with her.

4. After the expression *c'est* . . .

> **Ah! C'est toi.**

Oh! It's you.

ACTIVITY 9:   TAKE IT FOR A SPIN

Toi or *moi* ? Well, you! Make complete sentences or answer questions by combining the elements on the left with the elements on the right.

a)	Qui est-ce qui est là?	c)	chez lui?
b)	Delphine voyage avec	d)	Moi.
c)	Tu ne vas pas	e)	Vous aussi?
d)	Qui est-ce qui a besoin d'essence?	b)	eux.
e)	Ils ont faim.	a)	C'est nous, Maman!

WORDS TO LIVE BY

HAPPY ANNIVERSARY!: SHOPPING FOR A PRESENT

So, our friends seem to have solved their problem even on a Sunday (*dimanche*). *La boutique de la station d'essence,* the gas station store, may be indeed one of the rare open places, when you drive around Paris on a Sunday:

être ouvert, ouverte	to be open
être fermé, fermée	to be closed

But apart from shopping for a rubber boat, you can also do other things at the gas station:

prendre de l'essence	to get gas
faire le plein	to fill up

You can ask: *Le plein, s'il vous plaît!* (Fill it up, please!) By the way, you can get *l'essence sans plomb* (unleaded gas), *le super*, or *le diesel*.

And after such successful shopping, we're celebrating:

un anniversaire	birthday
un anniversaire de mariage	anniversary
le cadeau d'anniversaire	birthday / anniversary present
le bateau pneumatique	rubber boat

Heads Up!

Was the present *original* or *absurde?* Whatever it was, *cadeau* (the present) takes a final –*x* in its plural form, as do all the other words ending in –*au* or –*eau,* such as *le bateau.* So, the plural of *bateau* is *bateaux.*

The final –*x,* like the final –*s,* is silent. And remember the adjective *beau* (beautiful), from the previous lesson? Its plural is *beaux* as well.

Heads Up!

It takes time, of course, to think of the right present—you need to look for it and maybe you'll find it:

chercher	to look for
trouver	to find

Word on the Street

First, here are some more interjections:

Aïe! or **Aïe aïe aïe!**	You can say it once or three times, and it means "trouble" or "it hurts."
Zut!	Gosh! (used to express disappointment or anger)
Hmmm . . .	Yummy! (used when something smells or looks good)
Hé là!	Slow down!, Easy!

Now, a few more common expressions:

Que'est-ce que tu mijotes?	What are you up to? (very colloquial and informal) (Lit. "What are you cooking up?")

And two very basic ones—remember them, they might come in handy:

avoir faim	to be hungry
avoir soif	to be thirsty

When you really cannot take it any more, this slang term may come in handy:

J'ai la dalle.   *I'm starving.*

You should certainly not go hungry in France!

TAKE IT FOR A SPIN

Now, please fill in the blanks with the appropriate words listed below:

va / dimanche / faim / anniversaire / aller / frère / où / aussi / fermé / colère / retard / elle / essence / cadeau

    a)   *Lucien ne peut pas _____ plus vite.*

    b)   *_____ trouver un cadeau d'_____ ? Tout est _____ le dimanche.*

    c)   *On va à la station d'_____ . C'est ouvert le _____ .*

    d)   *Ça _____ barder! On est en _____ et on n'a pas de _____ d'anniversaire.*

    e)   *Lucien, le _____ de Delphine, est en _____ .*

    f)   *Delphine, _____ , a _____ . Jean-David _____ .*

Almost done, except for this final little challenge:

TAKE IT UP A NOTCH!

Complete this story from the dialogue by putting the verbs in parentheses into the appropriate form of the present tense.

    a)   *Delphine (être) en voiture avec Lucien et Jean-David.*

    b)   *Ils (aller) à la station d'essence.*

    c)   *Nous ne (pouvoir) pas trouver un cadeau à la boutique de la station!*

    d)   *Qu'est-ce qu'ils (aller) trouver?*

    e)   *Lucien (être) en colère et les autres (avoir) faim.*

CRIB NOTES

HEAR...SAY 1

Lucien:	We're going to be late again!
Jean-David:	Lucien, maybe you can drive faster . . .
Lucien:	No, I don't think so, Jean-David. Don't you see the traffic?
Delphine:	No need to rush, just leave on time.

Lucien:	Hey, Miss Smarty! Who is always late?
Delphine:	It's him. . . . Jean-David.
Jean-David:	Lucien, really, can you pass that car?
Lucien:	Maybe . . .
The horn beeps.	

Lucien:	Maybe not!
Delphine:	Ha! Men behind the wheel! And we won't say anything else . . . I'm willing to drive but . . .
Lucien:	One more word from you and . . .
Delphine:	But Lucien, why are you angry?

Lucien gets into the right lane and parks the car on the side of the road.

Lucien:	Delphine, get out!

Delphine:	Shoot! The present!
Jean-David:	A present? What for?
Delphine:	But it's our parents' wedding anniversary!

The car starts again and goes from lane to lane.

Jean-David:	Whoa. . . . We're going to arrive late and without a present! All hell will break loose . . .

HEAR...SAY 2

Jean-David:	Where do we go? On Sundays, everything is closed.
Delphine:	No, not everything . . .
Lucien:	What are you up to now?
Delphine:	You see, you can't live without women!
Jean-David:	C'mon, Delphine!
Delphine:	Lucien . . . do you see the next exit. . . . Here!
Lucien:	The Esso gas station?
Jean-David:	But we don't need gas!

At the gas station store . . .

Lucien:	What do you want to find here?
Delphine:	Hello, Madam! We're looking

	for a present . . . a present for a wedding anniversary . . .
Lady of the store:	You're looking for a wedding anniversary present here?
Delphine:	Yes, a very original present . . .

Shortly after, they arrive at their parents' home in the Parisian suburb of Vincennes.

Lucien:	This is absurd! They aren't going to like this . . .
Delphine:	But Mom wants to go on a cruise! Yum! I'm hungry!
Jean-David:	Me, too . . .
Lucien:	A cruise on a rubber boat?!

ANSWER KEY

ACTIVITY 1

a) FAUX—Lucien conduit.
b) VRAI—They are going to their parents.
c) FAUX—Delphine est toujours en retard.
d) FAUX—They forgot to get a present for their parents' wedding anniversary.
e) FAUX—Lucien est en colère.

ACTIVITY 2

a) À qui est-ce que Delphine parle?
b) Qui a une idée?
c) Qu'est-ce que vous cherchez?
d) Combien est-ce qu'ils sont?
e) Quand est-ce qu'ils arrivent?
f) Où est-ce qu'ils vont?

ACTIVITY 3

a) Est-ce que je peux aller à Paris?
b) Vous voulez conduire ma voiture.
c) Les parents ne veulent pas être en retard.
d) Nous pouvons garer la voiture.
e) Lucien ne peut pas doubler la voiture.
f) Maman veut aller à Perpignan.

ACTIVITY 4

a) Delphine et Lucien vont chez les parents.
b) Bien sûr, Delphine est en retard et Lucien va être en colère. (immediate future)
c) Est-ce que Jean-David va conduire? (immediate future)
d) Nous n'allons pas arriver sans cadeau! (immediate future)
e) On va passer sur la file de droite. (immediate future)
f) Les parents ne vont pas être en colère. (immediate future)

ACTIVITY 5

la route-la rue; souvent-toujours; plus-moins; sur-sous; garer-démarrer; avec-sans; la soeur-le frère.

ACTIVITY 6

a) Do you work on Sundays?: Oui, je travaille le dimanche. / Non, je ne travaille pas le dimanche.
b) Are you going to see your family?: Oui, je vais voir ma famille. / Non, je ne vais pas voir ma famille.

a) 3. La soeur.
b) 1. C'est la seule boutique ouverte.
c) 3. Un cadeau absurde.
d) 2. Dans une maison à Vincennes.

a) dix-sept
b) quatorze
c) vingt-neuf
d) onze

a) Qui est-ce qui est là?—C'est nous, Maman!
b) Delphine voyage avec eux.
c) Tu ne vas pas chez lui?
d) Qui est-ce qui a besoin de l'essence?—Moi.
e) Ils ont faim.—Vous aussi?

a) Lucien ne peut pas aller plus vite.
b) Où trouver un cadeau d'anniversaire? Tout est fermé le dimanche.
c) On va à la station d'essence. C'est ouvert le dimanche.
d) Ça va barder! On est en retard et on n'a pas de cadeau d'anniversaire.
e) Lucien, le frère de Delphine, est en colère.
f) Delphine, elle, a faim. Jean-David aussi.

a) Delphine est en voiture avec Lucien et Jean-David.
b) Ils vont à la station d'essence.
c) Nous ne pouvons pas trouver de cadeau à la boutique de la station!
d) Qu'est-ce qu'ils vont trouver?
e) Lucien est en colère et les autres ont faim.

4.

THE BRIDE WORE BLACK

La mariée était en noir

She's looking over here! Ooh! She looks upset.

COMING UP. . .

- *It's all in the family*: Talking about family and weddings
- *Here comes the bride*: Talking about weddings
- *The countdown*: Let's count from 30 to 100
- *Time to add up your possessions!*: Words that say you're an owner—*my, your, his, her*, etc., in French
- *I scream, you scream*: The irregular verbs *devoir* (to have to), *recevoir* (to receive), and *savoir* (to know) in the present tense
- *Living in the present*: The regular verbs ending in *–ir* in the present tense
- *Just say no!*: Using *never, nothing*, etc., in French

La mariée était en noir (*The Bride Wore Black*) was directed in 1968 by one of the most famous French directors, François Truffaut (1932–1984), starring, among others, the memorable Jeanne Moreau. It is the most explicit homage by Truffaut to Hitchcock. Truffaut was one of the founders of the New Wave movement (*la Nouvelle Vague*) in the French cinema, which introduced a more personal approach of the director to moviemaking.

LOOKING AHEAD

You've already learned enough basic words and structures to be able to almost "walk on your own." Great feeling, isn't it? *Félicitations!* Congratulations!

In this lesson, you'll be invited to a wedding ceremony.

Paco and his girlfriend Julienne (you met them briefly in Lesson 1) are attending the wedding (*le mariage*) of Marie-Thérèse and Antoine. Paco, Antoine's best friend, is, of course, his best man (*son témoin*). A beautiful *cérémonie* is about to take place (*avoir lieu*) in spite of the obnoxious attitude of Marie-Thérèse's stepmother (*belle-mère*), madame Gaudin. At the church (*à l'église*), during the ceremony, Paco chats (*discute*) with Julienne, telling her about the family and the guests.

But before we eavesdrop on the latest family gossip, let's take a look at Antoine and Marie-Thérèse's wedding invitation.

LET'S PUT IT IN WRITING

THE WEDDING INVITATION (*LE FAIRE-PART DE MARIAGE*)

> *Madame et Monsieur Lewoz*   *Madame Moreau, Monsieur Gaudin*
>
> SONT HEUREUX DE VOUS ANNONCER LE MARIAGE DE LEURS ENFANTS
>
> *Antoine Lewoz* et *Marie-Thérèse Gaudin*
>
> LE QUATORZE AVRIL DEUX MILLE DEUX
> LA RÉCEPTION A LIEU À QUINZE HEURES AU
> GRAND HÔTEL DU CASINO À ENGHIEN-LES-BAINS.
>
> R S V P

TAKE IT FOR A SPIN

Aren't you lucky! You're invited to our friends' wedding. So, make sure you got the following information right:

a)   The ceremony is taking place on:
     April 14, 2002   April 4, 2002   April 24, 2001
b)   The reception is at:
     1 PM   3 PM   5 PM
c)   The reception is taking place at:
     Antoine's house   the Casino   the Grand Hôtel

By the way, RSVP stands for *Répondez, s'il vous plaît*, literally, "please respond."

Heads Up!

Notice that *Madame* and *Monsieur* are capitalized when used alone, but not when followed by a name, e.g., *madame Lewoz* and *monsieur Lewoz*.

Heads Up!

Did You Know?

A PERFECT PLACE FOR A ROMANTIC WEDDING

The ceremony is taking place in (*a lieu à*) Enghien-Les-Bains, a very romantic place, indeed. Since the end of the 18th century, Enghien-Les-Bains, a town northwest of Paris, has been famous as a spa. It is surrounded with lakes and a forest, Forêt de Montmorency. In its vicinity are equally famous racetracks and a century-old casino.

Did You Know?

HEAR . . . SAY 1

Here Comes the Bride!   (Vive la mariée!)

Julienne:	Hmmm! Cette musique à l'orgue . . . C'est si émouvant . . .
Paco:	Ouais . . .
Julienne:	(*She's crying.* / Elle pleure.) . . . Ils sont beaux!
Paco:	Mais Julienne, ça ne va pas?
Julienne:	Ce n'est rien . . . Qui est-ce?
Paco:	Elle? C'est madame Gaudin, la belle-mère de Marie-Thérèse.

Julienne:	Elle regarde par ici. Ouh! Elle a l'air en colère.
Paco:	Oui, je sais. Ce n'est pas une personne sympathique.
Julienne:	Et pourquoi ça?
Paco:	Eh bien . . .
Un invité:	Chhutt!!!
Paco:	Eh bien, elle et sa famille n'aiment pas Antoine car . . .
Julienne:	Car il est noir?
Paco:	Ouais. C'est triste, non?

Outside the church. (À l'extérieur de l'église.)

Julienne:	Alors?
Paco:	Donc, les parents de Marie-Thérèse sont divorcés. Sa belle-famille a beaucoup de préjugés. Au contraire, sa mère et les parents d'Antoine sont des gens très chaleureux et ouverts!
Julienne:	Ah, les voilà! Nos meilleurs voeux de bonheur!
Les invités:	Vive la mariée!
Paco:	Et le marié alors? Vive les mariés!

Following tradition, the guests throw rice at the newlyweds. (Selon la tradition, les invités jettent du riz sur les mariés.)

ACTIVITY 2:   HOW'S THAT AGAIN?

The wedding promises to be a lot of fun. Well, we'll see that later . . . In the meantime, try to answer, in French, the following questions:

- a)   Who is getting married? Who are they?
- b)   Why is Julienne sobbing?
- c)   *Qui est le témoin d'Antoine?*
- d)   *Est-ce que Julienne et Paco sont mariés?*
- e)   What is the custom described at the very end of the dialogue?

Did You Know?

Since the late 1960s, attitudes toward marriage have changed dramatically in France and elsewhere. More and more *couples* decide to live together without officially tying the knot, in church or court. Simple cohabitation, however, doesn't provide the same social and economic benefits and advantages as *le mariage*.

In answer to the evolution in society, a new legal entity has recently been created. It is called *PACS* (*le pacte civil de solidarité,* "civil pact of solidarity") and it allows couples, both heterosexual and homosexual, to benefit from most of the advantages enjoyed by *les couples mariés.* **This is not the end of** *le mariage.* **It is just that men and women now have more options to choose from.**

Did You Know?

WORKSHOP 1

THE NITTY-GRITTY

THE COUNTDOWN: LET'S COUNT FROM 30 TO 100

How about if we work more on increasing your ability to count in French? It's difficult to say no to such an offer, isn't it?

All right, you already know how to count up to 29. Let's make sure of that—1, 2, 3, . . . 29! *Bravo!* And now, up to 100:

NUMBERS FROM 30 TO 59		
30: trente	40: quarante	50: cinquante
31: trente et un	41: quarante et un	51: cinquante et un
32: trente-deux	42: quarante-deux	52: cinquante-deux
33: trente-trois	43: quarante-trois	53: cinquante-trois
34: trente-quatre	. . .	. . .
35: trente-cinq		
36: trente-six		
37: trente-sept		
38: trente-huit		
39: trente-neuf		

NUMBERS 60 TO 100			
60: soixante	70: soixante-dix	80: quatre-vingts	90: quatre-vingt-dix
61: soixante et un	71: soixante et onze	81: quatre-vingt-un	91: quatre-vingt-onze
62: soixante-deux	72: soixante-douze	82: quatre-vingt-deux	92: quatre-vingt-douze
63: soixante-trois	73: soixante-treize	83: quatre-vingt-trois	93: quatre-vingt-treize
. . .	. . .	. . .	. . .
69: soixante-neuf	79: soixante-dix-neuf	89: quatre-vingt-neuf	99: quatre-vingt-dix-neuf

And . . . 100: *CENT!*

Okay . . . How does this look to you? Good!

And now, let's try to make some observations that may help you to memorize the numbers better.

LESSON 4 • THE BRIDE WORE BLACK

1. Only 21, 31, 41, 51, 61, and 71 use *et* to connect the number in the "tens" place and the number in the "ones" place.

   vingt *et* un, trente *et* un, soixante *et* onze . . .

2. All other numbers use a hyphen to connect the tens and the ones.

   vingt-deux, soixante-quatorze, quatre-vingt-neuf, quatre-vingt-quinze . . .

3. Basically, counting in French is as simple as math! Just kidding . . . The numbers from 70 to 100 involve some adding and multiplying. Look at this:

70 is 60 + 10:	**soixante-dix**
71 is 60 + 11:	**soixante et onze**
72 is 60 + 12:	**soixante-douze**
73 is 60 + 13:	**soixante-treize**
80 is 4 x 20:	**quatre-vingts**
81 is 4 x 20 + 1:	**quatre-vingt-un**
82 is 4 x 20 + 2:	**quatre-vingt-deux**
89 is 4 x 20 + 9:	**quatre-vingt-neuf**
90 is 80 + 10:	**quatre-vingt-dix**
91 is 80 + 11:	**quatre-vingt-onze**
etc.	

   So, now you understand what I mean? Interesting, don't you think?

TIME TO ADD UP YOUR POSSESSIONS!: WORDS THAT SAY YOU'RE AN OWNER—*MY, YOUR, HIS, HER,* ETC., IN FRENCH

Words like *my*, *your*, or *his* are called possessive adjectives. They describe the ownership of an item.

Like all adjectives in French, they agree with the noun they modify, both in number (one vs. many) and in gender (masculine vs. feminine). Just like the possessive adjectives in English, and unlike most other adjectives in French, possessive adjectives always come before the noun they modify.

THE POSSESSIVE ADJECTIVES			
SINGULAR		PLURAL	
Masculine	Feminine	Masculine	Feminine
mon	ma	mes	my
ton	ta	tes	your
son	sa	ses	his / her / its
notre	notre	nos	our
votre	votre	vos	your
leur	leur	leurs	their

Things are far more complicated in French than in English. I will give you that.

In contrast to English, where possessive adjectives agree with the possessor (e.g., _his_ book or _her_ book depending on who the owner is), possessive adjectives in French simply match the gender and number of the word (the noun) they describe and stand next to. For instance:

La femme d'Antoine. _Sa_ femme.

In French, the possessed object (Hmmm!!! . . .), _femme_, is feminine and so is the possessive adjective.

Heads Up!

When a feminine noun starts with a vowel or an "aspirated" h, one uses the masculine singular adjectives _mon, ton, son_ regardless of the gender of the noun. This is a pronunciation issue that you'll encounter over and over again as you study French.

mon, ton, son invitée (feminine singular)

my, your, his / her guest

mon, ton, son hôtel (masculine singular)

my, your, his / her hotel

Note that in the last example, _un hôtel_, the "h" is mute. So you should do the _liaison_ and say [uh<u>n</u> ohtehl].

Heads Up!

ACTIVITY 3: TAKE IT FOR A SPIN

La recherche! (Search!) Write down all the possessive adjectives contained in the dialogue. Make sure you write them down together with the nouns they modify. (Once you have listened to the second dialogue, find them there, too.)

WORDS TO LIVE BY

IT'S ALL IN THE FAMILY: TALKING ABOUT FAMILY AND WEDDINGS

Even if _le mariage_ is not as common as it used to be, it still important to many people. _Le mariage_ in French means both "wedding" and "marriage." (Did you notice the difference in spelling between the English and the French word? _Mariage_ takes only one "r.") And so do:

être marié   _to be married_

le marié, la mariée	*groom, bride*
le faire-part de mariage	*wedding invitation*

You can get married (*se marier*) at:

la mairie, l'hôtel de ville	*town hall, city hall*

or else at:

l'église (*fem.*)	*church*

where you'll hear the sounds of:

un orgue	*organ*

In all cases, a best man is indispensable. In French, *le témoin* means literally the witness (of the ceremony). Both the bride and the groom have *un témoin*. There is also:

la demoiselle d'honneur	*bridesmaid*

After the ceremony, *les mariés* have now become *mari et femme*, husband and wife.

It is a tradition (*la tradition*) for *les invités*, that is, the guests, and *la famille*, to throw rice (*jeter du riz*) on the newlyweds.

un invité, une invitée	*guest*
inviter	*to invite*

And now it's time for you to meet the whole family:

la belle-fille	*stepdaughter; daughter-in-law*
le beau-fils	*stepson; son-in-law*
le gendre	*son-in-law (a very common term)*
la belle-mère	*stepmother; mother-in-law*
le beau-père	*stepfather; father-in-law*
la fille	*daughter*
le fils	*son*
la grand-mère	*grandmother*
le grand-père	*grandfather*
la mère	*mother*
le père	*father*
le petit-fils	*grandson*
la petite-fille	*granddaughter*

Well, it's a real pleasure to meet you all! *Je suis enchanté / enchantée!*

As we all know, a wedding can be a very emotional moment for *les mariés* and for *les parents*.

The emotions . . .

French uses only one word for *to like* and *to love*, *aimer*. (Yes, this is a regular verb in —er.) This may be the reason why they use this verb with reserve . . . They say, more openly, *j'aime beaucoup* or *j'adore* (I adore) than *j'aime* . . .

embrasser	*to kiss; to hug*

And wishes . . .

Les *voeux* is more than one wish, and *le voeu* is just one. (Note the irregular plural —*x*.)

les félicitations	*congratulations*
meilleurs voeux de bonheur	*best wishes for happiness*

Here's a series of adjectives expressing *l'amour et le bonheur* (love and happiness):

chaleureux, chaleureuse	*warm-hearted*
cher, chère	*dear*
émouvant, émouvante	*moving*
heureux, heureuse	*happy*
merveilleux, merveilleuse	*wonderful*
ouvert, ouverte	*open*
sympathique	*nice*

Notice the adjectives *chaleureux, heureux,* and *merveilleux*. In the masculine form, they end in —*eux*. This ending changes to —*euse* in the feminine form.

In the plural form, *chaleureux* remains unchanged, whereas *chaleureuse* gets an —*s*, *chaleureuses*. The same goes for *heureux* and *merveilleux*.

Unfortunately, there's the bad stuff in life, too. *C'est si triste* . . . (It's so sad . . .)

pleurer	*to cry; to sob*
le divorce	*divorce*
divorcé, divorcée	*divorced*
divorcer	*to get a divorce*

Much worse and unacceptable is *le racisme*. One small word that has caused a lot of harm . . .

haïr, détester	*to hate*
blanc, blanche	*white*

Heads Up!

Note that the final —*c* of the adjective *blanc* is mute. You say (blah[n]).

noir, noire	*black*
un préjugé	*prejudice*
raciste	*racist*

Racism shows the lack of *le respect* for the universal values, *les valeurs universelles*.

respecter	*to respect*

So, let's cultivate some positive feelings:

In the following list, pick the words that imply "positive feelings."

merveilleux, les préjugés, peu sympathique, triste, s'embrasser, le respect, le divorce, meilleurs voeux, enchanté, le racisme

And now, let's get back to the wedding celebration. Are you ready for *la photo de famille* (the family picture)?

HEAR...SAY 2

The Family Picture   (La photo de famille)

Paco:	Alors, madame et monsieur Lewoz, madame Moreau, c'est une belle journée! Vos enfants sont mariés. Vos cent invités sont tous là!
Monsieur Lewoz:	Oh oui, nous sommes très heureux!
Paco:	Marie-Thérèse est une jeune femme merveilleuse!
Madame Moreau:	Antoine, aussi.
Paco:	Ça oui . . . Ah, voici mon amie, Julienne Nyollo . . .
Madame Gaudin:	C'est l'heure! C'est l'heure!
Madame Moreau:	Mais qu'est-ce qu'elle a . . . ? Enfin . . . Enchantée, Mademoiselle!
Antoine:	(Il embrasse sa famille.) Ouf! Eh bien!
Madame Lewoz:	Mon fils, nous sommes si heureux! Félicitations!
Antoine:	Merci à tous et à toi, Paco, mon témoin. Ah, Julienne, ça va? Belle-maman, toujours aussi belle!
Madame Gaudin:	Allez! On va être en retard.

In the Grand Hôtel d'Enghien. Following tradition, the newlyweds end by cutting the cake. (Dans le Grand Hôtel d'Enghien. Selon la tradition, les mariés finissent de couper la pièce montée.)

Madame Lewoz:	Les accras sont très bons.
Madame Moreau:	Hmmm . . . délicieux! Et la pièce montée, hmmm! Un peu de champagne, madame Lewoz? Monsieur Lewoz?
Marie-Thérèse:	Ouf! Bien voilà!
Monsieur Gaudin:	Eh bien, Antoine, vous devez désormais être sérieux . . . Marie-Thérèse est notre seule fille, vous savez.
Madame Moreau:	Ce sont là tes seuls voeux? Antoine n'a pas besoin de tes remarques. Il est sérieux. Et voilà l'autre . . .

Madame Gaudin:	Edouard, très cher, leur orchestre créole doit jouer maintenant. Tout est bien organisé dans notre pays.
Marie-Thérèse:	Papa, je t'avertis, je ne veux plus entendre ta femme!
Madame Moreau:	On ne veut plus entendre vos préjugés! Il est temps de respecter votre nouvelle famille et vos invités.
Marie-Thérèse:	Et le respect est une valeur universelle.
Le photographe:	Mesdames, Messieurs, plus près les uns des autres, s'il vous plaît. Prêts pour la photo de famille?

Did You Know?

FRANCE, A MULTICULTURAL COUNTRY?

La grande victoire of the multi-racial French team in the World Soccer Cup in 1998 spread a wind of *optimisme* and acceptance around the country. The French seemed to have finally realized that *leur pays* is a multicultural place and that life together can be wonderful.

During the 1990s the government started introducing integration policy plans and various support programs for the younger generation, whose parents or grandparents immigrated to France. It seems clear to most political sides in France that the country should count on and integrate new multiethnic and multicultural immigrant population.

Did You Know?

67

LESSON 4 • THE BRIDE WORE BLACK

ACTIVITY 5:   HOW'S THAT AGAIN?

Please answer the following questions:

- a) *Où est-ce que la réception a lieu?*
- b) *Est-ce que les invités sont en colère?*
- c) What does the young couple traditionally do at the reception?
- d) What is there to eat and drink?

WORKSHOP 2

THE NITTY-GRITTY

I SCREAM, YOU SCREAM: THE IRREGULAR VERBS *DEVOIR* (TO HAVE TO), *RECEVOIR* (TO RECEIVE), AND *SAVOIR* (TO KNOW) IN THE PRESENT TENSE

It's that time again . . . Add to your list of irregular verbs: *devoir* (to have to; to owe), *recevoir* (to receive) and *savoir* (know). They follow the same pattern.

All three verbs have the same endings in the present tense:

je: **–s**	nous: **–ons**
tu: **–s**	vous: **–ez**
il / elle: **–t**	ils / elles: **–ent**

1. The irregular verb *devoir* (to have to; to owe)

THE PRESENT TENSE OF THE IRREGULAR VERB *DEVOIR* (TO HAVE TO; TO OWE)	
je dois	nous devons
tu dois	vous devez
il / elle doit	ils / elles doivent

Note that the stem of the verb *devoir*, *dev-*, appears in the *nous* and *vous* forms. *Devoir* has several meanings. It means "to have to, must":

Nous devons respecter les gens.

We have to respect people.

Or "to owe":

Il me doit cent euros.

He owes me 100 euros.

Je dois quatre-vingts euros à Paco.

I owe 80 euros to Paco.

Finally, *devoir* can be used to express probability:

Il doit arriver dimanche.

He must arrive on Sunday.

Elle doit être en colère.

She must be angry.

2. The irregular verb *recevoir* (to receive)

THE PRESENT TENSE OF THE IRREGULAR VERB *RECEVOIR* (TO RECEIVE)	
je reçois	nous recevons
tu reçois	vous recevez
il / elle reçoit	ils / elles reçoivent

The pattern is the same as with *devoir*. The verb *recevoir* keeps its stem *recev–* in the *nous* and *vous* forms. Take a look at the examples:

Les mariés reçoivent beaucoup de cadeaux.

The newlyweds receive a lot of presents.

Je reçois le faire-part de mariage.

I am receiving the wedding invitation.

3. The irregular verb *savoir* (to know)

THE PRESENT TENSE OF THE IRREGULAR VERB *SAVOIR* (TO KNOW)	
je sais	*nous savons*
tu sais	*vous savez*
il / elle sait	*ils / elles savent*

Actually, in this case, the verb *savoir* keeps its stem *sav-* in the *nous*, *vous*, and *ils / elles* forms but it is irregular in the singular forms.

Ils sont mariés, vous savez.

They are married, you know.

Je ne sais pas.

I don't know.

ACTIVITY 6: **TAKE IT FOR A SPIN**

All those verbs! Is it *savoir* or *devoir* or *recevoir*? Fill in the blanks!

a) *Ils _____ arriver à treize heures.*
b) *Nous sommes en retard. Nous _____ être à l'église dans cinq minutes!*
c) *Je ne _____ plus le nom de l'hôtel.*
d) *L'orchestre _____ jouer maintenant.*
e) *Antoine _____ quatre-vingts euros à Paco.*
f) *Les mariés _____ des cadeaux de mariage.*

LIVING IN THE PRESENT: THE REGULAR VERBS ENDING IN –IR IN THE PRESENT TENSE

Don't worry, these verbs are really not difficult. To start with, they **are** regular.

To form the present tense, you drop the *–ir* off the *–ir* form of the verb, e.g., *fin–ir*, and add the present tense endings. They are:

je: –**is**	nous: –**issons**
tu: –**is**	vous: –**issez**
il / elle: –**it**	ils / elles: –**issent**

THE PRESENT TENSE OF THE VERB *FINIR* (TO FINISH)	
je finis	*nous finissons*
tu finis	*vous finissez*
il / elle finit	*ils / elles finissent*

Heads Up!

Some verbs ending in –*ir* are irregular. When such verbs are introduced, I'll let you know.

Heads Up!

ACTIVITY 7: TAKE IT FOR A SPIN

Voilà! Now try to write down all the forms for *avertir* (to warn). Let me get you started:

j'
tu
il / elle
. . .

Please go on!

JUST SAY NO!: USING *NEVER, NOTHING,* ETC., IN FRENCH

In Lesson 2, you learned how to use *non* and *ne . . . pas* to say "no" in French. Let me remind you:

Non, je ne veux pas.

No, I don't want to.

You put *ne* before the verb and *pas* after it.
  But the French have many ways of saying "no."

1. *Ne . . . plus* is used in the same fashion as *ne . . . pas. Plus* means "no longer."

Je ne vais plus à l'église.

I don't go to church any more.

Nous ne voulons plus entendre vos préjugés.

We don't want to hear your prejudices any longer.

2. *Ne . . . rien* is also used in this way. *Rien* means "nothing."

Non, nous ne voulons rien donner.

No, we don't want to give anything.

Ce n'est rien . . .

It's nothing . . .

3. *Ne . . . jamais* is a third way of saying "no" that's used just like the other two. *Jamais* means "never."

Il ne joue jamais dans des réceptions.

He never plays at receptions.

And here's a saying:

On ne doit jamais juger son prochain.

One should never judge a fellow human.

In sum, all expressions of negation follow the same word order: *ne* + verb + *pas / plus / rien / jamais.*

ACTIVITY 8: TAKE IT FOR A SPIN

Rewrite these sentences in the negative form. Use the most appropriate negative word: *ne . . . pas, plus, rien,* or *jamais.*

- a)   *Je vais toujours à l'église.*
- b)   *Nous savons tout.*
- c)   *Tu avertis tes amis.*
- d)   *Elles veulent toujours discuter.*
- e)   *Ils doivent trouver un cadeau de mariage.*
- f)   *Ils reçoivent encore des cadeaux.*

WORDS TO LIVE BY

HERE COMES THE BRIDE: TALKING ABOUT WEDDINGS

A good thing about *la cérémonie* is that there's *la reception* after it. (Have you noticed how similar these French words are to English words? Always try to make connections; this will help you memorize things.)

During the reception, the guests *discutent*, that is, chat, and of course, eat. . . . According to the tradition, newlyweds have to *couper la pièce montée*, must cut the wedding cake. . . .

Anyway, *si vous avez faim* or *soif*, there are *des accras*, an excellent Caribbean (*créole*) specialty. *Délicieux!* Delicious! And there's also *Champagne*.

Stop eating (that's *manger*), and get ready for . . .

la photo de famille	*family picture*
la photographie	*photograph*
le photographe	*photographer*
plus près les uns des autres	*closer to each other*

Don't forget to smile!

And now for some useful little words:

désormais	*from now on*
par ici	*around here*

Word on the Street

Allez!	Let's go!
C'est l'heure!, Il est temps!	It's time!
Ouf!	Interjection meaning "We made it!"
Ouh!	Interjection meaning "Doesn't look good!" or "It hurts"

ACTIVITY 9: **TAKE IT FOR A SPIN**

Write the words given below in their singular form. Draw a table with two columns and separate the feminine words from the masculine words. Then make up a sentence containing each word.

les champagnes, les mariées, les respects, les orgues, les invités, les préjugés, les photographies, les églises, les mariages, les cérémonies, les réceptions

ACTIVITY 10: **TAKE IT UP A NOTCH!**

Here's a little challenge for you. Put the verbs in parentheses into the appropriate form of the present tense.

a)   *Nous (manger) des accras. Ils sont bons.*
b)   *Ils (finir) de jouer de l'orgue.*
c)   *Est-ce que vous (vouloir) du champagne maintenant?*
d)   *Antoine (embrasser) toute sa nouvelle famille.*
e)   *Vous n'(avertir) jamais vos parents?*
f)   *Nous (devoir) respecter les autres.*
g)   *Les mariés (recevoir) des cadeaux.*

CRIB NOTES

Julienne:	Oh! This organ music . . . It's so moving.
Paco:	Yep . . .
Julienne:	(crying) They're beautiful!
Paco:	But, Julienne, what's the matter?
Julienne:	Nothing at all . . . Who is that?
Paco:	Her? It's Mrs. Gaudin. Marie-Thérèse's stepmother.
Julienne:	She's looking over here. Ooh! She looks upset.
Paco:	Yes, I know. She is not a nice person.
Julienne:	How come?
Paco:	Well . . .
Guest:	Shh!!!
Paco:	Well . . . She and her family don't like Antoine, because . . .
Julienne:	Because he's black?
Paco:	Yep. Sad, isn't it?

Outside the church.

Julienne:	So?
Paco:	So, Marie-Thérèse's parents are divorced. Her stepfamily is prejudiced. On the other hand, her mother and Antoine's parents are very warm and open!
Julienne:	Ah! Here they are! Our best wishes for happiness!
Guests:	Here comes the bride!
Paco:	And what about the groom? Here come the bride and the groom!

Following tradition, the guests throw rice at the newlyweds.

Paco:	So, Mr. & Mrs. Lewoz, Ms. Moreau, it's a beautiful day! Your children are married. Your 100 guests are all here!
Mr. Lewoz:	Oh, yes, we are very happy.
Paco:	Marie-Thérèse is a wonderful young woman.
Ms. Moreau:	Antoine, as well.
Paco:	Oh yes . . . Ah, here's my friend, Julienne Nyollo . . .
Mrs. Gauduin:	It's time! It's time!
Ms. Moreau:	But what does she . . . ? Oh, well. Pleased to meet you, young lady!
Antoine:	(he kisses his family) Ouf! Well . . .
Mrs. Lewoz:	My son, we're so happy! Congratulations!
Antoine:	Thank you everyone, and you, too, Paco, my best man. Julienne, how are you? And my beautiful stepmom!
Mrs. Gaudin:	Let's go! We're going to be late.

In the Grand Hotel in Enghien. Following tradition, the newlyweds end by cutting the cake.

Mrs. Lewoz:	The accras are very good!
Ms. Moreau:	Mmm . . . delicious! And the tiered cake, mmm! Some champagne, Mrs. Lewoz? Mr. Lewoz?
Marie-Thérèse:	Ouf! Here we are . . .
Mr. Gaudin:	Well, Antoine, you have to be serious now . . . You know, Marie-Thérèse is our only daughter.
Ms. Moreau:	Are those your only wishes? Antoine doesn't need your comments. He is serious. And here's the other one . . .
Mrs. Gaudin:	Edouard, dear, their creole orchestra has to play now. Things are well organized in our country.
Marie-Thérèse:	Dad, I'm warning you, I don't want to hear your wife any more!
Ms. Moreau:	We don't want to hear your prejudices any more. It's time to respect your new family and your guests.
Marie-Thérèse:	And respect is a universal value.
Photographer:	Ladies, gentlemen, closer to one another, please! Ready for the family picture?

ACTIVITY 1

a) The ceremony is taking place on April 14, 2002.
b) The reception is at 3 PM.
c) The reception is taking place at the Grand Hôtel.

ACTIVITY 2

a) C'est le mariage des amis de Paco, Antoine et Marie-Thérèse.
b) Car c'est émouvant.
c) Paco est le témoin.
d) Non.
e) Les invités jettent du riz sur les mariés.

ACTIVITY 3

sa famille; sa belle-famille; sa mère; nos meilleurs voeux; vos enfants; vos cent invités; mon amie; sa famille; mon fils; mon témoin; notre seule fille; tes seuls voeux; tes remarques; leur orchestre; notre pays; ta femme; vos préjugés; votre nouvelle famille; vos invités.

ACTIVITY 4

merveilleux, s'embrasser, le respect, meilleurs voeux, enchanté.

ACTIVITY 5

a) La réception a lieu dans le Grand Hôtel d'Enghien.
b) Non, les invités ne sont pas en colère.
c) Les mariés coupent la pièce-montée à la réception.
d) They eat *les accras* and *la pièce montée*. There is also *le champagne*.

ACTIVITY 6

a) Ils doivent arriver à treize heures.
b) Nous sommes en retard. Nous devons être à l'église dans cinq minutes!
c) Je ne sais plus le nom de l'hôtel.
d) L'orchestre doit jouer maintenant.
e) Antoine doit quatre-vingts euros à Paco.
f) Les mariés reçoivent des cadeaux de mariage.

ACTIVITY 7

j'avertis, tu avertis, il / elle avertit, nous avertissons, vous avertissez, ils / elles avertissent

ACTIVITY 8

a) Je ne vais jamais à l'église.
b) Nous ne savons rien.
c) Tu n'avertis pas tes amis.
d) Elles ne veulent jamais discuter.
e) Ils ne doivent pas trouver un cadeau de mariage.
f) Ils ne reçoivent plus de cadeaux.
(Notice that by rule, in a negative sentence, *des* (plural) must change to a simple *de*.)

ACTIVITY 9

Masculine	Feminine
le champagne, le respect, l'orgue, l'invité, le préjugé, le mariage	la mariée, la photographie, l'église, la cérémonie, la réception

While there are many different possibilities, here are some examples of sentences using these words.

J'aime le champagne.—Tu dois avoir du respect pour tes parents.—J'ai un orgue chez moi.—L'invité est en colère.—Le racisme est un préjugé.—Je dois préparer le mariage de ma fille.—La mariée est très belle.—Prêts pour la photographie de famille?—Ils sont à l'extérieur de l'église.–Je veux aller à la cérémonie de mariage d'Antoine et Marie-Thérèse.—Les mariés coupent la pièce montée à la réception.

ACTIVITY 10

a) Nous mangeons des accras. Ils sont bons.
b) Ils finissent de jouer de l'orgue.
c) Est-ce que vous voulez du champagne maintenant?
d) Antoine embrasse toute sa nouvelle famille.
e) Vous n'avertissez jamais vos parents?
f) Nous devons respecter les autres.
g) Les mariés reçoivent des cadeaux.

5.

THE DREAM LIFE OF ANGELS

La vie rêvée des anges

Darling, the water is great. Shall we go for a swim?

COMING UP. . .

- *In and out of the office*: Talking about work
- *A dream vacation*: Talking about vacations
- *What time is it?*: Telling time in French
- *To and fro*: Using *à* (to; in) and *de* (from; of) with articles
- *I scream, you scream*: The irregular verbs *faire* (to do) and *dire* (to say) in the present tense
- *Strut your stuff!*

In 1998, the director Erik Zonka surprised critics and audiences around the world with his first film, *La vie rêvée des anges* (*The Dream Life of Angels*), which brought him praise and awards around the globe. The main actresses, Elodie Bouchez and Nathalie Reigner, shared the Best Actress Award at the Cannes Festival. *The Dream Life of Angels* is a story of a close friendship between two poor twenty-something girls.

LOOKING AHEAD

In this lesson, *on révise!* In other words, you are going to review what you've studied so far. Therefore, there's little new material. Aren't you lucky? And there's a bonus, too: You'll soon learn how to tell time *en français*. Since the dialogues are taking place in an office, here's the opportunity to learn the related vocabulary . . .

In this lesson, you'll meet Harold Rigard at his office, on his first day back from vacation (*de retour de vacances*). Harold *travaille* (works) as the artistic director for a media company. But being back at work after his vacation is tough, and Harold sits at his *bureau* (desk) daydreaming (*il rêve*) about his *merveilleuses vacances* with his beloved *femme* (wife), Paule. . . . Fortunately, his devoted *secrétaire* is here to save his business day.

HEAR . . . SAY 1

It's Hard to Be Back . . .   (C'est dur d'être de retour . . .)

La voix de sa femme:	Chéri, l'eau est bonne. On va se baigner?
Harold Rigard:	Oh Paule. . . . Hmmmm, tu as raison, l'eau est bonne!
Sa secrétaire:	Monsieur Rigard . . . monsieur Rigard! Cela va être l'heure de votre rendez-vous.
Harold Rigard:	Euhh . . . oui . . . bien sûr. . . . Le rendez-vous. Oui . . .
Sa secrétaire:	C'est sur votre agenda! À 11h45 (onze heures quarante-cinq). C'est-à-dire, dans cinq minutes.
Harold Rigard:	Oh! Et où exactement?
Sa secrétaire:	Dans la salle de conférence. Bon, je vais faire les photocopies pour ce soir.
Harold Rigard:	Mais bien sûr, dans la salle de conférence. Et?
Sa secrétaire:	Avec M. Chouraki! Vous allez bien, vous êtes sûr?
Harold Rigard:	Oui, oui . . . je vais . . . très bien . . .
Sa secrétaire:	Voici les photocopies du dossier. Mais vous devez avoir une copie du contrat.
Harold Rigard:	Le contrat, bien sûr! Pauline, vous êtes merveilleuse.

La voix de sa femme:	C'est un vrai paradis pour les sens! Le mouvement des vagues, le vent parfumé. Tout ici est merveilleux!
Harold Rigard:	Oui, et toi aussi . . .
Sa secrétaire:	Vous dites . . . ? Ah! Et voici le fax de M7.
Harold Rigard:	Oui? Au sujet de . . .
Sa secrétaire:	Au sujet du mariage de la princesse!
Harold Rigard:	Bien sûr! Bon, quand faut y aller, faut y aller! Merci, Pauline. À tout à l'heure.

ACTIVITY 1: **HOW'S THAT AGAIN?**

Draw two large columns on a piece of paper. In the first one, copy down all the phrases from the dialogue related to Harold's daydreaming about his vacation. We'll take care of the business part a bit later.

Did You Know?

In order to reduce the unemployment rate, the French government introduced *La loi des 35 heures* (The Law of 35 Hours) in March 2000, which reduced the work week to a maximum of 35 hours.

While some people like having more free time for leisure and their families, others are critical about the law and the effects it might have on the French economy.

LET'S PUT IT IN WRITING

During *ses vacances de rêve* (his dream vacation), Harold Rigard sent a card to *ses amis* at the office!

> Chers tous,
>
> Meilleurs souvenirs de Point-à-Pitre d'Harold et de Paule. La vie ici est merveilleuse... C'est un vrai paradis!
>
>   À bientôt.

How can one make his colleagues jealous?! Answer these questions:

a) *Où est-ce que Paule et Harold passent leur vacances?*
b) Which words on Harold's card describe the mood of his holidays?

WORKSHOP 1

THE NITTY-GRITTY

WHAT *TIME IS IT*? TELLING TIME IN FRENCH

In everyday life, the French use the 12-hour system to tell time. They use *du matin* (AM or "in the morning"), *de l'après-midi* (PM or "in the afternoon"), *du soir* (PM or "in the evening") after the number in order to specify the time of the day.

Did You Know?

In France, as in most other European countries, in official and formal situations, the 24-hour system of telling time is used (also referred to as "military" system in the United States). This system is used for any type of schedule in order to avoid confusion: at the airports, the train stations, for TV programs, etc. There is a very simple way to get from the 12-hour to the 24-hour system or the opposite: Just add or deduct 12.

Did You Know?

1. On the hour

HOURS OF THE DAY IN FRENCH			
12 AM:	*zéro heure, minuit*	12 PM:	*douze heures* (rare), *midi*
1 AM:	*une heure du matin*	1 PM:	*une heure de l'après-midi, treize heures*
2 AM:	*deux heures du matin*	2 PM:	*deux heures de l'après-midi, quatorze heures*
3 AM:	*trois heures du matin*	3 PM:	*trois heures de l'après-midi, quinze heures*
4 AM:	*quatre heures du matin*	4 PM:	*quatre heures de l'après-midi, seize heures*
5 AM:	*cinq heures du matin*	5 PM:	*cinq heures de l'après-midi, dix-sept heures*
6 AM:	*six heures du matin*	6 PM:	*six heures du soir, dix-huit heures*
7 AM:	*sept heures du matin*	7 PM:	*sept heures du soir, dix-neuf heures*
8 AM:	*huit heures du matin*	8 PM:	*huit heures du soir, vingt heures*
9 AM:	*neuf heures du matin*	9 PM:	*neuf heures du soir, vingt et une heures*
10 AM:	*dix heures du matin*	10 PM:	*dix heures du soir, vingt-deux heures*
11 AM:	*onze heures du matin*	11 PM:	*onze heures du soir, vingt-trois heures*

The key is to practice! From now on, each time you are in a relaxed situation and you look at the time, read it *en français!*

2. Other possibilities

For the times between the full hour and the next half hour, just say the hour and then the number of minutes. For 15 minutes you can also use the term *et quart* (and a quarter).

3:15 pm: ***trois heures quinze de l'après-midi*** or

trois heures et quart de l'après-midi or

quinze heures quinze

For the times between the half hour and the following hour use *moins* (minus; less). First say the following hour, then *moins,* and then the number of minutes (or *moins le quart* when appropriate). (You can also say the preceding hour followed by the number of minutes.)

6:45 pm: ***sept heures moins le quart du soir*** or

six heures quarante-cinq du soir or

dix-huit heures quarante-cinq

2:55 am: ***trois heures moins cinq du matin*** or

deux heures cinquante-cinq du matin

The equivalent of "half" is, in French, *demie.* First comes the number of hours, then the number of minutes or *et demie* or *et quart.*

4:30 pm: ***quatre heures trente de l'après-midi*** or

quatre heures et demie or

seize heures trente.

3. Asking for the time

There are several ways to ask for the time. The most formal way is:

Quelle heure est-il, s'il vous plaît?

What time is it, please?

Avez-vous l'heure, s'il vous plaît?

Do you have the time, please?

Or slightly more colloquial:

Quelle heure est-ce qu'il est, s'il vous plaît?

Quelle heure il est, s'il vous plaît?

Vous avez l'heure, s'il vous plaît?

Est-ce que vous avez l'heure, s'il vous plaît?

The answer could be.

Il est dix-neuf heures quarante-trois.

It is 7:43 PM.

Or, if you want to ask at what time a plane is arriving, say:

À quelle heure est-ce que l'avion de New York arrive?

Or:

À quelle heure l'avion de New York arrive?

The answer could be.

L'avion arrive à seize heures dix.

The plane arrives at 4:10 PM.

ACTIVITY 3: TAKE IT FOR A SPIN

Quelle heure est-il? Spell out the times using the 12-hour and then the 24-hour system.

a) *Tu as l'heure, s'il te plaît? . . . Oui, il est* (3:30 PM).
b) *La secrétaire arrive à* (10:15 AM).
c) *Je peux finir mon dossier à* (11:35 PM).
d) *Le rendez-vous est à* (18:45 PM).
e) *L'avion est à* (6:54 AM).

TO AND FRO: USING À (TO; IN) AND DE (FROM; OF) WITH ARTICLES

Strange things happen when *à* (to; in) and *de* (from; of) stand in front of a definite article.

But first, let's see . . . which are the definite articles? *Oui!* The definite articles are *le* (masculine singular), *la* (feminine singular) and *les* (masculine / feminine plural). Good!

Two of these articles, *le* and *les*, get contracted when they are preceded by the prepositions *à* (to; in) and *de* (from; of). Look at the table:

THE CONTRACTED ARTICLES	
SINGULAR	*PLURAL*
à + le = au	*à + les = aux*
de + le = du	*de + les = des*

Je vais <u>au</u> (à + le) mariage d'Antoine et Marie-Thérèse.

I'm going to the wedding of Antoine and Marie-Thérèse.

J'habite <u>aux</u> (à + les) États-Unis.

I live in the United States.

Ils arrivent <u>des</u> (de + les) États-Unis.

They are arriving from the United States.

Nous sommes <u>du</u> (de + le) sud de la France.

We are from the south of France.

Note that with the feminine singular article *la*, there is no contraction.

Ils arrivent à la salle de conférence.

They are coming to the conference room.

When there is an elision between the article and the noun, as in *l'aéroport*, even if the noun is masculine (*un aéroport*), there is no contraction between the preposition and the article.

| ACTIVITY 4: | **TAKE IT FOR A SPIN** |

Au, aux, du, and the others . . . Fill in the blanks with the appropriate combination of *à* or *de* and the articles.

a)   *Je suis* ____au____ *nord* ____de l'____*Afrique.*
b)   *Ils vont* ____aux____ *États-Unis.*
c)   *Vous allez* ____de l'____ *église tous les dimanches?*
d)   *Nous arrivons* ____au____ *aéroport.*
e)   *Ce sont les bureaux* ____de la____ *compagnie de marketing.*

I SCREAM, YOU SCREAM: IRREGULAR VERBS *FAIRE* (TO DO) AND *DIRE* (TO SAY) IN THE PRESENT TENSE

The present tense endings for these verbs are the same as usual in the singular (*je, tu, il / elle*) forms: –s, –s, –t.

The *nous* form also uses the usual –ons, but endings for the *vous* and *ils / elles* forms are irregular.

THE PRESENT TENSE OF THE IRREGULAR VERB *FAIRE* (TO DO)	
je fais	nous faisons
tu fais	vous faites
il / elle fait	ils / elles font

THE PRESENT TENSE OF THE IRREGULAR VERB *DIRE* (TO SAY)	
je dis	nous disons
tu dis	vous dites
il / elle dit	ils / elles disent

Heads Up!

Note that *(nous) faisons* is pronounced (fuhzoh[n]). *(Vous) faites* and *(vous) dites* are pronounced (feht) and (deet). The ending on the *vous* forms is silent.

Heads Up!

Here are some expressions and phrases with the verbs *faire* and *dire*.

Vous dites?

What are you saying?

C'est-à-dire . . .

That is to say . . .

Fais / Faites attention!

Be careful!

Fais des photocopies!

Make photocopies!

ACTIVITY 5: TAKE IT FOR A SPIN

The verb *interdire* (to forbid) follows the same pattern as the verb *dire*, because, as you can see, *dire* is contained in *interdire*. (The only difference is the *vous* form, which is *vous interdisez*.) Can you write down and then read all of its different forms in the present tense?

WORDS TO LIVE BY

IN AND OUT OF THE OFFICE: TALKING ABOUT WORK

Back at work . . .

After a nice vacation (*les vacances*), it's the usual nine to five deal:

le bureau	office; desk
le contrat	contract
la copie	copy
le dossier	file
le fax	fax
la page	page
la photocopie	photocopy
la salle de conférence	conference room
la secrétaire, le secrétaire	secretary; assistant

You might know the French word *rendez-vous* (masc.) as meaning "a date," but you should know that a *rendez-vous* in French is not always romantic—it also means "appointment" or "meeting." So, if your business partner mentions the word, don't get the wrong idea!

Harold Rigard knows that his *rendez-vous* will be strictly business . . . and obviously has a hard time accepting it.

l'après-midi (*masc. / fem.*)	afternoon
le matin	morning
le soir	evening

A DREAM VACATION: TALKING ABOUT VACATIONS

At this point Harold can start dreaming about his next vacation:

nager	to swim
rêver	to dream
l'eau (*fem.*)	water
la vague	wave (of water)
le mouvement des vagues	movement of the waves
le paradis des sens	sensory paradise
la princesse	princess
les vacances de rêve	dream vacation
le vent	wind

Some useful little words:

alors	so; then
au sujet de	about; concerning

Word on the Street

à l'heure	on time
À tout à l'heure!	See you later
aller bien	to go well, to be well
Cela ne va plus!	This is not working!
Quand faut y aller, faut y aller.	When you have to go, you have to go.

ACTIVITY 6: **TAKE IT FOR A SPIN**

Fill in the gaps in the sentences with the appropriate word:

client; fax; vacances; photocopies; dur; faire; paradis; dossier; au travail; allez; sujet

a) *Monsieur Rigard, comment est-ce que vous* _allez_ *? Et vos* _____ *?*
b) *Ça va bien. Un vrai* _paradis_.
c) *C'est votre programme et voici le* ~~contrat~~ _dossier_ *et le* _fax_ *de M7!*
d) *Mais au* _____ *de . . .*
e) *S'il vous plaît, est-ce que vous pouvez téléphoner à notre* _vacances_ *d'Andalousie?*
f) *Est-ce que je dois* _photocopie_ *des* _____ *?*
g) *Oui, merci. Ah, c'est* _dur_ *d'être de retour* _au travail_

HEAR...SAY 2

84

FRENCH WITHOUT THE FUSS

It's Hard to Be Back (cont'd.) . . . (C'est dur d'être de retour . . .)

De retour au bureau, cinq heures de l'après-midi:

Harold Rigard:	Lalalalala . . . lalalala . . .
Sa secrétaire:	Hmmhmm!!! Est-ce que vous voulez les traductions des lettres et du rapport pour votre rendez-vous ce soir?
Harold Rigard:	Oui, chérie, bien sûr . . .
Sa secrétaire:	Pardon?!? M. Rigard, cela ne va vraiment plus!

Elle tape sur le bureau.

Harold Rigard:	Mademoiselle . . . Paule, Pauline . . . je. . . .
Une voix au téléphone:	Monsieur Rigard, c'est monsieur Mizogushi sur la ligne quatre.
Sa secrétaire:	Vous voulez . . . ?
Harold Rigard:	Non, non, merci, Pauline. Allô, bonjour, monsieur Mizogushi . . . oui . . . bien sûr . . . Oui . . . Non! Non . . . Oui! Eh bien, d'accord, à 18h45 (dix-huit heures quarante-cinq). Très bien. À plus tard.

Sa secrétaire:	Alors?
Harold Rigard:	Oui, toutes les traductions.
Sa secrétaire:	Est-ce que vous pouvez signer ici? Merci.
Harold Rigard:	Pauline. . . . Mes vacances sont bien finies! Ce soir, je vais dîner avec notre riche client, M. Mizogushi!

ACTIVITY 7: HOW'S THAT AGAIN?

Let's get back to our little game from Activity 1. In the second column, write all the phrases related to what Harold needs for a meeting with Mr. Mizogushi.

Let's check out the new vocabulary.

WORDS TO LIVE BY

At the end of the day *au bureau*, Harold is still daydreaming:

signer	to sign
taper sur le bureau	to tap on the desk

. . . until he hears he has *un dîner d'affaires* (a business dinner) with *un riche client* . . . Everything has to be ready:

la lettre	letter
le rapport	report
la traduction	translation

Some useful little words:

Pardon?	Excuse me?
d'accord	all right; okay

ACTIVITY 8: TAKE IT FOR A SPIN

Do these sentences make sense? If not, correct them.

a)   Le rápport *vent* est long et parfumé.

b)   Mes vacances sont trop difficiles: je ne fais rien, je suis dans l'eau toute la journée (the whole day).

c)   M. Rigard, est-ce que vous pouvez ~~manger~~ *signu* le contrat? Merci bien.

d)   M. Rigard va au bureau en avion.

e)   La secrétaire organise le ~~divorce~~ ^marriage^ de la princesse.
f)   Est-ce que vous voulez de l'essence ^le rapport^ avec le dossier?

And now it's time to show what you've learned so far . . .

STRUT YOUR STUFF!

TAKE IT FOR A SPIN

Enchantée! Why don't you start by telling me a few things about yourself:

a)   *Votre nom?*
b)   *Où est-ce que vous habitez?*
c)   *Qu'est-ce que vous faites?*
d)   *Où est-ce que vous travaillez?*
e)   *Est-ce que vous allez en vacances? Où?*   à l'île Capri
f)   *Vous êtes marié(e)?*
g)   *Vous avez des enfants?*

TAKE IT FOR A SPIN

Pretend someone is asking you questions. Write them down using a question word and
est-ce que. (The object of the question is underlined.)

Model: *Je suis au travail.*   →   *Où est-ce que tu es?*

a)   *Nous devons arriver <u>à l'aéroport Charles de Gaulle.</u>*   Est-ce que ^où^ vous devez arriver?
b)   *Mais l'avion a du retard <u>car il pleut.</u>*   Est-ce que l'avion a du retard?
c)   *Nous arrivons <u>à trois heures de l'après-midi.</u>*   Est-ce que l'heure que nous arrivons?
d)   *Notre famille est <u>à la maison.</u>*   Est-ce que où est notre famille?
e)   *Nous sommes <u>très bien.</u>*   Comment allons nous. Est ce que nous allons Comment?
f)   *On va à Paris <u>en bus.</u>*   Est-ce qu'on va à Paris?

TAKE IT FOR A SPIN

Put the verbs in parentheses into the appropriate form of the present tense.

a)   *Est-ce qu'elles (avoir) ^ont^ soif? Qu'est-ce qu'elles (vouloir) ^veulent^ manger?*
b)   *Harold ne (pouvoir) ^peut^ pas travailler. Il (rêver) ^rêve^ de ses vacances.*
c)   *Les mariés (être) ^sont^ en voyage. Ils (aller) ^vont^ aux États-Unis.*

d) *Nous (devoir) faire attention. Notre oncle (être) en colère.*

       devons   *est*

e) *Vous ne (dire) rien, d'accord?*

           dites

f) *Tes vacances (finir) donc dans le bonheur.*

        finis

ACTIVITY 12: TAKE IT FOR A SPIN

The ultimate test! Translate this little story told by Jeannie and Florine, who have just arrived in Paris.

a) *Here we are at the Paris airport.*   Nous Sommes ici à l'aeriport de Paris

b) *We are hungry and thirsty.*   nous avons faim et nous avons soif.

c) *The plane is late, so our family is not here.*   L'avion est tard, parceque notre famille n'est pas ici.

d) *In the afternoon, it's our cousin's wedding. The reception is well organized.*

e) *My uncle is the best man. He's also the groom's best friend.*

f) *We offer our best wishes for happiness. The couple looks very happy!*

CRIB NOTES

His wife's voice:	Darling, the water is great. Shall we go for a swim?
Harold Rigard:	Oh, Paule . . . Hmmm, you're right the water is great!
His secretary:	Mr. Rigard . . . Mr. Rigard! It's almost time for your appointment.
Harold Rigard:	Well . . . yes . . . of course. The appointment. Yes . . .
His secretary:	It's in your calendar! At 11:45 am. That is in 5 minutes.
Harold Rigard:	Oh. And where exactly?
His secretary:	In the conference room. Well, I'm going to make the photocopies for tonight.
Harold Rigard:	Yes, of course, in the conference room. And . . . ?
His secretary:	With Mr. Chouraki! Are you sure you're all right?
Harold Rigard:	Yes, yes . . . I'm . . . fine . . .
His secretary:	Here are the photocopies of the report. But you should have a copy of the contract.
Harold Rigard:	The contract, of course! Pauline, you are wonderful!
His wife's voice:	It's a real paradise for the senses! The movement of the waves, the scented wind. Everything here is wonderful!
Harold Rigard:	Yes, and you are, too . . .
His secretary:	What . . . ? And here's the fax from M7.
Harold Rigard:	Yes? About . . .
His secretary:	About the princess' wedding!
Harold Rigard:	Of course! Well, when it's time to go, it's time to go. Thank you, Pauline. See you later.

Back at the office, at five o'clock in the afternoon . . .

Harold Rigard:	Lalalalala . . .
His secretary:	Ahem!! Do you want the translations of the letters and the report for your appointment this evening?
Harold Rigard:	Yes, darling, of course . . .
His secretary:	Excuse me! Mr. Rigard, this really won't do!
She taps her fingers on the desk.	
Harold Rigard:	Miss . . . Paule, Pauline . . . I . . .
A voice on the telephone:	Mr. Rigard, it's Mr. Mizogushi on line four.

His secretary:	Do you want . . . ?
Harold Rigard:	No, thank you, Pauline. Hello, good day, Mr. Mizogushi. . . . Yes, of course. Yes . . . No! No . . . Yes! Well, all right, at 6:45 pm. Very well. See you later.
His secretary:	So?

Harold Rigard:	Yes, all the translations.
His secretary:	Can you sign here? . . . Thank you.
Harold Rigard:	Pauline. . . . My vacation really is over. Tonight I'm having dinner with our rich client, Mr. Mizogushi!

ANSWER KEY

ACTIVITY 1

1st column: chéri, l'eau est bonne, se baigner, un vrai paradis pour les sens, le mouvement des vagues, le vent parfumé, tout est merveilleux, toi aussi.

ACTIVITY 2

a) Paule et Harold passent leurs vacances à Point-à-Pitre.
b) Meilleurs / merveilleuse / paradis.

ACTIVITY 3

a) Tu as l'heure, s'il te plaît? Oui, il est quinze heures trente (trois heures et demie de l'après-midi).
b) La secrétaire arrive à dix heures et quart (dix heures quinze) du matin.
c) Je peux finir mon dossier à onze heures trente-cinq du soir (minuit moins vingt-cinq, vingt-trois heures trente-cinq).
d) Le rendez-vous est à six heures quarante-cinq du soir (sept heures moins le quart du soir, dix-huit heures quarante-cinq).
e) L'avion est à six heures cinquante-quatre du matin (sept heures moins six du matin).

ACTIVITY 4

a) Je suis du nord de l'Afrique.
b) Ils vont aux États-Unis.
c) Vous allez à l'église tous les dimanches?
d) Nous arrivons à l'aéroport.
e) Ce sont les bureaux de la compagnie de marketing.

ACTIVITY 5

j'interdis, tu interdis, il / elle interdit, nous interdisons, vous interdisez, ils / elles interdisent

ACTIVITY 6

a) Monsieur Rigard, comment est-ce que vous allez? Et vos vacances?
b) Ça va bien. Un vrai paradis.
c) C'est votre programme et voici le fax et le dossier de M7!

d) Mais au sujet de . . .
e) S'il vous plaît, est-ce que vous pouvez téléphoner à notre client d'Andalousie?
f) Est-ce que je dois faire des photocopies?
g) Oui, merci. Ah, c'est dur d'être de retour au travail.

ACTIVITY 7

2nd column: les traductions des lettres et du rapport; signer; dîner avec un client.

ACTIVITY 8

a) Le rapport est *long*.
b) Mes vacances sont *merveilleuses*: je ne fais rien, je suis dans l'eau toute la journée.
c) M. Rigard, est-ce que vous pouvez *signer* le contrat? Merci bien.
d) M. Rigard va au bureau *en bus / en voiture*.
e) La secrétaire organise *le mariage* de la princesse.
f) Est-ce que vous voulez *les traductions* avec le dossier?

ACTIVITY 9

a) Je m'appelle . . . / Je suis . . . / Mon nom est . . .
b) J'habite à . . .
c) Je suis étudiant(e). / Je travaille.
d) Je travaille à . . . / Je ne travaille pas.
e) Je vais / je ne vais pas en vacances à . . .
f) Je suis / je ne suis pas marié(e).
g) J'ai . . . enfants / Je n'ai pas d'enfants.

ACTIVITY 10

a) Où est-ce que vous devez arriver?
b) Pourquoi est-ce que l'avion a du retard?
c) Quand est-ce que vous arrivez? or À quelle, heure est-ce que . . . ?
d) Où est votre famille?
e) Comment est-ce que vous allez?
f) Comment est-ce qu'on va à Paris?

a) Est-ce qu'elles ont soif? Qu'est-ce qu'elles veulent manger?
b) Harold ne peut pas travailler. Il rêve de ses vacances.
c) Les mariés sont en voyage. Ils vont aux États-Unis.
d) Nous devons faire attention. Notre oncle est en colère.
e) Vous ne dites rien, d'accord?
f) Tes vacances finissent donc dans le bonheur.

a) Nous voici à l'aéroport de Paris.
b) Nous avons faim et soif.
c) L'avion est en retard, donc notre famille n'est pas ici.
d) L'après-midi, c'est le mariage de notre cousin / cousine. La réception est bien organisée.
e) Mon oncle est le témoin. C'est aussi le meilleur ami du marié.
f) Nous disons nos meilleurs voeux de bonheur. Le couple a l'air très heureux!

6.

THE LITTLE THIEF

La petite voleuse

Laetitia takes three frozen pizzas.

COMING UP...

- *Shopping list*: Going to the supermarket
- *On a shopping spree*: Shopping at the flea market
- *The countdown*: Let's count from 101 to 999
- *I scream, you scream*: The irregular verbs *vendre* (to sell) and *prendre* (to take) in the present tense
- *Talking about what "there is" and what "there isn't"*
- *I'll have a little bit of that*: Using the preposition *de* (of) with articles to talk about parts of things
- *Talking about "this" and "that"*: Pointing to things using *ce / cette* (this) and *ces* (these)

The script for *La petite voleuse* (*The Little Thief*) was originally written by the late François Truffaut in 1965. Before his death in 1984, he entrusted the script to Claude Miller, who turned it into a movie in 1989. The star of the film is Charlotte Gainsbourg, daughter of the famous French singer and actor, Serge Gainsbourg.

Did You Know?

MAKING LADIES HAPPY . . .

In his 1883 novel *Au bonheur des dames* (literally, *For the Happiness of the Ladies*), the famous French writer and social critique Émile Zola (1840–1902) describes the creation of the first *grand magasin* (department store) in Paris and the devastating consequences it had for the small neighborhood boutiques. Zola's story was inspired by the establishment of Le Bon Marché, the first Parisian department store.

Zola was also a political activist. He is famous for his open letter to the president, *"J'accuse!"* (I accuse!), published in January 1898 in the Parisian newspaper L'Aurore. In it, he denounces the arbitrary and immoral military trial of Officer Dreyfus and its underlying anti-Semitism. This letter, and the public outcry and debate that followed its publication, contributed greatly to Officer Alfred Dreyfus' later rehabilitation. Zola's ashes lie in the Panthéon, the tomb where the greatest French heroes are buried.

Did You Know?

LOOKING AHEAD

So, how did *les révisions* go? Don't you feel good that you've learned so much French already? And now, *vous êtes prêt pour une nouvelle leçon?* (Are you ready for a new lesson?) This one is about shopping, so let me first give you a few shopping tips.

Did You Know?

In France, as in most European countries, all taxes are included in the *prix de vente* (sales price). So, the ticketed price is what you will pay at the register. In *les grands magasins* (the department stores) and especially in *les supermarchés* (the supermarkets), the employees *à la caisse* (at the register) will not put your purchases into bags. It is not part of their job to do so in France. So don't take it personally!

Did You Know?

In the first dialogue, Pierre Eluard, a man in his forties, *fait les courses* (is shopping) with *sa fille* (his daughter), eight-year-old Laetitia, at the Monoprix *de leur quartier* (of their neighborhood). Monoprix is a very popular *supermarché*, found throughout France.

Pierre is trying to focus on what's on *sa liste des courses* (his shopping list), but *sa petite fille* (his little girl) decides to do some of her own shopping as well.

HEAR...SAY 1

Shopping with Dad Is so Sad!   (C'est si triste les courses avec Papa!)

Laetitia:	Papa, je peux aller dans le chariot?
Pierre:	Oui, ma puce . . . mais tu restes sage. Ah, la voilà!
Laetitia:	Quoi, Papa?
Pierre:	Ma liste de courses. Comme ça, je n'oublie rien. Bon, voyons. . . . On va aux fruits et légumes . . .
Laetitia:	Berk! J'aime pas les légumes.
Pierre:	C'est bon pour la santé. Il y a des vitamines et . . .
Laetitia:	Et des pesticides. J'ai faim, du pain, Papa . . .
Pierre:	Incroyable! Tu es comme ta mère. On prend des carottes, des pommes de terre. Ces tomates-ci sont bien mûres. On prend six tomates.
Laetitia:	Papa, on achète ces beaux champignons de Paris?
Pierre:	Très bonne idée, Laetitia!
Laetitia:	Du pain, Papa. Et ces fraises, si jolies . . . ?
Pierre:	Non, Laeti, il y a encore des fruits à la maison. Et tu ne veux jamais manger de fruits. C'est le dernier morceau de pain.
Laetitia:	C'est pas vrai! C'est triste les courses avec papa.
Pierre:	Mais . . . ! Bon, on va aux surgelés.

Laetitia prend trois pizzas surgelées. Et hop! Dans le chariot.

Pierre:	Tu aimes ces poissons panés, Laetitia? C'est une bonne idée? Non? Bon! Voyons, de la farine, du sucre . . .

Laetitia prend des oeufs en chocolat en cachette!

Laetitia:	Papa, on doit prendre du lait! Et des oeufs.
Pierre:	Du lait et des oeufs. Bravo, Laetitia, tu es comme ton Papa! Et voilà! On va à la caisse. Laeti, tu descends maintenant.
La caissière:	Bonjour, Monsieur, Mademoiselle . . .
Pierre:	Bonjour. . . . Ah! Mais Madame, attendez, je ne veux pas de ça.
La caissière:	Alors, pourquoi est-ce que ces pizzas sont dans votre chariot?
Pierre:	Laetitia! C'est. . . . Laetitia, où est-ce que tu es?
La caissière:	Ça fait 23 (vingt-trois) euros. Voici des sacs.
Pierre:	Merci, Madame. Laetitia, tu entends! On va à la maison!

À la sortie, l'alarme retentit. Laetitia a peur et lâche tous les oeufs en chocolat.

Please answer the following questions:

a)   Who are the characters (*personnages*) in the dialogue?
b)   *Qu'est-ce qu'ils font?*
c)   *Où est-ce qu'ils sont?*
d)   *Qu'est-ce que Laetitia veut?*
e)   *Qu'est-ce que la petite fille fait en cachette?*
f)   What happens *à la sortie?*

Did You Know?

WHAT'S FOR DINNER?

As unbelievable as it may sound to an American, food delivery service (apart from pizza delivery in the big cities) hasn't really caught on yet in the *Hexagone*. (*Hexagone* is a nickname for France, based on its shape.) However, great prepared food is easily available from *traiteurs* (caterers) and, more recently, from small neighborhood restaurants.

The supermarkets also have a wide selection of quality food products *en conserve* (canned) and *surgelé* (frozen) that can be quickly turned into a good meal. Supermarkets also carry *produits de luxe* (delicacy foods) and *produits régionaux* (regional specialties).

Did You Know?

WORKSHOP 1

THE NITTY-GRITTY

You'll need the following for a good shopping day:

THE COUNTDOWN: LET'S COUNT FROM 101 TO 999

NUMBERS FROM 101 TO 199
100: cent
101: cent un
102: cent deux
103: cent trois
. . .
199: cent quatre-vingt-dix-neuf

After 199, *cent* (one hundred) simply gets multiplied. Take a look:

NUMBERS FROM 200 TO 999

200: *deux cents*	500: *cinq cents*
201: *deux cent un*	600: *six cents*
202: *deux cent deux*	700: *sept cents*
. . .	800: *huit cents*
300: *trois cents*	900: *neuf cents*
400: *quatre cents*	999: *neuf cent quatre-vingt-dix-neuf*

Heads Up!

Note that *cent*, like *vingt* (twenty) takes an -s when it is multiplied, except when it's followed by other numbers.

Heads Up!

Did You Know?

The traditional French currency was the French franc. But in January 2002, a new currency called the euro, common to twelve (out of fifteen) countries of the European Union, was introduced. Euro bills *(les billets)* come in denominations of 5, 10, 20, 50, 100, 200, and 500. The coins *(les pièces)* have a "European face" common to all the member countries and a "national face" with symbols specific to each country.

Did You Know?

ACTIVITY 2: TAKE IT FOR A SPIN

Spell out and then read aloud the following amounts in euros.

a) 49 euros   *quarante-neuf*
b) 175 euros   *cent soixante quinze*
c) 490 euros   *quatre cents vingt-dix*
d) 770 euros   *sept cents soixante dix*
e) 231 euros   *deux cents trente et un*
f) 98 euros   *quatre-vingt-dix-huit*

I SCREAM, YOU SCREAM: THE IRREGULAR VERBS *VENDRE* (TO SELL) AND *PRENDRE* (TO TAKE) IN THE PRESENT TENSE

The verbs *vendre* (to sell), *entendre* (to hear), *attendre* (to wait), and *descendre* (to descend) follow the same pattern. The endings in the present tense are:

For *je, tu, il / elle:* **-s, -s, -ø.**
For *nous, vous, ils / elles:* **-ons, -ez, -ent.**

THE PRESENT TENSE OF THE VERB *VENDRE* (TO SELL)

je vends	nous vendons
tu vends	vous vendez
il / elle vend	ils / elles vendent

Heads Up!

As you know now, the final -s is not pronounced. Neither is the -d in *je / tu vends* and *il / elle vend*. All three forms of singular are pronounced as (vah^n).

Heads Up!

ACTIVITY 3: TAKE IT FOR A SPIN

À vous! Write down and then read aloud all the different forms of *entendre*, *attendre*, and *descendre* in the present tense.

The verb *prendre* (to take), like *comprendre* (to understand) and *apprendre* (to learn), is even more irregular than *vendre*. The stem of *prendre* (notice that both *comprendre* and *apprendre* contain *prendre* in them) changes in the different forms. But the endings remain the same. Take a look!

THE PRESENT TENSE OF THE VERB *PRENDRE* (TO TAKE)

je prends	nous prenons (pruh-noh^n)
tu prends	vous prenez (pruh-neh)
il / elle prend	ils / elles prennent (prehn)

The *je*, *tu*, *il/elle* forms of *prendre* are just like those of *vendre*. The verb gets really irregular with the *nous*, *vous*, and *ils/elles* forms. Note the pronunciations!

ACTIVITY 4: TAKE IT FOR A SPIN

And now, looking at the forms of *prendre*, write down all the different forms of *apprendre* and *comprendre*.

TALKING ABOUT WHAT "THERE IS" AND WHAT "THERE IS NOT"

Il y a is the equivalent of English "there is / there are." For example:

Il y a beaucoup de monde.

There are a lot of people.

Il y a des pesticides.

There are pesticides.

Il y a mon papa à la caisse.

There is my daddy at the register.

Note that *il y a* is invariable, i.e., either a singular or a plural noun can follow it without any change in the expression. Yes, for once, French is easier than English. *Incroyable!* "There isn't / aren't" is *il n y a pas.*

I'LL HAVE A LITTLE BIT OF THAT: USING THE PREPOSITION *DE* (OF) WITH ARTICLES TO TALK ABOUT PARTS OF THINGS

De (of) followed by a definite article (*le/la/les*) is used to talk about an unspecified quantity of something. These combinations are called partitive articles. In English, expressions "some of" or "any" are normally used in such contexts. For example:

Je veux de la tarte.

I want <u>some</u> pie.

You'll remember that when *de* (which can also mean "from") is followed by *le* and *les*, it is contracted or joined with the article. Take a look at the table below:

THE PARTITIVE ARTICLES		
	SINGULAR	PLURAL
MASCULINE	*du / de l'*	*des*
FEMININE	*de la / de l'*	*des*

And here are some more examples:

On prend <u>des</u> oeufs, <u>de la</u> farine et <u>du</u> sucre.

We are getting (some) eggs, flour, and sugar.

Il y a encore <u>des</u> fruits à la maison.

There is still some fruit at home.

Est-ce que tu veux <u>des</u> carottes?

Do you want (any) carrots?

J'ai faim, je veux <u>de la</u> pizza.

I'm hungry, I want some pizza.

When a sentence is negative, *du*, *de la*, *de l'*, and *des* become simply *de*.

Tu ne manges jamais _de_ fruits.

You never eat any fruit.

On n'a plus _de_ sucre.

We don't have any sugar left.

Je ne veux pas _de_ tomates.

I don't want any tomatoes.

TAKE IT FOR A SPIN

Complete the sentences by selecting the appropriate articles from the right column.

a)	*Nous allons au supermarché acheter* _de l'_ *eau.*	des
b)	*Mais tu ne prends pas* _de_ *fruits.*	de la
c)	*D'accord, et ensuite je vais prendre* _du_ *pain.*	de l'
d)	*Ils vendent aussi* _de la_ *pizza aux champignons.*	de
e)	*Vous avez faim? Prenez* _des_ *bananes.*	du
f)	*Tu ne veux pas* _de_ *pizza?*	~~de~~

WORDS TO LIVE BY

SHOPPING LIST: GOING TO THE SUPERMARKET

Some love it, others loathe it . . . but the words are:

faire les courses   *to shop*

About *acheter* (ahshuhteh): Although it is regular, its spelling and pronunciation change slightly in the different forms of the present tense. Look: *j'achète* (ah-sheht), *tu achètes* (ah-sheht), *il / elle achète* (ah-sheht), *nous achetons* (ah-shuh-toh^n), *vous achetez* (ah-shuh-teh), *ils / elles achètent* (ah-sheht). As usual, note that the *nous* and *vous* forms are different from all the others.

You already know:

prendre   *to take; to get*
vendre   *to sell*

From the verb *acheter* comes the noun:

l'achat (*masc.*)   *purchase*

From the verb *vendre* come the nouns:

la vente   *sale*
le vendeur   *salesman*
la vendeuse   *saleswoman*

Where do you go to shop?

Obviously, it all depends on what you want to buy:

le grand magasin   *department store*

It sells everything. For food, especially if you're busy, you go to:

le supermarché   *supermarket*

Or, if you don't have time to cook, you go to:

le traiteur   *caterer*

No meal is complete in France without bread, so you have to go to:

la boulangerie   *bakery*

There are many types of breads in France, like:

le pain complet	*whole wheat bread*
le pain de campagne	*country bread*
le pain d'épice	*gingerbread*
le pain de seigle	*rye bread*
le pain de son	*bran bread*
le pain de mie	*sandwich bread*
le pain azyme	*matzos*

Your *liste de courses* (shopping list) is ready. *Au supermarché*, you put all your items *dans un chariot* (a cart). And of course, you're paying attention *aux prix* (the prices). Here are some groceries:

la carotte	*carrot*
le champignon	*mushroom*
le chocolat	*chocolate bar*
la farine	*flour*
la fraise	*strawberry*
le fruit	*fruit*
le lait	*milk*
le légume	*vegetable*
l'oeuf (masc.)	*egg*
le poisson pâné	*breaded fish*
la pomme de terre	*potato*
le sucre	*sugar*
le surgelé	*frozen food*
la tomate	*tomato*

When you're done, you go *à la caisse* (to the register) to pay. The person behind the register gives you *quelques sacs* or *sachets* (a few bags) for your *achats* (purchases).

Word on the Street

à la maison	at home
en cachette	secretly; on the sly
Tu es comme . . .	You are just like . . .
Hop!	Interjection meaning "Jump!"
Voyons . . .	Let's see . . .

There are some interesting expressions using the word *pain* (bread) as a theme:

gagner son pain à la sueur de son front
to earn one's bread by working very hard (Lit. by the sweat of one's brow)
long comme un jour sans pain
long as a day without bread, i.e., a very long day
On a du pain sur la planche.
We have plenty of work.

And then . . .

recevoir un pain   to receive a blow

And, one last comment. . . . Remember when Laetitia says:

J'aime pas les legumes?

She says this instead of the more standard: *Je n'aime pas les légumes.* She also says:

C'est pas vrai.

instead of:

Ce n'est pas vrai.

The first part of the negation—*ne*—is dropped each time. Both children and adults speak that way in everyday situations.

ACTIVITY 6: TAKE IT FOR A SPIN

Time to shop around . . . In the previous dialogue, find all the food items and write a shopping list (*une liste des courses*). Which items has Laetitia "secretly" put under her jacket and dropped into the cart?

Did You Know?

The city of Paris is divided into *vingt arrondissements* (twenty sections) which are a rough equivalent of U.S. boroughs. Each *arrondissement* then contains one or more *quartier*s (neighborhoods). The first *arrondissement* is in the heart of Paris; the next ones unfold clockwise like the shell of a snail. Usually, the *arrondissement* number is given as part of an address. For example, you may hear someone say, *Le Bon Marché est dans, septième*, pronounced as (seh-tyehm) and often written as 7ème or 7e.

By the way, when you're in Paris, you'll notice that the addresses of stores, restaurants, movie theaters, etc., contain the name of the closest metro station (*la station de métro*) in addition to the regular street address. Very convenient, isn't it?

LET'S PUT IT IN WRITING

Take a look at this store ad:

La rentrée au BON MARCHÉ?
Des pages d'idées nouvelles pour toute la famille!

LE BON MARCHÉ Rive Gauche 24, rue des Sèvres, Paris 7ème
Métro: Sèvres-Babylone (lignes 10 et 12)
Service clientèle, tel: 01-44-39-82-80 - www.lebonmarche.fr

ACTIVITY 7: TAKE IT FOR A SPIN

You know what's next:

a)   What is Le Bon Marché?
b)   What is the ad about?
c)   What information is given about Le Bon Marché?
d)   *Combien est-qu'il y a d'arrondissements à Paris?*

LOOKING AHEAD

Our next scene is taking place *aux Puces de Montreuil*, one of the biggest flea markets in Paris. By the way, Montreuil is a nearby suburb located east of Paris (*Métro: Mairie de Montreuil-ligne 9*).

Two friends, Danielle Éluard and Frédérique Thomas, have *un stand aux Puces de Montreuil*. They sell untagged designer clothes, jewelry, and other knickknacks.

HEAR...SAY 2

The Thief! (Ah, la voleuse!)

Frédérique:	Et où est Laetitia, alors?
Danielle:	Elle est avec son père. Ils font les courses ce matin Bonjour. Monsieur, un petit bijou pour Madame? Non? Bon . . .
Frédérique:	Madame, bonjour! Je peux vous aider?
Danielle:	Voyez tous ces vêtements de marques dégriffés! La dernière mode! Et ceux-là ne sont vraiment pas chers . . .
La cliente:	Oui, vous avez de belles choses. Vous êtes là tous les week-ends?
Danielle:	Oui, Madame.
La cliente:	J'aime beaucoup cet ensemble Yves Saint Laurent. Oh, et ce manteau en daim! Je ne vois pas le prix . . .
Danielle:	Quatre-vingt-dix euros, Madame. C'est une affaire!

Frédérique turns toward other customers. (Frédérique se tourne vers des autres clients.)

Les jeunes clientes:	Ces bagues sont super! On peut voir?
Frédérique:	Oui, Mesdemoiselles! Ce sont des bijoux en argent.
Danielle:	(*sotto voce*) Fréd, fais attention à celles-là . . .
Un couple:	Bonjour, Mesdames. . . . Est-ce que vous avez d'autres lampes? C'est pour notre fille.
Danielle:	Oui, oui, il y a une autre lampe. . . . De l'autre côté. Mais où est-ce qu'elle est? Et ma cliente? Eh, Fréd, où elle est? Mais c'est incroyable! La voleuse est partie avec le manteau et la lampe! Frédérique, qu'est-ce que je fais?
Frédérique:	Il n'y a plus rien à faire maintenant! C'est trop tard! Il y a trop de monde. Vous prenez ces trois bagues? Vingt-huit euros. . . . Merci, Mesdemoiselles. Bien, voilà une bonne journée!
Danielle:	Incroyable! Si je vois cette voleuse . . .

ACTIVITY 8: HOW'S THAT AGAIN?

It looks like instant family karma, doesn't it? Of course, we can't use here all the words that come out of Danielle's mouth . . . Now, let's see if you can tell which of these sentences describe the situation correctly.

T a) *Les jeunes femmes sont heureuses.*

T b) *Danielle est vraiment en colère.*

F c) *Elles apprécient la voleuse.*

d) *Ça va barder!*

F e) *Frédérique a peur.*

T f) *La voleuse est partie, alors il n'y a plus rien à faire.*

Did You Know?

THE MARRIAGE OF FASHION AND ART

France is famous for its *haute couture* (high fashion), which has always flirted with art. As early as the 1930's, fashion designer Elsa Schiaparelli designed an embroidered jacket, based on a drawing by Jean Cocteau.

More recently, Fondation Cartier organized a sold-out Issey Miyake exhibition (and not a fashion show!), and John Galliano created a "surrealist" collection for Christian Dior. All top fashion boutiques on the Rive Gauche (Left Bank) display art, from paintings to video installations, in their windows: Castelbajac, Dior, Saint-Laurent, Rykiel. . . . Art is a must! Yves Saint-Laurent, a famous designer and a renowned art collector, is partly financing renovation work at the Beaubourg Center for Art. And Hermès is opening a gallery in Brussels.

Did You Know?

WORKSHOP 2

THE NITTY-GRITTY

TALKING ABOUT "THIS" AND "THAT": POINTING TO THINGS USING *CE / CETTE* (THIS) AND *CES* (THESE)

We use words like *this* and *that* to show or point to people, places, or things. Such words are also called demonstrative adjectives (think: "demonstrate").

1. The Demonstrative Adjectives

	SINGULAR		PLURAL	
THE DEMONSTRATIVE ADJECTIVES				
MASCULINE	*ce / cet*	this / that	*ces*	these / those
FEMININE	*cette*	this / that	*ces*	these / those

Like other adjectives, demonstrative adjectives agree in gender and number with the noun they modify. Take a look at the examples:

Ces champignons sont délicieux.

These mushrooms are delicious.

Cet ensemble est beau.

This outfit is beautiful.

Je prends cette lampe.

I'm taking that lamp.

Heads Up!

In front of a masculine noun starting with a vowel, e.g., *ensemble*, or a silent "h," e.g., *homme*, use *cet* instead of *ce*. This helps pronunciation. For example:

Cet enfant dans le chariot est sage.

This child in the carriage is well behaved.

Cet hôtel est à côté du supermarché.

This hotel is next to the supermarket.

Heads Up!

Demonstrative adjectives can also be used in combination with with *–ci* and *–là*. *–ci* indicates proximity in space and time and *–là* indicates a more distant time / place / object. *–ci* and *–là* attach to a noun as in the following examples:

Ces tomates-ci sont bien mûres.

These tomatoes are really ripe.

Cet enfant-là est ma fille.

That child is my daughter.

J'aime cette bague-ci.

I like this ring.

Ce supermarché-là a tout.

That supermarket has everything.

ACTIVITY 9: TAKE IT FOR A SPIN

Search! Please find all the demonstrative adjectives in the two Hear . . . Say sections and write them down together with the nouns they modify.

2. The Demonstrative Pronouns

Demonstrative pronouns are used to point to things without actually naming them. So, you can say, *I want these strawberries.* Or if the context is obvious, you can just say, *I want these. These*, as used in the latter example, is a demonstrative pronoun. In French, demonstrative pronouns are actually different from demonstrative adjectives.

THE DEMONSTRATIVE PRONOUNS				
	SINGULAR		PLURAL	
	CLOSE OBJECT	FAR OBJECT	CLOSE OBJECT	FAR OBJECT
MASCULINE	*celui-ci*	*celui-là*	*ceux-ci*	*ceux-là*
FEMININE	*celle-ci*	*celle-là*	*celles-ci*	*celles-là*

Let's look at the examples. (The noun which is replaced by a demonstrative pronoun is underlined.)

On va acheter <u>des fruits</u>. Ceux-ci semblent bien mûrs.

We're going to buy fruit. These look really ripe.

Nous vendons <u>des bagues</u>. Celles-ci ne sont pas chères.

We sell rings. These are not expensive.

Celle-là (fem.) est très belle.

That one is beautiful.

Celui-là (masc.) est dans mon quartier.

That one is in my neighborhood.

ACTIVITY 10: TAKE IT FOR A SPIN

Draw a line between a demonstrative adjective, a corresponding noun and an appropriate demonstrative pronoun that could replace them.

a)	ces	supermarché	celui-là
b)	cet	petite voleuse	celui-ci
c)	cet	tomates	celui-ci
d)	ce	ensemble	ceux-ci
e)	ces	homme-là	celle-ci
f)	cette	fruits	celles-ci

ON A SHOPPING SPREE: SHOPPING AT THE FLEA MARKET

Au marché aux puces or *aux puces* (at the flea market) you can find everything—furniture, clothes . . . old and new . . . all very *bon marché* (cheap) or not so *cher/chère* (expensive).

la bague	*ring*
le bijou (les bijoux)	*jewelry*
l'ensemble (*masc.*)	*suit; outfit*
la lampe	*lamp*
le manteau en daim	*suede coat*
le stand	*stand; table*
le vêtement de marque	*designer clothing*
dégriffé, dégriffée	*untagged*

By the way, *une puce*, you got it, is "a flea." The word is also used as a pet name, as in *ma puce*. . . . That's right, Pierre calls his daughter that . . .

The word *la rentrée* describes the period of the year when the schools start again in early September.

Word on the street

Cela fait ____ euros (€).	It's ____ euros.
C'est à la mode.	It's fashionable.
C'est une affaire.	It's a good deal.
être parti, partie	to be gone
Il n'y a plus rien à faire!	There's nothing else to do!

CRIB NOTES

HEAR...SAY 1

Laetitia:	Daddy, can I get into the cart?
Pierre:	Yes, sweetie. . . . But you have to be good. Ah, here it is!
Laetitia:	What, Daddy?
Pierre:	My shopping list. That way, I don't forget anything. Well, let's see. . . . Let's go to the fruit and vegetables . . .
Laetitia:	Yuck! I don't like vegetables.
Pierre:	They're healthy. There are vitamins and . . .
Laetitia:	And pesticides. I'm hungry. Give me some bread, Daddy.
Pierre:	Incredible! You're like your mother. We'll get carrots, potatoes. These

	tomatoes are just ripe. We'll get six tomatoes.
Laetitia:	Daddy, shall we buy these beautiful mushrooms?
Pierre:	Very good idea, Laetitia!
Laetitia:	Some bread, Daddy. And those strawberries, so lovely . . . ?
Pierre:	No, Laeti, there's still some fruit at home. And you never want to eat any fruit. That's the last piece of bread.
Laetitia:	Can't be! Shopping with Dad is so sad.
Pierre:	But . . . ! Well, let's go to the frozen food section.

Laetitia takes three frozen pizzas. And into the cart they go.

Pierre: Do you like breaded fish, Laetitia? A good idea? No? Well! Let's see, flour, sugar . . .

Laetitia takes some chocolate eggs on the sly!

Laetitia: Dad, we need to get milk! And eggs.
Pierre: Milk and eggs. Good, Laetitia, you're like your Dad! That's it! We're going to the register. Laeti, get down now.

The cashier: Hello, Sir, Miss.
Pierre: Hello . . . ! But wait, Ma'am, I don't want that.
The cashier: So why are those pizzas in your cart?
Pierre: Laetitia! It's . . . Laetitia, where are you?
The cashier: That's 23 euros. Here are some bags.
Pierre: Thank you, Ma'am. Laetitia, do you hear me? We're going home!

At the exit, the alarm rings. Laetitia is scared and drops all the chocolate eggs.

HEAR...SAY 2

Frédérique: So where is Laetitia?
Danielle: She's with her father. They're going shopping this morning. Hello, Sir, a nice piece of jewelry for Madam? No? Well . . .
Frédérique: Madam, good morning! Can I help you?
Danielle: Look at these untagged designer clothes! The latest fashion! And those are really not expensive . . .
The customer: Yes, you have beautiful things. Are you here every weekend?
Danielle: Yes, Madam.
The customer: I like this Yves Saint-Laurent outfit very much. Oh, and this suede coat! I don't see the price . . .
Danielle: 90 euros, Madam. A real deal!
Frédérique: Yes, ladies! These pieces of jewelry are silver.

The young customers: These rings are great! Can we see?
Danielle: (sotto voce) Fréd, be careful with them . . .
A couple: Good morning, ladies. . . . Do you have other lamps? It's for our daughter.
Danielle: Yes, yes, there is another lamp. . . . On the other side. . . . But where is it? And my customer? Hey, Fréd, where is she? That's incredible! The thief is gone with the coat and the lamp! Frédérique, what do I do?
Frédérique: There's nothing you can do now! It's too late! There are too many people. Are you taking these three rings? 28 euros. . . . Thank you, ladies. Well, this is a fine day!
Danielle: Incredible! If I see that thief . . .

ANSWER KEY

ACTIVITY 1

a) Le personnages sont Pierre Éluard et sa fille Laetitia.
b) Ils font les courses.
c) Ils sont au supermarché Monoprix.
d) Laetitia veut des fraises.
e) La petite fille prend des pizzas et des oeufs en chocolat en cachette.
f) L'alarme retentit à la sortie.

ACTIVITY 2

a) quarante-neuf euros
b) cent soixante-quinze euros
c) quatre cent quatre-vingt-dix euros
d) sept cent soixante-dix euros
e) deux cent trente et un euros
f) quatre-vingt-dix-huit euros

ACTIVITY 3

j'entends, tu entends, il / elle entend, nous entendons, vous entendez, ils / elles entendent

j'attends, tu attends, il / elle attend, nous attendons, vous attendez, ils / elles attendent

je descends, tu descends, il / elle descend, nous descendons, vous descendez, ils / elles descendent

ACTIVITY 4

j'apprends, tu apprends, il / elle apprend, nous apprenons, vous apprenez, ils / elles apprennent

je comprends, tu comprends, il / elle comprend, nous comprenons, vous comprenez, ils / elles comprennent

ACTIVITY 5

a) Nous allons au supermarché acheter de l'eau.
b) Mais tu ne prends pas de fruits.
c) D'accord, et ensuite je vais prendre du pain.
d) Ils vendent aussi de la pizza aux champignons.
e) Vous avez faim? Prenez des bananes.
f) Tu ne veux pas de pizza?

ACTIVITY 6

La liste des courses: des fruits et des légumes, des carottes, des pommes de terre, des tomates, des champignons, du pain, des fraises, des pizzas, des poissons pânés, de la farine, du sucre, des oeufs en chocolat, du lait, des oeufs.

Laetitia prend en cachette des pizzas et des oeufs en chocolat.

ACTIVITY 7

a) Le Bon Marché est le premier grand magasin parisien.
b) The ad is about *la rentrée au Bon Marché*.
c) The address, the phone number, and the Web site are given.
d) Il y a vingt arrondissements à Paris.

ACTIVITY 8

b) Danielle est vraiment en colère.
d) Ça va barder!
f) La voleuse est partie, alors il n'y a plus rien à faire.

ACTIVITY 9

First dialogue: ces tomates-ci, ces beaux champignons, ces fraises, ces poissons panés, ces pizzas

Second dialogue: ce matin, ces vêtements, cet ensemble, ce manteau, ces bagues (2 times), cette voleuse

ACTIVITY 10

a) ce supermarché—celui-ci
b) cette petite voleuse—celle-ci
c) ces tomates—celles-ci
d) cet ensemble—celui-ci
e) cet homme-là—celui-là
f) ces fruits—ceux-ci

7. VINCENT, FRANÇOIS, PAUL AND THE OTHERS

Vincent, François, Paul et les autres

Mmmm! That smells good!

COMING UP. . .

- *Enjoy your meal*: Talking about food
- *Mix it up!*: Making crepes
- *Give it to me*: Personal pronouns like *(to) me, (to) you, (to) him / her*, etc.
- *I scream, you scream*: The irregular verbs *venir* (to come), *tenir* (to hold), and *servir* (to serve) in the present tense
- *I've just done it*: Talking about what's just happened

Vincent, François, Paul et les autres (*Vincent, François, Paul, and the Others*) (1974) is a bittersweet comedy by the late Parisian director, Claude Sautet. Sautet was a master at depicting relationships with both realism and tenderness. Romy Schneider, his favorite actress, Emmanuelle Béart, who starred in a few of his later films, Yves Montand and Serge Reggiani, both singers and actors also featured in this film, all belonged to Claude Sautet's movie "family." And guess who had his first important role in this movie? Gérard Depardieu!

Did You Know?

Gathering for dinner around a well-garnished table remains an important tradition *en France*. It doesn't need to be Christmas or someone's birthday. *Les familles* and *les amis* enjoy sharing a cooked meal as much as they would enjoy going to a theater or a concert. It's an opportunity to meet, share, catch up, and of course, eat! In spite of an increasingly fast-paced life in France, in which most adults—men and women—work outside their homes, *faire un dîner à la maison* (having dinner at home) is a tradition still holding strong there. And, by the way, if you are invited for dinner, don't forget to bring a present to the *maîtresse de maison* (the hostess), such as *une bouteille de vin* (a bottle of good wine) or liquor, or *un bouquet de fleurs* (a bouquet of flowers)!

Did You Know?

LOOKING AHEAD

Here we are in a very "tasteful" chapter! You'll find out what's on *le menu* (muh-nü) (the menu) for a delicious dinner, get *la recette* (the recipe) for a popular dessert, hear the captivating story of a *photographe* (photographer) who decided to take care of his family's *vignobles* (vineyards), learn about delicious *produits régionaux* (regional foods), and much more. Are you still here? Good, for as one says in French, *il y a du pain sur la planche*! (There's a lot to do!)

In the dialogues, *un nouveau personnage*, Nathalie, is having *un dîner chez elle* (a dinner party at her house). *C'est lundi soir.* (It's Monday evening.) She has invited several of *ses amis*. *Son ami* (her boyfriend), Luc, has come earlier *pour l'aider* (to help her) cook. We hear their secret—Nathalie is *enceinte* (pregnant), but *chutt*!!! No one else knows it yet.

Later on, as *les amis* are finishing *le dîner*, there's a little battle about what they should be doing next—watch a soccer game *à la télé*, play a game or . . .

Who's Coming to Dinner Tonight?   (Qui vient dîner ce soir?)

Luc: Hmmm! Ça sent bon! Nat, tu es le plus joli des cordons-bleus.

Nathalie: Oh, tu sais, ce n'est pas difficile. Je me demande si . . .

Luc: Si c'est un garçon ou une fille? Moi, je ne veux pas le savoir! Et, ce menu? Qu'est-ce que tu nous prépares de bon?

Nathalie: Eh bien, en entrée, il y a une tarte au saumon. . . . Tiens, tu peux faire la salade, s'il te plaît?

Luc: Mais bien sûr. . . . Et après cette délicieuse tarte au saumon?

Nathalie: Il y a de la lotte à l'armoricaine, de la salade verte aux crottins de chèvre et des crêpes pour le dessert. Voici la tarte. Tu peux la tenir? Attention, c'est chaud. . . . Je veux juste prendre le dessous de plat. . . . Merci. Eh bien, tout est prêt, je crois.

Luc: Un vrai festin! Où est-ce que tu ranges les saladiers?

Nathalie: Je les range dans le placard, en haut. Bon . . . je vais finir de mettre la table, car nos invités vont arriver.

Plus tard, Aziza, Paco et Julienne sont déjà là. On sonne à la porte.

Nathalie: Je viens! Florence, Momar, bonsoir! Comment ça va?

Momar: Ça va. On n'est pas en retard? Car avec Florence . . .

Florence: Mais dis donc! Luc, salut! Aziza! Paco! Comment allez-vous? Nathalie, on t'apporte du vin blanc.

Nathalie: Ah, merci bien. C'est parfait pour ce repas.

Luc: Vous n'êtes même pas les derniers, Momar, on attend encore Jason. Alors, quoi de neuf, Flo?

Florence: Eh bien, je suis à l'heure! (Rires.) Ça va, Juju? Mais les gars, ça sent super bon! Qu'est-ce que vous nous mijotez?

Luc: Qu'est-ce que vous croyez, je suis un vrai chef cuisinier!

Aziza: Mais oui, on te croit. . . . Tu nous donnes la recette de la lotte?

Paco: Luc, je te sers un peu de rosé? Pour l'inspiration . . . Momar, Flo, vous arrivez au bon moment. . . . Et la maîtresse de maison?

Julienne: Nathalie, viens . . . Paco va te servir à boire.

Luc: Non . . .

En français, whenever you can.

a)   Is it a potluck party?
b)   *Est-ce que c'est un dîner ou un déjeuner?*
c)   *Qu'est-ce que Luc fait?*
d)   *Quel est le menu?*
e)   *Est-ce que Momar et Florence sont en retard?*

LET'S PUT IT IN WRITING

You get hungry as you eat . . .

. . . or, as the French say, *L'appétit vient en mangeant*. If you go to a restaurant or are invited to a dinner, you should know what to expect. Here's a little text telling you all you need to know about a typical French meal.

Pour ouvrir l'appétit, on peut servir un apéritif, c'est-à-dire, une boisson avec des ca-cahuètes (peanuts), par exemple. Le repas commence avec un hors-d'oeuvre (ou une entrée); puis, il y a le plat principal. Avant le dessert, on peut proposer une salade verte et du fromage. Enfin, après le dessert, beaucoup de personnes aiment boire du café. À la fin, on peut prendre un digestif! Oh! Et au restaurant, on ne peut absolument pas demander un "doggy bag"! Bon appétit!

ACTIVITY 2:   TAKE IT FOR A SPIN

Translate the above text on French meals using the glossary in the back of the book or your dictionary.

WORKSHOP 1

THE NITTY-GRITTY

GIVE IT TO ME: PERSONAL PRONOUNS LIKE *(TO) ME*, *(TO) YOU*, *(TO) HIM / HER*, ETC.

So far you've learned about the pronouns that correspond to English "I," "you," "he / she," "it," etc. Let's review them: *je, tu, il / elle / on, nous, vous, ils / elles.*

There are two more types of pronouns that you need to learn—those that correspond to English "me," "you," "him / her," etc. and those that correspond to "to me," "to you," "to him / her," etc.

1. Direct Object Pronouns

Let's brush up a bit on some grammar terms: We know that a noun is the direct object in a sentence if it answers the question "whom?" or "what?" So, in the sentence *Luc helps Nathalie*, "Nathalie" is the answer to the question "whom?", and "Nathalie" is the object in the sentence. Now, this object can be replaced by the pronoun *her* to avoid repetition, and we call "her" a direct object pronoun. Here are all the direct object pronouns in French:

THE DIRECT OBJECT PRONOUNS			
SINGULAR		**PLURAL**	
me, m'	me	*nous*	us
te, t'	you	*vous*	you
le, l'	him / it	*les*	them
la, l'	her / it	*les*	them

How do the direct object pronouns work?
First, let's take a look at a few examples from the dialogue.

> **Où est-ce que tu ranges <u>les saladiers</u>? —Je <u>les</u> range dans le placard.**

Where do you keep the salad bowls? —I keep them in the cupboard.

> **Luc aide <u>Nathalie</u>. Il <u>l'</u>aide.**

Luc helps Nathalie. He helps her.

> **Tu peux tenir <u>la tarte</u>? —Oui, je peux <u>la</u> tenir.**

Can you hold the pie? —Yes, I can hold it.

a) Placing object pronouns
In a positive sentence, the direct object pronoun comes right in front of the verb.

> **On <u>te</u> croit.**

We believe you.

In a negative sentence, the direct object pronoun comes between *ne* and the verb (or again, right in front of the verb).

> **On ne croit pas <u>Luc</u>. On ne <u>le</u> croit pas.**

We don't believe Luc. We don't believe him.

In questions, the direct object pronoun also comes directly before the verb.

> **Est-ce que tu invites <u>ton amie</u>? Est-ce que tu <u>l'</u>invites?**

Are you inviting your friend? Are you inviting her?

But when there are two verbs, as in *Je peux faire la salade*, the direct object pronoun always comes before the second verb.

Je peux faire <u>la salade</u>. Je peux <u>la</u> faire.

I can make the salad. I can make it.

Est-ce que tu veux <u>m'</u>aider?

Do you want to help me?

Vous n'allez pas servir <u>la tarte</u> chaude. Vous n'allez pas <u>la</u> servir chaude.

You're not going to serve the pie hot. You're not going to serve it hot.

b) The object pronouns and the *élision*

The rule of *élision* applies here as well. That is, in front of a noun starting with a vowel or a silent *h*, *me* becomes *m'*:

Tu veux <u>m'</u>aider?

You want to help me?

Te becomes *t'*:

Nous <u>t'</u>attendons.

We are waiting for you.

Le/la become *l'*:

Elles <u>l'</u>invitent.

They invite him / her.

ACTIVITY 3: **TAKE IT FOR A SPIN**

Your turn! *À vous!* Replace the direct object noun (underlined in the examples below) by an object pronoun.

a)   *Lundi, j'invite <u>mes amis</u>.*
b)   *Si tu veux, tu peux faire <u>les courses</u>.*
c)   *Mais tu ne prépares pas <u>le menu</u>.*
d)   *Est-ce que mes invités aiment <u>le poisson</u>?*
e)   *Je sais faire <u>la tarte au saumon</u>.*
f)   *Et pourquoi est-ce que tu ne fais pas <u>les crêpes</u>?*

2. Indirect Object Pronouns

Okay, it's time for the next set of pronouns. This time, it's those that replace nouns that are indirect objects of a sentence. A noun is an indirect object of a sentence when it answers to the question "to whom?" or "for whom?" For example, in the sentence *Luc gives the recipe to Aziza*, "to Aziza" is the indirect object, which could be replaced by *to her*. *To her* is the indirect object pronoun.

We can recognize an indirect object by the preposition that precedes it, such as *à* (to) or *pour* (for). In French, the indirect object pronoun replaces the noun **and** the preposition that precedes it. For example:

On apporte du vin blanc <u>à Nathalie</u>.   →   **On <u>lui</u> apporte du vin.**

We bring white wine to Nathalie.   We bring her white wine.

THE INDIRECT OBJECT PRONOUNS			
SINGULAR		**PLURAL**	
me, m'	to me	*nous*	to us
te, t'	to you	*vous*	to you
lui	to him / her / it	*leur*	to them

As you can see, there is in fact little difference between the direct and the indirect object pronouns. Only the *lui* (to him / her) form and the *leur* (to them) form are different.

Let's look at the following examples:

Elles sert des crêpes <u>à ses amis</u>. →   **Elle <u>leur</u> sert des crêpes.**

She's serving crepes to her friends.   She's serving them crepes.

Est-ce qu'on <u>t'</u>apporte du vin?

Should we bring you wine?

Tu ne parles pas <u>à son ami</u>. →   **Tu ne <u>lui</u> parle pas.**

You don't speak to his friend.   You don't speak to him.

Tu peux <u>nous</u> passer le sucre?

Can you pass us the sugar?

Il ne veux pas donner du fromage <u>à Nathalie</u>. →

He doesn't want to give cheese to Nathalie. →

Il ne veux pas <u>lui</u> donner du fromage.

He doesn't want to give her cheese.

In conclusion, the indirect object pronouns (like the direct object ones) always come directly in front of the verb.

TAKE IT FOR A SPIN

Replace the underlined indirect object nouns with the corresponding pronouns.

a) *Nathalie demande <u>à Luc</u> de faire la salade.*
b) *Est-ce que vous voulez passer le saladier <u>à Jason</u>?*
c) *Ils parlent <u>à leur amis</u>.*
d) *Tu ne telephones pas <u>à Paco</u>?*
e) *Tu sers de la tarte au saumon à Julienne <u>et Aziza</u>.*

And what if you have them both together?

You're in for trouble. Just joking! What happens when a verb has two objects? Let's see:

Nathalie <u>nous</u> donne <u>la recette</u>. →   **Elle <u>nous la</u> donne.**

Nathalie gives us the recipe.   She gives it to us.

Pourquoi est-ce que vous <u>le leur</u> apportez?

Why do you bring it to them?

Elle ne <u>nous le</u> passe pas.

She doesn't give it to us.

You'll just have to remember that:
Me, te, nous, and *vous* always come before *le, la,* and *les,* which always come before *lui* and *leur.*

TAKE IT FOR A SPIN

Help me, please! Rewrite these sentences by putting the words in the right order.

a) *donner / pas / je / le / peux / ne / te.*
b) *leur / quand / le / est-ce / vas / que / tu / dire?*
c) *pouvons / vous / passer / les / nous.*
d) *elle / nous / sert / chaude / la / est-ce que?*
e) *ce / le / apportent / leur / ils / soir.*

***I SCREAM, YOU SCREAM:* THE IRREGULAR VERBS *VENIR* (TO COME),
TENIR (TO HOLD) AND *SERVIR* (TO SERVE) IN THE PRESENT TENSE**

Yes, this is the time to learn more *irrrrregular* verbs.

The verb *venir* (to come) and the verb *tenir* (to hold)—and all the verbs that have the same root, such as *prévenir* (to warn), *devenir* (to become) and *contenir* (to contain)—follow the same pattern.

THE PRESENT TENSE OF THE IRREGULAR VERB *VENIR* (TO COME)	
je viens (vyeh^n)	*nous venons* (vuh-noh^n)
tu viens	*vous venez* (vuh-neh)
il / elle vient	*ils / elles viennent* (vyehn)

THE PRESENT TENSE OF THE IRREGULAR VERB *TENIR* (TO HOLD)	
je tiens (tyeh^n)	*nous tenons* (tuh-noh^n)
tu tiens	*vous tenez* (tuh-neh)
il / elle tient	*ils / elles tiennent* (tyehn)

The verb *tenir* is used in a few useful expressions.

One of them is *Tiens!* which can be translated as "by the way"; it can also express a slight surprise.

Tiens! Tu es là!

Hey! You're here!

Tiens! Il revient de New York.

By the way, he's returning from New York.

ACTIVITY 6: TAKE IT FOR A SPIN

Fill in the blanks in each sentence with the appropriate verb form on the right.

a)	*Je ne peux pas _____ à 3 heures.*	vient
b)	*Qui est-ce qui _____ dîner ce soir?*	Tiens
c)	*_____ ! Vous êtes de retour.*	venons
d)	*Est-ce que vous pouvez _____ ce saladier?*	venir
e)	*Nous _____ vous voir ce soir.*	tenir

Let's take a look at the irregular verb *servir.* The verb *servir* is actually an important verb in this chapter. It is used in the following constructions:

servir de quelque chose à quelqu'un

or

servir quelque chose à quelqu'un

In the first case, you use the verb *servir* followed by partitive articles—*du, de la,* or *des.* You'll remember that you need to use a partitive article when what you serve cannot be counted, like cake, salad, wine, etc. Look at the examples:

Je vous sers <u>du</u> saumon?

Can I serve you (some) salmon?

Il sert <u>de la</u> salade à Aziza.

He's serving (some) salad to Aziza.

Nous ne servons pas <u>de vin</u> à Nathalie.

We don't serve (any) wine to Nathalie.

Note that *servir du / de la / des* becomes *servir de* in a negative sentence.

If what is served is a countable item (like glass, plate, apple, etc.), a regular article (*un / une / des* or *le / la / les*) is used after *servir.* For example:

Je te sers un verre de vin?

Can I serve you a glass of wine?

THE PRESENT TENSE OF THE IRREGULAR VERB *SERVIR* (TO SERVE)	
je sers	nous servons
tu sers	vous servez
il / elle sert	ils / elles servent

WORDS TO LIVE BY

ENJOY YOUR MEAL: TALKING ABOUT FOOD

It's always fun to prepare *un dîner à la maison* for your friends:

la maîtresse de maison	the hostess
aider à + infinitif	to help to (do something)
cuisiner	to cook
faire à dîner	to make dinner
mettre la table	to set the table
préparer à manger	to fix a meal, to cook
ranger	to put in order / in place

Note that if you go to visit a person, you say *rendre visite à,* e.g., *Ils rendent visite à Nathalie;* but if you go to visit a place, you say *visiter,* e.g., *Je vais visiter Paris.*

When you speak to a person, you use *parler à,* e.g., *Je parle à Nathalie,* but when you speak about something or somebody, you use *parler de,* e.g., *Je parle de Paris.*

The meal (*le repas*):

le festin	*feast*
le déjeuner	*lunch*
le dîner	*dinner*
un hors-d'oeuvre / une entrée	*appetizer*
le menu	*menu*
le plat	*dish*
le plat principal	*main course*
la cacahuète	*peanut*
le crottin de chèvre	*type of goat cheese*
la crêpe	*crepe*
le dessert	*dessert*
le fromage	*cheese*
la lotte à l'armoricaine	*fish dish*
la salade verte	*green salad*
le saumon	*salmon*
la tarte au saumon	*salmon pie*

On the table (*sur la table*):

l'assiette (fem.)	*plate*
la cuillère à café	*teaspoon*
la cuillère à soupe	*tablespoon*
le dessous de plat	*table mat*
le saladier	*salad bowl*

The drinks (*la boisson*):

boire du vin	*to drink wine*
servir du vin	*to serve wine*
l'apéritif (*masc.*)	*aperitif*
la bouteille	*bottle*
le café	*coffee, espresso*
l'eau, de l'eau (*fem.*)	*water, some water*
le verre	*glass*
le (vin) blanc	*white wine*
le (vin) rosé	*rosé*
le (vin) rouge	*red wine*

Notice that you can omit the word *vin* when speaking about it, and just say *le blanc* (white), *le rosé* (rosé), *le rouge* (red).

And some useful little words:

à la fin	*at the end*
après	*after*
avant	*before*
petit à petit	*little by little*

Word on the Street

à la maison	at home, at one's house
Bon appétit!	Enjoy your meal!
Ça sent bon!	It smells good!
chez quelqu'un	at someone's place
Mais dis donc!	But . . . !; Oh, please . . .
On sonne à la porte.	The doorbell is ringing.
ouvrir l'appétit	to whet the appetite
Quoi de neuf?	What's new?

ACTIVITY 7: **TAKE IT FOR A SPIN**

Separate the following words into two columns: Use one column for the feminine words, and the other for the masculine words.

les assiettes, les saumons, les invitées, les festins, les vins, les crottins de chèvre, les crêpes, de l'eau, les tables, les repas, les desserts, les menus, les amies, les dîners, les salades

HEAR . . . SAY 2

Let's Watch the Soccer Game! (On regarde le foot!)

À la fin du dîner:

Momar: Nathalie, tu peux venir cuisiner à la maison quand tu veux!

Aziza: On vient de faire un délicieux repas. Merci, Nat, euh, Luc!

Jason: Qui est-ce qui veut des crêpes? Avec du sucre ou du miel ou du sirop d'érable ou du nutella ou . . .

Julienne: Tout le monde, je crois. Je viens de les goûter. Hmmm!

Luc: Et qui est-ce qui veut un peu de Muscat La Casenova avec les crêpes?

Aziza: Hmmm, c'est la potion d'amour de ton pays, le Roussillon?

Luc: Oui, et c'est un excellent muscat! Flo?

Florence: Non, pas maintenant, je viens de boire du rosé. Merci, Luc. Mais, je veux bien goûter ces crêpes! Vous pouvez nous passer l'assiette de crêpes? Et le sucre, s'il vous plaît? Merci.

Paco: Voilà, Flo. Tiens, on peut peut-être regarder le match de foot!

Julienne: Pourquoi pas? C'est la finale en plus . . .

Luc: Ils ont raison, pourquoi est-ce qu'on ne regarde pas la fin du match au moins?

Nat et Flo: Ah non! Pas ce soir! Et pourquoi pas faire un jeu?

Momar:	Pfff! Allez, on regarde le match!
Aziza, Flo	
et Nathalie:	Non! Non! Non!
Nathalie:	Non, je . . . vais mettre de la musique. Ou Paco, est-ce que tu veux jouer ta musique?

ACTIVITY 8:   **HOW'S THAT AGAIN?**

a)	*Les invités n'aiment pas le dîner.*	*VRAI OU FAUX*
b)	*Julienne ne veut pas regarder la télé.*	*VRAI OU FAUX*
c)	*Aziza, Florence et Nathalie ne veulent pas voir le foot.*	*VRAI OU FAUX*
d)	*Jason n'est pas arrivé.*	*VRAI OU FAUX*
e)	*Ils mangent des fruits pour dessert.*	*VRAI OU FAUX*

Did You Know?

WINE TALK

A meal without wine is somehow just not complete. To the French, it's close to blasphemy. France has a wide variety of wonderful wines. Remember that French wines don't list the grape variety. Rather, they rely on regions and estates to identify the type of wine. Here are the major wine regions of France with the grape varieties they use:

- Alsace (white wines—riesling, gewürtztraminer, sylvaner)
- Bordeaux (red wines—blends of cabernet sauvignon, cabernet franc, and merlot; white wines—blend of sauvignon blanc and Semillon)
- Burgundy (sub-regions are Beaujolais and Chablis) (red wines—pinot noir; white wines—chardonnay)
- Loire (white wines—sauvignon blanc; red wines—cabernet franc)
- Rhône (red wines—syrah)

The *"appellation d'origine contrôlée"* label is the title officially awarded to quality wines.

There is a simple rule for choosing a wine to go with your meal: Drink white wines with light, delicate foods (fish, chicken, vegetable dishes), and red wines with heavier foods (red meat, dark fish, and tomato sauce).

Did You Know?

THE NITTY-GRITTY

I'VE JUST DONE IT: TALKING ABOUT WHAT'S JUST HAPPENED

The irregular verb *venir* (to come) is used to talk about the immediate past. The immediate past is used to describe an action that has just happened.

The immediate past in French is formed using the present tense form of the verb *venir* + *de* + infinitive verb. Take a look at the examples:

Nous <u>venons de manger</u>.

We've just eaten.

Tu <u>viens de boire</u> deux verres!

You've just drunk two glasses!

On <u>vient de faire</u> un délicieux repas.

We've just had a delicious meal.

ACTIVITY 9: TAKE IT FOR A SPIN

Modify the following sentences by making the verb indicate the immediate past.

a) *Ta famille mange à la maison.*
b) *Le match de foot finit.*
c) *Je sers du muscat de mon pays à tout le monde.*
d) *Nous n'arrivons pas.*
e) *Qu'est-ce qu'elles font?*

WORDS TO LIVE BY

MIX IT UP!: MAKING CREPES

The crepe recipe (*la recette à crêpes*):

ajouter	to add
goûter	to taste
mélanger	to mix
le citron	lemon
le zeste de citron	lemon peel
la farine	flour
l'huile (fem.)	oil

le lait	milk
le miel	honey
le rhum	rum
le sel	salt
le sirop d'érable	maple syrup

Wines (*les vins*):

l'étiquette (fem.)	label
le muscat	muscat wine
le raisin	grape
le terroir	soil; agricultural region
le vignoble	vineyard

LET'S PUT IT IN WRITING

La recette à crêpes

...

POUR 6 PERSONNES

*200 grammes de farine,
1 quart de litre de lait, 1 quart de litre d'eau,
4 oeufs,
1 demie cuillère à café de sel,
3 cuillères à soupe d'huile,
3 cuillères à soupe de rhum (ou un autre parfum),
un zeste de citron,
3 cuillères à soupe de sucre.*

...

Dans un grand saladier, mettre les oeufs, le sel, le sucre et l'huile. Bien mélanger tous les ingrédients. Puis, ajouter petit à petit la farine et le lait. À la fin, ajouter l'eau, le rhum et le zeste de citron. C'est fait! Attendre 20-30 minutes avant de faire les crêpes.

Notice that the instructions in the recipe are all given using the infinitive form of the verb—*mettre, mélanger, ajouter, attendre,* and *faire.*

Pay attention to the following pronunciations: *un oeuf* (uh<u>n</u> uhf), "one egg," but *deux oeufs* (duh<u>z</u> uh), "two eggs," without the sound *f* at the end. Also, because the word starts in a vowel, the rule of *liaison* applies.

Did You Know?

In one pound, there are 454 grams. In a gallon, about 3.75 liters. The French, like most Europeans, use the metric system. In recipes they normally give quantities in grams and liters rather than in cups.

ACTIVITY 10: TAKE IT FOR A SPIN

Now it's your turn to do some cooking! Follow the crepes recipe. But first, look for the necessary ingredients and write your shopping list.

Did You Know?

The *terroir du Languedoc-Roussillon* (the Languedoc-Roussillon agricultural region) in southwest France is the oldest and largest in the world. It spreads from the Mediterranean Sea to the Pyrenees Mountains and has been known since antiquity. This region is second in wine production in France.

ACTIVITY 11: TAKE IT UP A NOTCH

Write a short dialogue by translating the following sentences into French:

a) Hey, what's new? How's it going?
b) My friend is cooking a dinner this Monday.
c) Do you want to come with us?
d) You can bring a bottle of wine.
e) I'm going to help her set the table and prepare the salmon.
f) My friend knows how to make delicious recipes from her region.

CRIB NOTES

Luc:	Mmmm! That smells good! Nat, you are the most beautiful chef.
Nathalie:	Well, you know, nothing difficult. I'm wondering . . .
Luc:	If it's a boy or a girl? I don't want to know! And the menu is? What goodies are you preparing for us?
Nathalie:	Well, as an hors d'oeuvre, there's a salmon tart. . . . By the way, can you prepare the salad, please?
Luc:	But of course. . . . And after this delicious salmon tart?
Nathalie:	There is the *lotte à l'armoricaine*. Then, salad with goat cheese, and crepes for dessert. Here's the tart. Can you hold it? Be careful, it's hot. I just want to grab the table mat. Thank you. Well, I think everything is ready.
Luc:	This is a real feast! Where do you keep the salad bowls?
Nathalie:	I keep them in the cupboard, on the top. Good. . . . I'm going to finish setting the table, because our guests are going to arrive.

Later: Aziza, Paco, and Julienne are already here. The doorbell rings.

Nathalie:	I'm coming! Florence, Momar, good evening! So, how it's going?
Momar:	Fine. We're not late? Because you know with Florence . . .
Florence:	Oh please . . . ! Hi, Luc! Aziza! Paco! How are you doing? Nathalie, we are bringing you some white wine.
Nathalie:	Oh, thank you. It's perfect for this meal.
Luc:	No, Momar, you aren't the last to arrive, we're still waiting for Jason. So, what's new, Flo?
Florence:	Well, I'm on time! (Laughs.) How's it going, Juju? Hey, guys, it smells really good! What's cooking?
Luc:	What do you think? I'm a real chef!
Aziza:	Yes, sure. We believe you. You'll give us the recipe for the *lotte*!
Paco:	Luc, maybe a little rosé? For inspiration . . . Momar, Flo, you're coming at the right time . . . And what about the hostess?
Julienne:	Nathalie, come on . . . Paco is going to pour you a drink.
Luc:	No . . .

At the end of the dinner . . .

Momar:	Nathalie, you can come to cook at my house whenever you want!
Aziza:	We've just had a delicious meal. Thank you, Nat, I mean Luc!
Jason:	Who wants some crepes? With sugar or honey or maple syrup or Nutella or . . .
Julienne:	Everyone, I think. I've just tasted them. Mmmm!
Luc:	And who wants a little Muscat La Casenova with the crepes?
Aziza:	Mmm, is this the love potion of your country, the Roussillon?
Luc:	Yep, and it's an excellent muscat! Flo?
Florence:	No, not now, I've just had some rosé. Thank you, Luc. But I want to taste these crepes! Can you pass us the plate of crepes? And some sugar, please? Thank you.
Paco:	Here, Flo. Hey, we could watch the soccer game!
Julienne:	Why not? Besides, it's the final game.
Luc:	They're right. Why not watch the end of the game at least?
Nat and Flo:	Oh, no! Not tonight! Why don't we play a game?
Momar:	Pfff! C'mon, let's watch the game!
Aziza, Flo, and Nathalie:	No! No! No!
Nathalie:	No, I . . . I'm going to put on some music. Or, Paco, do you want to play your music?

ACTIVITY 1

a) Non, Nathalie prépare le repas.
b) C'est un dîner chez Nathalie.
c) Luc aide son amie; il fait la salade.
d) Il y a une tarte au saumon, de la salade aux crottins de chèvre, de la lotte à l'armoricaine, et des crêpes pour le dessert.
e) Non, Jason est le dernier. *or* Non, ils attendent encore Jason.

ACTIVITY 2

To whet your appetite, one could serve an aperitif, that is, a drink and some peanuts, for example. The meal starts with an appetizer (*hors d'oeuvre* or *entrée*); then, there is the main course. Before the dessert, one could offer salad or cheese. Finally, after the dessert, many people like to have (*Lit.* drink) coffee. Oh! And at the restaurant, one absolutely cannot ask for a "doggy bag." Enjoy your meal!

ACTIVITY 3

a) Lundi, je les invite.
b) Si tu veux, tu peux les faire.
c) Mais tu ne le prépares pas.
d) Est-ce que mes invités l'aiment?
e) Je sais la faire.
f) Et pourquoi est-ce que tu ne les fais pas?

ACTIVITY 4

a) Nathalie lui demande de faire la salade.
b) Est-ce que vous voulez lui passer le saladier?
c) Ils leur parlent.
d) Tu ne lui téléphones pas?
e) Tu leur sers de la tarte au saumon.

ACTIVITY 5

a) Je ne peux pas te le donner.
b) Quand est-ce que tu vas le leur dire?
c) Nous pouvons vous les passer.
d) Est-ce qu'elle nous la sert chaude?
e) Ils le leur apportent ce soir.

ACTIVITY 6

a) Je ne peux pas venir à 3 heures.
b) Qui est-ce qui vient dîner ce soir?

c) Tiens! Vous êtes de retour.
d) Est-ce que vous pouvez tenir ce saladier?
e) Nous venons vous voir ce soir.

ACTIVITY 7

Feminine nouns: les assiettes, les invitées, les crêpes, de l'eau, les tables, les amies, les salades.

Masculine nouns: les saumons, les festins, les vins, les crottins de chèvre, les repas, les desserts, les menus, les dîners.

ACTIVITY 8

a) FAUX
b) FAUX
c) VRAI
d) FAUX
e) FAUX

ACTIVITY 9

a) Ta famille vient de manger à la maison.
b) Le match de foot vient de finir.
c) Je viens de servir du muscat de mon pays à tout le monde.
d) Nous ne venons pas d'arriver.
e) Qu'est-ce qu'elles viennent de faire?

ACTIVITY 10

On a besoin d'eau, de lait, d'oeufs, de farine, de sucre, d'huile, de sel, de rhum, d'un citron. J'aime manger les crêpes avec du sucre, du citron, du miel, du nutella, du sirop d'érable . . .

ACTIVITY 11

a) Quoi de neuf? Comment ça va?
b) Mon amie prepare un dîner ce lundi.
c) Tu veux venir avec nous? *or* Est-ce que tu veux venir avec nous?
d) Tu peux apporter une bouteille de vin.
e) Je vais l'aider à mettre la table et à préparer le saumon.
f) Mon amie sait faire de délicieuses recettes de son pays.

8.

THE TELEPHONE

Téléphone

But Aziza, is this you in the picture?

COMING UP. . .

- *Hello?*: Talking on the phone and leaving a message
- *Arts and leisure*: Going to an art show
- *She's so talented!*: Chatting at a photo exhibition
- *Who's calling?*: More on using telephones
- *Just say no!*: Using *ni . . . ni . . .* (neither . . . nor . . .)
- *Been there, done that*: Talking about past events using the *passé composé*
- *Been there, done that, Part 2*: The *passé composé* of *avoir*, *être*, and *aller*

When the group Téléphone first appeared on the French music scene in the late 1970s, some were satisfied to see that finally *le rock français* was born! This *groupe de musique*, which was originally put together over the phone, more or less by chance and for what was supposed to be just a single concert, immediately became very popular . . .

Did You Know?

WIRELESS OR NOT . . .

There are several phone companies *en France* today, but this is a fairly recent situation. France Télécom, which remains the main phone company, used to be a part of the government-administered Postes, Téléphones et Télécommunications or PTT, which had had a complete monopoly over telecommunications in France since the creation of the telephone. Recently, many companies have appeared, encouraged by the great success of *les portables* (cellular phones). The French fully embraced cell phones—so much so that the government felt that their use needed to be regulated. As a result of that, it is forbidden to use a cell phone while driving. Signs asking for discretion, posted in the trains or other public places, are also quite common. So watch out for the traffic police, and *Chut!*

LOOKING AHEAD

In this lesson, you'll get practical tips about how to use *le téléphone*, *les portables*, and *le Minitel*, in France and in French.

In the dialogues, we're back with Luc, his girlfriend, Nathalie, and Aziza, who in spite of their very busy lives (*vies bien remplies*) try to go out in the evenings. *C'est vendredi* (it's Friday) and tonight, they're planning to go to *le vernissage d'une exposition de photographies* (the opening of a photo exhibition). The young women have all the information for tonight, but Luc has no idea where to go. He's been waiting *en vain* (in vain) for a phone call from his friends. *Est-ce qu'elles l'ont vraiment oublié?* (Did they actually forget him?) It's getting late and he's trying desperately to reach them.

HEAR . . . SAY 1

Always on the Phone! (Toujours au téléphone!)

Luc:	Ce n'est pas vrai! Elle est toujours au téléphone. . . . Eh bien, tant pis pour ce soir. A moins que . . .

Il fait un autre numéro.

Luc:	Allô Flo? Euh. . . . Est-ce que Florence est là, s'il vous plaît?
Une voix au téléphone:	Ah non, vous avez fait un mauvais numéro.
Luc:	Oh, pardon, Madame.
La voix au téléphone:	Mademoiselle.
Luc:	Mademoiselle, bonsoir! (Il raccroche.) Mais je n'ai vraiment pas de chance avec le téléphone aujourd'hui!

Il refait le numéro.

Luc:	Bon, 01–41–02–02–01 (zéro un, quarante et un, zéro deux, zéro deux, zéro un) . . . Florence? Ah salut, c'est Luc, ça va?
Florence:	Oui, ça va. Et toi?
Luc:	Eh bien, ça va. Oui, j'ai essayé de téléphoner à Nat au travail, mais sans succès. Sa ligne est toujours occupée.
Florence:	Est-ce que tu as téléphoné chez elle?
Luc:	Oui, bien sûr, mais son répondeur n'est pas branché! En fait, je dois la retrouver à une expo. Aziza va être là-bas aussi. Mais je n'ai ni l'adresse, ni le nom de la galerie.
Florence:	Ah, je ne suis pas au courant, Luc. Mais, est-ce que tu as appelé Aziza au bureau?
Luc:	Oui, bien sûr. Je l'ai appelée au bureau plusieurs fois et sur son portable, mais sans succès. Puis là, elle est sûrement partie.
Florence:	Oui, elle a travaillé au studio aujourd'hui. Tu lui as laissé un message?
Luc:	Non, sa messagerie vocale ne prend plus de messages. Elle est sûrement partie retrouver Nat.
Florence:	Je suis désolée, Luc, je ne sais pas où elles sont allées. Mais elles vont te téléphoner bientôt.
Luc:	Oui, sûrement. Bon, merci Florence, passe une bonne soirée.
Florence:	Toi aussi. Bonsoir, Luc.
Luc:	(Il raccroche.) Mais qu'est-ce que je m'embête! En plus, cela ne me dit rien d'y aller! Et puis, je peux maintenant aller boire un pot avec Ricardo et Paco.

ACTIVITY 1: HOW'S THAT AGAIN?

Too bad for Luc! Now, let's see if you got the message.

a) *Pourquoi est-ce que Luc doit parler à ses amies?* Parce que il doit trouver le nom et l'adresse de galerie.

b) *Où est-ce qu'ils sont supposés aller ce soir?* à une expo

c) Est-ce qu'il a essayé de téléphoner à Nathalie? *Oui, àu son travail et à son repondeur mais son repondeur n'est pas branché.*

d) Est-ce qu'il a parlé à Aziza? *Oui, beccoup de temps.*

e) Qu'est-ce qu'il va faire? *Il peux aller un pot avec Ricardo et Paco.*

LET'S PUT IT IN WRITING

Take a look at this ad:

"Avec le forfait complet (flat rate) de nos téléphones portables,
plus rien ne vous retient! Vous êtes partout en un instant!
Soury Télécom vous donnent des ailes...

ACTIVITY 2: TAKE IT FOR A SPIN

Take your French for a spin and translate this little ad.

WORKSHOP 1

THE NITTY-GRITTY

JUST SAY NO!: USING NI ... NI ... (NEITHER ... NOR ...)

In previous chapters, you learned how to say "no" using *ne ... pas, ne ... plus, ne ... rien,* and *ne ... jamais.* As you remember, they are all used in the same fashion: *ne* + verb + *pas / plus / rien / jamais.*

Ni ... ni ... is the equivalent of the English "neither ... nor ...." See how it is used by taking a look at the following examples:

Elle n'est <u>ni</u> au travail, <u>ni</u> chez elle.

She's neither at work, nor at her place.

Je n'ai <u>ni</u> le nom, <u>ni</u> l'adresse de cette galerie.

I have neither the name nor the address of this gallery.

You can see that *ni* is placed right before the noun it refers to. Unlike English, the expression *ni ... ni* is used together with *ne* (not), which comes before the verb. So, the structure is:

ne + verb + ni + _____ + ni + _____

130

FRENCH WITHOUT THE FUSS

Make these sentences negative using *ni . . . ni . . .*

a)   *Tu téléphones à Nathalie et à Aziza.*   Tu ne telephones ni a Nat, ni à Aziza.
b)   *Elles vont au vernissage et boire un verre.*   Elles ne vont ni au vernissage, e m'boire un verre
c)   *Nous avons un répondeur et une messagerie vocale.*
d)   *Il laisse un message au travail et à la maison.*
e)   *Son amie a le nom et l'adresse de la galerie.*

BEEN THERE, DONE THAT: TALKING ABOUT PAST EVENTS USING THE *PASSÉ COMPOSÉ*

Don't panic! It's not that hard and you already know half of it. Really!

1. What Is the Passé Composé and How to Use It

Passé composé is the most commonly used past tense in French. Most of the time, it is used to describe a past action that was completed in the past. *Passé composé* is a compound tense, i.e., it has two pieces to it. Here are some examples, straight from the first dialogue:

> **Nous <u>avons essayé</u> de téléphoner à notre amie.**
>
> We've tried to call our friend.
>
> **J'<u>ai appelé</u> mais sa ligne est toujours occupée.**
>
> I called but her line's always busy.
>
> **Elle <u>a travaillé</u> au studio.**
>
> She worked at the studio.

You can see that *passé composé* can be translated by either present perfect (*we have tried . . .*) or the simple past tense (*I called . . .* , *She worked . . .*) in English.

Now let's see how this tense is formed.

Most verbs use *avoir* (to have) in *passé composé*, but several others use *être* (to be). (I'll come back to that point later.) Normally, you take the present tense form of *avoir* (*j'ai, tu as, il/elle a, nous avons, vous avez, ils/elles ont*) and follow it with a special form of the main verb, called the "past participle." Let's look at a few examples:

> **Je lui <u>ai parlé</u> hier soir.**
>
> I talked to her last night.
>
> **Elles ne m'<u>ont donné</u> ni l'adresse ni le nom de la galerie.**
>
> They gave me neither the address nor the name of the gallery.

Here's the basic structure for *passé composé*:

subject + *avoir* / *être* in the present tense + past participle of main verb

In negative sentences, *ne . . . pas* is placed around the forms of *avoir* (or *être*), the structure is:

subject + *ne* + *avoir* / *être* + *pas* + past participle of main verb

For example:

Tu n'as pas retrouvé tes amis.

You didn't meet your friends.

In the interrogative form, the structure is:

***Qu'est-ce que* + subject + *avoir* / *être* + past participle of verb?**

As in:

Est-ce que tu as retrouvé tes amis?

Did you meet your friends?

In a sentence containing an object pronoun, the structure is:

subject + object pronoun + *avoir* / *être* + past participle of the main verb

Tu les a retrouvés ce soir.

You met them tonight.

And in a negative sentence with an object pronoun, the structure is:

subject + *ne* + object pronoun + *avoir* / *être* + *pas* + past participle of the main verb

Tu ne les a pas retrouvés ce soir.

You haven't met them tonight.

2. How to Form the Past Participles of *-er* Verbs

The past participle of verbs ending in *-er* is easily formed: remove the ending *-er* from the infinitive verb and add *-é*.

PAST PARTICIPLES OF SOME VERBS ENDING IN *-ER*					
parler	to speak	*retrouver*	to meet	*appeler*	to call
parlé	spoken	*retrouvé*	met	*appelé*	called

And now, let's look at all the different forms of *passé composé* for the verb *téléphoner* "to make a call."

THE PASSÉ COMPOSÉ OF THE VERB TÉLÉPHONER (TO MAKE A CALL)	
j'ai téléphoné	nous avons téléphoné
tu as téléphoné	vous avez téléphoné
il / elle a téléphoné	ils / elles ont téléphoné

As mentioned earlier, some verbs use *être* to form the *passé composé. Arriver* (to arrive) is one of them, e.g., *Je suis arrivé* (I arrived). In general, verbs expressing motion are used with *être*, for example: *aller* (to go), *rentrer* (to return), *entrer* (to enter), *passer* (to stop by), *venir* (to come), *partir* (to leave), *descendre* (to come down), etc. Another example you've encountered earlier is *se marier* (to get married), e.g., *Je me suis marié* (I got married). A verb like *se marier* is called a reflexive verb because it is always used with a reflexive pronoun *se*.

THE *PASSÉ COMPOSÉ* OF THE VERB ARRIVER (TO ARRIVE; TO COME)	
je suis arrivé(e)	nous sommes arrivé(e)s
tu es arrivé(e)	vous êtes arrivé(e)(s)
il / elle est arrivé(e)	ils / elles sont arrivé(e)s

Here are some more examples using *—er* verbs:

Elle <u>est sûrement</u> <u>rentrée</u>.

She probably went back home.

Nous <u>sommes allés</u> voir une exposition géniale.

We went to see a great exhibition.

Heads Up!

Some verbs of motion, like *marcher* (to walk), are exceptions to this general rule and form their *passé composé* with *avoir*, e.g., *J'ai marché pendant une heure* (I walked for an hour). The verb *passer* is also used with *avoir* when it means "to spend time," rather than "to pass," as in:

J'ai passé une bonne soirée avec mes amis.

I spent a good evening with my friends.

ACTIVITY 4:	TAKE IT FOR A SPIN

Time to jump in! Write these sentences in the *passé composé.*

a) J'appelle mon ami toute la journée. *J'ai appellé ...*

b) Ils ne téléphonent pas ce soir. *ils m'ont téléphonés pas ce soir.*

c)   *Elle invite ses amis à son exposition.*   *Elle a invité ses amis ....*

d)   *Vous ne me donnez pas votre numéro de téléphone.*   *Vous ne m'avez pas votre ..*

e)   *Où est-ce qu'elles travaillent?*   *Où est-ce qu'elles ont travaillé.*

The Fine Print

If you looked carefully at the examples, you may have noticed that the past participles, normally ending in –é, ended sometimes in –ée, –ées, or –és. When used with *être*, past participles agree in number (–s marks the plural) and gender (–e marks the feminine) with the subjects. So, in that way, they behave just like adjectives. For example:

il est arrivé   (masculine singular)

elle est arrivée   (feminine singular)

ils sont arrivés   (masculine plural)

elles sont arrivées   (feminine plural)

When the subject refers to both feminine and masculine nouns, the masculine gender always wins. For instance:

Luc et son amie sont allés voir une exposition de photographie.

Luc and his friend went to see a photography exhibition.

These changes are a matter of spelling only, because the pronunciation stays the same throughout.

And if you think this was bad, wait, there's more:

You know that when the auxiliary *avoir* is used to form the *passé composé,* the past participle does not change. Except . . . when a direct object pronoun is placed before the verb. Then, there is an agreement between this pronoun and the past participle. For instance:

Voilà la photographe; je l'ai rencontrée à M7.

Here's the photographer; I met her at M7.

C'est une invitation pour le vernissage. Ils l'ont envoyée à nos amis.

It's an invitation for the opening. They sent it to our friends.

Nous les avons rencontrés à cette expo.

We met them at this exhibition.

Fill in the gaps by selecting the appropriate past participle for each sentence:

a) Nathalie a *téléphoné* un message à Luc. dîné
b) Vous avez _dîné_ après le vernissage? téléphoné
c) Aziza n'est pas là. Je lui ai _appelé_. présentés
e) Luc a _laissé_ Florence. laissé
f) Leur ami les a _présentés_ à la photographe. appelé

WORDS TO LIVE BY

HELLO?: TALKING ON THE PHONE AND LEAVING A MESSAGE

Let's learn how to use the *téléphone* in French!

First, you have to *faire le numéro de téléphone* (to dial the phone number) of the person you want to talk to. For instance, let's take the number Luc dials in order to reach Florence:

Son numéro de téléphone est le 01–41–02–02–01. Here's how you would read this number: *zéro un, quarante et un, zéro deux, zéro deux, zéro un.* In other words, the numbers are grouped in twos.

Mais attention de ne pas faire un mauvais numéro! Be careful not to dial a wrong number! When someone answers your phone call, you say *Allô!* and you start to speak.

If *la ligne est occupée* (the line is busy) you can hang up or *raccrocher*. If you get an answering machine (*un répondeur*) or voice mail (*une messagerie vocale*), you may want to leave a message (*laisser un message*). This is the message Luc could have left for Nathalie:

> **"Allô, oui, c'est moi. Je n'ai ni le nom ni l'adresse de la galerie. Rappelle-moi, s'il te plaît! À plus tard!"**

Rappeler, you guessed it, means "to call back." You're right again—it comes from *appeler* "to call." The prefix *r–/re–* expresses the repetition of an action, just like the prefix *re–* in English.

Heads Up!

By the way, throughout the chapter, we've been using the verb *appeler*, an easy *–er* verb, but with some spelling changes in the different forms of the present tense. *Appeler,* in the infinitive form, is spelled with one "l," and pronounced [ah-puh-leh]. The same pronunciation is used for the past participle, *appelé.*

In the present tense, *vous appelez* (ah-puh-leh) and *nous appelons* (ah-puh-lohn) still have only one "l." But in *j'appelle, tu appelles, il / elle appelle, ils / elles appellent,* there are two "l"s. This spelling change reflects the difference in the pronunciation, which is the same for all the forms with double "l": (ah-pehl).

Here are a few more useful terms and expressions:

le portable	cell phone
le téléphone sans fil	cordless phone
être branché (e)	to be hooked up; in slang, also, to be hip *(connected)*

ARTS AND LEISURE: GOING TO AN ART SHOW

Luc thinks that *il n'a pas de chance* (he has no luck). He can't get his friends on the phone and, therefore, won't be able to go to the exhibition (*l'exposition*):

la chance	luck
chanceux, chanceuse	lucky
avoir de la chance (avec)	to have luck (with)

And Florence, who doesn't know what's going on (*elle n'est pas au courant*), is sorry (*désolée*), because she can't help (*aider*) Luc.

Nevertheless, this bad luck serves Luc's real desires, since he didn't want to go to the exhibition in the first place!

He says:

Mais qu'est-ce que je m'embête!	What do I care!

Luc prefers to spend a good evening (*passer une bonne soirée*) having a drink (*boire un pot*) with his buddies. *Tant pis!* Too bad!

la galerie de photos	photo gallery
une exposition (une expo)	exhibition
le vernissage	opening
présenter quelqu'un à	to introduce someone to
rencontrer quelqu'un	to meet someone (for the first time or by chance)
retrouver quelqu'un	to meet someone (you already know)
le copain, la copine	pal

And the more colloquial . . .

le pote, la pote	buddy

And some useful little words . . .

à moins que	unless
après tout	after all
aujourd'hui	today
en fait	in fact
en vain	in vain
plusieurs fois	several times
sûrement	surely

TAKE IT FOR A SPIN

Fill in the blanks with an appropriate word from the list:

essayer / téléphoner / messages / une bonne soirée / occupée / téléphone / numéro / messagerie vocale

a) Salut Florence, ça va? Est-que tu as le _numéro_ de la galerie?
b) Ah non, tu dois _téléphoner_ à Aziza.
c) Mais sa ligne est _occupée_ et sa _messagerie vocale_ ne prend plus de _messages_
d) Oui, je sais, elle est toujours au _téléphone_
e) Merci, Flo. Je vais _essayer_ de la rappeler. Passe _une bonne soirée_ !.

LET'S WARM UP

Let's see! In the light of past events, which of the following is true?

a) Luc va rester chez lui tout seul. TRUE / FALSE / I DOUBT IT
b) Florence va boire un pot avec Aziza. TRUE / FALSE / I DOUBT IT
c) Les filles sont désolées pour Luc. TRUE / FALSE / I DOUBT IT
d) Luc est un amateur de photographie. TRUE / FALSE / I DOUBT IT

And now, let's see what's up at this *vernissage d'exposition de photo*. Nat and Aziza seem to have a fun time. Maybe they're a bit bothered by an American guy, but . . . And, as a reminder, M7 is a TV channel for which Aziza, Florence, and other characters you'll meet work.

HEAR . . . SAY 2

After All . . . (Après tout . . .)

Aziza: Nika Nesgoda habite à New York. Elle a beaucoup de talent.
Nathalie: Sa vision est très intéressante. J'aime ce portrait couleur et cette série de visages en noir et blanc. Tu l'a déjà rencontrée? *Have you already seen it?*
Aziza: Oui, à M7. Elle est supposée être ici d'ailleurs. *was supposed / somewhere*
Un homme: Vous l'avez déjà rencontrée? *en comptes*
Aziza: Qui, Nika Nesgoda?
L'homme: Non, madame Lafaure, la propriétaire de la galerie.
Nathalie: Non, non . . . (Nathalie prend son téléphone.)
L'homme: Mesdemoiselles, je dois vous présenter. . . . Pardon, je m'appelle Gregory Stevens.

Aziza:	Enchantée, je suis Aziza Bensaïd et voici Nathalie . . . Ah . . .
Nathalie:	(Elle range son portable.) Enchantée, Monsieur. Mais, Aziza, c'est toi sur cette photo? Et là aussi?
Aziza:	Hmmm?. . . Ah, oui . . .
Nathalie:	Aziza, tu me surprends toujours! Ces portraits sont très beaux. Ah! Tu m'as eue!
L'homme:	Voilà Madame Elysée Lafaure. Vous venez?
Nathalie:	Un moment, Monsieur, s'il vous plaît. . . . Mais qu'est-ce qu'il a celui-là? Dis, c'est étrange, il est huit heures, Luc est censé être ici. C'est bizarre. . . . Et il n'est pas chez lui, je viens d'appeler.
Aziza:	Quand est-ce que tu l'as eu au téléphone?
Nathalie:	Et bien, ce matin. Il n'a peut-être pas eu ton fax. Tu ne lui as pas envoyé le fax pour ce soir?
Aziza:	Bien, non, je. . . . J'ai pensé. . . . Oh là là! Il va gueuler *bawl (cry)* . . .
Nathalie:	Je lui laisse l'adresse sur son répondeur. Mais, après tout, il ne m'a pas téléphoné non plus. Il est sûrement allé boire un pot avec ses potes!

ACTIVITY 8: HOW'S THAT AGAIN?

Correct the following statements.

a)   *Le nom du photographe est Gregory Stevens.*   Le nom du ph est Nike Nusjour
b)   *Cette exposition de photos est peu intéressante.*   Cette est très interesante.
c)   *Nathalie a rencontré la photographe.*   No, Aziza à l'ii rencontré
d)   *La photographe est là et elle parle avec les invités.*   no, elle n'est pas ici.
e)   *Aziza a envoyé un fax à Luc.*   Elle n'a pas envoyé un fass à Luc.

Did You Know?

WORKSHOP 2

THE NITTY-GRITTY

BEEN THERE, DONE THAT, PART 2: THE *PASSÉ COMPOSÉ* OF *AVOIR*, *ÊTRE*, AND *ALLER*

When *avoir* and *être* are used as main verbs, in the *passé composé*, they both use *avoir* as a helping verb. Their participles are irregular. For *avoir*, it's *eu*, and for *être*, it's *été*.

Tu m'as eu.	You got me.
J'ai été là.	I was there.
Tu l'as eu au téléphone?	You got him on the phone?
Nous n'avons pas été au vernissage.	We weren't at the gallery opening.

THE *PASSÉ COMPOSÉ* OF *AVOIR* (TO HAVE) AND *ÊTRE* (TO BE)			
AVOIR		**ÊTRE**	
j'ai eu	nous avons eu	j'ai été	nous avons été
tu as eu	vous avez eu	tu as été	vous avez été
il / elle a eu	ils / elles ont eu	il / elle a été	ils / elles ont été

ACTIVITY 9: TAKE IT FOR A SPIN

Pretend the story told below happened yesterday. Modify the sentences using the *passé composé*.

a) Les amies sont à un vernissage d'une exposition de photo.
b) Mais Luc n'a ni le nom de la galerie, ni l'adresse.
c) Aziza a les informations.
d) Luc n'est pas au vernissage.

Aller is a verb expressing motion; therefore, it is used with *être*. Its past participle is *allé* and it agrees in gender and number with the subject. Here are some examples:

Il est sûrement allé boire un pot avec ses potes.

He probably went to have a drink with his buddies.

Nathalie et son amie sont allées à la galerie.

Nathalie and her friend went to the gallery.

THE *PASSÉ COMPOSÉ* OF *ALLER* (TO GO)	
je suis allé(e)	nous sommes allé(e)s
tu es allé(e)	vous êtes allé(e)s
il / elle est allé(e)	ils / elles sont allé(e)s

TAKE IT FOR A SPIN

Complete each sentence by selecting the appropriate form of the verb *aller* on the right.

a) Je ne _suis allé_ jamais _allé_ à cette galerie.   sont allés

b) N'y _est_ -tu pas _allé_ la semaine dernière?   suis allé

c) Cette photographe _est_ _allé_ chaque année à Visa.   est allé

d) Beaucoup de gens _sont allés_ là-bas.   est allée

e) Si Luc n'est pas ici, il _es_ _allé_ voir ses amis.   es allé

WORDS TO LIVE BY

SHE'S SO TALENTED!: CHATTING AT A PHOTO EXHIBITION

A photo exhibition is *une exposition de photographie*.

La photographe a beaucoup de talent (the photographer is very talented), thought the people at the exhibition.

The expression is *avoir du talent*. If you use it in the negative form or with an adverb, such as *beaucoup*, the partitive article *du* changes to *de*. Take a look again:

J'ai *du* talent. / Elle a *beaucoup de* talent. / Elle *n'*a *pas de* talent.

About photography . . .

la couleur, en couleur	color, in color
le noir et blanc, en noir et blanc	black-and-white, in black-and-white
le portrait	portrait
le visage	face

By looking more carefully at some photos, Nathalie realizes that she's actually looking at Aziza. She's so surprised! *Elle est si surprise!*

surprendre	to surprise
la surprise	surprise

Word on the Street

Nathalie tells her friend: *Tu m'as eue!* "You got me!"

avoir quelqu'un	to trick someone

The photographer is supposed to be here (*est supposée être là*).

And Luc is supposed to be here as well (*est censé être là*). These two expressions are two different ways of saying the same thing.

WHO'S CALLING?: MORE ON USING TELEPHONES

Here are some additional words you might need:

un annuaire	telephone directory
un appel PCV	collect call
la cabine téléphonique	phone booth
la carte de téléphone à unités	prepaid phone card
composer un numéro	to dial a number
la double ligne	call waiting
le numéro payant	toll number
la présentation du numéro	caller I.D.
ranger son téléphone	to put away one's phone
les renseignements téléphoniques	telephone information

Did You Know?

When you call France from the United States, dial 011 for international and 33 for the country, then *le numéro de téléphone* in France without the first zero. When you call the United States from France, *faites le 00–1–,* and the number in the States.

France is divided into five calling regions. The following prefixes are the first digits of the phone numbers:

01 for the Parisian region
02 for the northeast of France
03 for the northwest of France
04 for the southeast of France
05 for the southwest of France

If you're lost, *pour les renseignements* (for information), dial 12.

Did You Know?

ACTIVITY 11:   TAKE IT FOR A SPIN

Select the right word from the list and fill in the blanks:

carte de téléphone / portables / annuaire / renseignements / faux numéro / numéro de téléphone / raccroche

a)   Si je n'ai pas un _numéro de tél_, je peux regarder dans l' _annuaire_.

b)   Ou j'appelle les _renseignements_ lls me donnent le numéro de téléphone.

c) Je fais ce numéro et "Ah non, Madame, vous avez fait un ~~faux numéro~~".

d) Alors, je ~~raccroche~~ et je refais le numéro.

e) Mais dans une cabine téléphonique, on a besoin d'une ~~carte de télé~~

f) Aujourd'hui, beaucoup de gens ont des ~~portable~~ C'est plus facile!

CRIB NOTES

HEAR...SAY 1

Luc:	This can't be! She's always on the phone. . . . Well, too bad for this evening. Unless . . . (He dials another number.)
Luc:	Hello, Flo? Umm. . . . Is Florence there, please?
A voice on the phone:	No, you dialed a wrong number.
Luc:	Oh, sorry, Madame.
Voice on the phone:	Miss.
Luc:	Miss, have a good evening! (He hangs up.) I'm really having no luck with the phone today! (He dials the number again.)
Luc:	So, 01–41–02–02–01 . . . Florence? Hi, it's Luc. How are you?
Florence:	I'm fine. . . . And you?
Luc:	Well, I'm okay. . . . You know, I've tried to call Nat at work, but with no luck. Her line is always busy.
Florence:	Did you call her at home?
Luc:	Yes, of course, but her answering machine isn't hooked up! Actually, I have to meet her at an exhibition. Aziza is going to be there, too. But I have neither the address, nor the name of the gallery . . .

Florence:	Hmmm, I don't know anything about it, Luc. But did you call Aziza at the office?
Luc:	Yes, of course, I've called her at the office several times and on her cell phone, but with no luck. Now she's probably gone.
Florence:	Yes, she worked at the studio today. Did you leave her a message?
Luc:	No, her voice mail doesn't take any more messages. She probably went to meet Nat.
Florence:	I'm sorry, Luc, I don't know where they are. But they'll call you soon.
Luc:	Yes, probably. Well, thanks, Florence. Have a good evening.
Florence:	You, too. Bye, Luc.
Luc:	(He hangs up.) But what do I care! Besides, I don't even feel like going! Now I can go and have a drink with Ricardo and Paco.

HEAR...SAY 2

Aziza:	Nika Nesgoda lives in New York. She's quite gifted.
Nathalie:	Her view is very interesting. I like this color portrait and this series of faces in black-and-white. Have you ever met her?
Aziza:	Yes, at M7. She is supposed to be here, actually.
A man:	Have you ever met her?
Aziza:	Who, Nika Nesgoda?
The man:	No, Mrs. Lafaure, the owner of the gallery.
Nathalie:	No, no . . . (Nathalie takes her phone.)
The man:	Ladies, I have to introduce you. . . . I'm sorry, my name is Gregory Stevens.

Aziza:	Pleased to meet you. I'm Aziza Bensaïd and this is Nathalie. . . . Hmm . . .
Nathalie:	(She puts away her cell phone.) Nice to meet you, sir. But Aziza, is this you in this picture? And there, too?
Aziza:	Hmm. . . . Well, yes . . .
Nathalie:	Aziza, you always surprise me! These portraits are very beautiful. You really got me!
The man:	Here is Mrs. Elysée Lafaure. Are you coming?
Nathalie:	A moment, sir, please. . . . What's the matter with him? You know, it's strange. It's eight o'clock, Luc is supposed to be here. It's weird. . . . And he's not at home; I just called.

142

FRENCH WITHOUT THE FUSS

Aziza:	When did you get him on the phone?
Nathalie:	Well, this morning. He may not have gotten your fax. Didn't you send him a fax for tonight?
Aziza:	Well, no . . . I . . . I thought. . . . Whoa! He's gonna be mad . . .

| Nathalie: | I'm leaving the address on his answering machine. Well, after all, he didn't call me either. I'm sure he went to have a drink with his buddies! |

ANSWER KEY

ACTIVITY 1

a) Car elles ont l'adresse de la galerie.
b) Ils sont supposés aller à un vernissage.
c) Oui, mais sa ligne est toujours occupée.
d) Oui, mais sa messagerie vocale ne prend plus de messages.
e) Il va boire un pot avec ses amis.

ACTIVITY 2

With the flat rate on our cellular phones, nothing is holding you back any more! You're every-where in a second. Soury Télécom gives you wings . . .

ACTIVITY 3

a) Tu ne téléphones ni à Nathalie, ni à Aziza.
b) Elles ne vont ni au vernissage, ni boire un verre.
c) Nous n'avons ni un répondeur, ni une messagerie vocale.
d) Il ne laisse un message ni au travail, ni à la maison.
e) Son amie n'a ni le nom, ni l'adresse de la galerie.

ACTIVITY 4

a) J'ai appelé mon ami toute la journée.
b) Ils n'ont pas téléphoné ce soir.
c) Elle a invité ses amis à son exposition.
d) Vous ne m'avez pas donné votre numéro de téléphone.
e) Où est ce qu'elles ont travaillé?

ACTIVITY 5

a) Nathalie a laissé un message à Luc.
b) Vous avez dîné après le vernissage?
c) Aziza n'est pas là. Je lui ai téléphoné.
d) Luc a appelé Florence.
e) Leur ami les a présentés à la photographe.

ACTIVITY 6

a) Salut Florence, ça va? Est-que tu as le numéro de la galerie?
b) Ah non, tu dois téléphoner à Aziza.
c) Mais sa ligne est occupée et sa messagerie vocale ne prend plus de messages.
d) Oui, je sais, elle est toujours au téléphone.
e) Merci, Flo. Je vais essayer de la rappeler. Passe une bonne soirée.

ACTIVITY 7

a) I DOUBT IT
b) FALSE
c) I DOUBT IT
d) I DOUBT IT

ACTIVITY 8

a) Le nom de la photographe est Nika Nesgoda.
b) Cette exposition de photos est très intéressante.
c) Nathalie n'a jamais rencontré la photo-graphe.
d) La photographe n'est pas là.
e) Aziza n'a pas envoyé de fax à Luc.

ACTIVITY 9

a) Les amies ont été à un vernissage d'une exposition de photo.
b) Mais Luc n'a eu ni le nom de la galerie, ni l'adresse.
c) Aziza a eu les informations.
d) Luc n'a pas été au vernissage.

ACTIVITY 10

a) Je ne suis jamais allé à cette galerie.
b) N'y es-tu pas allé la semaine dernière?
c) Cette photographe est allée chaque année à Visa.
d) Beaucoup de gens sont allés là-bas.
e) Si Luc n'est pas ici, il est allé voir ses amis.

ACTIVITY 11

a) Si je n'ai pas un numéro de téléphone, je peux regarder dans l'annuaire.
b) Ou j'appelle les renseignements. Ils me donnent le numéro de téléphone.
c) Je fais ce numéro et "Ah non, Madame, vous avez fait un faux numéro."
d) Alors, je raccroche et je refais le numéro.
e) Mais dans une cabine téléphonique, on a besoin d'une carte de téléphone.
f) Aujourd'hui, beaucoup de gens ont des portables. C'est plus facile!

That's enough! I've been waiting for twenty minutes.

COMING UP. . .

- *You've got mail!*: Going to the post office
- *Say it when you need something*: Using *il faut* (it's necessary) and *il me faut* (I need)
- *Any questions?*: A third way of asking questions in French
- *Been there, done that*: *The passé composé* of the *–ir* verbs
- *I scream, you scream*: The *passé composé* of several irregular verbs

IN THE SPOTLIGHT

Subway (1985) is a film by Luc Besson, starring Christophe Lambert, Jean Réno, Jean-Hugues Anglades, and Isabelle Adjani. Besson is well known in the United States for his more recent movies, such as *Le grand bleu* (*Big Blue*), *Nikita* (*La femme Nikita*), and *The Fifth Element*. The most American of the French directors, Besson became famous at age 25 when he made his first film, *Le dernier combat* (*Final Combat*) in black-and-white, without dialogue, featuring *son acteur fétiche* (favorite actor), Jean Réno.

LOOKING AHEAD

Ça va? In this chapter, you'll get plenty of information about the French post office and the Parisian subway system.

Our friend Julienne is going through an ordinary day, *un jour ordinaire*. *Elle ne travaille pas aujourd'hui*, so, she takes the opportunity to do all her errands, like going to the post office and *faire des courses*. She needs to go to the post office (*il lui faut aller à la poste*) to send some mail (*du courrier*) and a couple of parcels (*des colis*) to her family back in Cameroon. Plus, *elle veut acheter* some stamps (*des timbres*), and a money order (*un mandat*). At the end of the day (*en fin de journée*), after her classes at the university (*ses cours à l'université*) she takes the subway (*prend le métro*) to go pick-up her boyfriend Paco at the recording studio (*le studio d'enregistrement*), where he's working with his band.

HEAR... SAY 1

An Ordinary Day ...   (Une journée ordinaire ...)

L'agent de la poste:	Bonjour, Mademoiselle.
Julienne:	Bonjour, Madame, voici du courrier; c'est pour Douala, au Cameroun, et ces trois colis aussi ...
L'agent de la poste:	Voulez-vous les envoyer par avion?
Julienne:	Oui, s'il vous plaît. Et j'ai besoin d'acheter des timbres. Et il me faut aussi un mandat de 40 (quarante) euros.
L'agent de la poste:	Une chose à la fois, s'il vous plaît ...
Une femme:	Dites donc, j'attends depuis vingt minutes!
Julienne:	Comme tout le monde, Madame!
La femme:	D'ailleurs, qu'est-ce que vous avez besoin d'envoyer tout ce bazar?!
Julienne:	Mais vraiment, ce ne sont pas vos affaires!
L'agent de la poste:	Il faut être patient dans la vie, Madame. Alors, s'il vous plaît, retournez à la file d'attente.

L'agent de la poste:	Bah . . . il ne faut pas faire attention! Que vous faut-il comme timbres?
Julienne:	Deux carnets de timbres à 46 (quarante-six) cents, s'il vous plaît.
L'agent de la poste:	Et que m'avez-vous dit? Un mandat de . . .
Julienne:	Un mandat de 40 (quarante) euros, Madame.
L'agent de la poste:	Comment allez-vous payer, Mademoiselle?
Julienne:	Avec ma carte banquaire.
L'agent de la poste:	Bien. . . . Voilà, cela fait 72 (soixante-douze) euros.
Julienne:	Voici.
L'agent de la poste:	Merci. Voici votre mandat, vos timbres et votre reçu. Voilà, Mademoiselle.
Julienne:	Merci, Madame. Bonne journée.
L'agent de la poste:	À vous aussi. . . . Suivant!

ACTIVITY 1: HOW'S THAT AGAIN?

Just a few questions . . .

- a) *Où est-ce que Julienne envoie son courrier?*
- b) *Qu'est-ce qu'elle envoie aussi?*
- c) *Est-ce qu'elle prend autre chose?*
- d) *Pourquoi la femme est-elle en colère?* (This is a new type of question. Any difficulty? Look first in the Nitty-Gritty section.)

WORKSHOP 1

THE NITTY-GRITTY

SAY IT WHEN YOU NEED SOMETHING: USING IL FAUT (IT'S NECESSARY) AND IL ME FAUT (I NEED)

Both *il faut* (it's necessary) and *il me faut* (I need) use the irregular verb *falloir*, "to have to, must." You don't have to worry though, because this verb is used most commonly, almost exclusively, in these two expressions. So, that's all you need to know.

1. The expression *il faut*

This expression is roughly equivalent to the English "It is necessary to . . ." *Il faut*, as we will learn here, is always followed by an infinitive verb. Here are some examples:

Il faut y aller.

It is necessary to go. / We must go.

Il faut aller à la poste.

It is necessary to go to the post office.

Il faut être patient.

One has to be patient. / It is necessary to be patient.

2. The expression *il me faut*

   In the expression *il me faut*, the verb is preceded by an indirect object pronoun. Of course, *me* could be replaced with any other indirect object pronoun depending on who experiences the necessity of something, *Il lui faut . . .* (He needs . . .), *Il nous faut . . .* (We need . . .), etc. Then you follow the expression with the object needed or the action that needs to be performed.

   Il me faut un mandat.

   I need a money order.

   Il lui faut aller.

   He / she needs to go.

   Once again, the expression is formed as follows:

   il + indirect object pronoun + *faut* + object noun / infinitive verb

ACTIVITY 2: TAKE IT FOR A SPIN

Look at this mess! Rewrite each sentence by putting the words in the right order.

   a)   *Il / attendre / son / faut / tour.*
   b)   *la poste / Il / aller / faut / à.*
   c)   *Cameroun / faut / au / colis / Il / envoyer / ces.*
   d)   *faut / pas / attention / Il / faire / ne.*
   e)   *il / des / Est-ce qu' / faut / timbres / vous?*
   f)   *en / ne / être / Il / retard / faut / pas.*

ANY QUESTIONS?: A THIRD WAY OF ASKING QUESTIONS IN FRENCH

In the previous chapters, you've already studied a few ways of forming questions:

—Using intonation:

   Tu peux aller à la poste?

   Can you go to the post office?

—Using *est-ce que:*

Est-ce que tu vas à la poste?

Are you going to the post office?

—Using different question words + *est-ce que:*

Où est-ce que tu vas?

Where are you going?

All these question types belong to a rather informal style. A more formal and written style requires the use of "inversion questions." The inversion happens between the verb and the subject, which switch places in the sentence. No need for *est-ce que* here. For example:

Tu vas à la poste. →   **Vas-tu à la poste?**

You're going to the post office.   Are you going to the post office?

An *est-ce que* question can be easily turned into an inversion question:

Comment est-ce que vous allez payer? →   **Comment allez-vous payer?**

How are you going to pay?

Pourquoi est-ce que tu arrives en retard? →   **Pourquoi arrives-tu en retard?**

Why are you late?

Basically, you need to first put the question word, if any, followed by the verb, then a hyphen to tie the verb to the subject pronoun, and then the rest of the sentence.

Heads Up!

When the subject is a noun, a question with inversion is formed differently. The subject is expressed twice, first with the noun and then, again after the verb, with the corresponding subject pronoun. Weird but true!

Est-ce que Julienne va à la poste? →   **Julienne va-t-elle à la poste?**

Does Julienne go to the post office?

Pourquoi est-ce que les clients doivent faire la queue? →
Pourquoi les clients doivent-ils faire la queue?

Why do customers have to wait on line?

When the subject of the question is a human being (*who*), use the interrogative pronoun *qui.* For instance, with *est-ce que,* the question is:

> **Qui est-ce qui va venir au studio?**
>
> Who's going to come to the studio?

Without *est-ce que,* the question is:

> **Qui va venir au studio?**

In other words, there is no inversion between the subject and the verb, since the question word itself is the subject. Here's another example:

> **Qui est-ce qui va aller à la poste?** →   **Qui va aller à la poste?**
>
> Who is going to the post office?

When the verb is in the *passé composé,* which is a compound tense, we treat the helping verb *être* or *avoir* as main verbs, so it will be inverted or placed before the subject in a question.

> **Où est-ce que tu es allé?** →   **Où es-tu allé?**
>
> Where did you go?

> **Pourquoi est-ce qu'elles ont envoyé ces colis?** →
> **Pourquoi ont-elles envoyé ces colis?**
>
> Why have they sent those parcels?

When there is an object pronoun in a question with inversion, it comes directly before the verb, as always. This means that if the verb is placed before the subject in the question, the pronoun "travels" with it. Ah, French is so easy . . .

> **Est-ce que tu <u>les</u> as achetés?** →   **<u>Les</u> as-tu achetés?**
>
> Did you buy them?

Où est-ce que Julienne l'a envoyé? → **Où Julienne l'a-t-elle envoyé?**

Where did she send it?

'Nuff said! Let's practice!

TAKE IT FOR A SPIN

Please change these *est-ce que* questions into inversion questions:

a) *Est-ce que vous allez bien?*
b) *Est-ce que nous pouvons venir?*
c) *Où est-ce que tes amies habitent?*
d) *Quand est-ce qu'il faut arriver?*
e) *Qui est-ce qui va à la poste?*

WORDS TO LIVE BY

YOU'VE GOT MAIL!: GOING TO THE POST OFFICE

These days it's become quite rare to *écrire du courrier* (write letters), or *faire son courrier* (do one's mail). But if you do it, always make sure to write the right address (*la bonne adresse*), and the right zip code (*le code postal*). For everywhere in the world, in this age of electronic and digital communication, the post office hasn't improved its service. The stamps are more colorful, though . . .

By the way, the verb *envoyer* (to send), pronounced (ah^n-vwah-yeh), although regular, has a peculiarity:

PRESENT TENSE OF THE VERB *ENVOYER* (TO SEND)	
j'envoie	*nous envoyons*
tu envoies	*vous envoyez*
il envoie	*ils envoient*

The *nous* and *vous* forms and the past participle, *envoyé*, have the "y" letter (and sound) in them. The *je, tu, il/elle* and *ils/elles* forms are pronounced (eh^n-vwah).

Waiting on line is *faire la queue* (or more rarely, *la file* or *la file d'attente*). Literally, *la queue* means "tail". And you wait at the *guichet* (window; counter).

Things to send are:

la lettre à poster	letter to be mailed
la carte postale	postcard
une enveloppe (with two "p"s!)	envelope
un expéditeur	sender

And some related adjectives:

postal, postaux (pl.)	postal
patient, patiente	patient
impatient, impatiente	impatient
suivant, suivante	the next on line

The funny thing is that people always seem to be in a rush (*être pressé*) when going to such places and then, they get angry or frustrated. That's when more colloquial words come out.

Word on the Street

Quel bazar!	What a mess!
le bazar	jumble, stuff
Ce ne sont pas vos affaires!	It's none of your business!

ACTIVITY 4: TAKE IT FOR A SPIN

Fill in the blanks with the appropriate word from the list below:

mandat / courrier / journée / patient / faut / reçu / file / carte / Poste / carnets / guichet / timbres / à la fois

Ce matin, je suis allée poster mon _____. À la poste, il y a toujours une longue d'attente. Il _____ vraiment être _____ dans la vie. C'est à mon tour, je vais au _____. L'agent de la poste me salue. "Il me faut un _____ de 60 euros et deux carnets de _____. à 46 cents." "Une chose _____" l'agent de la _____ me dit. "Comment allez-vous payer?" "Avec ma _____ de crédit". "Très bien, voici vos _____ de timbres, votre mandat et le _____. Bonne _____, Mademoiselle!"

ACTIVITY 5: LET'S WARM UP

The second dialogue invites you to visit the Parisian subway. *En fin de journée*, Julienne is in the subway station. *C'est l'heure de pointe* (it's rush hour) and there are a lot of people *sur les quais* (on the platforms), waiting impatiently for the train to arrive. Julienne is *pressée* (in a rush), *parce que* (because) *elle est supposée retrouver Paco* (she's supposed to meet Paco) at the recording studio at 6:30 PM. But the subway train has not come yet.

Before diving in, can you answer these questions?

a) *Écrivez-vous beaucoup de courrier?*
b) *Aimez-vous prendre le métro?*

Did You Know?

Le 19 juillet 2000, le métro parisien a eu cent ans! (On July 19, 2000, the Parisian subway turned 100!)

Paris started seriously growing in size in the 1880s and underground transportation was becoming imperative. The Métropolitain, or the Parisian subway, was inaugurated on July 19, 1900, the year of the famous Exposition Universelle of 1900. *La première ligne de métro* (the first subway line) was 30 km long. The first train had three wooden cars. Ten years later, six new lines were opened, but a season of hard rain and, later, World War I greatly slowed down the construction. With the dramatic advent of World War II, work was completely paralyzed once again. *Le métro* became a strategic point for *la Résistance* (the French anti-German resistance movement). During the German occupation, the subway company was required to keep the last wagon, named *La Synagogue*, for Jewish passengers.

In the 1950s, the newly formed RATP, the Parisian transportation company, greatly modernized and expanded *le métro*.

Did You Know?

HEAR . . . SAY 2

Rendez-vous at the Studio (Rendez-vous au studio)

Un homme: Trente minutes! Ils sont encore en grève.
Julienne: Non, je ne crois pas. Il y a peut-être eu un accident.
Le métro arrive enfin. Dans le wagon:
Julienne: Avez-vous l'heure, s'il vous plaît, Madame?
La dame: Oui . . . Ah, voilà . . . il est six heures trente-cinq, Mademoiselle.
Julienne: Oh là là. . . . Merci!

À la station suivante, les passagers descendent ou montent.
Julienne: Ouh!!! Mais faites attention!

Un musicien de rue joue des vieux airs sur son accordéon. Julienne lui donne un peu d'argent. Beaucoup de monde descend à cette station.
La dame: Ah! On respire enfin!
Julienne: C'est vrai. . . . Mais je descends aussi. Bonne soirée!

Dehors, il pleut. Julienne arrive à son rendez-vous.
Julienne: Désolée, Paco, je suis en retard!
Paco: Mais Julienne, c'est pas grave. . . . Alors, est-ce que tu as passé une bonne journée?

Julienne:	Ça va. Je n'ai pas travaillé aujourd'hui; alors je suis allée poster les colis pour ma famille. Ensuite, j'ai eu mon cours à la fac, puis voilà! Et toi?
Paco:	On a fini d'enregistrer un morceau. . . . Mais tu cherches quoi?
Julienne:	. . . mon porte-monnaie pour ranger ma carte orange. Mais je ne le trouve pas. J'ai dû le perdre dans le métro.
Paco:	Tu es sûre?
Julienne:	Ou alors, on me l'a volé.
Paco:	On va au commissariat de police, si tu veux.
Julienne:	Ça ne sert jamais à rien! Bien, voilà. . . . On rentre?

ACTIVITY 6: HOW'S THAT AGAIN?

a) *Que s'est-il passé dans le métro?*
b) *Qu'est-ce que Paco lui propose?*
c) *Est-ce que Julienne est d'accord? Pourquoi?*
d) *Est-ce qu'un pickpocket vous a déjà volé?*
e) *Qu'est-ce que vous avez fait?*

WORKSHOP 2

THE NITTY-GRITTY

BEEN THERE, DONE THAT: THE *PASSÉ COMPOSÉ* OF THE *–IR* VERBS

The past participles of regular verbs ending in *–ir* are all formed the same way. You drop the *–r* at the end of the infinitive, and that's it, as in *finir* (to finish) → *fini* (finished).

THE *PASSÉ COMPOSÉ* OF THE VERB *FINIR* (TO FINISH)	
j'ai fini	*nous avons fini*
tu as fini	*vous avez fini*
il / elle a fini	*ils / elles ont fini*

For example:

On a fini le diner à minuit. →

We finished dinner at midnight.

J'ai choisi ces timbres. →

I've chosen the stamps.

On l'a fini.

We finished it at midnight.

Je les ai choisis.

I have chosen them.

I SCREAM, YOU SCREAM: THE *PASSÉ COMPOSÉ* OF SEVERAL IRREGULAR VERBS

Irregular verbs, alas, have irregular participles.

Croire (to believe), *savoir* (to know), *voir* (to see), *devoir* (to have to), *recevoir* (to receive), *pouvoir* (to be able to), and *boire* (to drink) follow a similar pattern. Here they are:

THE *PASSÉ COMPOSÉ* OF SOME IRREGULAR VERBS						
CROIRE (TO BELIEVE)	SAVOIR (TO KNOW)	VOIR (TO SEE)	DEVOIR (MUST)	RECEVOIR (TO RECEIVE)	POUVOIR (CAN)	BOIRE (TO DRINK)
j'ai cru . . .	j'ai su . . .	j'ai vu . . .	j'ai dû . . .	j'ai reçu . . .	j'ai pu . . .	j'ai bu . . .

This table gives only the *je* form. But you know the game, don't you? Try writing down the rest of the forms for yourself.

Heads Up!

Notice the accent on the *–û* of *dû*? Yes, this is one more irregularity, but *devoir* is the only verb in this list to have it. However, in its feminine form, *due*, the past participle of *devoir*, loses its accent: *due*.

Vouloir (to want) and *falloir* (need; must), which is always used in the expression *il faut* (it is necessary), follow a slightly different pattern in the *passé composé*. You drop the ending *–oir* and replace it with the past participle ending *–u*.

THE *PASSÉ COMPOSÉ* OF THE VERBS *VOULOIR* AND *FALLOIR*	
VOULOIR (TO WANT)	FALLOIR (NEED; MUST)
j'ai voulu	il a fallu

As we mentioned in Lesson 8, most verbs use the helping verb *avoir* to form the *passé composé*. Others (verbs of motion and verbs used with the reflexive pronoun *se*) use *être*.

And again, remember the rules for agreement:

J'ai vu Julienne. →   **Je l'ai vue.**

I saw Julienne.   I saw her.

Vue (feminine) agrees with *l'*, the direct object pronoun which precedes the verb, because *l'* refers to a female.

With *être*, the subject and the participle always agree in gender and number. For instance:

Julienne et Paco sont allés au bureau de poste.

Julienne and Paco went to the post office.

Les amies sont arrivées en métro.

The friends have arrived by subway.

TAKE IT FOR A SPIN

Fill in the appropriate form of *être* or *avoir*.

a)   *J' _____ été à la maison.*

b)   *Vous _____ dû aller à la poste.*

c)   *Nos cousines _____ reçu les colis de Julienne ce matin.*

d)   *Il _____ fallu aller au commissariat.*

e)   *Est-ce que tu _____ pu prendre le métro?*

f)   *Où _____ -elles vu les musiciens de rue?*

WORDS TO LIVE BY

Here you are, ready to take the subway (*prendre le métro*) It can get crowded during rush hour (*aux heures de pointe*), when so many *passagers* get off (*descendent*) and get on (*montent)* the subway train.

Did You Know?

The Parisian subway (when it's not on strike or *en grève*) runs very smoothly and frequently. A train comes every two minutes or so.

Since the mid 1990s, a new subway line, number 14, called Météor, has been introduced. This high-speed line without a conductor (!!!) crosses Paris from the southeast to the station called La Madeleine.

Did You Know?

And more subway words:

le quai	platform
la station de métro	subway station
le train	train
le wagon, la voiture du train	wagon, car
la carte orange	subway card (called "orange" because of its color)

Did You Know?

The RATP, the Parisian subway and transportation company, has made a huge effort to prevent people from getting free rides. So beware! Once you have bought *votre ticket*, keep it in a safe place. There are a lot of RATP *contrôleurs* (ticket checkers) who may ask you to show it to them. And you can be checked anywhere: in the train, on the platform, and in the halls.

Unfortunately, in Paris, as in every big city, there are a lot of homeless people, called *les sans domicile fixe* (Lit., without a stable residence) or *les SDF*, who inhabit the subway in the cold months. Also, many street musicians (*les musiciens de rue*) play in the subway station.

And then, there are also *les pickpockets* (you recognize the English word here). Yes, they exist everywhere. . . . Actually, the RATP regularly makes announcements in the hardest-hit stations: *"Mesdames, Messieurs, attention aux pickpockets dans cette station!"*

If something happens, go to the *commissariat de police* (police station) to report your bag (*sac*) or wallet (*porte-monnaie*) stolen (*volé*).

Did You Know?

La carte orange (a subway card, orange in color) was introduced in the 1970s, and has since allowed passengers to travel all over the Parisian area for a bargain price. Concerned about its image, the RATP has also worked on the beautification of its largest stations, turning them into performance and exhibition spaces for various artists. The RATP has also developed a huge marketing operation around a line of products that use the subway ticket as a logo.

LET'S PUT IT IN WRITING

Read some of the RATP's slogans:

La RATP, votre deuxième voiture.	*RATP, your second car.*
L'esprit libre.	*Free spirit.*
La meilleure façon d'avancer.	*The best way to move along /advance.*

Finally, the RATP started the new millennium with:
Un bout de chemin ensemble.   *Let's walk together a bit.*

Word on the Street

A few more exclamations and expressions:
Ah!   *Finally!; Good!*
Bah!   *Interjection expressing indifference; Pooh!*

Dites / dis donc!	Hey! What do you mean?
Oh là là!	Well, it's not good . . .
Ouh!	Interjection expressing surprise;

TAKE IT FOR A SPIN

Place the following actions in the order in which they might logically take place:

descendre du train; acheter un ticket; marcher dans les couloirs; monter dans le train; aller au métro; faire la queue au guichet; sortir (to get out of) de la station de métro.

TAKE IT UP A NOTCH!

The ultimate test! Translate the following sentences.

a) I have finished my work.
b) Do you have a date with Paco now?
c) Yes, but I have to go to the post office. I need stamps.
d) I went to the post office and there were a lot of people.
e) Is the subway on strike?
f) Yes, the subway is on strike.
g) So, how am I going to go to my date?

CRIB NOTES

HEAR...SAY 1

The post office clerk:	Hello, Miss.
Julienne:	Hello, Madam, here is some mail; it goes to Douala, in Cameroon, and these three parcels, too.
The post office clerk:	Do you want to send them by air mail?
Julienne:	Yes, please. And I need to buy stamps. And I also need a money order for 40 euros.
The post office clerk:	One thing at a time, please . . .
A woman:	That's enough! I've been waiting for twenty minutes.
Julienne:	Like everybody, Madam!
A woman:	Besides, what do you need to send all this jumble for?!
Julienne:	Really, it's none of your business!
The post office clerk:	You have to be patient in life, Madam. So, please, go back to the line.
The post office clerk:	Well . . . you can't pay attention to things like that. What kind of stamps do you need?
Julienne:	Two booklets of 46-cent stamps, please.
The post office clerk:	And what did you tell me? A money order for . . .
Julienne:	A money order for 40 euros, Madam.
The post office clerk:	How are you going to pay, Miss?

Julienne:	With my bank card.		and your receipt. Here you are, Miss.
The post office clerk:	All right . . . here, that's 72 euros.	Julienne:	Thank you, Madam. Have a good day.
Julienne:	Here it is.	The post office clerk:	You, too. . . . Next in line!
The post office clerk:	Thank you. Here's your money order, your stamps,		

HEAR...SAY 2

A man: 30 minutes! They're on strike again.

Julienne: No, I don't think so. There may have been an accident.

The subway finally arrives. In the subway car.

Julienne: Do you have the time, please, Madam?

The lady: Yes. . . . Ah, here. . . . It's 6:35 PM, Miss.

Julienne: Whoa. . . . Thank you!

At the next station, people get off and on.

Julienne: Hey!!! Be careful!

A street musician plays some old tunes on his accordion. Julienne gives him a little money. Many people get off at this station.

The lady: Finally, we can breathe.

Julienne: True. But I'm getting off, too. Have a good evening!

Outside, it's raining. Julienne gets to her appointment.

Julienne: Sorry, Paco, I'm late!

Paco: But Julienne, it's okay. . . . So, did you have a good day?

Julienne: Okay. I didn't work today, so I went to the post office to send some parcels to my family. After that, I had my class at the university, and that's it! And what about you?

Paco: We finished recording a track. . . . What are you looking for?

Julienne: My purse, to put away my subway card. But I can't find it. I must have lost it in the subway.

Paco: Are you sure?

Julienne: Or somebody stole it from me.

Paco: We'll go to the police station if you want.

Julienne: That never helps! Well, that's that. Shall we go home?

ANSWER KEY

ACTIVITY 1

a) Julienne envoie son courrier à Douala au Cameroun.

b) Elle envoie aussi trois colis.

c) Oui, elle prend des timbres et un mandat de 40 (quarante) euros.

d) La femme est en colère car elle attend depuis vingt minutes.

ACTIVITY 2

a) Il faut attendre son tour.

b) Il faut aller à la poste.

c) Il faut envoyer ces colis au Cameroun.

d) Il ne faut pas faire attention.

e) Est-ce qu'il vous faut des timbres?

f) Il ne faut pas être en retard.

ACTIVITY 3

a) Allez-vous bien?

b) Pouvons-nous venir?

c) Où tes amies habitent-elles?

d) Quand faut-il arriver?

e) Qui va à la poste?

ACTIVITY 4

Ce matin, je suis allée poster mon courrier. À la poste, il y a toujours une longue file d'attente. Il faut vraiment être patient dans la vie. C'est à mon tour, je vais au guichet. L'agent de la poste me salue. "Il me faut un mandat de 60 euros et deux carnets de timbres à 46 cents." "Une chose à la fois," l'agent de la poste me dit. "Comment allez-vous payer?" "Avec ma carte de crédit." "Très bien, voici vos carnets de timbres, votre mandat et le reçu. Bonne journée, Mademoiselle!"

ACTIVITY 5

a) Oui, j'écris beaucoup de courrier. / Non, je n'écris pas beaucoup de courrier.

b) Oui, j'aime prendre le métro. / Non, je n'aime pas prendre le métro.

ACTIVITY 6

a) Dans le métro, on a volé le porte-monnaie de Julienne.

b) Paco lui propose d'aller au commissariat de police.

c) Julienne n'est pas d'accord, car ça ne sert jamais à rien.
d) Oui, un pickpocket m'a déjà volé(e). / Non, un pickpocket ne m'a jamais volé(e).
e) Je suis allé(e) au commissariat de police. *or* Je n'ai rien fait. (I didn't do anything.)

ACTIVITY 7

a) J'ai été à la maison.
b) Vous avez dû aller à la poste.
c) Nos cousines ont reçu les colis de Julienne ce matin.
d) Il a fallu aller au commissariat.
e) Est-ce que tu as pu prendre le métro?
f) Où ont-elles vu les musiciens de rue?

ACTIVITY 8

aller au métro; faire la queue au guichet; acheter un ticket; marcher dans les couloirs; monter dans le train; descendre du train; sortir de la station de métro.

ACTIVITY 9

a) J'ai fini mon travail.
b) As-tu un rendez-vous avec Paco maintenant? *or* Est-ce que tu as . . .?
c) Oui, mais je dois aller à la poste. Il me faut des timbres.
d) Je suis allé(e) à la poste et il y a eu beaucoup de monde.
e) Le métro est-il en grève? *or* Est-que le métro est . . .?
f) Oui, le métro est en grève.
g) Mais comment vais-je aller à mon rendez-vous? *or* Mais comment est-ce que je vais aller . . .?

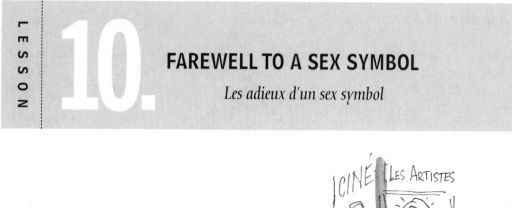

Four tickets for The Little Girl
Who Sold the Sun, *please.*

COMING UP...

- *Every day is not a holiday*: The French calendar and saying dates
- *It's a classic*: Talking about movies
- *Out on the town*: All the French you need to have fun
- *Been there, done that*: The *passé composé* of *attendre* (to wait), *prendre* (to take), and other similar verbs
- *Any questions?*: Asking questions using *which?*
- *Like it or not*: The irregular verbs *plaire* "to like" and *nuire* "to hurt" in the present tense and the *passé composé*
- *Strut your stuff!*

"Les adieux d'un sex symbol" ("Farewell to a Sex Symbol") is a famous song from *Star-mania*, the French musical written by Michel Berger and Luc Plamondon in 1978. This is a song about the downfall of an aging movie star, wonderfully interpreted by *la chanteuse canadienne* (the Canadian singer) Diane Dufresne.

LOOKING AHEAD

Ready for an evening out on the town and a taste of French nightlife (*la vie nocturne*)? In this lesson, you'll learn how to have fun in French, but in addition, you'll get a chance to strut your stuff and show and review all the things you've learned from Lesson 5 on.

In the dialogues, you'll find again Frédérique, a character you may remember from the *marché aux puces* (flea market) story. You'll also get to meet her husband, her sister, and her sister's husband. *Leur programme* for this evening: *aller au ciné! C'est mercredi soir* (Wednesday evening). Frédérique and *son mari* Étienne are in front of *un cinéma d'art et d'essai dans le quartier latin*. By the way, *un cinéma d'art et d'essai*, literally, a movie theater for art and experimental films, is an independent movie theater showing old classics or independent art movies. There are still several *cinémas d'art et d'essai* left in Paris, but fewer than there used to be. Frédérique and Étienne *font la queue au guichet* (they stand in line at the box office) as they wait for Frédérique's sister, Marianne, and her husband, Wolfgang. After the movie, they will go *prendre un pot* at a hip little bar where they'll meet more friends.

Did You Know?

THE FIRST STEPS OF THE FRENCH CINEMA!

In 1893, the Lumière brothers (and their father) invented the first all-in-one camera and projector that they named *le cinématographe*.

The first motion pictures shown by the Lumière brothers in 1895 became an instant success in France and in Europe. The Lumière brothers' work consisted mostly of short movies documenting scenes from everyday life. Louis Lumière's first film was *La sortie des usines Lumière* (*Workers Leaving the Lumière Factory*). The famous *L'arrivée d'un train à Ciotat* (*A Train Pulling into the Ciotat Station*) scared audiences not used to the moving image medium—they screamed and ducked for cover as a steam train was shown pulling into the train station in the direction of the camera.

Did You Know?

Feel Like Going to the Movies? (On s'fait une toile?)

Marianne:	Ah, bonsoir! On n'est pas en retard?
Frédérique:	Vous avez pris le métro, je parie . . .
Wolfgang:	Oui, et on l'a attendu pendant longtemps. Bon, quoi de neuf?
Étienne:	Toujours d'accord pour le film de Diop Mambety?
Wolfgang:	Oui! J'ai entendu de bonnes critiques sur France Inter.
Marianne:	Son émission de radio favorite, "Le masque et la plume."
Frédérique:	C'est une bonne émission. Est-ce que vous avez vu d'autres films de ce réalisateur?
Marianne:	Eh bien, on a juste vu *Touki Bouki.*
Étienne:	Un ami sénégalais m'a parlé récemment de ce réalisateur. Il est d'ailleurs supposé venir. C'est à nous . . .
Wolfgang:	Bonsoir, Madame, quatre places pour *La petite vendeuse de soleil,* s'il vous plaît. Le film n'a pas commencé au moins?
La caissière:	Non, Monsieur, dans cinq minutes. Ça fait trente euros.
Wolfgang:	Voilà, Madame. Merci.

Ils entrent dans la petite salle de cinéma.

Frédérique:	C'est gentil, Wolfgang. Eh bien, on vous invite à boire un pot après le film. Tenez, j'ai pris des programmes.
Marianne:	Merci, Fréd.
Une voix masculine:	Étienne! Eh, Étienne!
Étienne:	Momar! Mais par où es-tu passé?
Momar:	Ah ah! Ça va? Étienne, je te présente Florence.
Étienne:	Enchanté, Florence!
Florence:	Bonsoir. . . . Oh! Mais ce n'est pas Wolfgang?
Étienne:	Bien oui, c'est mon beau-frère.
Momar:	Avec Florence, c'est toujours comme ça.
Florence:	Il travaille avec moi à M7. Il va être surpris.
Momar:	Ah, le couvre-feu! On s'parle après.

ACTIVITY 1:   HOW'S THAT AGAIN?

Just a few questions . . . *En français, s'il vous plaît.*

   a)   *Quel est le nom du beau-frère de Frédérique?*
   b)   *Pourquoi Marianne et son mari arrivent-ils un peu tard?*

c) Quel film vont-ils voir? *La petite vendeus ...*
d) Combien coûte la place de ciné? *7.50 Euro*
e) Qui est-ce qu'Étienne retrouve dans la salle de cinéma? *M. Momar*

LET'S PUT IT IN WRITING

Portrait...

director

DJIBRIL DIOP MAMBETY (1945–1998), réalisateur et poète sénégalais, a laissé une série unique de fables allégoriques sur son pays. Mambety est considéré par beaucoup, comme un des précurseurs (*forerunners*) du cinéma sénégalais post-colonialiste.

Sa filmographie: *Contras City* (1968), *Badou Boy* (1970), *Touki Bouki* (1973), *Parlons Grand-Mère* (1989), *Hyènes* (1992) (en compétition au Festival de Cannes), *Le Franc* (1994), *La petite vendeuse de soleil* (1999) (présenté à la Quinzaine des réalisateurs au Festival de Cannes). *FORTNIGHT*

Did You Know?

Le Festival international du film de Cannes (The Cannes Film Festival) first opened in September 1946. Since 1951, this event has taken place every spring and is considered to be the greatest international film festival. Its highest award, *La Palme d'Or* (The Golden Palm), was first given out in 1955. Over the years, several parallel categories were added to the official selection, such as *La semaine de la critique* (The Critic's Week), *La quinzaine des réalisateurs* (The Directors' Fortnight), and *Un certain regard* (A Certain Look).

Did You Know?

WORKSHOP 1

THE NITTY-GRITTY

BEEN THERE, DONE THAT: THE *PASSÉ COMPOSÉ* OF *ATTENDRE* (TO WAIT), *PRENDRE* (TO TAKE), AND OTHER SIMILAR VERBS

1. The *passé composé* of the verbs *attendre* (to wait for), *entendre* (to hear), *vendre* (to sell), and *descendre* (to go / come down)

The verb *attendre*, like *entendre* and *vendre*, uses the auxiliary *avoir* in the *passé composé*. To form the past participle, drop the ending –*re* and add the ending –*u*.

THE *PASSÉ COMPOSÉ* OF
ATTENDRE, ENTENDRE, AND *VENDRE*

ATTENDRE (TO WAIT)	*ENTENDRE* (TO HEAR)	*VENDRE* (TO SELL)
j'ai attendu . . .	*j'ai entendu . . .*	*j'ai vendu . . .*

For example:

Nous l'avons attendu longtemps.

We waited for him for a long time.

J'ai entendu de bonnes critiques.

I've heard good reviews.

Ils ont vendu toutes les places.

They sold every seat.

Heads Up!

The verb *descendre* (to go / come down) can be used with either *avoir* or *être*.

It is used with *être* when it is followed by an indirect object (a noun followed by a preposition).

Je suis descendu <u>du train</u> rapidement.

I got off the train quickly.

It is used with *avoir* when it has a direct object.

J'ai descendu <u>les escaliers</u>.

I went down the stairs. (*Les escaliers* is a direct object.)

2. The *passé composé* of the verbs *prendre* (to take) and its derivatives *apprendre* (to learn; to teach), *comprendre* (to understand), and *surprendre* (to surprise)

These verbs are used with the auxiliary *avoir*. The past participle of *prendre* is *pris*. The past participles for *surprendre*, *apprendre* and *comprendre* follow the same pattern, so the forms are *surpris*, *appris*, and *compris* respectively.

THE *PASSÉ COMPOSÉ* OF THE VERBS
PRENDRE, APPRENDRE, COMPRENDRE, AND *SURPRENDRE*

PRENDRE (TO TAKE)	APPRENDRE (TO LEARN; TO TEACH)	COMPRENDRE (TO UNDERSTAND)	SURPRENDRE (TO SURPRISE)
j'ai pris . . .	*j'ai appris . . .*	*j'ai compris . . .*	*j'ai surpris . . .*

For example:

J'ai pris des programmes.

I took programs.

Vous avez pris le métro?

You took the subway?

Je n'ai rien compris au film.

I didn't understand anything in this film.

Je l'ai surpris au cinéma avec des amis.

I caught him at the movies with friends.

As-tu appris quelque chose?

Did you learn anything?

Heads Up!

Pris (the past participle of *prendre*) also functions as an adjective. It means "busy." Its feminine form is *prise*.

Je ne peux pas aller au cinéma, je suis trop prise.

I can't go to the movies; I'm too busy.

In *pris*, the letter "s" is not pronounced, but in *prise*, which has the final "e," you've guessed it, it is—hence, (preez).

Surpris also functions as an adjective. When in the feminine form, it becomes *surprise*, pronounced (sürpreez).

Elle va être surprise.

She's going to be surprised.

Heads Up!

ACTIVITY 2: TAKE IT FOR A SPIN

Help! *À l'aide!* Complete the following sentences by picking the appropriate past participle from the column on the right.

a)   J'ai ___pris___ plusieurs places de cinéma.   prises

b)   Est-ce que vous avez ___attendu___ l'émission sur ce film?   attendu

c)   Je n'ai rien ___compris___ à ce film.   descendus

d) Avez-vous _entendu_ le métro longtemps?
e) Elles ne peuvent pas venir, elles sont _prises_ .
f) Ils sont _descendus_ du train à l'heure.

pris
~~entendu~~
compris

Did You Know?

You're in Paris and you want to go out tonight? Well, there are several sources that can help you make your pick. There are the big *quotidiens* (daily newspapers), such as *Le Monde* or *Libération,* or *des hebdomadaires* (weekly magazines), such as *Télérama. Télérama* is both an intelligent TV guide and a magazine, with a whole section devoted to the cultural life of Paris. You can also go for a very handy *Pariscope* or *L'officiel des spectacles,* pocket-size weekly magazines that list all events—films, concerts, exhibitions, etc.—happening in the capital for less than 50 cents! And if you have access to the Internet, check out *www.paris-premiere.fr.*

ANY QUESTIONS?: ASKING QUESTIONS WITH *WHICH?*

Which in French is *quel,* as in the following example:

Quel jour sommes-nous?

Which / what day is it today?

Because *quel* is always accompanied by a noun, to which it refers, it is really an adjective, and as such, it must agree in gender and number with the noun it modifies. The different forms of *quel* are:

THE FORMS OF *QUEL* (WHICH? / WHAT?)		
	SINGULAR	PLURAL
MASCULINE	quel	quels
FEMININE	quelle	quelles

For example:

Quel homme?	Which man?
Quelle femme?	Which woman?
Quels hommes?	Which men?
Quelles femmes?	Which women?

It's time to nail down the elements of the French calendar, but before we get into details . . .

Did You Know?

THE FRENCH REPUBLICAN CALENDAR

Did you know that after the French Revolution (1789), the revolutionary government decided to get rid of the traditional Gregorian Calendar and replace it by *le calendrier républicain* (the French Republican Calendar)? The calendar, officially adopted in October 1793, was divided into twelve 30-day months each containing three 10-day weeks, eliminating Sundays. It symbolized the effort to break away from the old Christian traditions in the name of reason and progress. The French Republican Calendar was abolished by Napoleon in 1805.

Did You Know?

EVERY DAY IS NOT A HOLIDAY!: THE FRENCH CALENDAR AND SAYING DATES

Or in French: *Ce n'est pas tous les jours fête!*

The Days of the Week

I've got an idea . . . Let's see if you remember when the following events from this lesson and the past lessons took place:

Le dîner at Natalie's took place on: *un lundi, un mardi,* or *un mercredi?*
Un lundi, good!

Most stores are closed on: *le vendredi, le samedi,* or *le dimanche?*
Le dimanche!

Le vernissage that Luc missed was on: *un vendredi, un samedi,* or *un dimanche?*
Un vendredi!

And the scene from the last dialogue takes place on . . . ?
Un mercredi, you're right again!

See, you know most days of the week in French already.
Now, let's put them all together: *les jours de la semaine* (the days of the week) are:

THE DAYS OF THE WEEK IN FRENCH						
lundi (Monday)	*mardi* (Tuesday)	*mercredi* (Wednesday)	*jeudi* (Thursday)	*vendredi* (Friday)	*samedi* (Saturday)	*dimanche* (Sunday)

Note that all names of the days of the week are masculine in French, but articles *le* or *un* are not normally used in front of them.

Also note that in French, the week starts with *(le) lundi* and ends with *(le) dimanche*. And this is how the names of the days of the week are used within a sentence:

Je vais au cinéma lundi.

I'm going to the movies on Monday.

Notice that there is no preposition before the name of the day of the week in French, unlike in English, where "on" is required.

When the article is used with the name of the day of the week, as in the following example, the meaning changes. *Le lundi* means "on Mondays."

Je vais au cinéma <u>le</u> lundi.

I go to the movies on Mondays.

Another way to say the same thing is:

Je vais au cinéma tous les lundis.

I go to the movies every Monday.

The Fine Print

Capitalization rules are very different in French and in English. English words are capitalized much more often than French words. The days of the week, like the months of the year (and ethnic and language names, remember?), are not capitalized in French.

The Months of the Year

In brief, *les mois de l'année* (the months of the year) are:

THE MONTHS OF THE YEAR IN FRENCH					
janvier (January)	*février* (February)	*mars* (mahrs) (March)	*avril* (April)	*mai* (May)	*juin* (June)
juillet (July)	*août* (oot) (August)	*septembre* (September)	*octobre* (October)	*novembre* (November)	*décembre* (December)

For example:

Juin a trente jours.

June has thirty days.

Octobre a trente et un jours.

October has thirty-one days.

You can say *juin* (June) or *le mois de juin* (the month of June).

To say when something is happening, use *en* before the name of the month. For example:

En octobre, je vais étudier à l'Institut Louis Lumière.

In October, I'm going to study at the Louis Lumière Institute.

Or, you can be more specific and use the expressions *à la fin de* (at the end of) or *au début de* (at the beginning of) before the name of the month:

Les grandes vacances commencent à la fin de juin.

The summer holidays start at the end of June.

Le nouveau film d'Emir Kusturica sort au début du mois d'octobre.

Emir Kusturica's new movie is coming out at the beginning of October.

And remember that the names of the months, like the names of the days of the week, are not capitalized and are always masculine in gender.

Saying Dates in French

Here's an example: *dimanche, le 14 avril, 2002* means "Sunday, April 14, 2002." The date is read as follows: *le quatorze avril deux mille deux.*

French doesn't use the ordinal numbers (1st, 2nd, 3rd, etc.) in dates except for the first day of the month, which is *le 1er* or *le premier*.

le 1er septembre	**(le premier septembre)**	September 1st
le 2 septembre	**(le deux septembre)**	September 2nd

The word for a year is either *un an* or *une année*. When talking about a person's age, *an* is always used.

Il a trente-quatre ans.

He's thirty-four.

An is also used instead of *année* to put emphasis on the date.

Nous sommes en l'an 2002.

We are in the year 2002.

Here are the questions you can use to inquire about days, months or dates:

Quel jour sommes-nous?

What day is it?

Quelle est la date d'aujourd'hui?

What's the date?

En quelle année sommes-nous?

What year is it?

Did I forget anything? Yes, here are a few more expressions:

la fête	holiday, festival
le jour de fête	holiday
le jour férié	public / official holiday
le jour ouvrable	working day, weekday
le jour de travail	working day

ACTIVITY 3: TAKE IT FOR A SPIN

Which months have *trente jours*? Which ones have *trente et un jours*? And a question for extra points: what's the French name of the month that has 28 or 29 days?

IT'S A CLASSIC: TALKING ABOUT MOVIES

And now, let's go back to the movies:

You can say: *On va au cinéma* (We're going to the movies) or, more colloquially speaking, *On s'fait une toile* (*Lit.* We get ourselves a canvas).

Movies are very popular in France. You can buy *une place de cinema*, a movie ticket, through the Minitel or on the Web, or simply by going to *le guichet* (box office) before the screening.

What makes a film?

le réalisateur	director
réaliser	to direct (also: to realize)
un acteur, une actrice	actor, actress
la bande originale	soundtrack
le scénario	script
le succès	success
la version originale (v.o.)	original version
la version sous-titrée (v.s.t.)	subtitled version

Who or what tells you about a film?

le cinéphile	film buff / lover
la critique de film	film review
le critique	(film) critic
la sortie d'un film	movie opening

Some useful little words:

au moins	at least
d'ailleurs	besides

récemment	*recently*
longtemps	*for a long time*
sortir	*to come out; to go out*

Finally, *juste* can mean "fair," but also "only" and "just." Just a little word, I tell you!

Word on the Street

Did You Know?

RAPPING IN FRENCH

Can one rap in French? Of course. MC Solaar, a famous French rap artist, originally from Senegal, has proven it. In addition to a series of successes throughout the 1990s, MC Solaar was also featured on *Guru's Jazzmatazz*, an album produced in the United States. MC Solaar's songs, penned in French, carried positive messages at a time when most rap music still fed on a culture of violence.

Did You Know?

LET'S PUT IT IN WRITING

Read from *L'officiel des spectacles* to find a couple of *endroits branchés et sympas* (some cool and fun places).

La Mère Michel, RESTAURANT-BAR, ouvert de 20 h à 4 h (5, rue Rennequin, 17è.);
La Mercerie, café (98, rue Oberkampf, 11è.);
La Poste, restaurant (22, rue de Douai, 9è.);
Le Baiser Salé, bar (58, rue de Lombards, 1er).

And the full ad for le Baiser Salé:

Le Baiser Salé-Paris (1er)

58, rue des Lombards 75001 PARIS

Métro: Châtelet Plan d'accès

Tel : 01.42.33.37.71 • Fax : 01.42.36.24.40

Genres jazz, fusion, rock, blues, chanson, latin jazz/afro jazz

> *a)*   *Quelle est l'adresse du bar Le Baiser Salé?*
> *b)*   *On peut y voir des films ou y entendre des concerts?*
> *c)*   *La Mère Michel est une salle de cinéma?*

After the movie, *nos amis vont prendre un pot tous ensemble* (all together). *Momar et Flo invite leurs amis dans un petit bar-resto branché du 9ème (neuvième) arrondissement.*

HEAR . . . SAY 2

We're Treating You to a Drink! (On vous invite à boire un pot!)

Momar:	Alors, qu'avez-vous pensé du film?
Étienne:	C'est comme une fable, avec plusieurs messages.
Frédérique:	C'est vrai, à la fois onirique et réaliste.
Marianne:	Son style de narration est très intéressant.
Wolfgang:	Oui, c'est très bien. Vraiment. Est-ce que tu as vu ses autres films?
Momar:	J'ai vu *Touki Bouki, Hyènes, Le Franc.* Et avec Flo, on s'est fait ses courts-métrages en vidéo.

Frédérique et Étienne prennent une cigarette.

Florence:	Alors, ça vous plaît comme endroit?
Marianne:	Oui, c'est sympa, mais il y a trop de fumée! Je ne vous comprends absolument pas.
Frédérique:	Oui, on le sait, cela nuit à la santé.
Étienne:	Tu ne vas pas nous changer, Marianne, ça fait vingt ans.
Florence:	Tiens! Paco. . . . Salut! Et où est Julienne?
Paco:	Bonsoir tout le monde! Mademoiselle étudie.
Momar:	Ouh . . . Ça va? Voilà, Étienne, Frédérique, Marianne et Wolfgang. On a vu *La petite vendeuse de soleil.*
Paco:	Ah, c'est bien. Ça vous a plu?
Wolfgang:	Oui, beaucoup! Vous prenez un verre avec nous?
Paco:	Volontiers! Je suis allé au Baiser Salé. . . . Tiens, voilà MC!
Florence:	Salut, MC! Ça va?
Étienne et Wolfgang:	MC???
Paco:	Hey, man! Quoi de neuf?
Frédérique:	C'est MC Solaar?!

a) *La scène se passe chez Momar.*   VRAI OU FAUX

b) *Ils discutent du travail.*   VRAI OU FAUX

c) *Le mari de Marianne fume beaucoup.*   VRAI OU FAUX

d) *Florence ne connaît pas tout le monde.*   VRAI OU FAUX

e) *Julienne arrive à la fin de la scène.*   VRAI OU FAUX

WORKSHOP 2

THE NITTY-GRITTY

LIKE IT OR NOT: THE IRREGULAR VERBS *PLAIRE* (TO LIKE) AND *NUIRE* (TO HURT) IN THE PRESENT TENSE AND THE *PASSÉ COMPOSÉ*

These two peculiar irregular verbs follow a similar pattern.

1. The verb *plaire* (to like)

Plaire is the equivalent of "to like," but it is used in a very different type of construction. Take a look:

Ces films plaisent beaucoup à mes amis.

My friends like these movies a lot.

In literal translation, this sentence would be something like, "These movies are very pleasing to my friends." Here are more examples:

Cet endroit vous plaît?

Do you like this place? (*Lit.* Is this place pleasing to you?)

Il me plaît.

I like it. (*Lit.* It is pleasing to me.)

So, the construction in which *plaire* is used is:

(something / somebody, sg.) *plaît à* (somebody)
(something / somebody, pl.) *plaisent à* (somebody)

You know this verb from the expression *s'il vous plaît* or *s'il te plaît,* meaning *please.* Now you know that it literally means "if it is pleasing to you" or "if it pleases you."

The verb agrees with the object of liking in French, and here are its different present tense forms.

THE PRESENT TENSE OF THE VERB *PLAIRE* (TO LIKE)

je plais	nous plaisons
tu plais	vous plaisez
il / elle plaît	ils / elles plaisent

Note the accent on the letter "i" in the third person singular form.

2. The verb *nuire* "to hurt; to be harmful to"

The verb *nuire* is used in the same type of construction as *plaire*. In this case, a similar construction is used in English, so not much to worry about here. For example:

Les cigarettes nuisent la santé.

Cigarettes are harmful to your health.

Les armes nous nuisent à tous.

Guns are harmful to all of us.

THE PRESENT TENSE OF THE VERB *NUIRE* (TO HURT; TO BE HARMFUL)

je nuis	nous nuisons
tu nuis	vous nuisez
il / elle nuit	ils / elles nuisent

3. *Plaire* and *nuire* in the *passé composé*

In the *passé composé*, *plaire* and *nuire* both use the auxiliary *avoir*.

THE PAST PARTICIPLE OF THE IRREGULAR VERBS *PLAIRE* AND *NUIRE*

NUIRE	PLAIRE
J'ai nui . . .	J'ai plu . . .

ACTIVITY 6: TAKE IT FOR A SPIN!

Étienne discute avec Momar et d'autres amis. Fill in the blanks with either *plaire* or *nuire* depending on what he means.

a) Ils te trouvent charmant. Tu leur ____ beaucoup.

b) Toutes ces cigarettes ont ____ à sa santé.

c) Ce bar-restaurant ne ____ pas à ma belle-soeur car il y a trop de fumée.

d) Les films de ce réalisateur leur ont vraiment ____ .

e) Les préjugés ____ à la communication.

OUT ON THE TOWN: ALL THE FRENCH YOU NEED TO HAVE FUN

How do you like your *vie nocturne* in Paris with our friends?

There isn't just one particular hip, *branché* or *sympa*, neighborhood in the French capital, but various places in different *arrondissements*. The multi-cultural arrondissements in the northeast of Paris may be the new thing . . . In any event, there are many small restaurants or *bars-restaurants*, where you can either eat or *prendre un verre-pot* as you listen to some good music.

l'alcool (*masc.*)	liquor; alcohol
le bar	bar
le barman	bartender
trinquer	to clink glasses
Santé!	Cheers! (Lit. To your health!)
Tchin, tchin!	Cheers!

Prendre or *boire un verre* is a social ritual and not an end in itself for most French people. Between the sips, the French love to discuss issues, such as movies, music, or the arts. And there is much to do and see in Paris. *Oui, il y a beaucoup de cinémas, de galeries, de musées, de boutiques, de concerts* . . .

Here's some vocabulary for your discussion about movies:

le court métrage	short film
la fable	fable
le long métrage	feature
onirique	dreamlike
réaliste	realistic
le style de narration	narrative style

ACTIVITY 7: TAKE IT FOR A SPIN!

All these words! Please write all these nouns in their singular form:

les films / les styles / les bars-restaurants / les cigarettes / les amis / les courts-métrages / les fils / les soeurs

And now, the time has come for you to . . .

STRUT YOUR STUFF !

You've learned a lot since Lesson 5. Do these exercises to get a sense of where you stand. And remember, there's nothing wrong with going back for a little refresher.

Corinne is talking about a dinner that Nathalie, her sister, has just had at her place. She's used the *passé composé* to tell her story. Rewrite each sentence using the immediate past [e.g., *Je viens de voir* un bon film (I've just seen a good movie)], which would be just as good.

a) *Je suis allée chez ma soeur.*
b) *Elle nous a préparé ce dîner délicieux.*
c) *Mon beau-frère nous a apporté du muscat de son pays.*
d) *Et j'ai bu deux verres. C'est si bon!*
e) *J'ai goûté aussi le vin blanc.*
f) *Au dessert, enfin, j'ai pris un verre d'eau.*
g) *Rico nous a joué sa musique.*

It's time for you to be a bit more formal! Pretend you are speaking to Julienne. Rewrite the following questions using the inversion questions [e.g., *Qui as-tu vu?* (Whom did you see?)].

a) *Est-ce que tu es allée à la poste de ton quartier?*
b) *Où est-ce que tu as envoyé tes colis?*
c) *Tu as acheté plusieurs carnets de timbres aussi?*
d) *Comment est-ce que tu as payé?*
e) *Pourquoi est-ce que tu as pris cette ligne de métro?*
f) *Qui est-ce que tu as rencontré?*

Imagine you are invited to Nathalie's for dinner. You're introducing to her some friends of yours. Replace the English pronouns with their French equivalents.

a) *(I) (you) présente mes amis.*
b) *Peux-(you) (them) passer ces assiettes?*
c) *(They) ne vont pas manger. Ils viennent de manger avec leurs parents.*
d) *C'est dommage! (I) (you) ai préparé des crêpes délicieuses.*
e) *(you) ne peux pas (them) inviter une autre fois?*
f) *D'accord! Aziza, peux-(you) (me) apporter du sirop d'érable?*

Now that you see you know it all, try this as well. Translate the following sentences.

a) Good evening! Did you have a good day?
b) Yes, it's ok. I worked all day at the office, and I had a few appointments. And you?

c)   Well, I went to the post office in the 1ˢᵗ arrondissement. I went to the University. And now, I've just finished studying.

d)   Our friend has just left us a message. She's going to have a dinner at her place, and she wants to invite us.

e)   Great! That's a good idea! Can you call her back?

f)   I tried but she's neither home nor at her office.

g)   Do we need to go to the supermarket and buy some wine?

CRIB NOTES

HEAR...SAY 1

Marianne:	Ah, good evening! We're not late?
Frédérique:	You took the subway, I bet . . .
Wolfgang:	Yes, and we waited for it for a long time. So, what's new?
Étienne:	Still okay for the Diop Mambety film?
Wolfgang:	Yes! I heard some good reviews on France Inter.
Marianne:	His favorite radio show, "The mask and the feather!"
Frédérique:	It's a good show. Have you seen other movies by this director?
Marianne:	Well, we just saw *Touki Bouki*.
Étienne:	A Senegalese friend spoke to me recently about this director. He's supposed to come, actually. It's our turn . . .
Wolfgang:	Hello, Madam, four tickets for *The Little Girl Who Sold the Sun*, please. The film hasn't started, I hope.
The ticket lady:	No, Sir, in five minutes. That's 30 euros.
Wolfgang:	Here you are, Madam. Thank you.

They enter the small movie theatre.

Frédérique:	That's nice (of you), Wolfgang. Well, we're inviting you for a drink after the movie. Here. I picked up programs.
Marianne:	Thanks, Fréd.
A male voice:	Étienne! Hey, Étienne!
Étienne:	Momar! How did you get in?
Momar:	Hey! How are you? Étienne, let me introduce you to Florence.
Étienne:	Pleased to meet you, Florence!
Florence:	Good evening. . . . Hey! Isn't that Wolfgang?
Étienne:	Well, yes, he's my brother-in-law.
Momar:	With Florence, it's always like that.
Florence:	He works with me at M7! He's going to be surprised.
Momar:	Ah, the show is starting! We'll talk later.

HEAR...SAY 2

Momar:	So what did you think of the film?
Étienne:	It's like a fable with several messages.
Frédérique:	That's true, dreamlike and realistic at the same time.
Marianne:	His narrative style is very interesting.
Wolfgang:	Yes, it is very good. Really. Have you seen his other films?
Momar:	I saw *Touki Bouki*, *Hyenas*, and *The Franc*. And with Flo, we've just seen his short films on video.

Frédérique and Étienne have a cigarette.

Florence:	So, how do you like this place?
Marianne:	Yes, it's cool, but there's too much smoke! I don't get you at all.
Frédérique:	Yes, we know, it's bad for the health.
Étienne:	You're not going to change us, Marianne, it's been twenty years.
Florence:	Hey! Paco. . . . Hi! And where's Julienne?
Paco:	Good evening, everyone! The girl is studying.
Momar:	Oh . . . How are you? This is Étienne, Frédérique, Marianne, and Wolfgang. We saw *The Little Girl Who Sold the Sun*.
Paco:	Oh, that's nice. Did you like it?
Wolfgang:	Yes, a lot! Are you having a drink with us?
Paco:	Sure! I went to the Baiser Salé. Hey, here comes MC!

Florence:	Hi, MC! How are you?	Paco:	Hey, man! What's up?
Étienne et Wolfgang:	MC???	Frédérique:	That's MC Solaar?!

ANSWER KEY

ACTIVITY 1

a) Le nom du beau-frère de Frédérique est Wolfgang.
b) Ils arrivent un peu tard car ils ont attendu le métro longtemps.
c) Ils vont voir *La petite vendeuse de soleil.*
d) La place de ciné coûte environ 7,5 euros.
e) Étienne retrouve Momar et Florence dans la salle de cinéma.

ACTIVITY 2

a) J'ai pris plusieurs places de cinéma.
b) Est-ce que vous avez entendu l'émission sur ce film?
c) Je n'ai rien compris à ce film.
d) Avez-vous attendu le métro pendant longtemps?
e) Elle ne peuvent pas venir, elles sont prises.
f) Ils sont descendus du train à l'heure.

ACTIVITY 3

Avril, juin, septembre et novembre ont trente jours. Janvier, mars, mai, juillet, août, octobre et décembre ont trente et un jours. Février a vingt-huit ou vingt-neuf jours.

ACTIVITY 4

a) L'adresse du bar Le Baiser Salé est 58, rue des Lombards, dans le 1er arrondissement au Métro Châtelet.
b) On peut y entendre des concerts.
c) Non, La Mère Michel est un restaurant-bar.

ACTIVITY 5

a) Faux. La scène se passe dans un restaurant-bar.
b) Faux. Ils discutent du film.
c) Faux. Le mari de Marianne ne fume pas.
d) Faux. Florence connaît tout le monde.
e) Faux. MC Solaar arrive à la fin de la scène.

ACTIVITY 6

a) Ils te trouvent charmant. Tu leur plais beaucoup.
b) Toutes ces cigarettes ont nui à sa santé.
c) Ce bar-restaurant ne plaît pas à ma belle-soeur car il y a trop de fumée.
d) Les films de ce réalisateur leur ont vraiment plu.
e) Les préjugés nuisent à la communication.

ACTIVITY 7

le film / le style / le bar-restaurant / la cigarette / l'ami / le court-métrage / le fils / la soeur

ACTIVITY 8

a) Je viens d'aller chez ma soeur.
b) Elle vient de nous préparer ce dîner délicieux.
c) Mon beau-frère vient de nous apporter du muscat de son pays.
d) Et je viens de boire deux verres. C'est si bon!
e) Je viens de goûter aussi le vin blanc.
f) Au dessert, enfin, je viens de prendre un verre d'eau.
g) Rico vient de nous jouer sa musique.

ACTIVITY 9

a) Es-tu allée à la poste de ton quartier?
b) Où as-tu envoyé tes colis?
c) As-tu acheté plusieurs carnets de timbres aussi?
d) Comment as-tu payé?
e) Pourquoi as-tu pris cette ligne de métro?
f) Qui as-tu rencontré?

ACTIVITY 10

a) Je vous / te présente mes amis.
b) Peux-tu leur passer ces assiettes?
c) Ils ne vont pas manger. Ils viennent de manger avec leurs parents.
d) C'est dommage! Je vous ai préparé des crêpes délicieuses.
e) Tu ne peux pas les inviter une autre fois?
f) D'accord! Aziza, peux-tu m'apporter du sirop d'érable?

ACTIVITY 11

a) Bonsoir! Est-ce que tu as passé une bonne journée? (*or* As-tu passé . . .?)
b) Oui, ça va. J'ai travaillé toute la journée au bureau et j'ai eu quelques rendez-vous. Et toi?
c) Eh bien, je suis allée à la poste dans le premier arrondissement. Puis, je suis allée à l'université. Et maintenant, je viens de finir d'étudier.
d) Notre amie vient de nous laisser un message. Elle fait un dîner chez elle et elle veut nous inviter.
e) Super! C'est une bonne idée. Tu peux la rappeler? (*or* Peux-tu . . . ? *or* Est-ce que tu peux . . . ?)
f) J'ai essayé mais elle n'est ni chez elle, ni au bureau.
g) Faut-il aller au supermarché acheter du vin? (*or* Est-ce qu'il faut . . . ?)

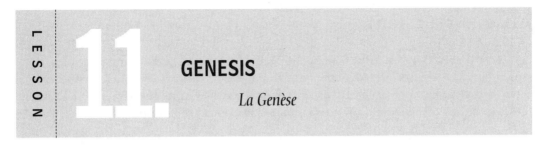
GENESIS

La Genèse

I guess your old grandpa is not that dumb.

La Genèse (*Genesis*), a beautiful film by the Malian director Cheick Oumar Sissoko, starring internationally acclaimed singer Salif Keita, was first shown within the competition section *Un certain regard* (*A Certain Look*) during the 1999 Cannes Festival. Cheick Oumar Sissoko studied directing at L'Atelier Lumière, a famous French film school.

LOOKING AHEAD

We just couldn't avoid it any longer: The topic of this lesson is computers and the Internet! But don't cringe! Internet language in French will be truly simple for you because it mostly consists of words borrowed from English. Isn't that *pratique* (handy)?

Now, not everyone feels at ease with the Internet revolution . . . for instance, the older generation. In our first dialogue, we will see how a boy teaches *son grand-père* (his grandfather) how to use the Internet, only to discover that the Internet already knows about his grandpa. (Wait to see how.) Nicolas, *un internaute de onze ans* (an 11-year-old cybernaut), shows Papi Ernest how to log onto the Web, where to *cliquer sur l'écran* (click on the screen), how to use *la souris* (the mouse), how to *faire des recherches* (do searches), and so on. Papi Ernest is really *attentif* (attentive) and interested in *l'informatique* (computer science). *Il fait de son mieux* (he does his best) but *il a besoin de prendre son temps* (he needs to take his time). At the end, there is a surprise waiting for Nicolas.

Did You Know?

Compared to other industrialized countries, France was relatively slow to catch up with the craze surrounding the Internet. Even now, the number of *utilisateurs d'ordinateurs* (computer users) in France remains inferior to other industrial countries. However, in the last three years the percentage of *internautes*, Internet users, has increased from 7% to 24%.

HEAR ... SAY 1

It's Easy, Grandpa! (C'est facile, Papi!)

Nicolas: Aie confiance en moi, Papi! Tu vas voir, c'est facile.

Ernest: Facile? Pas pour moi, Nicolas! Pour moi, cet Internet, c'est vraiment un autre monde. C'est la Genèse. Oui, le commencement de tout.

Nicolas: Ne t'inquiète pas, j'suis là! Regarde! Tape, oui, sur les touches du clavier, y, a, h, o, o, puis sur le point et sur f, r.

Ernest: Et qu'est-ce que ça veut dire tout ça?

Nicolas: Yahoo, c'est comme une bibliothèque géante, mais plus cool. On appelle ça un serveur. Il y en a plusieurs.

Ernest: Hmmm. . . . Je viens de taper une adresse.

Nicolas: T'as compris. Maintenant, choisis quelque chose dans cette liste de recherche. C'est pour aller vers un autre site.

Ernest: Ton vieux Papi n'est donc pas trop retardé?

Nicolas: Ça va. Allez, Papi, choisis quelque chose.

Ernest: Voyons. . . . Qu'est ce que je veux savoir? Yahoo?

Nicolas: Mais non, on en vient! Vas-y! Vite!

Ernest: Ah! Vite! Il faut toujours aller vite avec vous les jeunes! Je ne marche pas comme ça, moi! Je préfère prendre mon temps et réfléchir. Hmmm. . . . Ça y est. . . . Allons aux inventions!

Nicolas: Allons-y! Papi, prends la souris. Mais ne sois pas si tendu. Oui, comme ça, et clique là, sur "inventions".

Ernest: Arrh . . . Ah, enfin . . . je clique . . . Et, alors?

Nicolas: Attends. . . . On y est! Là, tu as tous les liens, c'est-à-dire les autres sites en ligne. Il y en a des pages!

Ernest: Je vois. Tu ne veux pas t'occuper de cette bestiole?

Nicolas: Cette bestiole! T'es marrant, Papi! OK, je m'en occupe.

Ernest: Voyons. . . . Oui! Essayons ce lien. Non. Reviens là.

Nicolas: Qu'est-ce que tu cherches?

Ernest: Ah! Ne sois pas si impatient, Nicolas. Voilà!

Nicolas: Et alors? "Les inventeurs des années 50". Et alors? Mais Papi, c'est ton nom là? "Ernest Akrich, l'inventeur du tobanabo . . ." Papi, t'es sur Internet?!?

ACTIVITY 1: HOW'S THAT AGAIN?

Just a few questions. . . . Please write down the answers.

a) Quels sont les noms du grand-père et du petit-fils? *Ernest et Nicolas*

b) Est-ce que le grand-père sait se servir de l'ordinateur? *No*

c) Est-ce que Nicolas est patient? *No*

d) Qu'est-ce que le grand-père n'aime pas faire?

e) Quelle section choisit-il? Pourquoi? *Le section de recherche, parce que il est très famous.*

WORKSHOP 1

THE NITTY-GRITTY

PLEASE SIT DOWN! HOW TO GIVE ORDERS IN FRENCH

When you give orders and commands in French you need to use a special form of the verb called the imperative. This verb form only exists for the *tu*, *nous*, and *vous* persons. Look at the examples:

Tu me regardes. →	*Regarde-moi!*
You look at me.	Look at me!
Nous allons sur Internet. →	*Allons sur Internet!*
We're logging onto the Internet.	Let's log onto the Internet!
Vous partez. →	*Partez!*
You leave.	Leave!

As you will see, the imperative is actually very similar to, and sometimes exactly the same as, the present tense in French.

1. The Imperative of the –er Verbs

The *nous* and *vous* imperative forms are identical to the present tense. The *tu* imperative form loses its final –s. Note that this does not change the pronunciation.

THE IMPERATIVE OF THE VERB *TRAVAILLER* (TO WORK)	
travaille	work
travaillons	let's work
travaillez	work

Travaillez vite!

Work fast!

Clique ensuite sur "ok".

Then, click "ok".

Note that subject pronouns are not used in front of the imperative form of the verb.

2. The Imperative of the −ir Verbs

The imperative forms of the −ir verbs are exactly the same as their present tense forms.

THE IMPERATIVE OF THE REGULAR VERB FINIR (TO FINISH)	
finis	finish
finissons	let's finish
finissez	finish

Choisis quelque chose sur le site.

Choose something on the site.

Finissons notre leçon.

Let's finish our lesson.

3. The Imperative of the Helping Verbs Avoir (to have) and Être (to be)

The helping verbs *avoir* and *être* are irregular, so their imperative forms are irregular as well.

THE IMPERATIVE OF THE HELPING VERBS AVOIR AND ÊTRE			
AVOIR (TO HAVE)		*ÊTRE* (TO BE)	
aie	have	*sois*	be
ayons	let's have	*soyons*	let's be
ayez	have	*soyez*	be

Aie confiance en moi!

Have confidence in me!

Soyons prêts à l'heure!

Let's be ready on time!

4. The Imperative of Other Irregular Verbs

Like regular verbs, most irregular verbs take the *tu*/*nous*/*vous* forms of the present tense to form their imperative. Nothing else!

THE PRESENT AND IMPERATIVE OF THE IRREGULAR VERB *ALLER* (TO GO)

PRESENT	IMPERATIVE
tu vas	va
nous allons	allons
vous allez	allez

Just like a regular verb in *–er*, *aller* loses its *–s* in the *tu* person.

Va chez toi!

Go home.

Heads Up!

Note that when *Va!* is followed by *y*, as in *Vas-y!* (Go ahead!), the "s" is there again, and the pronunciation is (vah-zee). The same rule applies to other *–er* verbs.

Heads Up!

THE IMPERATIVE OF IRREGULAR VERBS *VENIR* AND *TENIR*

VENIR (TO COME)	TENIR (TO HOLD)
viens	tiens
venons	tenons
venez	tenez

Venez demain chez mon grand-père!

Come tomorrow to my grandfather's!

Tenons bon!

Let's hold on!

THE IMPERATIVE OF THE IRREGULAR VERBS *FAIRE* AND *DIRE*

FAIRE (TO DO)	DIRE (TO SAY)
fais	dis
faisons	disons
faites	dites

Fais tes devoirs!

Do your homework!

Dites la verité!

Tell the truth!

THE IMPERATIVE OF THE IRREGULAR VERBS *VOIR* AND *CROIRE*	
VOIR (TO SEE)	*CROIRE* (TO BELIEVE)
vois	crois
voyons	croyons
voyez	croyez

Voyez tous ces sites . . .

See all these sites . . .

Crois en le futur!

Believe in the future!

THE IMPERATIVE OF THE IRREGULAR VERBS *BOIRE* AND *RECEVOIR*	
BOIRE (TO DRINK)	*RECEVOIR* (TO RECEIVE)
bois	reçois
buvons	recevons
buvez	recevez

Buvons à notre rencontre!

Let's drink to our meeting!

Recevez tous nos meilleurs voeux!

Receive our best wishes!

THE IMPERATIVE OF THE IRREGULAR VERBS *APPRENDE* AND *PRENDRE*	
APPRENDRE (TO LEARN; TO TEACH)	*PRENDRE* (TO TAKE)
apprends	prends
apprenons	prenons
apprenez	prenez

Apprends leurs paroles!

Learn their words!

Prenez votre temps!

Take your time!

5. The Verb Savoir (to know) is Like Aller (to go) in That it Also has an Irregular Imperative

THE IMPERATIVE OF THE IRREGULAR VERB SAVOIR (TO KNOW)	
sache	know
sachons	let us know
sachez	know

Sachons nous servir de l'ordinateur!

Let's learn how to use the computer!

Sachez dire l'heure en français!

Know how to tell time in French!

ACTIVITY 2: TAKE IT FOR A SPIN

Are you starting to get the hang of it? Let's see . . . .*Voyons!* Write the following sentences in the imperative.

- a) *Tu as confiance en nous.*
- b) *Vous venez voir notre nouvel (new) ordinateur.*
- c) *Vous voyez comme c'est pratique.*
- d) *Nous apprenons nos cours d'informatique.*
- e) *Nous allons acheter un livre sur Internet.*

When an imperative verb is combined with an object pronoun, the latter is attached to the end of the verb with a hyphen.

Object pronouns? Well, here they are again. (*C'est pratique, n'est-ce pas?*)

The direct object pronouns are: *me, te, le, la, nous, vous, les.*
The indirect object pronouns are: *me, te, lui, nous, vous, leur.*

Good! Remember that, when used in an imperative sentence, *me* changes to *moi.*

Parle-moi!

Talk to me!

Finissons-<u>les</u> maintenant!

Let's finish them now!

Donne-<u>la</u>!

Give it!

Dites-<u>lui</u> la vérité!

Tell him the truth!

6. The Imperative in the Negative Form

To make a negative command, add the negation words *ne . . . pas* (not) in the usual fashion: *ne* goes before the verb and *pas* after the verb.

Papi, ne tape pas le point trois fois!

Grandpa, don't type the dot three times!

Ne sois pas si tendu!

Don't be so tense!

Ne t'inquiète pas!

Don't worry!

Curiouser and curiouser . . . When the imperative verb is negative, the object pronouns go back to their usual place in front of the verb and *moi* becomes *me* again.

Ne me parle pas!

Don't talk to me!

Ne les finissons pas maintenant!

Let's not finish them now!

| ACTIVITY 3: | **TAKE IT FOR A SPIN** |

Write down all the imperative verbs you can find in the first dialogue.

| ACTIVITY 4: | **TAKE IT FOR A SPIN** |

Rewrite the following text by turning it into imperative. To be nice, I underlined the verbs you can turn into commands. *Allez!*

Soyez
<u>Vous êtes</u> sûrs que la prise (the plug) *est bien branchée.* <u>Vous pressez</u> (push) *le bouton en bas de l'écran* (the screen). <u>Vous attendez</u> *quelques secondes, et voilà! Vous pouvez commencer à vous servir de votre ordinateur.*

Si vous avez un problème, <u>vous ne paniquez pas.</u> (You don't panic.)

<u>Vous n'hésitez pas</u> à nous contacter pour toutes questions.
<u>Vous nous téléphonez</u> au 800–800–80–80. Bon courage!

LITTLE WORDS SAY A LOT: USING *EN* (FROM THERE) AND *Y* (THERE)

1. How to Use *En* and *Y*?

En and *y* show location. They replace phrases that describe a location and are always placed in front of the verb. (In the examples below, the location phrases replaced by *en* and *y* are underlined.)

Je viens <u>de chez papi</u>. →	**J'en viens.**
I've just come from Grandpa's.	I've just come from there.
Nous allons <u>sur Internet</u>. →	**Allons-y.**
We're logging onto the Internet.	Let's log on!
Tu es <u>sur le site de Yahoo</u>. →	**Tu y es!**
You are on Yahoo's site.	You are there!

En and *y* can also be used to replace nouns introduced by *à* and *de* (or their different combinations like *au, aux, du, des*, etc.).

Generally, the pronoun *en* replaces a noun introduced by *de*; the pronoun *y* replaces a noun introduced by *à*.

Il pense <u>aux cours d'informatique</u>. →	**Il y pense.**
He's thinking about taking computer classes.	He's thinking about it.
Tu peux t'occuper <u>de la souris</u>? →	**Tu peux t'en occuper?**
Can you take care of the mouse?	Can you take care of it?
Il y a des pages <u>de serveurs</u>. →	**Il y en a des pages.**
There are pages of servers.	There are pages of them.

2. The Position of *En* and *Y*

In the interrogative and negative forms, *en* and *y* precede the verb.

Allez-vous <u>à votre cours d'informatique</u>? →	**Y allez-vous?**
Are you going to your computer class?	Are you going there?
Je n'ai plus besoin <u>de ce logiciel</u>. →	**Je n'en ai plus besoin.**
I don't need this software anymore.	don't need it anymore.
On ne se sert pas <u>de l'ordinateur</u>. →	**On ne s'en sert pas.**
We don't use the computer.	We don't use it.

In the *passé composé*, *en* and *y* are placed before the helping verb *avoir* or *être*.

Nous sommes allés <u>sur son site</u>. →	***Nous y sommes allés.***
We went to his site.	We went there.
Tu n'as pas vu <u>d'informations intéressantes</u>. →	***Tu n'en as pas vues.***
You haven't seen any interesting information.	You haven't seen any.

In the imperative, *en* and *y* come after the verb, attached to it with a hyphen, just like other pronouns.

Va <u>sur Wanadoo</u>! →	***Vas-y!***
Go to Wanadoo!	Go there!
Choisis <u>un site</u>! →	***Choisis-en un!***
Choose a site!	Choose one!
Pensez <u>à prendre une adresse e-mail</u>! →	***Pensez-y!***
Think about getting an e-mail address!	Think about it!

When an imperative sentence is negative, *en* and *y* go back to the position before the verb.

Ne va pas <u>sur Internet</u>! →	***N'y va pas!***
Don't log onto the Internet!	Don't log onto it!
Ne choisis pas <u>de site</u>! →	***N'en choisis pas!***
Don't choose a site!	Don't choose any!
Ne prenez pas <u>d'adresse e-mail</u>! →	***N'en prenez pas!***
Don't get an e-mail address!	Don't get one!

Word on the Street

A few common expressions using *en* and *y*. All of them really useful:

Il y a . . .	There is / are . . .
Allez-y!	Go ahead!
Allons-y!	Let's go (there)!
Ça y est!	That does it!
Je m'en vais.	I'm leaving.
J'en ai assez!	I've had enough!
Va-t-en!	Go!
On y est!	Here we are!

Allez-y! Rewrite this little scene by replacing the underlined nouns with *en* or *y* as appropriate.

>   *Regarde! Ça y est! On est connecté . . .*
>
>   a)   *C'est facile, on tape son mot de passe et on est <u>sur Internet</u>.*
>   b)   *Allez! Essaie d'aller <u>sur ton site préféré</u>.*
>   c)   *Tu vas voir, il y a des pages <u>de liens</u>.*
>   d)   *Alors, est-ce que c'est difficile de se servir <u>de cet ordinateur</u>?*

WORDS TO LIVE BY

LIFE IN CYBERSPACE: COMPUTERS AND THE INTERNET IN FRENCH

For those of us whose goal in life is to keep learning, well, we can't complain—technology is doing its best (*fait de son mieux*) to keep us busy. Our natural curiosity is always pushing us to *penser* (think) and to *faire des recherches* (research things; do searches).

la bibliothèque	library
la pensée	thought
penser	to think
la recherche	search; research
rechercher	to research; to do a search
la refléxion	thought, reflection
réfléchir	to think

If every beginning, *tout commencement*, seems *difficile*, we should not *s'inquiéter* (worry). We should remain *attentif* (attentive, vigilant) and *avoir confiance* (have confidence) in ourselves. The most important thing is to *essayer* (try) and *persévérer* (persevere).

Papi Ernest has learn this and much more. But he still prefers to take his time, *il préfère prendre son temps. Les jeunes aiment aller vite*, the young people like to go fast. He's aware of the importance of this new tool, *l'ordinateur*. It's indispensable and *bien pratique*. Therefore, he decides to *prendre une leçon* (take a lesson) from his grandson.

And now for *l'informatique* (computer science) terms.
Un ordinateur (a computer) has:

l'écran (*masc.*)	screen
le clavier	keyboard
la touche	key
la souris	mouse

And there is more . . . how many are borrowed from English?

cliquer	to click
taper	to type
envoyer	to send

la banque de données	database
le courrier électronique, l'e-mail, le mèl	electronic mail, e-mail
en pièce jointe	as an attachment
Internet	Internet
l'internaute (masc. / fem.)	Internet user, cybernaut
les chaînes, les liens	links
en ligne, online	on-line
le mot de passe	password
le point	dot
la salle de tchatche	chatroom
le fournisseur d'accès Internet (FAI)	Internet Service Provider (ISP)
le serveur	server
le site	site
le web	Web

See what I mean?

In order to use the Internet, you often need to register, *s'abonner*. The price of the registration, *abonnement*, varies slightly from one provider to another.

Did You Know?

The name of the ubiquitous sign @ is *arrobas* (ah-roh-bahs) in French.

Did You Know?

Word on the Street

Are you catching on to the colloquial language? For instance, did you learn the following common exclamations?

Allez!	C'mon!
Bon!	Well!
Vas-y!	Go ahead!

And did you notice something strange about *t'as compris* or *t'es marrant*? In spoken language, the pronoun *tu* is often clipped off and pronounced together with the word that follows. When we speak we like to make it short and quick, and so do the French.

While Papi Ernest may lack speed, he certainly has humor, even according to his grandson's standards.

Marrant or *rigolo* both mean "funny" (in informal spoken language). The more formal word is *amusant*. And from *rigolo* comes the verb *rigoler* (to laugh). From *marrant* comes the verb *se marrer* (to laugh). The more neutral term is *rire*.

I've received this message from a friend of mine. Her French is only in a budding stage (unlike yours!) and she missed some words. The message is about computers. Here are a bunch of words she missed. Can you put them in the right places?

sites / ordinateur / serveurs / pratique / liens / Internet / souris / informatique / recherches / abonner

L'_____est partout. Un_____vous permet de travailler, de communiquer avec des correspondants de l'autre côté de la planète, d'envoyer des documents . . . _____est un outil très_____et très facile à utiliser. Il faut s'y_____bien sûr. En quelques secondes, si vous faites_____, vous avez accès à une banque de données énorme grâce aux (thanks to) différents_____et aux_____. Mais il faut savoir choisir les _____intéressants. Vous pouvez aussi y lire tous les journaux. Une chose . . . N'ayez pas peur de la_____!

LET'S PUT IT IN WRITING

A few sites you can visit. *Quelques sites à consulter:*

WWW.ARTE-TV.COM: *Site de la chaîne de télévision culturelle Arte.*

WWW.RADIO-FRANCE.FR: *Site de toutes les radios publiques françaises.*

WWW.RFI.FR: *Site de la Radio France Internationale.*

WWW.LEMONDE.FR: *Site du quotidien* Le Monde.

LOOKING AHEAD

In the next dialogue, Audrey Leduc, a young mother, is resting after a long day. *Elle vient d'avoir un bébé* (she's just had a baby). Whenever she finds a quiet moment, *elle allume son ordinateur* (she turns on her computer). *Elle s'apprête* (she's getting ready) to look at her e-mail or *son courrier électronique. Elle tape son mot de passe* (she types her password). She has received several e-mails from her Parisian friends. And just then, she receives an e-mail from her Corsican friend and *collègue de travail* (colleague from work), Michèle. Audrey quickly types a response to her. While Audrey is typing her message, how about a little warm-up?

LET'S WARM UP

Tell me about your computer habits by answering these questions:

a) *Avez-vous un ordinateur?*

b) *Avez-vous accès à Internet?*

c) *Quel serveur utilisez-vous souvent?*

HEAR . . . SAY 2

SEND (Envoyer)

Audrey: Chère Michèle, je m'installe juste devant mon écran et te voilà! J'ai bien reçu ton courrier! Merci. Et comment va la vie à Paris? Et au studio? (Elle clique sur "Envoyer".)

Michèle: Audrey! Enfin, on arrive à communiquer "live" sur le web! Ici, tout va bien. Enfin, c'est Paris, il pleut. Et toi, jolie maman, comment te débrouilles-tu dans ton nouveau rôle? Comment vont les hommes? (Elle clique sur "Envoyer".)

Audrey: Sasha et El'hadj vont bien. Moi aussi, ça va. Je commence à m'y habituer! Sasha grandit si vite, de jour en jour, il change. Bien sûr, mes parents sont heureux de nous avoir. ("Envoyer".)

Michèle: Tu dois être heureuse aussi. Profites-en! Au boulot, ça a été un peu difficile. On a appris à utiliser de nouveaux logiciels . . . Vivement les vacances! ("Envoyer".)

Audrey: Quand penses-tu aller en Corse? ("Envoyer".)

Michèle: J'ai acheté mon billet aller-retour pour Noël! J'y vais peut-être aussi pour un reportage à la fin du mois.("Envoyer".)

Audrey: Bien! Moi, je rentre dans deux semaines et El'hadj à la fin de la semaine. As-tu des nouvelles de Laurence? ("Envoyer".)

Michèle: Elle va bien. Audrey, il me faut y aller. On se parle bientôt? S'il te plaît, pense à ouvrir le dossier joint. Bises. ("Envoyer".)

Audrey: Ne t'inquiète pas pour le dossier. J'essaie de le lire ce soir. Passe une bonne nuit, Audrey. ("Envoyer".)

Audrey continue à regarder son courrier.

HOW'S THAT AGAIN?

a) *D'où est Audrey?*

b) *Pourquoi est-elle à Montréal?*

c)   *Que s'apprête-t-elle à faire?*
d)   *Est-ce que Michèle est sa soeur?*
e)   *Est-ce que Audrey est seule à Montréal?*

Did You Know?

Did You Know?

WORKSHOP 2

THE NITTY-GRITTY

KNOW THYSELF: REFLEXIVE PRONOUNS LIKE *MYSELF, YOURSELF,* ETC., AND VERBS USING THEM

1. Reflexive Pronouns

Words such as *myself, yourself, herself,* etc. are called reflexive pronouns. Reflexive pronouns are used with the so-called reflexive verbs, as in *I washed myself quickly* or *I saw myself in the window.*

THE REFLEXIVE PRONOUNS			
SINGULAR		**PLURAL**	
me, m'	myself	*nous*	ourselves
te, t'	yourself	*vous*	yourselves
se, s'	himself / herself	*se, s'*	themselves

In French, unlike in English, reflexive verbs are extremely common and many verbs can only be used with an accompanying reflexive pronoun. In the dictionary, you'll always find those verbs preceded by *se*, as in *s'installer* (to install oneself, to sit down).

Je m'installe juste devant mon écran.

I've just sat down in front of the screen.

Je commence à m'y habituer.

I'm starting to get used to it.

The same reflexive pronouns can also have the meaning of English "each other," as in the following example:

Elles se parlent grâce aux e-mails.

They talk to each other thanks to e-mail.

2. Verbs Using Reflexive Pronouns

With typical reflexive verbs, the subject performs an action on itself, as in *se regarder* (to look at oneself) or *se laver* (to wash oneself). This "reflexive" action is not always obvious with all French reflexive verbs. In many cases, you'll just have to remember that the verb comes with a reflexive pronoun, even if its English translation doesn't: *s'inquiéter* (to worry), *s'apprêter* (to get ready, to be about to), *se reposer* (to rest), *s'arrêter* (to stop) . . .

Nous nous apprêtons à lire nos messages.

We're getting ready to read our messages.

Elle se repose dans l'après-midi.

She rests in the afternoon.

Ils s'arrêtent.

They stop.

Ne t'inquiète pas!

Don't worry!

Then there are verbs where two or more subjects perform the action on each other, as in *s'aimer* (to love each other), *se téléphoner* (to call each other), *se parler* (to speak to each other), *se plaire* (to like each other), etc. Note that not all verbs with this meaning are used with *each other* in English, e.g. *se rencontrer* (to meet) or *se marier* (to get married).

Marie-Thérèse et Antoine se marient.

Marie-Thérèse and Antoine are getting married.

Les deux amis se téléphonent.

The two friends call each other.

Nous nous envoyons beaucoup de e-mails.

We send a lot of e-mails to each other.

On s'est rencontrés sur Internet!

We met on the Internet!

Many verbs used with reflexive pronouns don't have any clear reflexive or reciprocal ("each other") sense, for example, *s'appeler* (to be called) or *se souvenir de* (to remember).

Elle s'appelle Audrey Leduc.

Her name is Audrey Leduc.

Papi Ernest se souvient des jours anciens.

Grandpa Ernest remembers the old days.

By the way, you know how to say *Je m'appelle . . .* meaning "My name is . . . ." Now here's your chance to learn how to use the verb *s'appeler* (to be called) in other forms of the present tense.

THE PRESENT TENSE OF *S'APPELER* (TO BE CALLED)	
je m'appelle	nous nous appelons
tu t'appelles	vous vous appelez
il / elle s'appelle	ils / elles s'appellent

Note that all the forms containing two "l"s are pronounced (ah-pehl), and the forms containing one "l" are: *appelons* (ah-puh-loh^n), *appelez* and *appeler* (ah-puh-leh).

ACTIVITY 9: TAKE IT FOR A SPIN

It's just a matter of following the same pattern. Write down the present tense forms of *se souvenir*. Here's a tip: *se souvenir* is just like *venir*.

3. Reflexive Verbs in Questions and Following Other Verbs

The reflexive pronoun always precedes the verb. Here are two examples where the reflexive verb follows another verb (the reflexive pronoun is underlined):

Ils doivent <u>se</u> téléphoner.

They have to call each other.

Nous ne pouvons pas <u>nous</u> voir.

We can't see each other.

Here are examples of these verbs used in questions (the reflexive pronoun is under-lined again):

Pourquoi _vous_ inquiétez-vous?

Why are you worrying?

Est-ce que tu _te_ reposes?

Are you resting?

4. Reflexive verbs in the Passé Composé

It's important to remember that all reflexive verbs always use *être* in the *passé composé*. For this reason, the past participle must agree in gender and number with the subject!

Je me suis souvenu de ce site intéressant.

I remembered this interesting site.

Nous ne nous sommes pas téléphonés hier.

We didn't call each other yesterday.

Elle ne s'est pas inquiétée au moins?

She didn't worry, at least?

ACTIVITY 10: TAKE IT FOR A SPIN

Put the verbs in parentheses into the appropriate form of the present tense. (In the ex-ample b, use *passé composé* instead.)

a)   Comment (s'appeler) vous?
b)   Nous (s'envoyer in the *passé composé*) des e-mails.
c)   Vous ne devez pas (se téléphoner).
d)   Il ne (se préparer) pas à travailler sur l'ordinateur.
e)   Est-ce que tu (se souvenir) de ce lien?

LET'S PUT IT IN WRITING

Read this little *annonce* (ad):

> *Bernard Pivot* arrive sur le Net avec un site consacré *(devoted)*
> à la langue française et à l'orthographe: *www.dicosdor.com!*

Bonne nouvelle pour les internautes!

Did You Know?

ACTIVITY 11: TAKE IT FOR A SPIN

Of course, I could ask you to do a *dictée* (dictation) . . . but instead, just decide whether these statements are *vrai ou faux*.

- a) Bernard Pivot hosted a sport show.
- b) *Bouillon de Culture est une émission de radio.*
- c) *Le nouveau website, dicosdor.com, est consacré à la cuisine française.*

WORDS TO LIVE BY

Thanks to the Internet, we are now able to *communiquer, avoir des nouvelles de notre famille et ami(e)s* (get the news from our family and friends) and *s'envoyer des documents* in a matter of seconds.

Audrey is not working; that's because she just gave birth to *(a donné naissance à)* a little boy. Speaking of work, the word is *travail* or more colloquially, *boulot*. Audrey is amazed to see how fast her baby son is growing and changing.

changer	*to change*
grandir	*to grow (up)*
profiter de	*to enjoy; to take advantage of*

According to the labor laws in France and Canada, women are allowed several weeks of paid maternity leave, or *le congé de maternité*, during pregnancy and after they give birth.

And let's take a second look at reflexive verbs from the lesson:

s'habituer à	*to be / get used to*
avoir l'habitude de	*to be used to*
s'installer à	*to settle, to sit down*

se préparer à faire	to prepare oneself to do
se souvenir de	to remember
s'apprêter à	to get ready, to be about to
se débrouiller	to manage, to handle, to cope

TAKE IT FOR A SPIN

Put the following words into pairs based on their meanings.

au boulot / allumer / e-mail / passer une bonne nuit / se reposer / grandir / travailler / l'ordinateur / changer / envoyer

CRIB NOTES

HEAR...SAY 1

Nicolas:	Trust me, Grandpa. You'll see, it's easy.
Ernest:	Easy? Not for me, Nicolas! This Internet is really another world for me. It's the genesis. Yes, the beginning of it all.
Nicolas:	Don't worry! I'm here! Look. Type, here on the keyboard, "y," "a," "h," "o," "o," then the dot and "f," "r."
Ernest:	And what does it all mean?
Nicolas:	Yahoo is like a giant library, but better. It's called a server. There are several of them.
Ernest:	Hmmm. . . . So, I just typed an address.
Nicolas:	You got it. Now choose something in this research list; it's to go to another site.
Ernest:	I guess your old Grandpa is not that dumb.
Nicolas:	You're OK. C'mon, Grandpa, choose something . . .
Ernest:	Let's see. What do I want to know? Yahoo?
Nicolas:	No, we've just been there! Go ahead! Quick!
Ernest:	Ah! Quick! Everything has to be quick with you young people! For me it doesn't work that way! I prefer to take my time

and think. Hmmm. . . . That's it. . . . Let's go to the inventions!

Nicolas:	Let's go! Grandpa, take the mouse. But don't be so tense. Yes, like that, and click here on "Inventions."
Ernest:	Arrh. . . . Ah, finally . . . I click. . . . And then?
Nicolas:	Wait. . . . Here we are! Here you have all the links, that is, the other sites online. There are pages of them!
Ernest:	I see. Do you want to take care of this bug?
Nicolas:	This bug! You're funny, Grandpa! OK, I'm taking care of it.
Ernest:	Let's see! Yes! Let's try this link. No. Come back there.
Nicolas:	What are you looking for?
Ernest:	Ah! Don't be so impatient, Nicolas. That's it!
Nicolas:	So? "The inventors of the 1950s." So? But Grandpa, that's your name there? "Ernest Akrich, the inventor of the tobanabo . . ." Grandpa, you're on the Internet?!?

HEAR...SAY 2

Audrey:	Dear Michèle, I have just sat down in front of my screen and here you are! I received your mail! Thank you. And how's life in Paris? And at the studio? (She clicks "Send".)
Michèle:	Audrey! Finally, we manage to communicate "live" on the web! Here everything is fine. Well, it's Paris, it's

raining. And you, sweet mommy, how are you handling your new role? How are the men? (She clicks "Send".)

Audrey:	Sasha and El'hadj are doing well. Me too, I'm fine. I'm starting to get used to it! Sasha is growing up so quickly, from day to day, he changes. Of course, my parents are happy to have us. ("Send".)

Michèle:	You must be happy too. Enjoy it! At work, it's been a little hard. We learned to use some new software. . . . I can't wait for the holidays! ("Send".)
Audrey:	When are you thinking of going to Corsica? ("Send".)
Michèle:	I've bought a round-trip ticket for Christmas! I may also go there to do a story at the end of the month. ("Send".)
Audrey:	Good! As for me, I'm coming back in two weeks and El'hadj at the end of the week. Have you heard from Laurence? ("Send".)
Michèle:	She's doing well. Audrey, I have to go. We'll talk soon? Please, don't forget to open the report I've attached. Kisses. ("Send".)
Audrey:	Don't worry about the report. I'll try to read it tonight. Have a good night, Audrey. ("Send".)

Audrey continues to look at her mail.

ANSWER KEY

ACTIVITY 1

a) Le nom du grand-père est Ernest et le nom du petit-fils est Nicolas.
b) Non, le grand-père ne sait pas se servir de l'ordinateur.
c) Non, Nicolas n'est pas toujours patient.
d) Le grand-père n'aime pas travailler vite.
e) Il choisit la section "Inventions" car il y a son nom là.

ACTIVITY 2

a) Aie confiance en nous.
b) Venez voir notre nouvel ordinateur.
c) Voyez comme c'est pratique.
d) Apprenons nos cours d'informatique.
e) Allons acheter un livre sur Internet.

ACTIVITY 3

Aie confiance / Ne t'inquiète pas / Regarde / Tape / Choisis / Allez / Choisis / Voyons / Vas-y / Allons / Allons-y / Prends /
Ne sois pas / Clique / Attends / Voyons / Essayons / Reviens / Ne sois pas.

ACTIVITY 4

Soyez sûrs que la prise est bien branchée. Pressez le bouton en bas de l'écran. Attendez quelques secondes, et voilà! Vous pouvez commencer à vous servir de votre ordinateur.

Si vous avez un problème, ne paniquez pas!

N'hésitez pas à nous contacter pour toutes questions.

Téléphonez-nous au 800–800–80–80. Bon courage!

ACTIVITY 5

Regarde! Ça y est! On est connecté.

a) C'est facile, on tape son mot de passe et on y est.
b) Allez! Essaie d'y aller.
c) Tu vas voir, il y en a des pages.
d) Alors, est-ce que c'est difficile de s'en servir?

ACTIVITY 6

L'informatique est partout. Un ordinateur vous permet de travailler, de communiquer avec des correspondants de l'autre côté de la planète, d'envoyer des documents. Internet est un outil très pratique et très facile à utiliser. Il faut s'y abonner bien sûr. En quelques secondes, si vous faites des recherches, vous avez accès à une banque de données énorme grâce aux différents serveurs et aux liens. Mais il faut savoir choisir les sites intéressants. Vous pouvez aussi y lire tous les journaux. Une chose: N'ayez pas peur de la souris!

ACTIVITY 7

a) Oui, j'ai un ordinateur. / Non, je n'ai pas d'ordinateur.
b) Oui, j'ai accès à Internet. / Non, je n'ai pas accès à Internet.
c) J'utilise souvent . . .

ACTIVITY 8

a) Audrey est de Montréal mais elle habite à Paris.
b) Elle est à Montréal car elle vient d'avoir un bébé et elle se repose cher ses parents.
c) Elle s'apprête à regarder son courrier électronique / son e-mail / ses e-mails.
d) Non, Michèle est sa collègue de travail.
e) Non, Audrey est avec El'hadj, leur fils Sasha et ses parents.

ACTIVITY 9

je me souviens, tu te souviens, il / elle se souvient, nous nous souvenons, vous vous souvenez, ils / elles se souviennent

a) Comment vous appelez-vous?
b) Nous nous sommes envoyés des e-mails.
c) Vous ne devez pas vous téléphoner.
d) Il ne se prépare pas à travailler sur l'ordinateur.
e) Est-ce que tu te souviens de ce lien?

ACTIVITY 11

a) FAUX—Bernard Pivot hosted a show on literature and culture.

b) FAUX—*Bouillon de Culture* est une émission de télévision.
c) FAUX—Le nouveau website, dicosdor.com, est consacré à la langue française.

ACTIVITY 12

au boulot–travailler, allumer–l'ordinateur, e-mail–envoyer, passer une bonne nuit–se reposer, grandir–changer

12.

A SUNDAY IN THE COUNTRY

Un dimanche à la campagne

Wait for us, Mister Train!

COMING UP...

- *There are no more seasons!*: Talking about the weather and seasons
- *Round-trip to Brest, please!*: Traveling by train
- *A Sunday in the country*: Talking about a weekend in the countryside
- *As time goes by*: Expressing time using *since, during, ago,* etc.
- *Take a seat, please*: The verb *s'asseoir* (to sit down) in the present and past tenses, and the imperative
- *I scream, you scream*: The irregular verbs *venir* (to come), *tenir* (to hold), and *se souvenir* (to remember) in the past tense and the imperative
- *How perfect!*: Using exclamations with *quel* (what) and *comme* (how)

IN THE SPOTLIGHT

It was a good day for the film industry when Bertrand Tavernier decided to drop out of Law School and devote his life to filmmaking instead. A subtle observer of French society, Tavernier, filmmaker, screenwriter, and producer, has won many prizes in the course of his fruitful film career. *Un dimanche à la campagne* (*A Sunday in the Country*) (1984) won two prizes at the Cannes Film Festival: Tavernier got a prize for *mise en scène* (directing) and Sabine Azéma won a César (an award equivalent to an Oscar) for her *interprétation* (acting).

LOOKING AHEAD

This is a chapter about *des voyages en France* and many of its beautiful regions. As elsewhere in Europe, traveling by train is very common and comfortable in France. That's why in Paris alone, there are several *gares* (railway stations), with each station serving a group of regions. All trains are regulated by the SNCF (*Société nationale des chemins de fer*), the French national railways. In this lesson, you'll get a lot of useful info about traveling by train: how to *acheter un billet de train* (buy a train ticket), how to ask about the *différents tarifs* (different prices), etc.

In the first dialogue, a family, Françoise, Marc, and *leur fils* (their son), Mathieu, *profite d'un long week-end de fête* (takes advantage of a long holiday weekend) to go to meet some friends in *Bretagne* (Brittany). In the morning, *ils se précipitent* (they are rushing) to catch an early train. But where is Brittany? Well, it's *cette belle région* located in the northwest of France, across the ocean from the U.S.

Did You Know?

A FRENCH INVENTION—THE HIGH-SPEED TRAIN

You may have heard of the TGV (teh-zheh-veh) (*train à grande vitesse*), the network of streamlined, usually bright orange high-speed trains, that are the pride of France. Since the early 1980s, when the first line from Paris to Lyon was inaugurated, TGV trains seduced many travelers with their high speed of about 300 km / hour or 186 miles / hour. New lines toward the west and north of Paris were introduced during the 1990s. Yet, each new TGV line raises an outcry among environmentalists. The latest SNCF project was the 250-kilometer TGV line between Valence-Marseille and Nîmes. The plans, made by a group of well-known architects and engineers, made every attempt to preserve the countryside surrounding the new line. Originally, the line was going to cut through the heart of such beautiful sites as La Vallée du Rhône (the valley of the river Rhône) and La Haute Provence (the northern part of Provence), but the SNCF opted for a better solution: The line passes west of these regions.

Did You Know?

Everything is Ready! (Tout est prêt!)

Françoise: Lève-toi, Mathieu! Allez, poussin.

Mathieu: Ouh, j'ai sommeil, maman!

Françoise: Oui, je sais, mais il faut se préparer. Tu te souviens? On va prendre le train et . . .

Mathieu: On va voir Sonia à la campagne!

Après la toilette et le petit déjeuner, dans le taxi.

Marc: Ah, on arrive. Monsieur, pouvez-vous vous garer près de l'entrée de la gare, là? Oui, merci. Combien je vous dois?

Françoise: Bon, j'y vais. Ouh! Quel froid ce matin!

Mathieu: Maman, où tu vas? Maman!!! Je veux venir avec toi!

Marc: Sois sage, Mathieu! Elle va acheter des croissants. Tiens, prends ton sac et ta valise.

Dans le hall de la gare Montparnasse, au guichet "Grandes lignes," Marc et son fils font la queue depuis un quart d'heure.

Marc: On va rater ce train! Cela fait une demi-heure qu'on attend! Ah . . . Bonjour, trois aller-retours pour Brest. Le prochain train.

Mathieu: Sois patient, papa. Voilà maman!

Marc: Ça y est, j'ai les billets. On a six minutes! Quai 1.

Sur le quai, les contrôleurs de la SNCF arrêtent les voyageurs.

Mathieu: Attendez-nous, monsieur Train!

Le contrôleur: Bonjour, vos billets, s'il vous plaît. Merci. C'est en tête de train, voiture 3. Montez maintenant, le train va bientôt partir.

Françoise: Allez, monte, Mathieu! Marc, prends-le avec toi.

Le coup de sifflet retentit, les portes du train se ferment automatiquement. Ils arrivent à leurs places dans un wagon non-fumeur de 2ème (deuxième) classe.

Marc: Ah! On a eu de la chance d'avoir trois places à côté. Mathieu, assieds-toi.

Mathieu: Je veux m'asseoir à côté de la fenêtre. Je veux voir le paysage.

Marc: Si tu veux changer de place, demande-le gentiment. Allez . . .

Just a few questions to make sure you're still with me. Decide: *vrai* (true) or *faux* (false).

a) Cette scène se passe le soir. *F - matin*

b) La famille prend le métro pour aller à la gare. *F - taxi*

c) Mathieu va acheter les croissants. *F - Maman*

d) Ils font la queue au guichet pendant une heure. *F (demi-quart heure)*

e) Leurs places se trouvent en fin de train. *F (à tête de train)*

Did You Know?

FRANCE *EN VÉLO* *(bike)*

One type of tourism on the rise in France is *cyclo-tourisme* (bike tourism), to the great satisfaction of environmentalists and the various regional tourist associations. The *conseils départementaux* (departmental councils) have been willing to do their part to make bike riding safer around France. As a result, many new bicycle tracks (*voies cyclables* or *voies vertes*) have been built. Even the SNCF started reorganizing its trains and stations, by making more room for the *vélos* or *bicyclettes* (bikes).

Did You Know?

WORKSHOP 1

THE NITTY-GRITTY

AS TIME GOES BY: EXPRESSING TIME USING *SINCE*, *DURING*, *AGO*, ETC.

The time has come to learn several useful ways of talking about time in French.

1. How long have you been doing it?

The expression *depuis* (since, ever since; for) expresses the starting time of an action or the length of time it has been taking place.

Je vais en Bretagne depuis trois ans.

I've been going to Brittany for three years.

Nous sommes ici depuis juin.

We've been here since June.

Note that *depuis* is used with the present tense in French.

Another expression that can be used with the same meaning is *il y a . . . que*.

Il y a trois ans que je vais en Bretagne.

I've been going to Brittany for three years.

Il y a six mois que nous sommes ici.

We've been here for six months.

The expression *cela fait . . . que* is equivalent to *il y a . . . que*.

Cela fait trois ans que je vais en Bretagne.

I've been going to Brittany for three years.

Cela fait six mois que nous sommes ici.

We've been here for six months.

The questions corresponding to *depuis, il y a . . . que* and *cela fait . . . que* are:

Depuis combien de temps vas-tu en Bretagne?

How long have you been going to Brittany?

Depuis quand êtes-vous ici?

Since when have you been here?

2. How long ago did you do it?

Use the expression *il y a . . .* when you want to express how long ago an action took place. The tense used in French is the *passé compose*.

Je suis allée en Bretagne il y a trois ans.

I went to Brittany three years ago.

Nous sommes arrivés à la campagne il y a une semaine.

We arrived in the country a week ago.

To ask a question about *il y a* use *quand* (when; how long ago):

Quand es-tu allée en Bretagne?

When did you go to Brittany?

Quand êtes-vous arrivés?

When did you arrive?

3. To express a duration of time, use *pendant* or *durant*, which both mean "during; for."

Ils ont voyagé pendant six heures.

They traveled for six hours.

Ils sont en vacances pendant l'été.

They are on vacation during the summer.

Le train s'est arrêté durant trois minutes.

The train stopped for three minutes.

To ask a question about *pendant* and *durant* use *pendant combien* (for how long)

Pendant combien de temps ont-ils voyagé?

For how long did they travel?

Pendant combien de temps sont-ils en vacances?

For how long are they on vacation?

Pendant combien de temps le train s'est-il arrêté?

For how long did the train stop?

Seem like too much information? Here it is, all in one quick-reference table.

EXPRESSIONS OF TIME		
	TIME EXPRESSION	CORRESPONDING QUESTION
since, ever since, for	*depuis . . .* *il y a . . . que . . .* *cela fait . . . que . . .*	*depuis combien de temps?, quand . . . ?*
. . . ago	*il y a . . .*	*quand . . . ?*
during, for	*pendant . . .* *durant . . .*	*pendant combien de temps . . . ?*

ACTIVITY 2: TAKE IT FOR A SPIN

Fill in the gaps by inserting the appropriate time expression:

cela fait / il y a / depuis / pendant / depuis quand

a)   *Nous avons voyagé en deuxième classe* _pendant_ *tout le voyage .*

b)   _depuis quand_ *font-ils la queue?*

c)   *Il s'est installé à la campagne* _il y a_ *un an.*

d)   _cela fait_ *deux ans qu'elle est contrôleur à la SNCF.*

e)   *Je prends le train tous les matins* _cela fait_ *le début de septembre.*
     depuis

TAKE A SEAT, PLEASE: THE VERB S'ASSEOIR (TO SIT DOWN) IN THE PRESENT AND PAST TENSES, AND THE IMPERATIVE

1. The Present Tense of s'asseoir (to sit down)

Not only is the verb *s'asseoir* irregular, but it also has two forms of conjugation in the present tense. What's next?! I'm sorry to say that both forms are used frequently, which means you need to learn them both. As for the *nous, vous* and *ils / elles* forms, the second set consisting of *asseyons / asseyez / asseyent* is more common.

THE PRESENT TENSE OF THE VERB S'ASSEOIR (TO SIT DOWN)			
je m'assois	nous nous assoyons	je m'assieds	nous nous asseyons
tu t'assois	vous vous assoyez	tu t'assieds	vous vous asseyez
il / elle s'assoit	ils / elles s'assoient	il / elle s'assied	ils / elles s'asseyent

2. The Passé Composé of s'asseoir (to sit down)

In the *passé composé, s'asseoir* is used with *être* for two reasons. First, it's a reflexive verb and second, it expresses a motion. So, don't forget about agreement.

What agreement? The past participle agrees in gender and number with the subject.

The past participle of *s'asseoir* is *assis* (masculine singular or plural) and *assise / assises* (feminine singular / plural).

THE *PASSÉ COMPOSÉ* OF THE VERB S'ASSEOIR (TO SIT DOWN)	
je me suis assis(e)	nous nous sommes assis(es)
tu t'es assis(e)	vous vous êtes assis(es)
il / elle s'est assis(e)	ils / elles se sont assis(es)

3. The Imperative Present of s'asseoir (to sit down)

In the imperative, *s'asseoir* has two forms just like in the present tense.

THE IMPERATIVE OF THE IRREGULAR VERB S'ASSEOIR (TO SIT DOWN)	
assois-toi	assieds-toi
assoyons-nous	asseyons-nous
assoyez-vous	asseyez-vous

The second form, *assieds-toi*, etc., is commonly used in everyday language.

Rewrite the sentences in the imperative form and then the *passé composé*:

a)   Nous nous asseyons dans le taxi.

asseyons nous · · · *,*   *Nous nous sommes assis*

b)   Rico, tu t'assieds et tu me dis tout maintenant.

assieds toi et dis moi   *Rico, tu t'es t'assis et tu de m'as dis*

c)   Vous vous asseyez dans une voiture non-fumeur du train.

asseyez vous vous   *Vous vous êtes assis* · · ·

WORDS TO LIVE BY

THERE ARE NO MORE SEASONS!: TALKING ABOUT THE WEATHER AND SEASONS

Here's a common comment—*Il n'y a plus de saisons!* (There are no more seasons!) Whether you agree or not, it refers to the seasons and the weather, the very subjects of this section.

By the way, the French word *le temps* means both "weather" and "time."

1. The Seasons

These are the names for the four *saisons* in French:

THE SEASONS			
l'hiver	*le printemps*	*l'été*	*l'automne*
winter	spring	summer	fall

And too quickly, we are back to *l'hiver* again!

In French, the names of seasons are masculine, just like those of the months of the year and the days of the week.

The preposition *en* precedes the names of seasons, again, just like the names of the months, e.g., *en hiver* (in winter), *en été* (in summer), *en automne* (in fall). The only exception is the word for spring, *printemps*, which is used with *au*. So, it's *au printemps* (in spring). Don't ask why . . .

Here are some examples:

Noël est en hiver.

Christmas is in winter.

Avril est au printemps.

April is in spring.

En été, beaucoup de gens sont en vacances.

In the summer, a lot of people are on vacation.

En automne, c'est la rentrée.

In the fall, it's the back-to-school / work time.

2. The Weather Report

Want to know the *météo* (weather report)? If you want to talk about the weather in French, the most useful expression is *il fait . . .* Most weather expressions use it. Let's see:

THE WEATHER, PART I					
Il fait froid.	*Il fait beau.*	*Il fait humide.*	*Il fait chaud.*	*Il fait du vent.*	*Il fait nuageux.*
It's cold.	It's nice.	It's humid.	It's hot.	It's windy.	It's cloudy.

Il ne fait pas froid.	It's not cold.
Est-ce qu'il a fait beau?	Has the weather been nice?
Il fait trop humide!	It's too humid!
Il ne fait pas très chaud.	It's not very hot.
Fait-il du vent?	Is there any wind?

By the way, you can also say:

Il y a du vent.	It's windy.

Or . . .

Il y a des nuages.	It's cloudy.

In other cases, you need a specific verb, such as *pleuvoir* (to rain), an irregular verb, and *neiger* (to snow), a regular verb. Both verbs are used with *il*.

THE WEATHER, PART II	
Il pleut.	*Il neige.*
It's raining.	It's snowing.

Il ne pleut pas.	It isn't raining.
Est-ce qu'il a plu?	Has it rained?
Va-t-il neiger?	Is it going to snow?
Il n'a pas neigé cet hiver.	It didn't snow this winter.

And if you need to ask a question:

Quel temps fait-il?	What is the weather like?
Quel temps fera-t-il demain?	What will the weather be like tomorrow?
Quel temps a-t-il fait hier?	What was the weather like yesterday?

And, as a result of the weather, you may have to say:

J'ai chaud.	I'm hot.
J'ai froid.	I'm cold.

Make sure that you use the verb *avoir* (to have) in these expressions and not *to be* as you would in English.

It's always a good idea to get the information about the weather before your *voyage* (trip). As mentioned earlier, *les voyages en train* (train trips) are very common in France. You can go everywhere by train, although you may have to *changer de train* (switch trains) a couple of times. *Ne râtez pas votre train* (don't miss your train)! I know this can be hard when you take an early train. *Il faut se lever tôt*, that is, you have to get up early, and chances are that you'll have to rush (*se précipiter*) anyway.

By the way, here are some common "morning" expressions:

J'ai sommeil!	I'm sleepy!
Debout!	Get up!

Or:

Lève-toi!	Get up!

Then:

prendre le petit déjeuner	to have breakfast
se doucher	to take a shower
se laver	to wash oneself

Of course, a smart thing to do is to buy your *billet de train* (train ticket) in advance. There are several possibilities: *Sur le minitel ou le web* . . . or you can buy a ticket *à la gare* (at the train station), a SNCF office or a travel agency (which may take a small commission for its service).

Now, let's see what you need to say to buy a train ticket:

Je voudrais aller à Brest.	I'd like to go to Brest.

Or:

Il me faut un aller pour Brest.	I need a one-way (ticket) to Brest.

Or:

J'ai besoin d'un aller-retour pour Brest en deuxième classe.

I need a round-trip (ticket) to Brest, second class.

There are two classes: *la première* (first) and *la deuxième classe* (second class). Then:

Je préfère une place non-fumeur, s'il vous plaît.

I prefer a non-smoking seat, please.

Côté fenêtre ou côté couloir, ça m'est égal.

Window or aisle, it doesn't matter to me.

And:

Est-ce que vous avez les horaires des trains pour Brest?

Do you have the train schedule for Brest?

Y-a-t-il des trains directs pour Brest?

Are there any direct trains to Brest?

Y-a-t-il des changements?

Do you need to change trains?

Finally . . .

À quelle heure part le prochain train pour Brest?

At what time does the next train to Brest leave?

De quel quai part le prochain train pour Brest?

From which platform does the next train to Brest leave?

If you have only a few minutes left, you'd better run . . .

And as they say, *quand le coup de sifflet retentit,* when the whistle blows, *attention à la fermeture automatique des portes!* Be careful of the automatic closing of the train doors!

Did You Know?

The SNCF, the French national railways, offers many different prices for the same trip. It depends, for example, upon how long in advance you buy your ticket, what time of the day you're traveling (*période normale* "off hours" vs. *période de pointe* "peak hours") or on whether you're spending a week-end in the place of your destination or not. The truth is that the French are getting confused with all the different *tarifs*! I suggest you buy your ticket from a SNCF clerk *à la gare* (at the station). It may save you some euros.

TGV and Eurostar trains require a reservation, for which you are charged an additional fee. For other trains, a reservation is not required but you can make one if you wish to have *une place* (a seat) assigned to you. You may be asked to show your ticket on the train or on the platform before entering the train.

Here's more vocabulary you can use at the railway station:

descendre du train	*to get off the train*
monter dans le train	*to get on the train*
le couloir	*aisle; hallway*
le contrôleur	*inspector*

en queue de train	at the end of the train
en tête de train	at the beginning of the train
la fenêtre	window
le hall de gare	station terminal
un horaire	schedule
le paysage	countryside; scenery
le tableau d'affichage / des horaires	schedule, timetable
la valise	suitcase

Look for the following signs:

| Trains à l'arrivée | arrivals (Lit. arriving trains) |
| Trains au départ | departures (Lit. departing trains) |

Or simply: *arrivée* and *départ*.
    Biking around:

| la piste cyclable, la voie cyclable | bicycle track |
| le vélo / la bicyclette | bike, bicycle |

ACTIVITY 4: TAKE IT FOR A SPIN

Pick the words that are feminine.

    les gares / les croissants / les places / les contrôleurs / les saisons / les vents /
    les automnes / les portes / les têtes / les coups de sifflet

ACTIVITY 5: TAKE IT FOR A SPIN

Marc is buying the train tickets *à la gare Montparnasse*. He's missing some words. Can you fill them in?

couloir / billets / de crédit / aller-retour / -fumeur / à côté / aller-retours / retour / quai / direct / fenêtre / classe / part

— Bonjour Monsieur, je voudrais (I would like) trois billets *aller-retours* pour Brest. Pour un départ à 7h30 et un retour lundi vers 16h.
— Oui, vous voulez voyager en quelle *classe* ? *à côté*
— En deuxième. Si possible trois places *couloir*. En non-*fumeur*.
— Voilà, trois *aller-retours* sur le Paris-Brest, départ à 7h30 et *retour* lundi à 16h06. Vous avez une place côté *fenêtre* et deux places côté *couloir*. C'est bon?
— Parfait. Doit-on changer de train?
— Non, c'est un train *direct*. Alors, ça fait 200 euros. Vous payez comment?
— Avec ma carte *de crédit*. Voici.
— Merci. Voilà vos trois *billets*. Le train *part* dans sept minutes du *quai* 1. Bon voyage!

Françoise, Marc, and *leur fils* arrive at their friends' *maison de campagne* (country house) in Brittany. Françoise, Frédérique, Étienne, Marianne and Wolfgang *finissent de déjeuner*. In front of the house, *les enfants*, Sonia *et* Mathieu, *s'amusent*, whereas Marc *fait la sieste* (is taking a nap).

HEAR . . . SAY 2

Listen to Nature's Silence!   (Écoute le silence de la nature!)

Frédérique:	Bon, je vais faire du café. Qui en veut?
Étienne:	Tout le monde. Et Alice, où est-elle?
Frédérique:	Elle est allée se promener à vélo. Ça lui fait du bien de prendre l'air.

Un peu plus tard, durant la promenade de l'après-midi:

Wolfgang:	Ah! Quel bel après-midi d'octobre!
Étienne:	Nous aimons tant cette région. Comme l'air de l'automne sent bon!
Frédérique:	Oui, c'est très agréable, mais il fait très humide. Cela vous dit, ce soir, de dîner à la crêperie en ville?
Marianne:	Quelle bonne idée! Comme ça, pas de cuisine. Tenez, ce n'est pas Alice là-bas?

Alice, la fille de vingt ans de Frédérique, arrive à bicyclette.

Alice:	Alors, Françoise et Marc ne sont pas venus avec vous?
Sonia:	Alice! Ils sont allés faire du cheval. Mais pas Mathieu. Tu sais, ce soir on va tous manger des crêpes. Viens avec nous!
Alice:	Quelle bonne idée! Pas de vaisselle à faire!
Étienne:	Toujours avec ce walkman! Mais, Alice, écoute le silence de la nature! Comment veux-tu . . . Ouh! Je sens des gouttes.
Alice et les enfants:	(Ils rigolent.) Il pleut, il pleut!
Frédérique:	Ça commence à tomber. Sauve qui peut!

ACTIVITY 6:   HOW'S THAT AGAIN?

Please answer the following questions.

a) *Est-ce que les amis viennent de finir de dîner?*

b) *Que fait Marc?*

c) *Où sont Sonia et Mathieu?*

d)   *Que fait la fille de Frédérique?*   *Elle arrive à bicyclette.*
e)   *Quelle saison est-ce?*   — *en automne*
f)   *Quel temps fait-il à la fin de la scène?*   *Il pleut.*

Did You Know?

WELCOME TO BREST, BRITTANY.

Brest is one of two major towns in Brittany. It is accessible from Paris *par le TGV* or *par avion*. The region of North Finistère, where Brest is located, provides some breathtaking scenery consisting of almost 700 miles of coastline. Its international ports attract fishers and sailors from all over, and numerous sailing events take place in the region. Since 1990, there has been a new attraction, Océanopolis, the premier European ocean discovery theme park and a fantastic complex paying tribute to the underwater world.

Did You Know?

WORKSHOP 2

THE NITTY-GRITTY

I SCREAM, YOU SCREAM: **THE IRREGULAR VERBS *VENIR* (TO COME), *TENIR* (TO HOLD), AND *SE SOUVENIR* (TO REMEMBER) IN THE PAST TENSE AND THE IMPERATIVE**

1. The Irregular Verbs venir *(to come)* and tenir *(to hold)* in the Passé Composé

The past participles of the verbs *venir* and *tenir* and their derivative, *se souvenir* (to remember), are formed by simply dropping the ending *–ir* and adding the ending *–u*. Not that bad, right?

Ils ne sont pas venus avec vous?

They didn't come with you?

Il a tenu la porte.

He held the door.

Vous vous êtes souvenu de Sonia?

Did you remember Sonia?

Note that *venir*, being a verb expressing a motion, uses *être* in the *passé composé*. So does the reflexive verb *se souvenir*. You know what that means: The participles must agree in gender and number with the subject.

THE *PASSÉ COMPOSÉ* OF THE VERB *VENIR* (TO COME)	
je suis venu(e)	*nous sommes venu(e)s*
tu es venu(e)	*vous êtes venu(e)s*
il / elle est venu(e)	*ils / elles sont venu(e)s*

THE *PASSÉ COMPOSÉ* OF THE VERB *TENIR* (TO HOLD)	
j'ai tenu	*nous avons tenu*
tu as tenu	*vous avez tenu*
il / elle a tenu	*ils / elles ont tenu*

ACTIVITY 7: TAKE IT FOR A SPIN

Write down all the different forms of *se souvenir* in the *passé composé*. Just look at *venir* and you'll see, it's not difficult at all.

2. The Verbs venir, tenir, and se souvenir in the Imperative

The easiest tense! (You remember—only three persons, *tu, nous, vous*, which are taken from the present tense.)

Tiens ça!

Hold this!

Viens avec nous!

Come with us!

The imperative tense of *se souvenir* is like *venir*, except for the fact that it comes with a reflexive pronoun attached to the end of the verb with a hyphen.

THE IMPERATIVE OF THE VERBS *VENIR* (TO COME) AND *SE SOUVENIR* (TO REMEMBER)	
Viens!	*Souviens-toi!*
Venons!	*Souvenons-nous!*
Venez!	*Souvenez-vous!*

Souvenons-nous de cet automne!

Let's remember this fall!

HOW PERFECT! USING EXCLAMATIONS WITH *QUEL* (WHAT) AND *COMME* (HOW)

The use of *quel* (what) and *comme* (how) depends on the sentence.

1. What a Beautiful Day!

You know *quel?* as a question word meaning "what" or "which." It is an adjective always followed by a noun with which it must, of course, agree in gender and number. Its different forms are *quel* (masculine singular), *quelle* (feminine singular), *quels* (masculine plural) and *quelles* (feminine plural).

Quel is also commonly used in exclamations, similar to English "what." Take a look at the examples:

Quelle belle journée d'automne!

What a beautiful fall day!

Quelle bonne idée!

What a good idea!

Quel bel après-midi d'octobre!

What a beautiful October afternoon!

The Fine Print

Note the expression *bel après-midi* (beautiful afternoon) in the last example. *Bel* is a form of *beau* (beautiful) used in front of masculine nouns starting with a vowel. The feminine form of the adjective is *belle*. And by the way, the word *après-midi* can also be feminine, so you could also write *belle après-midi*, without a change in meaning or pronunciation.

2. How Interesting!

Comme (how) is another useful word to know when it comes to exclamations. Take a look:

Comme il fait froid!

How cold it is!

Comme il pleut!

How hard it's raining!

Comme on s'est précipité!

How we rushed!

These sentences are a mess! Can you correct them?

a) *Quel il faisons beau aujourd'hui!* ~~fait~~
b) *Quelle belle temps!* ~~beaux~~
c) *Comme elle fait chaud!* ~~il~~
d) *Quel il pleut en Bretagne!* ~~Comme~~
e) *Quel le train va vite!* ~~Quand~~
f) *Comme fait cela du bien!* ~~Quel~~

Comme vous êtes merveilleux! How wonderful you are!

WORDS TO LIVE BY

A SUNDAY IN THE COUNTRY: TALKING ABOUT THE WEEKEND IN THE COUNTRYSIDE

Enfin . . . Our friends are away from Paris, in the beautiful *campagne bretonne*! And here are all the simple things you can enjoy when you go back to Mother Nature. *Ça fait du bien!* It feels so good!

faire du vélo / de la bicyclette	to ride a bike
faire du cheval	to go horseback riding
faire une sieste	to take a nap

Or:

prendre l'air	to get some fresh air
respirer	to breathe
se promener	to go for a walk
le brouillard	fog
la feuille morte	fallen leaf (Lit. dead leaf)
les gouttes de pluie	raindrops
le silence	silence

En Bretagne, these pleasures often get interrupted by the rain. But on a quiet fall weekend, it can be so *amusant* (fun) to run *sous la pluie* (in the rain).

Word on the Street

Here are a few very colloquial and sometimes quite colorful ways of saying *il pleut* (it's raining):

Ça commence à tomber!	It's starting to rain. (Lit. It's starting to fall.)
Il tombe des cordes!	It's raining hard! (Lit. It's raining ropes.)
Il pleut comme vache qui pisse!	It's raining cats and dogs. (Lit. It's raining like a peeing cow.)

LET'S PUT IT IN WRITING

And now, enjoy a few beautiful lines from the famous poem *"Chanson d'automne"* ("An autumn song"):

> *Et je m'en vais*
> *   Au vent mauvais*
> *Qui m'emporte*
> *   Deça, delà*
> *Pareil à la feuille morte.*
> —PAUL VERLAINE *(1844–1896)*

And if this has whetted your appetite for more beautiful verse in French, go to this Web site: www.poesie.webnet.fr.

ACTIVITY 9: TAKE IT FOR A SPIN

Gather all the words you've learned in this lesson that remind you of fall. A few of them appear in the verses you just read.

ACTIVITY 10: TAKE IT UP A NOTCH

Quel temps fait-il? Here's a chart with a weather report for a week. Today is *samedi 14 avril.* Look at the chart and then answer the questions that follow.

LES JOURS	lundi	mardi	mercredi	jeudi	vendredi	samedi	dimanche
LA MÉTÉO							

- a) *Quel temps fait-il aujourd'hui?*
- b) *Quel temps a-t-il fait hier?*
- c) *Est-ce qu'il va pleuvoir dimanche 15 avril?*
- d) *Est-ce qu'il a plu jeudi 12 avril?*
- e) *Quels jours ont été nuageux cette semaine?*
- f) *Est-ce qu'il a plu toute la semaine?*

CRIB NOTES

Françoise:	Get up, Mathieu! C'mon, sweetie.
Mathieu:	Oh, I'm sleepy, Mommy!
Françoise:	Yes, I know, but we need to get ready. Do you remember? We're taking the train and . . .
Mathieu:	We're going to see Sonia in the country!

After washing up and breakfast, in the taxicab.

Marc:	Good, we're here. Sir, could you park near the station entrance, there? Yes, thank you. How much do I owe you?
Françoise:	All right, I'm going. Oh! How cold it is this morning!
Mathieu:	Mommy, where're you going? Mommy! I want to come with you!
Marc:	Behave, Mathieu! She's going to buy some croissants. Here, take your bag and your suitcase.

At the terminal of the Montparnasse station, at the "Long distance trains" ticket desk, Marc and his son have been waiting on line for a quarter of an hour.

Marc:	We're going to miss that train! We've been waiting for half an hour already! Finally . . . Hello, three round-trips for Brest—the next train.
Mathieu:	Be patient, Dad. Here comes Mommy!
Marc:	Here, I have the tickets. We have six minutes. Platform 1.

On the platform, the SNCF inspectors stop the passengers.

Mathieu:	Wait for us, Mister Train!
The inspector:	Good morning, tickets, please. Thank you. It's at the head of the train, car 3. Get in now, the train is leaving soon.
Françoise:	C'mon, get in, Mathieu! Marc, take him with you.

The whistle blows; the doors shut automatically. They arrive at their seats in a non-smoking second-class car.

Marc:	Oh! We were lucky to get three seats next to each other. Mathieu, sit down.
Mathieu:	I want to sit next to the window. I want to see the countryside.
Marc:	If you want to change seats, ask nicely. C'mon . . .

Frédérique:	Well, I'm going to make some coffee. Who wants some?
Étienne:	Everyone. Where's Alice?
Frédérique:	She went for a ride on her bike. It's good for her to get some fresh air.

Later on, during the afternoon walk . . .

Wolfgang:	Ah! What a beautiful October afternoon!
Étienne:	We like this region so much. The autumn air smells so good!
Frédérique:	Yes, it's very pleasant, but it's very humid. How about having dinner at the *crêperie* in town this evening?
Marianne:	What a good idea! That way, no cooking. Look, isn't that Alice up there?

Alice, Frédérique's 20-year-old daughter, arrives on her bike.

Alice:	So, Françoise and Marc didn't come with you?
Sonia:	Alice! They went horseback riding. But not Mathieu. You know, this evening we are all going to eat crêpes. Come with us!
Alice:	What a good idea! No dishes to wash!
Étienne:	Always with a walkman! But, Alice, listen to the silence of nature! How do you expect . . . Oh! I feel raindrops.
Alice and the children:	(They laugh.) It's raining, it's raining!
Frédérique:	It's starting to rain. Run for your life!

ACTIVITY 1

a) FAUX. Cette scène se passe le matin.
b) FAUX. La famille prend un taxi pour aller à la gare.
c) FAUX. Françoise va acheter les croissants.
d) FAUX. Ils font la queue au guichet pendant un quart d'heure.
e) FAUX. Leurs places se trouvent en tête de train.

ACTIVITY 2

a) Nous avons voyagé en deuxième classe pendant tout le voyage.
b) Depuis quand font-ils la queue?
c) Il s'est installé à la campagne il y a un an.
d) Cela fait deux ans qu'elle est contrôleur à la SNCF.
e) Je prends le train tous les matins depuis le début de septembre.

ACTIVITY 3

a) Asseyons-nous dans le taxi. / Nous nous sommes assis(es) dans le taxi.
b) Rico, assieds-toi et dis-moi tout maintenant. / Rico, tu t'es assis et tu m'as tout dit.
c) Asseyez-vous dans une voiture non-fumeur du train. / Vous vous êtes assis(es) dans une voiture non-fumeur du train.

ACTIVITY 4

la gare / la place / la saison / la porte / la tête

ACTIVITY 5

—Bonjour Monsieur, je voudrais trois billets aller-retour pour Brest. Pour un départ à 7h30 et un retour lundi vers 16h.
—Oui, vous voulez voyager en quelle classe?
—En deuxième. Si possible trois places à côté. En non-fumeur.
—Voilà, trois aller-retours sur le Paris-Brest, départ à 7h30 et retour lundi à 16h06. Vous avez une place côté fenêtre et deux places côté couloir. C'est bon?
—Parfait. Doit-on changer de train?

—Non, c'est un train direct. Alors, ça fait 200 euros. Vous payez comment?
—Avec ma carte de crédit. Voici.
—Merci. Voilà vos trois billets. Le train part dans sept minutes du quai 1. Bon voyage!

ACTIVITY 6

a) Non, ils viennent de finir de déjeuner.
b) Marc fait la sieste / se repose.
c) Sonia et Mathieu sont dehors, ils s'amusent.
d) La fille de Frédérique se promène à vélo / bicyclette.
e) C'est l'automne.
f) À la fin de la scène, il pleut.

ACTIVITY 7

je me suis souvenu(e) / tu t'es souvenu(e) / il s'est souvenu / elle s'est souvenue / nous nous sommes souvenu(e)s / vous vous êtes souvenu(e)s / ils se sont souvenus / elles se sont souvenues

ACTIVITY 8

a) Comme il fait beau aujourd'hui!
b) Quel beau temps!
c) Comme il fait chaud!
d) Comme il pleut en Bretagne!
e) Comme le train va vite!
f) Comme cela fait du bien!

ACTIVITY 9

la pluie, la feuille morte, l'automne, octobre, le vent, humide, le brouillard

ACTIVITY 10

a) Aujourd'hui, samedi 14 avril, il fait beau, mais il y a des nuages.
b) Hier, vendredi 13 avril, il a plu.
c) Non, dimanche 15 avril, il va faire beau.
d) Non, jeudi 12 avril, il a fait nuageux.
e) Mardi et jeudi, il a fait nuageux.
f) Non, il a fait beau lundi, mercredi et aujourd'hui, samedi.

13. THE PORT OF SHADOWS

Le quai des brumes

I do, Camille, I feel sick! Very sick!

COMING UP. . .

- *Lights, camera, action!*: Talking about acting and theater
- *More or less the same*: Making comparisons
- *What will be, will be*: Talking about the future
- *I scream, you scream*: The irregular verb *partir* (to leave) and its look-alikes
- *Write that down*: The irregular verbs *écrire* (to write) and *lire* (to read)

IN THE SPOTLIGHT

The film *Le quai des brumes* (*The River Bank in the Mist*), directed in 1938 by internationally acclaimed director Marcel Carné, is based on a *scénario* by *le poète* Jacques Prévert. It features the big stars of the classic French film, Jean Gabin and Michèle Morgan. The film, representative of Carné's work, depicts a pessimistic picture of life where evil battles good and wins, while eternal love is doomed. In answer to those who reproached him for this pessimism, Carné said that the artist is "the barometer of his or her time and shouldn't be held responsible for the tempests he or she announces." In 1940, Paris fell under German occupation.

LOOKING AHEAD

You're in Lesson 13—already! I decided we should celebrate, so I made this chapter *le chapitre du théâtre* (theater), *de la poésie* (poetry), and *des mots* (words).

In the dialogues, *deux acteurs répètent* (two actors are rehearsing), one on one, for a stage production of *Orphée* (*Orpheus*), a play written by the great French artist Jean Cocteau. Cocteau's surrealist play is a unique adaptation of the Greek myth of Orpheus, a man in search of his beloved, deceased wife, Eurydice. Determined to bring her back, Orpheus faces the greatest *perils* (dangers).

Camille et Émile répètent la scène finale d'Orphée. Émile interprète (interprets / is) *Orphée et Camille interprète Eurydice. Émile a du mal à se concentrer* (has trouble concentrating) on his part because he is deeply *déprimé* (depressed) and heartbroken: *Son amie l'a quitté* (his girlfriend left him). Camille is trying to get him to work. Later on, they have to rehearse *au théâtre* with other *acteurs* (actors) in front of the *metteur en scène* (director) and the *producteur* (producer).

Did You Know?

JEAN COCTEAU

Jean Cocteau (1889–1963) was the embodiment of the French avant-garde of the first half of the 20th century. He was a poet, a writer, a playwright, a scriptwriter, a director, and a painter.

His first film, in 1930, was *Le sang d'un poète* (*The Blood of a Poet*) based on a play he wrote; then came *La Belle et la Bête* (*The Beauty and the Beast*), and in 1950, *Orphée* (*Orpheus*), also based on his own play, starring Maria Casares, Jean Marais, and Marie Dea. He created movies as a poet writes poetry, using imagination in the place of technology.

Did You Know?

Let's Rehearse!   (Répétons!)

Émile: La vie est bizarre. Un jour, tu es heureux, tu es aimé et tu aimes. Mais le jour suivant . . .

Camille: Mais elle t'appellera, Émile. Allez, répétons!

Émile: "Le silence avance à reculons." Tu vois, Cocteau a toujours su. Mais est-ce qu'il est meilleur que moi? Ah, que faire?

Camille: Le mieux, Émile, est de te concentrer sur ton rôle.

Émile: Oui. "Tu ne te sens pas mal?" Hmmm . . . "Tu ne te sens pas mal?"

Camille: "Non . . ."

Émile: Moi, oui, Camille, je me sens mal! Très mal!

Camille: Émile, ça suffit! Tino et Clavier seront super en colère ce soir! Ils finiront le spectacle sans nous. Ce sera pire . . .

Émile: Qu'importe, c'est mon dernier spectacle! Puis, je partirai au bout du monde. Dans un pays sans femmes! Elle aura la paix.

Camille: Mais Émile, tu es le plus talentueux des Orphées, tu . . .

Émile: Tu crois? Oui . . . "Mes livres ne s'écrivent pas tout seuls."

Camille: "Tes livres s'écrivent tout seuls . . ."

Émile: "Je les aide. Comment se comporte le garçon?"

Camille: "Orphée, c'est . . ."

Émile: "Il sera aussi insupportable que son père." Dis, Camille, on ira boire un pot après la répétition?

Camille: Jason sera là ce soir.

Émile: Tu as Jason, toi. C'est bien. Je suis heureux pour vous.

Le portable de Camille sonne.

Camille: Allo? Monsieur Clavier? Tout marche bien. On répète avec Émile là . . . Nous serons prêts, bien sûr. À ce soir.

ACTIVITY 1:   HOW'S THAT AGAIN?

Please answer the following questions:

  a) *Que font les deux acteurs?*
  b) *Quels sont les rôles des deux acteurs?*
  c) *Est-ce qu'Émile est concentré?*
  d) *Que veut faire Émile après la répétition?*
  e) *Que se passe-t-il à la fin du dialogue?*

Did You Know?

WORKSHOP 1

THE NITTY-GRITTY

MORE OR LESS THE SAME: MAKING COMPARISONS

1. You're Better than I Am: Comparative Form of Adjectives

When we say, "She's taller than he is," we make a comparison. The comparison between two objects or two people usually involves two adjectives or two adverbs, which in English, take a special form—*taller* instead of *tall*, for example.

This "comparative of superiority" can also be expressed using *more . . . than* in English. For instance, "Camille is more talented than Émile." French always uses the equivalent of these English words when making comparisons. *More . . . than* in French is *plus . . . que*. For once, French is simpler! Take a look at the examples:

Camille est plus talentueuse que cette actrice.

Camille is more talented than this actress.

La pièce est plus intéressante que le scénario.

The play is more interesting than the script.

Camille est plus heureuse qu'Émile.

Camille is happier than Émile.

To express a "comparative of inferiority," English uses *less . . . than*, while the French equivalent is *moins . . . que*. For example:

Ce théâtre est moins grand que l'autre.

This theater is less large than the other.

Émile est moins concentré que Camille.

Émile is less focused than Camille.

Il se sent moins fatigué que les autres acteurs.

He feels less tired than the other actors.

Finally, to express a "comparative of equality," English uses *as . . . as*, while the French equivalent is *aussi . . . que*. For example:

Notre travail est aussi important que votre oeuvre.

Our work is as important as your piece.

Il sera aussi insupportable que son père. (Jean Cocteau)

He'll be as unbearable as his father.

Note that it is also possible to omit the second part of the comparison phrase introduced by *que*, just as in English.

Tu es aussi déprimé.

You are as depressed.

Aujourd'hui, tu es moins concentrée.

Today, you are less focused.

Heads Up!

Of course, there are also irregular comparatives. The most notable ones are the adjectives *bon* (good) and *mauvais* (bad).

Heads Up!

THE COMPARATIVE FORMS OF THE ADJECTIVES *BON* (GOOD) AND *MAUVAIS* (BAD)			
bon (good)	meilleur (better)	moins bon (less good)	aussi bon (as good)
mauvais (bad)	pire / plus mauvais (worse)	moins mauvais (less bad)	aussi mauvais (as bad)

Cet écrivain est meilleur que l'auteur de ce livre.

This writer is better than the author of this book.

The adjective *mauvais* is a bit tricky. The regular form of the comparative, *plus mauvais* (worse), is used with concrete objects, while the irregular form of the comparative, *pire* (worse), is used with abstract ideas.

Ce texte est plus mauvais que celui-là.

This text is worse than that one.

Les souffrances de l'amour sont pires que tout.

Love troubles are worse than anything.

ACTIVITY 2: **TAKE IT FOR A SPIN**

Who's better? Let's see . . . Write these sentences using the comparative form of the adjectives. Example:

Les enfants sont de bons acteurs / les adultes. (plus) →
Les enfants sont de meilleurs acteurs que les adultes.

a) *Elles sont talentueuses / leurs amies. (plus)*
b) *Il veut être bon acteur / lui. (plus)*
c) *Nous allons vite / eux. (moins)*
d) *Elles récitent le texte bien / toi. (moins)*
e) *Cet écrivain est intéressant / celui-ci. (aussi)*

2. You're the Best: Superlative Forms of Adjectives

When we want to say that an object or a person are one of a kind, we use the superlative, as in "He's *the best*." Again, we can say that something is the best of all (superlative of superiority), by using *le plus* (the most), or that something is the worst of all (superlative of inferiority), by using *le moins* (the least). *Le plus* or *le moins* can be followed by *de . . .* (of . . .) if we wish to name the item we are comparing an object or a person to.

For example:

Elle est la meilleure actrice.

She's the best actress.

Nous avons joué la plus mauvaise pièce de l'année.

We played the worst play of the year.

C'est le théâtre le moins vieux de la ville.

This is the least old theater in town.

Remember, the superlative forms are:

le / la / les + plus + adjective (+ de . . .)

le / la / les + moins + adjective (+ de . . .)

Heads Up!

Again, *bon* (good) and *mauvais* (bad) have irregular superlatives, but only those of superiority.

Heads Up!

THE SUPERLATIVE FORMS OF THE ADJECTIVES *BON* (GOOD) AND *MAUVAIS* (BAD)		
bon (good)	*le / la / les meilleur(e)(s)* (the best)	*le / la / les moins bon(ne)(s)* (the least good)
mauvais (bad)	*le / la / les pire(s)* or *le / la / les plus mauvais(e)(s)* (the worst)	*le / la / les moins mauvais(e)(s)* (the least bad)

Again, if the compared object is a concrete object, the regular superlative is used, *le plus mauvais* (the worst); if it is an abstract object, the superlative is irregular, *le pire* (the worst).

Le pire problème est l'ignorance.

The worst problem is ignorance.

Tu as fait le plus mauvais travail.

You did the worst work.

ACTIVITY 3: TAKE IT FOR A SPIN

Put the words in the right order to create sentences.

a) vous / jeunes / que / moins / sommes / nous.
b) intéressant / est / film / moins / ce.
c) plus / les / Molière / de / sont / faciles / textes.
d) ses / sont / meilleurs / les / films.
e) que / dramatiques / sont / de / celles-là / auteur / cet / pièces / les / aussi.

3. Faster!: Comparative and Superlative Forms of Adverbs

Fast is an adverb, and *faster* is its comparative form. The comparatives and superlatives of adverbs are formed just like those of adjectives.

The comparative of superiority: *plus* + adverb (+ *que* . . .)

Mais parlez plus fort!

But speak louder!

The comparative of inferiority: *moins* + adverb (+ *que* . . .)

Tu travailles moins sérieusement qu'au début.

You work less seriously than in the beginning.

The comparative of equality: *aussi* + adverb (+ *que* . . .)

Il l'aime aussi passionnément que son ancienne amie.

He loves her as passionately as his former girlfriend.

The superlative of superiority: *le plus* + adverb

Marche le plus lentement possible.

Walk as slowly as you can.

The superlative of inferiority: *le moins* + adverb

Il travaille le moins soigneusement.

He works the least carefully.

Heads Up!

Four adverbs have irregular forms of comparative and superlative.

Heads Up!

	BEAUCOUP (A LOT)	PEU (A LITTLE)	BIEN (WELL)	MAL (BADLY)
ADVERBS WITH IRREGULAR FORMS OF COMPARATIVE AND SUPERLATIVE				
COMPARATIVE FORMS	plus (more)	moins (less)	mieux (better)	pire (worse)
SUPERLATIVE FORMS	le plus (the most)	le moins (the least)	le mieux (the best)	le pire (the worst)

C'est toi qu'elle aime le plus.

She loves you the most.

J'aime moins cette pièce que l'autre.

I like this play less than the other.

Tu vas aller mieux.

You are going to get better.

Word on the Street

Note the expressions *de mieux en mieux* (better and better) and *de pire en pire* (worse and worse).

Cela va de pire en pire.

This is getting worse and worse.

Elle joue de mieux en mieux.

She's acting better and better.

And now, for better or for worse, or as the French say, *pour le meilleur ou pour le pire*, let's learn how to talk about the future in French.

WHAT WILL BE, WILL BE: TALKING ABOUT THE FUTURE

1. The Future Tense of the Regular –er Verbs

Very simple: Just take the *–er* form of the verb (e.g., *concentrer* [concentrate] and add the future tense endings, which are:

For *je, tu, il / elle*: **–ai, –as, –a**.
For *nous, vous, ils / elles*: **–ons, –ez, –ont**.

Let's try it out: *concentrer + ai → concentrerai*.

THE FUTURE TENSE OF THE *–ER* VERB *SE CONCENTRER* (TO CONCENTRATE)			
je me concentrerai	I will concentrate	*nous nous concentrerons*	we will concentrate
tu te concentreras	you will concentrate	*vous vous concentrerez*	you will concentrate
il / elle se concentrera	he / she will concentrate	*ils / elles se concentreront*	they will concentrate

Heads Up!

Some verbs in *–er*, such as *appeler* (to call), modify their spelling slightly in the future.

THE FUTURE TENSE OF THE VERB *APPELER* (TO CALL)

j'appellerai	nous appellerons
tu appelleras	vous appellerez
il / elle appellera	ils / elles appelleront

This spelling modification affects the pronunciation: *app<u>e</u>ler* is (ah-p<u>uh</u>-leh) and *app<u>e</u>llerai*, etc., is (ah-p<u>eh</u>-luh-reh).

THE FUTURE TENSE OF THE VERB *RÉPÉTER* (TO REPEAT; TO REHEARSE)

je répèterai	nous répèterons
tu répèteras	vous répèterez
il / elle répètera	ils / elles répèteront

The accent on the second vowel changes from *–é* to *–è* in the future forms.

ACTIVITY 4: TAKE IT FOR A SPIN

So easy to do . . . *acheter* is just like *répéter*. Write down all its forms of the future tense.

2. The Future Tense of the Regular –ir and –re Verbs

There are no complications at all for these verbs. (Can you believe it?)

The endings are exactly the same as before, so all you do is add them to the *–ir* or *–re* form of the verb, e.g., *finir* (to finish).

For *je, tu, il / elle*: **–ai, –as, –a**.
For *nous, vous, ils / elles*: **–ons, –ez, –ont**.

THE FUTURE TENSE OF THE REGULAR *–IR* VERB *FINIR* (TO FINISH)

je finirai	I will finish	nous finirons	we will finish
tu finiras	you will finish	vous finirez	you will finish
il / elle finira	he / she will finish	ils / elles finiront	they will finish

For *–re* verbs, you need to drop the final "e" before you add the endings.

THE FUTURE TENSE OF THE REGULAR *–RE* VERB *ATTENDRE* (TO WAIT)			
j'attendrai	I will wait	*nous attendrons*	we will wait
tu attendras	you will wait	*vous attendrez*	you will wait
il / elle attendra	he / she will wait	*ils / elles attendront*	they will wait

3. The Future Tense of the Helping Verbs *Être* and *Avoir*

The endings are the same, but let's be real—they're otherwise completely irregular.

THE FUTURE TENSE OF THE AUXILIARY VERB *ÊTRE* (TO BE)			
je serai	I will be	*nous serons*	we will be
tu seras	you will be	*vous serez*	you will be
il / elle sera	he / she will be	*ils / elles seront*	they wil be

THE FUTURE TENSE OF THE AUXILIARY VERB *AVOIR* (TO HAVE)			
j'aurai	I will have	*nous aurons*	we will have
tu auras	you will have	*vous aurez*	you will have
il / elle aura	he / she will have	*ils / elles auront*	they will have

4. The Future Tense of the Irregular Verb *Aller* (to go)

Again, the stem changes completely, but the endings stay the same for this verb as well.

THE FUTURE TENSE OF THE IRREGULAR VERB *ALLER* (TO GO)			
j'irai	I will go	*nous irons*	we will go
tu iras	you will go	*vous irez*	you will go
il / elle ira	he / she will go	*ils / elles iront*	they will go

ACTIVITY 5: TAKE IT FOR A SPIN

Find all the verbs in the future tense in the dialogue. Write them down together with their subjects. What is their infinitive (*–er/–ir/–re*) form?

LIGHTS, CAMERA, ACTION!: TALKING ABOUT ACTING AND THEATER

Let's start with the theater, *le théâtre*. You'll notice that many of these words are similar in English and in French:

un acteur, une actrice	actor, actress
le comédien, la comédienne	theater actor, actress
la comédie	comedy
le / la comique	comedian
la comédie dramatique	drama
le rôle	part
la tragédie	tragedy
jouer (la comédie)	to play; to act
sur scène	on stage
à l'écran	on the screen

Note that *jouer la comédie* doesn't refer to playing a comic (*comique*) role only. It can be a dramatic (*dramatique*) part as well.

Everyone works hard on the stage during *la répétition*, that is, the rehearsal. The word *répétition*, which comes from the verb *répéter* (to rehearse; to repeat), also means "a repetition."

Les comédiens have to:

se concentrer	to concentrate
réciter	to recite

They can be in an original play, *une pièce originale*, or in a classical play, *une pièce classique*.

Le metteur en scène directs the play:

mettre en scène	to direct (a play)
diriger les acteurs	to direct (the actors)

Le producteur produces it.

produire	to produce

They all start with *la littérature* (literature)—note the difference in spelling.

un auteur dramatique	playwright
la pièce	play
un écrivain, une femme écrivain /	
une romancière	writer
le livre	book
le poète, la poétesse	poet
la poésie	poetry
le poème	poem

And then, there is *le théâtre de la vie* (the everyday drama of life).

avancer	to move forward
quitter quelqu'un	to leave someone
se comporter	to behave
sentir	to feel; to smell
souffrir	to suffer
l'amour (masc.)	love
le bien	good
le mal	evil
la souffrance	suffering
déprimé, –e	depressed
fatigué, –e	tired
insupportable	unbearable; difficult to handle / to be with

But as unbearable as the pains *de l'amour* might be, the show must go on! *Le spectacle doit continuer!* Yes, the show is *le spectacle* in French.

Word on the Street

à reculons	going backward
au bout du monde	at / to the end of the world
avoir du mal à	to have trouble (doing something)
se sentir mal	to feel sick
avoir mal	to feel hurt; to be in pain
Ça suffit!	Enough!
Qu'importe!	It doesn't matter!

ACTIVITY 6: TAKE IT FOR A SPIN

Complete each sentence by finding the missing word in the right column.

a)	Les _____ jouent la comédie.	écrivains
b)	Les _____ écrivent des livres.	en vers
c)	Les _____ écrivent des pièces.	scène
d)	Le _____ dirige les acteurs.	acteurs
e)	Au théâtre, les acteurs jouent sur une _____ .	auteurs dramatiques
f)	Les poésies sont écrites _____ .	metteur en scène

Back to our friends again. On the stage (*sur la scène*) of the theater, Camille, Émile and other actors are rehearsing a play under the direction of the *metteur en scène*, Tino.

You want to know what poor Émile is thinking. Here, rewrite this little paragraph by putting the verbs in parentheses into the appropriate form (present or future tense, or *passé composé*) and you'll find out.

Mon amie m' (quitter). C'est fini! Je ne (croire) plus en l'amour. Il (être) mieux de travailler. Et à la fin du mois, je (partir) en voyage aux États-Unis. Là-bas, je (travailler) sur ma prochaine pièce.

HEAR . . . SAY 2

My Darlings! (Mes chéris!)

Tino: Émile, il faut te secouer, mon vieux. Oublie ta triste vie ou Clavier, lui, va t'oublier vite fait!

Émile: (à voix basse) Tout le monde m'oublie . . .

Tino: On reprend! Delphine, tu as failli renverser le miroir. Toi et Jean-David, vous vous approcherez d'Orphée par la droite. Le plus lentement possible! C'est mieux. Oui, parfait! Et n'oubliez pas de parler plus fort et plus vite que les autres personnages.

Delphine: Tino, on sort de ce côté?

Tino: Mais oui! Et la princesse? Aziza! Tu dors ou quoi!

Aziza: Je suis là, Tino. Je suis juste très fatiguée aujourd'hui.

Tino: Bien sûr, tu es toujours plus fatiguée que les autres. La vérité, Aziza, c'est qu'on n'est pas moins fatigué que toi!

Clavier, le producteur, arrive sur scène.

Clavier: Mes chéris, mes chéris! Comment allez-vous tous? Ah! Quel plaisir d'être avec sa petite famille!

Tino: Bonsoir, George.

Clavier: Qu'est-ce qui se passe, Tino? Ne sont-ils pas les meilleurs acteurs?

Tino: Excellents, George. Et fatigués, et déprimés, et . . .

Clavier: Arrrh! Tu es juste de mauvaise humeur. Hier soir, je suis allé à la première du *Misanthrope* de ce Chirat. Épouvantable! Je ne mens pas. La pire représentation de ma vie! Ah! J'ai bien fait de m'occuper de vous, mes chéris! Allez, montrez-moi tout!

You know the routine, *mes chéris!*

    a)   *Qui est Tino?*

    b)   *Est-ce qu'Émile se sent mieux?*

    c)   *Qui interprète la princesse?*

    d)   *Comment va-t-elle?*

    e)   *Est-ce que Tino est content du travail des acteurs?*

    f)   *Quel est le nom du producteur?*

Did You Know?

CLASSICAL FRENCH THEATER

The classical French theater was born toward the end of the 17th century. It was modeled on the classical Greek theater and its strict precepts. The French classical theater included *la comédie,* represented most notably by the playwright and actor Jean-Baptiste Poquelin Molière (1622–1673), and *la tragédie,* represented by the famous playwrights Pierre Corneille (1606–1684) and Jean-Baptiste Racine (1639–1699).

The tragedies, such as *Cinna* and *Le Cid* by Corneille or *Phèdre* and *Andromaque* by Racine, were all based on great stories drawn from Greek mythology or adapted from ancient Greek playwrights.

The comedies depicted and ridiculed ordinary characters and the everyday lives of the new middle class, *la bourgeoisie,* such as Molière's most famous comedies *Les précieuses ridicules (Miladies Precious), Le misanthrope (The Misanthrope),* and *Le Tartuffe (Tartuffe).*

Did You Know?

239

LESSON 13 • THE PORT OF SHADOWS

WORKSHOP 2

THE NITTY-GRITTY

I SCREAM, YOU SCREAM: THE IRREGULAR VERB *PARTIR* (TO LEAVE) AND ITS LOOK-ALIKES

Here's a bunch of irregular verbs, just for you! They are: *partir* (to go), *dormir* (to sleep), *sortir* (to go out), *sentir* (to feel; to smell), *mentir* (to lie). But it's a five-for-one kind of deal—they all follow a single pattern.

1. The Present Tense of the Irregular Verbs partir *(to go),* dormir *(to sleep),* sortir *(to go out),* sentir *(to feel; to smell),* and mentir *(to lie)*

While these irregular verbs end in *–ir,* they are very different from the regular verbs in *–ir* you studied earlier, such as *finir.*

To form the present tense of these verbs, in the singular form, drop their last syllable "tir" and add the already familiar present endings: −s, −s, −t. In the plural form, drop the ending −ir and add the plural present endings: −ons, −ez, −ent. Et voilà!

THE PRESENT TENSE OF THE IRREGULAR VERB PARTIR (TO LEAVE)	
je pars	nous partons
tu pars	vous partez
il / elle part	ils / elles partent

THE PRESENT TENSE OF THE IRREGULAR VERB DORMIR (TO SLEEP)	
je dors	nous dormons
tu dors	vous dormez
il / elle dort	ils / elles dorment

ACTIVITY 9:   TAKE IT FOR A SPIN

So far, so simple. Now write down the different forms of *sortir*, *sentir*, and *mentir*.

2. The Passé Composé of the Irregular Verbs partir (to go), dormir (to sleep), sortir (to go out), sentir (to feel; to smell), and mentir (to lie)

To get the past participle of these verbs, just remove the final −r. And . . . that's it! *Voilà: parti* (left), *dormi* (slept), *sorti* (went out), *senti* (felt), *menti* (lied).

Remember that all verbs expressing movement are conjugated with *être*, e.g., *sortir* and *partir*.

THE *PASSÉ COMPOSÉ* OF THE IRREGULAR VERB SENTIR (TO FEEL; TO SMELL)			
j'ai senti	I (have) felt	nous avons senti	we (have) felt
tu as senti	you (have) felt	vous avez senti	you (have) felt
il / elle a senti	he / she (has) felt	ils / elles ont senti	they (have) felt

THE *PASSÉ COMPOSÉ* OF THE IRREGULAR VERB SORTIR (TO GO OUT)			
je suis sorti(e)	I went / have gone out	nous sommes sorti(e)s	we went / have gone out
tu es sorti(e)	you went / have gone out	vous êtes sorti(e)(s)	you went / have gone out
il / elle est sorti(e)	he / she went / has gone out	ils / elles sont sorti(e)s	they went / have gone out

MENTIR (TO LIE)	*DORMIR* (TO SLEEP)	*PARTIR* (TO LEAVE)
j'ai menti . . . (I (have) lied)	*j'ai dormi . . .* (I (have) slept)	*je suis parti(e) . . .* (I (have) left)

3. The Imperative of the Irregular Verbs partir *(to go)*, dormir *(to sleep)*, sortir *(to go out)*, sentir *(to feel; to smell)*, and mentir *(to lie)*

In the imperative, there are only three forms: the *tu, nous* and *vous* forms. To make it even easier, they are the same as the *tu, nous, vous* forms of the present tense.

THE IMPERATIVE OF THE IRREGULAR VERBS *PARTIR* (TO GO), *DORMIR* (TO SLEEP), *SENTIR* (TO FEEL; TO SMELL), *SORTIR* (TO GO OUT), AND *MENTIR* (TO LIE)

PARTIR (TO LEAVE)	*DORMIR* (TO SLEEP)	*SENTIR* (TO FEEL; TO SMELL)	*SORTIR* (TO GO OUT)	*MENTIR* (TO LIE)
pars (Leave!)	*dors* (Sleep!)	*sens* (Smell!)	*sors* (Go out!)	*mens* (Lie!)
partons (Let's leave!)	*dormons* (Let's sleep!)	*sentons* (Let's smell!)	*sortons* (Let's go out!)	*mentons* (Let's lie!)
partez (Leave!)	*dormez* (Sleep!)	*sentez* (Smell!)	*sortez* (Go out!)	*mentez* (Lie!)

4. The Future Tense of the Irregular Verbs partir *(to go)*, dormir *(to sleep)*, sortir *(to go out)*, sentir *(to feel; to smell)*, and mentir *(to lie)*

Admit it. The future tense may be a tense you've just learned but the truth is that it is so easy. Like the regular verbs ending in *-er* and *-ir*, just add the future endings to the *–ir* form of the verb.

For *je, tu, il / elle*: **–ai,–as, –a**.
For *nous, vous, ils / elles*: **–ons, –ez, –ont**.

C'est tout! That's it!

THE FUTURE TENSE OF THE IRREGULAR VERB *MENTIR* (TO LIE)

je mentirai	I will lie	*nous mentirons*	we will lie
tu mentiras	you will lie	*vous mentirez*	you will lie
il / elle mentira	he / she will lie	*ils / elles mentiront*	they will lie

Just follow the same pattern for *sortir, partir, sentir, dormir.*

WRITE THAT DOWN: THE IRREGULAR VERBS *ÉCRIRE* (TO WRITE) AND *LIRE* (TO READ)

1. To form the present tense of *écrire* and *lire* you'll use the usual present tense endings for the *–re* verbs: *–s, –s, –t, –ons, –ez, –ent*. Pay attention, however, to the irregularity of the *nous, vous,* and *ils/elles* forms.

THE PRESENT TENSE OF THE IRREGULAR VERB *ÉCRIRE* (TO WRITE)

j'écris	I write	*nous écrivons*	we write
tu écris	you write	*vous écrivez*	you write
il / elle écrit	he / she writes	*ils / elles écrivent*	they write

THE PRESENT TENSE OF THE IRREGULAR VERB *LIRE* (TO READ)

je lis	I read	*nous lisons*	we read
tu lis	you read	*vous lisez*	you read
il / elle lit	he / she reads	*ils / elles lisent*	they read

2. In the *passé composé*, *écrire* and *lire* use the verb *avoir* (to have). Their past participles are *écrit* (written) and *lu* (read) respectively.

THE *PASSÉ COMPOSÉ* OF THE IRREGULAR VERBS *ÉCRIRE* (TO WRITE) AND *LIRE* (TO READ)

ÉCRIRE	TO WRITE	*LIRE*	TO READ
j'ai écrit	I wrote / have written	*j'ai lu*	I (have) read
tu as écrit	you wrote / have written	*tu as lu*	you (have) read
il / elle a écrit	he / she wrote / has written	*il / elle a lu*	he / she (has) read
nous avons écrit	we wrote / have written	*nous avons lu*	we (have) read
vous avez écrit	you wrote / have written	*vous avez lu*	you (have) read
ils / elles ont écrit	they wrote / have written	*ils ont lu*	they (have) read

3. For the imperative form of the verbs *écrire* and *lire*, just use the *tu, nous, vous* forms of the present tense.

THE IMPERATIVE OF THE IRREGULAR VERBS *ÉCRIRE* (TO WRITE) AND *LIRE* (TO READ)

ÉCRIRE	TO WRITE	*LIRE*	TO READ
écris	Write!	lis	Read!
écrivons	Let's write!	lisons	Let's read!
écrivez	Write!	lisez	Read!

4. And the future. . . . It's as easy as with the other verbs. Yes, just add the future endings (after you've dropped the final "e" on *écrire* and *lire*).

THE FUTURE TENSE OF THE IRREGULAR VERB *ÉCRIRE* (TO WRITE)

j'écrirai	I will write	nous écrirons	we will write
tu écriras	you will write	vous écrirez	you will write
il / elle écrira	he / she will write	ils / elles écriront	they will write

THE FUTURE TENSE OF THE IRREGULAR VERB *LIRE* (TO READ)

je lirai	I will read	nous lirons	we will read
tu liras	you will read	vous lirez	you will read
il / elle lira	he / she will read	ils / elles liront	they will read

ACTIVITY 10:   **TAKE IT FOR A SPIN**

Select the appropriate verb from the right column to complete the sentences in the left column.

a)	La comédienne a bien _____ cette nuit.	écris
b)	La nouvelle pièce de cet auteur _____ bientôt.	partie
c)	_____-moi les plus beaux vers de ton coeur.	sortis
d)	Après la répétition, je me _____ fatiguée.	mentiras
e)	Nous sommes _____ tous les soirs au théâtre.	écrit
f)	Pourquoi est-elle _____ ?	dormi
g)	Dis, tu ne me _____ plus?	sens
h)	Je lui ai _____ durant des années.	sortira

Did You Know?

MODERN FRENCH THEATER

In addition to the Comédie-Française, there are numerous modern theater companies in France. One of the most famous is *Le Théâtre du Soleil*, founded by Ariane Mnouchkine, one of the greatest French *metteurs en scène* of modern times.

    Events such as *Le Festival d'Avignon* (Avignon Theater Festival), which takes place every summer in the beautiful old town of Avignon in Provence, keep the theater tradition alive and draw thousands of people in front of a stage every year.

Did You Know?

Take a look at the announcement for a play in the program of the Avignon Theater Festival:

DANS LA RUBRIQUE THÉÂTRE, À VOIR . . .

Dans le cadre du **Festival D'Avignon, Médée, d'Euripide, mise en scène de Jacques Lassale**, avec Isabelle Huppert, Bernard Verley, Jean-Quentin Châtelain, et Michel Peyrelon. • *Du 12 au 22 juillet, à 22 heures, à la Cour d'Honneur du Palais des Papes. Loc: 04-90-14-14-14.*

ACTIVITY 11: TAKE IT FOR A SPIN

Tell me:

a) *Quel est le titre de cette pièce?*
b) *Durant quelles dates pouvez-vous voir cette pièce?*
c) *Quel est le numéro à appeler pour la location des places (reservations)?*

WORDS TO LIVE BY

And the show must go on. *Le spectacle doit continuer:*

le miroir	mirror
la représentation	performance
la première	premiere

And what do the artists say when they go on stage? According to an old superstition, it's the moment to say *Merde!* (Shit!), rather than *Bonne chance!* (Good luck!). This is not unlike the English "Break a leg!"

oublier	to forget
se souvenir de	to remember

Or:

se rappeler de	to remember
rappeler quelque chose à quelqu'un	to remind someone of something

The useful little words of the day are:

de ce côté	from that side
lentement	slowly
par la droite	from / on the right
par la gauche	from / on the left

Word on the Street

à voix basse	in a low voice
avoir failli + infinitive	to have almost + past participle

For example:

J'ai failli renverser le miroir.	I almost knocked the mirror over.
être de bonne humeur	to be in a good mood
être de mauvaise humeur	to be in a bad mood
Secoue-toi, mon vieux!	Wake up, buddy!
vite fait	in a blink (of an eye)

ACTIVITY 12: TAKE IT FOR A SPIN

Show off your vocabulary! Find the opposites of the following words. You may refresh your memory by looking at the Words To Live By sections in Workshops 1 and 2.

le pire; à voix forte; lentement; être de bonne humeur; gauche; merveilleux; la dernière; se rappeler; jeune; partir; le bien; heureux.

LET'S PUT IT IN WRITING

Read some inspiring words by Jean Cocteau:

About the artist:	*"Tout grand artiste, même s'il peint des volets* (shutters) *ou des pavots* (poppies), *trace toujours son propre portrait."*
About inspiration:	*"Il faudrait dire expiration, au lieu d'inspiration. C'est de notre réserve, de notre nuit que les choses nous viennent. Notre oeuvre préexiste en nous . . ."*
About the artwork:	*"L'oeuvre est posthume. À la fin de la création, le moi qui l'a créé, n'existe plus."*

Would you like to try to translate Cocteau's paragraph about inspiration? Let me get you started: *il faudrait* can be translated as *one should* or *we should.*

CRIB NOTES

HEAR...SAY 1

Émile: Life is strange. One day you're happy, you're loved and you love. But the next day . . .

Camille: But she'll call you, Émile. C'mon, let's rehearse!

Émile: "Silence moves forward by going backwards." You see, Cocteau always knew. But is he better than me? What can I do?

Camille: It'd be better, Émile, to concentrate on your part.

Émile: Yes. "You don't feel sick?" Hmmm . . . "You don't feel sick?"

Camille: "No . . ."

Émile: I do, Camille, I feel sick! Very sick!

Camille: Émile, that's enough! Tino and Clavier will be really upset tonight! They'll finish the show without us. It'll be worse if . . .

Émile: It doesn't matter, it's my last show! Then I'll go to the end of the world. To a country without women! She'll have peace.

Camille: But Émile, you're the most talented Orpheus, you . . .

Émile: You think so? Yes . . . "My books don't get written on their own."

Camille: "Your books get written on their own . . ."

Émile: "I help them. How is the boy behaving?"

Camille: "Orpheus, it's . . ."

Émile: "He'll be as unbearable as his father." Hey, Camille, shall we go and have a drink after the rehearsal?

Camille: Jason will be there tonight.

Émile: You have Jason. That's good. I'm happy for you.

Camille's cell phone rings . . .

Camille: Hello, Mr. Clavier. Everything's going well . . . We're rehearsing with Émile just now. We'll be ready, of course. See you tonight.

HEAR...SAY 2

Tino: Émile, you have to get your act together, buddy. Forget your sad life or Clavier will forget you in a blink!

Émile: (*sotto voce*) Everyone forgets me . . .

Tino: Let's start again! Delphine, you almost knocked the mirror over. You and Jean-David are approaching Orpheus from the right. As slowly as you can (*Lit.* the slowest possible)! That's better. Yes, perfect! And don't forget to talk louder and faster than the other characters.

Jean-David: Tino, do we go out on this side?

Tino: Yes! And the princess? Aziza! Are you sleeping or what!

Aziza: I'm here, Tino. I'm just very tired today.

Tino: Of course, you are always more tired than the others. The truth is, Aziza, that we're no less tired than you!

Clavier, the producer, arrives on stage.

Clavier: My darlings, my darlings! How are you all doing? What pleasure to be with my family!

Tino: Good evening, George.

Clavier: What's happening, Tino? Aren't they the best actors?

Tino: Excellent, George. And tired, and depressed, and . . .

Clavier: Ah! You're just in a bad mood. Last night I went to the premiere of Chirat's *Misanthrope*. Horrendous! I'm not kidding. (*Lit.* I'm not lying.) The worst performance in my life! Ah! How right I was to take care of you, my darlings! C'mon, show me everything!

ACTIVITY 1

a) Les deux acteurs répètent la scène finale d'Orphée.
b) Émile interprète Orphée et Camille Eurydice.
c) Non, Émile a du mal à se concentrer.
d) Il veut aller boire un pot.
e) À la fin de la scène, le portable de Camille sonne.

ACTIVITY 2

a) Elles sont plus talentueuses que leurs amies.
b) Il veut être meilleur acteur que lui.
c) Nous allons moins vite qu'eux.
d) Elles récitent le texte moins bien que toi.
e) Cet écrivain est aussi intéressant que celui-ci.

ACTIVITY 3

a) Nous sommes moins jeunes que vous.
b) Ce film est moins intéressant.
c) Les textes de Molière sont plus faciles.
d) Ses films sont les meilleurs.
e) Les pièces de cet auteur sont aussi dramatiques que celles-là.

ACTIVITY 4

j'achèterai, tu achèteras, il / elle achètera, nous achèterons, vous achèterez, ils / elles achèteront

ACTIVITY 5

elle t'appellera (appeler); Tino et Clavier seront (être); ils finiront (finir); ce sera (être); je partirai (partir); elle aura (avoir); il sera (être); on ira (aller); Jason sera (être); nous serons (être)

ACTIVITY 6

a) Les acteurs jouent la comédie.
b) Les écrivains écrivent des livres.
c) Les auteurs dramatiques écrivent des pièces.
d) Le metteur en scène dirige les acteurs.
e) Au théâtre, les acteurs jouent sur une scène.
f) Les poésies sont écrites en vers.

ACTIVITY 7

Mon amie m'a quitté. C'est fini! Je ne croirai plus en l'amour. Il est mieux de travailler. Et à la fin du mois, je partirai en voyage aux États-Unis. Là-bas, je travaillerai sur ma prochaine pièce.

ACTIVITY 8

a) Tino est le metteur en scène.
b) Non, Émile ne va pas mieux. Il est toujours aussi déprimé.
c) Aziza interprète la princesse.
d) Elle est fatiguée.
e) Tino n'est pas très content du travail des acteurs.
f) Clavier est le nom du producteur.

ACTIVITY 9

sortir: je sors, tu sors, il / elle sort, nous sortons, vous sortez, ils / elles sortent
sentir: je sens, tu sens, il / elle sent, nous sentons, vous sentez, ils / elles sentent
mentir: je mens, tu mens, il / elle ment, nous mentons, vous mentez, ils / elles mentent

ACTIVITY 10

a) La comédienne a bien dormi cette nuit.
b) La nouvelle pièce de cet auteur sortira bientôt.
c) Écris-moi les plus beaux vers de ton coeur.
d) Après la répétition, je me sens fatiguée.
e) Nous sommes sortis tous les soirs au théâtre.
f) Pourquoi est-elle partie?
g) Dis, tu ne me mentiras plus?
h) Je lui ai écrit durant des années.

ACTIVITY 11

a) Le titre de cette pièce est *Médée*.
b) Nous pouvons voir cette pièce du 12 au 22 juillet.
c) Pour la location des places, il faut appeler le 04–90–14–14–14.

ACTIVITY 12

le pire-le meilleur; à voix forte-à voix basse; lentement-vite; être de bonne humeur-être de mauvaise humeur; gauche-droite; merveilleux-épouvantable; la dernière-la première; se rappeler-oublier; jeune-vieux; partir-arriver; le bien-le mal; heureux-déprimé.

ACTIVITY 13

"We should say expiration, rather than inspiration. It is from our internal sources, from our nights that things come to us. Our work already exists within us."

14. PRÉVERT'S SONG

La chanson de Prévert

Hey! Hello, El'hadj! Long time no see!

COMING UP. . .

- *It's music to my ears*: Talking about music and the French *chanson*
- *Let's celebrate!*: Talking about events in life worth celebrating
- *Give them some applause!*: Going to a concert
- *What will be, will be*: The future tense of some irregular verbs
- *I could have been somebody*: Using *somebody* or *nobody* in French
- *I scream, you scream*: More irregular verbs—*offrir* (to offer) and its look-alikes
- *It's worth the effort*: Using the expressions *cela vaut* (it's worth) and *il vaut mieux* (it's better)

IN THE SPOTLIGHT

"La chanson de Prévert" ("Prévert's Song") is one of the many beautiful songs by Serge Gainsbourg (1928–1991), legendary icon of French pop music. Gainsbourg started writing music and songs and performing in *cabarets* in the late 1950s. He quickly became famous for his talent as a songwriter and also, for his sense of provocation and a special style. Several of his songs created scandals, such as *"Je t'aime, moi non plus"* and *"La Décadanse,"* playing with the concept of love and sex, and *"La Marseillaise,"* his unorthodox version of the French national anthem. His texts are uniquely poetic, and his music flirts with different styles. He worked with many icons of French and international film and music: Actrices Brigitte Bardot and Catherine Deneuve, singers France Gall, Françoise Hardy, Petula Clark, Marianne Faithful, and of course, his third wife, actress and singer, Jane Birkin.

LET'S PUT IT IN WRITING

Written by Serge Gainsbourg, the last great French *chansonnier*, "La chanson de Prevért" talks about great love. It is filled with references to the poem *"Les feuilles mortes"* ("Fallen Leaves") written by Jacques Prévert, the beloved 20th century French poet. Here are a few lines from the song:

LA CHANSON DE PRÉVERT

> *Jour après jour*
> *Les amours mortes*
> *N'en finissent pas de mourir.*

LOOKING AHEAD

In the first dialogue, we're back with Jason . . . *Vous vous rappelez de lui?* Yes, Jason from Canada. During his lunch break, he decides to go to a record store to buy some CDs for his girlfriend, Camille, the sweet *actrice* you met in Lesson 13. *L'anniversaire de Camille* (Camille's birthday) is coming *bientôt* (soon)! And to celebrate, on Saturday evening, her friends are taking them *à un concert* . . . . But it's a surprise!

Au rayon musique (in the music section) *de la FNAC*, a famous department store in Paris, Jason is looking for the right jazz CDs for Camille—*les chanteuses de jazz surtout* (mostly female jazz singers). *Un vendeur* (a salesman) approaches him.

La FNAC, pronounced as (fnahk), is a large media store *spécialisé* in audio, video, photo equipment, books, and all types of recordings (*CDs, cassettes, disques,* and *vidéos*). FNAC also sells *des billets de concert* (concert tickets) and *des places de théâtre* (theater tickets) and organizes cultural events, such as *des expositions* (exhibitions) or *des concerts* (concerts). You can find FNAC stores in many French cities.

Did You Know?

HEAR . . . SAY 1

What to Buy? (Qu'acheter?)

Une voix derrière lui:	Vous cherchez quelque chose?
Jason:	Eh! Salut, El'hadj! Il y a un bail! Comment vas-tu?
El'hadj:	Ça va, et toi?
Jason:	Bon . . . rien de spécial. Je ne travaille pas loin d'ici. Alors, je viens de temps en temps. Et toi, tu travailles ici?
El'hadj:	Oui, quelques jours par semaine; ça fait trois mois.
Jason:	Tu es toujours avec . . .
El'hadj:	Audrey! Oui. On s'est même mariés à New York! Et il y a deux mois, un petit garçon est né!
Jason:	Quelle surprise! Tu es papa! Félicitations à tous les deux! Tu es donc bien revenu des États-Unis.
El'hadj:	Ouais. Sinon, tu cherches quelque chose?
Jason:	En fait, oui, je voudrais offrir plusieurs CDs à ma copine, Camille. Ce sera son anniversaire samedi.
El'hadj:	En jazz . . . un instrumental?
Jason:	Oui, elle écoute beaucoup de jazz. Ou peut-être une chanteuse . . . Ella Fitzgerald ou Helen Merrill . . . En fait, je les écoute aussi. Tiens, samedi, on ira probablement à un concert avec d'autres amis. Tu te souviens de Flo et d'Aziza?
El'hadj:	Oui, on se parle parfois au téléphone avec Aziza. Voici un très bon d'Helen Merrill avec l'orchestre de Quincy Jones.
Jason:	Ah . . . . J'ai découvert cette chanteuse, il y a peu de temps. Mais je n'ai jamais entendu celui-là.
El'hadj:	Tu pourras l'écouter là-bas. Il vaut quinze euros.
Jason:	Bien. Je te fais confiance. Je le prends et je vais aussi prendre ce coffret d'Ella. Eh! Tu veux venir samedi?

El'hadj:	Okay. Et qui allez-vous voir en concert?
Jason:	On le saura seulement samedi. Florence et Aziza veulent nous faire une surprise. Après, on ira arroser ça au champagne. _su again_
El'hadj:	C'est sympa. Oui, c'est une bonne idée. Comme ça, je reverrai tout le monde.

ACTIVITY 1: HOW'S THAT AGAIN?

Just a few questions:

a)   *Est-ce que la scène se passe le weekend?*

b)   *Qu'est-ce qui se passe à la FNAC?*

c)   *Que cherche Jason? Pourquoi?*

d)   *Que lui annonce son copain?*

e)   *Qu'est-ce que Jason propose à El'hadj?*

Did You Know?

VIVE LA CHANSON FRANÇAISE!

From Edith Piaf, Yves Montand, Jacques Brel and Juliette Gréco to Serge Gainsbourg and Barbara, the golden age of *la chanson française* has slowly faded away with the passing of these unique artists. Next to the legends such as Charles Aznavour, Françoise Hardy, Jacques Dutronc, or William Sheller, the style and quality of some younger, currently popular singers may seem somewhat doubtful.

The 1980s and the 1990s brought a new wave of songwriters, singers, and ideas. Aside from the perpetually strong Anglo-Saxon influence, *la chanson française* has started to dance with melodies and rhythms coming from many other, often distant horizons (FFF, Les Négresses Vertes, Rita Mitsouko, Manu Chao, la Mano Negra). Numerous artists from Canada (Céline Dion, Diane Dufresnes, Diane Tell), Spain (Nilda Fernandez, Cyrius), Haiti (Beethova Obas), and various countries of Africa (Sally Nyollo, Bonga, Henri Dikongué, Richard Bona, Zap Mama) have been thriving in France.

Although *la musique du monde* (world music) has seduced French audiences and critics, due to the politics of cultural protectionism, *très franchouillard* (overbearingly French) indeed, quotas were imposed a few years ago in order to reduce the playing time of foreign language songs on radios and television. Should music, in essence international, be carrying a passport around?

Did You Know?

WORKSHOP 1

THE NITTY-GRITTY

***WHAT WILL BE, WILL BE*: THE FUTURE TENSE OF SOME IRREGULAR VERBS**

The Future Tense of Irregular Verbs in –oir(e)

No matter how irregular the verbs can otherwise be, the endings added to form the future tense are always the same. One more time, here they are:

For *je, tu, il / elle* forms: ***–ai, –as, –a***
For *nous, vous, ils / elles* forms: ***–ons, –ez, –ont***

The verbs *vouloir* (to want), *pouvoir* (can, to be able to), *savoir* (to know), and *voir* (to see) are especially unpredictable. So, again, be patient with yourself and don't worry about making mistakes. (Don't forget that you can also always refer to Appendix B to look up the various forms of these and many other irregular verbs.)

THE FUTURE TENSE OF THE IRREGULAR VERB *VOULOIR* (TO WANT)

je voudrai	I will want	*nous voudrons*	we will want
tu voudras	you will want	*vous voudrez*	you will want
il / elle voudra	he / she will want	*ils / elles voudront*	they will want

THE FUTURE TENSE OF THE IRREGULAR VERB *POUVOIR* (CAN, TO BE ABLE TO)

je pourrai	I will be able to	*nous pourrons*	we will be able to
tu pourras	you will be able to	*vous pourrez*	you will be able to
il / elle pourra	he / she will be able to	*ils / elles pourront*	they will be able to

THE FUTURE TENSE OF THE IRREGULAR VERB *SAVOIR* (TO KNOW)

je saurai	I will know	*nous saurons*	we will know
tu sauras	you will know	*vous saurez*	you will know
il / elle saura	he / she will know	*ils / elles sauront*	they will know

THE FUTURE TENSE OF THE IRREGULAR VERB *VOIR* (TO SEE)

je verrai	I will see	*nous verrons*	we will see
tu verras	you will see	*vous verrez*	you will see
il / elle verra	he / she will see	*ils / elles verront*	they will see

THE FUTURE TENSE OF THE IRREGULAR VERB *DEVOIR* (MUST, TO HAVE TO)			
je devrai	I will have to	*nous devrons*	we will have to
tu devras	you will have to	*vous devrez*	you will have to
il / elle devra	he / she will have to	*ils / elles devront*	they will have to

THE FUTURE TENSE OF THE IRREGULAR VERB *RECEVOIR* (TO RECEIVE)			
je recevrai	I will receive	*nous recevrons*	we will receive
tu recevras	you will receive	*vous recevrez*	you will receive
il / elle recevra	he / she will receive	*ils / elles recevront*	they will receive

As for the verbs *boire* (to drink) and *croire* (to believe), their future forms are practically regular. Drop the final "e," and add the endings.

boire (to drink) → **je boirai** (I will drink), etc.
croire (to believe) → **je croirai** (I will believe), etc.

ACTIVITY 2: TAKE IT FOR A SPIN

To complete each sentence, select the appropriate verb from the right column.

a) Ce soir, je _____ du champagne.   *pourrons*
b) Il ne me _____ pas.   *verrez*
c) Nous _____ lui acheter des CDs.   *recevront*
d) Pour son anniversaire, tu _____ aller au magasin.   *croira*
e) Elles _____ bientôt nos cadeaux.   *sauront*
f) Vous _____ ce soir, c'est une surprise.   *boirai*
g) Ils ne _____ rien.   *devras*

The Future Tense of Verbs Ending in −endre

Even French grammar can be easy. Verbs such as *entendre* (to hear), *attendre* (to wait), *vendre* (to sell), and *descendre* (to come down), as well as *prendre* (to take) and its derivatives, such *as apprendre* (to learn; to teach) and *comprendre* (to understand), follow the same, regular pattern in the future tense. Drop the last letter "e" and add the future endings.

THE FUTURE TENSE OF THE VERB *ATTENDRE* (TO WAIT)			
j'attendrai	I will wait	*nous attendrons*	we will wait
tu attendras	you will wait	*vous attendrez*	you will wait
il / elle attendra	he / she will wait	*ils / elles attendront*	they will wait

THE FUTURE TENSE OF THE IRREGULAR VERB *PRENDRE* (TO TAKE)

je prendrai	I will take	*nous prendrons*	we will take
tu prendras	you will take	*vous prendrez*	you will take
il / elle prendra	he / she will take	*ils / elles prendront*	they will take

The other verbs follow the same pattern:

entendre (to hear) → **j'entendrai** (I will hear)

descendre (to come down) → **je descendrai** (I will come down)

vendre (to sell) → **je vendrai** (I will sell)

comprendre (to understand) → **je comprendrai** (I will understand)

apprendre (to learn; to teach) → **j'apprendrai** (I will learn/teach)

For the verbs *dire* (to say), *interdire* (to forbid), *écrire* (to write), and *lire* (to read), it's the same story! Drop the final letter "e" from the verb and add the future endings.

THE FUTURE TENSE OF THE VERB *DIRE* (TO SAY)

je dirai	I will say	*nous dirons*	we will say
tu diras	you will say	*vous direz*	you will say
il / elle dira	he / she will say	*ils / elles diront*	they will say

interdire (to forbid) → **j'interdirai** (I will forbid)

écrire (to write) → **j'écrirai** (I will write)

lire (to read) → **je lirai** (I will read)

Back to trouble . . . . As for the verbs *venir* (to come), *tenir* (to hold), and *faire* (to do; to make), they are completely irregular. Yes, the stem of each verb has a special, irregular form in the future tense. (The endings are still the same.)

THE FUTURE TENSE OF THE IRREGULAR VERB *VENIR* (TO COME)

je viendrai	I will come	*nous viendrons*	we will come
tu viendras	you will come	*vous viendrez*	you will come
il / elle viendra	he / she will come	*ils / elles viendront*	they will come

THE FUTURE TENSE OF THE IRREGULAR VERB *TENIR* (TO HOLD)

je tiendrai	I will hold	*nous tiendrons*	we will hold
tu tiendras	you will hold	*vous tiendrez*	you will hold
il / elle tiendra	he / she will hold	*ils / elles tiendront*	they will hold

THE FUTURE TENSE OF THE IRREGULAR VERB FAIRE (TO DO; TO MAKE)			
je ferai	I will do	*nous ferons*	we will do
tu feras	you will do	*vous ferez*	you will do
il / elle fera	he / she will do	*ils / elles feront*	they will do

TAKE IT FOR A SPIN

Write the verbs in parentheses in the future tense.

a) *Nous te (attendre) au concert.*

b) *Quel plaisir, on (entendre) bien le son.*

c) *Je ne (comprendre) pas ces paroles.*

d) *Tu me (dire) si tu peux venir à la répétition demain.*

e) *Cela te (prendre) du temps d'enregistrer tout ça?*

f) *Tu (faire) du bon boulot.*

I COULD HAVE BEEN SOMEBODY: USING SOMEBODY OR NOBODY IN FRENCH

Une bonne nouvelle! Good news for you! You already know some of these words.

1. The Indefinite Pronouns

Because words like *nobody* or *somebody* don't refer to any particular person, they are called indefinite pronouns. Some indefinite pronouns are invariable—there is no change for number or gender.

SOME INVARIABLE INDEFINITE PRONOUNS			
personne	nobody	*quelqu'un*	someone
rien	nothing	*quelque chose*	something
plusieurs	several	*on*	one

Personne n'a téléphoné.

Nobody called.

Plusieurs pourront acheter des CDs de jazz.

Several people will be able to buy jazz CDs.

Il ne fait rien toute la journée.

He does nothing all day long.

Voilà quelqu'un.

Someone is coming.

On ne fait pas ça en France.

One does not do that in France. / You don't do that in France.

J'ai quelque chose dans l'oeil.

I have something in my eye.

Other indefinite pronouns are variable, that is, they must be modified to agree in gender and number with the nouns they replace.

SOME VARIABLE INDEFINITE PRONOUNS			
aucun(e)	none	le / la même, les mêmes	the same
l'autre, les autres	the other, the others	tout(e), tous, toutes	all
certain(s), certaine(s)	some, certain	pas un, pas une	not one
chacun(e)	each		

Les mêmes sont vendus partout.

The same things (masc./fem. pl.) are sold everywhere.

Chacun recevra son cadeau.

Each one (masc. sing.) will receive his present.

Certaines seront au concert.

Some of them (fem. pl.) will be at the concert.

Toutes sont bonnes.

All (fem. pl.) are good.

2. The Indefinite Adjectives

And here are the indefinite words that can be used next to a noun. Because these words are really adjectives, they often have a different form depending on the gender and the number of the noun they modify.

SOME INDEFINITE ADJECTIVES			
quelque(s)	a few, several	différent(e)(s)	different
certain(e)(s)	some	plusieurs	several
divers(e)(s)	various	tel(s), telle(s)	such
même	same	tout(e), tous, toutes	all
autre(s)	other	chaque	each
pas un(e)	not one		

J'ai passé quelques (pl.) heures à la FNAC.

I spent a few hours at the FNAC.

Il n'y aura pas un bruit durant le concert.

There won't be a sound (masc. sing.) during the concert.

Plusieurs artistes pourront jouer.

Several artists will be able to play.

C'est toujours la même chose!

It's always the same (old story)!

Heads Up!

As you may have noticed, some of these words function as both adjectives and pronouns, such as *aucun, autre, certain, même, plusieurs,* and *tout.*

Another important thing about these words: When the negative words *personne, aucun, pas un,* or *rien* are used in a sentence, the verb of the sentence is preceded only by *ne* instead of the full negation *ne . . . pas.* This double negation is actually the rule in French, unlike in English.

Aucun de mes amis ne téléphonera.

None of my friends will call. (*Lit.* None of my friends will not call.)

Personne ne sait rien.

No one knows anything. (*Lit.* No one doesn't know nothing.)

Rien ne me plaît.

I like nothing. (*Lit.* Nothing doesn't please me.)

Heads Up!

ACTIVITY 4:   TAKE IT FOR A SPIN

Fill in the blank with the appropriate word from the list:

tous / personne / rien / chaque / quelque chose / quelqu'un

a)   Je n'entends _____ (nobody).
b)   C'est l'anniversaire de mon ami, je dois lui trouver _____.
c)   _____ mes amis sont venus à mon anniversaire.
d)   Elle est très difficile. _____ (nothing) ne lui plaît jamais.
e)   Est-ce que _____ veut du champagne?
f)   _____ moment d'une vie est important.

Time to do some shopping. Some love it and others hate it.

Un grand magasin (a department store) is very *pratique* once you know the *heures d'ouverture* (opening hours) and *les heures de fermeture* (closing hours).

fermer	to close
la fermeture	closing time
ouvrir	to open
l'ouverture (fem.)	opening time

In each *rayon*, that is "department" or "section," salespeople, *des vendeurs* (masc. pl.) or *vendeuses* (fem. pl.) are here to help you.

le prix d'ami	sale price (Lit. friendly price)
les soldes	sales
la promotion	special offer
le rayon	department, section
bon marché, meilleur marché	cheap, cheaper
cher, chère	expensive

IT'S MUSIC TO MY EARS: LET'S TALK ABOUT MUSIC

There are many different styles of music: *La musique classique* (classical music), *la musique de jazz* (jazz music), *la musique du monde* (world music), *reggae* (reggae), *rock*, *punk*, *fusion*, *la music contemporaine* (contemporary music) . . . Everyone can listen to music, *écouter de la musique*.

la chanson	song
le chanteur, la chanteuse	singer
le concert	concert
le coffret de disques	CD box
la culture musicale	musical culture
le disque compact, le CD	compact disc, CD
le goût musical	musical taste

LET'S CELEBRATE!: TALKING ABOUT EVENTS IN LIFE WORTH CELEBRATING

Life is full of surprises (*plein de surprises*).

arroser la nouvelle	to drink to the good news
attendre un bébé	to expect a baby
avoir un enfant	to have a child; to give birth
célébrer	to celebrate
découvrir	to discover
offrir	to offer
revoir	to see again
souffrir	to suffer

And here are the events of life, *les évènements de la vie*, we like to celebrate:

un anniversaire	birthday
la naissance (d'un enfant)	birth (of a child)
les retrouvailles	reunion

Finally, here are our useful little words:

de temps en temps	from time to time
en particulier	in particular
parfois	at times
probablement	probably
seulement	only
sinon	otherwise
surtout	above all

Word on the Street

Since this lesson is largely about wants and wishes, we should also learn a very important expression:

Je voudrais	I would like to

Remember Jason when he says:

> **. . . je voudrais offrir plusieurs CDs à ma copine.**

> . . . I'd like to buy (*Lit.* offer) several CDs for my girlfriend.

> *Je voudrais* that you remember this useful expression. Don't leave home without it!

And here are some other useful expressions:

C'est sympa!	That's cool!
Il y a un bail!	It's been a while!
rien de spécial	nothing new; as usual

By the way, the colloquial term franchouillard expresses with irony the fact that a French person or an institution is being over-protective of French culture and territory.

ACTIVITY 5: TAKE IT FOR A SPIN

Please find the opposites of the following words:

tout le monde / en general / plusieurs / triste / peu sympathique / souvent / être bien / il y a peu de temps / même

ACTIVITY 6: LET'S WARM UP

C'est samedi soir. Pour célébrer l'anniversaire de Camille, Florence, Aziza, and Paco take their friends to a surprise concert. *Personne ne sait rien* (Nobody knows anything.) Their two cars stop in front of *Le New Morning*, a concert hall in Paris. There's a big crowd there already. And what about you?

a)   *Quels sont vos goûts musicaux?*

b)   *Avez-vous déjà vu des artistes francophones sur scène?*

HEAR ... SAY 2

At the Concert   (Au concert)

Aziza: On y est!

Florence: Ils ont déjà ouvert les portes.

Julienne: On va voir Richard Bona? Ah, tu m'as eue, Paco! J'ai failli acheter des places!

Camille: Super! Ah, merci!

Paco: De notre part à tous, joyeux anniversaire, Camille!!!

Jason: Bon anniversaire! Et à tous les trois, un grand merci.

Les autres: Joyeux anniversaire, Camille! Alors, quel âge as-tu?

Camille: J'ai toujours vingt ans! Oui, merci beaucoup. C'est super sympa de nous inviter. Jason m'a offert le CD de cet artiste. J'ai adoré . . .

Aziza: Eh bien, attends de le voir jouer, c'est un grand musicien et un auteur-compositeur talentueux!

Julienne: Oui, sans aucun doute, cela vaut le déplacement.

Paco: Il vaut mieux y aller, avec tout ce monde.

Florence: Oui, le concert commence dans peu de . . . Tu as vu ça, Ziza, il y a le tout-Paris de la musique.

À l'intérieur de la salle, la scène est prête, le public attend avec impatience le groupe, puis applaudit.

Jason: Ah, voilà El'hadj . . . Aziza, Flo . . .

Florence: El'hadj, quel plaisir de te voir! Tu arrives juste à temps. Les voilà! Bravo!

Après un concert chaud et émouvant, les amis vont dans les coulisses pour saluer les musiciens. Puis, ils iront tous chez Paco, célébrer les nouveaux vingt ans de Camille, les retrouvailles avec El'hadj et ce super concert.

ACTIVITY 7:   HOW'S THAT AGAIN?

a)   *Où vont les amis?*

b)   *Est-ce que les amis sont contents de la surprise?*

c)   *Est-ce que le public est patient?*

d)   *Comment est le concert?*

e)   *Et ensuite, où iront-ils?*

Did You Know?

LET'S PUT IT IN WRITING

World music *a beaucoup de succès en France* (is very successful in France). Two notable singers are MC Solaar and Khaled.

Here are some lyrics from a very original MC Solaar song, *"J'ai vu la concubine de l'hémoglobine"*:

> "Parce que la science nous balance sa science,
>
> Science sans conscience égale science de l'inconscience
>
> Elle se fout du progrès, mais souhaite la progression
>
> De tous les processus qui mènent à l'élimination".
>
> —© by MC Solaar

And another example from the rai singer Khaled's song *"Le Jour Viendra"*:

> "Et la nuit tendait les bras, pour y bercer le jour,
>
> Et les ombres de nos pas marchaient au pas de l'amour".
>
> —© by J.J.Goldman / Khaled

Take a Tip from Me!

Now that you've learned so much about old and new French singers and musicians, I hope you'll get to liking and listening to some of them. It's fun and it's great practice for your French to try and figure out what the lyrics are saying. By the way, you can find the lyrics to most songs on the Web: print them out and sing along.

Take a Tip from Me!

But before you run off to the record store, there's some more nitty-gritty stuff to do.

WORKSHOP 2

THE NITTY-GRITTY

I SCREAM, YOU SCREAM: MORE IRREGULAR VERBS—*OFFRIR* (TO OFFER) AND ITS LOOK-ALIKES

A new and really simple pattern of irregular verbs! *Offrir* (to offer), *souffrir* (to suffer), *ouvrir* (to open), and *découvrir* (to discover) are all formed in the same way.

1. To conjugate these verbs in the present tense, just drop *-ir* and add the same endings as for the regular verbs in *–er*. Incredible, but true! And just in case you need a little help, here are the present endings for the *–er* verbs:

   For *je, tu, il / elle* forms: **–e, –es, –e.**
   For *nous, vous, ils / elles* forms: **–ons, –ez, –ent.**

THE PRESENT TENSE OF THE IRREGULAR VERB *OFFRIR* (TO OFFER)			
j'offre	I offer	*nous offrons*	we offer
tu offres	you offer	*vous offrez*	you offer
il / elle offre	he / she offers	*ils / elles offrent*	they offer

There are no suprises with *souffrir* and *ouvrir*:

   souffrir (to suffer) → **je souffre** (I suffer), etc.
   ouvrir (to open) → **j'ouvre** (I open), etc.

2. In the *passé composé*, these verbs use the verb *avoir*. The past participles are: *offert* (offered), *souffert* (suffered), and *ouvert* (opened).

THE *PASSÉ COMPOSÉ* OF THE IRREGULAR VERB *OFFRIR* (TO OFFER)	
j'ai offert	*nous avons offert*
tu as offert	*vous avez offert*
il / elle a offert	*ils / elles ont offert*

Your turn. Continue with the rest of the forms after my prompt:

   j'ai souffert (I (have) suffered) . . .
   j'ai ouvert (I (have) opened) . . .

And now discover that *découvrir* (to discover) in the *passé composé* is just as easy. Write down its different forms.

3. As for the imperative, yes, use the *tu*, *nous*, *vous* forms of the present tense.

THE IMPERATIVE OF THE VERBS *OFFRIR*, *SOUFFRIR* AND *OUVRIR*		
OFFRIR (TO OFFER)	*SOUFFRIR* (TO SUFFER)	*OUVRIR* (TO OPEN)
offre	souffre	ouvre
offrons	souffrons	ouvrons
offrez	souffrez	ouvrez

4. You know what? These verbs have perfectly regular future forms. Yes! That is, just like with other *–ir* or *–er* verbs, you add the future endings to the infinitive. Just to hammer things in one more time, here are the forms for *offrir* (to offer):

THE FUTURE TENSE OF THE IRREGULAR VERB *OFFRIR* (TO OFFER)			
j'offrirai	I will offer	*nous offrirons*	we will offer
tu offriras	you will offer	*vous offrirez*	you will offer
il / elle offrira	he / she will offer	*ils / elles offriront*	they will offer

Things are really getting too easy for you . . .

These sentences are a mess! Can you correct them for me, please? Pay special attention to the form of the verb. Does it make sense?

a)   *Les hommes aiment souffriront.*
b)   *Qu'est-ce qu'on t'a offriras pour ton anniversaire?*
c)   *Il y a tant de choses à découvert.*
d)   *Personne n'ouvriront son cadeau maintenant.*
e)   *Tu découvert bientôt son album.*

IT'S WORTH THE EFFORT: USING THE EXPRESSIONS *CELA VAUT* (IT'S WORTH) AND *IL VAUT MIEUX* (IT'S BETTER)

It really is worth the effort: The expressions *cela vaut* (it's worth; it costs) and *il vaut mieux* (it's better) are extremely common and useful. Both expressions contain the verb *vaut*, a form of *valoir* (to be worth).

The expression *il vaut mieux* is generally followed by the *–er/-ir/-re* form of the verb. For example:

Il vaut mieux acheter les places pour le concert maintenant.

It's better to buy the tickets for the concert now.

Il vaut mieux partir de bonne heure.

It's better to leave early.

Il vaut mieux y aller.

It's better to go in now.

The expression *cela vaut* (it's worth; it costs) can be followed by a noun, or a number expressing cost. In everyday language, *cela vaut* is almost always shortened to *ça vaut*. For example:

Ça vaut le déplacement.

It's worth the trip.

Ça vaut quatre cents euros.

It costs 400 euros.

Combien est-ce que ça vaut?

How much does it cost?

And here are the various present tense forms of *valoir* (to be worth), an irregular verb, of course.

THE PRESENT TENSE OF THE IRREGULAR VERB *VALOIR* (TO BE WORTH)	
je vaux	nous valons
tu vaux	vous valez
il / elle vaut	ils / elles valent

(Note: The forms other than the third person are infrequently used.)

In the *passé composé*, the expression is *il a mieux valu* (it would have been better) or *cela a valu* (it was worth). And in the future tense, it's *il vaudra mieux* (it will be better) and *cela vaudra* (it will be worth).

Fill in the blanks with the corresponding phrases.

a)	*Ces coffrets de jazz _____ très chers.*		vaut mieux
b)	*Il _____ acheter les places aujourd'hui.*		valent
c)	*Combien _____ ces CDs?*		vaut
d)	*Rien ne _____ une chanson bien écrite.*		valent

LET'S PUT IT IN WRITING

You know of *la très célèbre* Céline Dion, right? But maybe not in French. Here are a couple of lines from her song "Pour que tu m'aimes encore":

> *J'irai chercher ton coeur si tu l'emportes ailleurs*
>
> *Même si dans tes danses d'autres dansent . . ."*
>
> © *J. J. Goldman / Céline Dion*

Ah! French is such a romantic language.

a) Translate the title of Céline Dion's song.

b) In this song, is Céline Dion speaking about: *la musique; le temps; l'amour?*

WORDS TO LIVE BY

GIVE THEM SOME APPLAUSE: GOING TO A CONCERT

A lot of musical events take place in Paris every night:

adorer	to love
aller dans les coulisses	to go backstage
applaudir	to applaud
saluer	to pay one's regards
le concert	concert
les coulisses	backstage
la place	seat
la porte	door
le public	audience
la salle	hall; room

Time to celebrate a birthday with a *Joyeux anniversaire!* (Happy birthday!)

Quel âge as-tu maintenant?	*How old are you now?*
J'ai trente-trois ans.	*I am 33.*
l'âge (masc.)	*age*
la bougie	*candle*
le gâteau d'anniversaire	*birthday cake*

And the expressions:

attendre de faire	*to wait to do*
arrêter de faire	*to stop doing*
commencer à faire	*to start doing*
faire plaisir à quelqu'un	*to please someone*

Some useful little words are:

juste à temps	*just in time*
sans aucun doute	*no doubt*

Word on the Street

Cela vaut le déplacement.	*It's worth going.*
de notre part	*from us*
le tout-Paris	*the Paris in-crowd, the Paris smart set*

ACTIVITY 12: **TAKE IT FOR A SPIN**

Off to a word hunt! Find all the sentences related to Camille's birthday in the dialogues.

CRIB NOTES

HEAR...SAY 1

A voice behind him:	Are you looking for something?	Jason:	Are you still with . . . ?
Jason:	Hey! Hello, El'hadj! Long time no see! How are you?	El'hadj:	Audrey! Yes. And we even got married in New York! And a couple of months ago, our little boy was born!
El'hadj:	I'm fine, and you?		
Jason:	Well . . . as usual. I work not far from here. So, I come here from time to time. And you, you work here?	Jason:	What a surprise! You're a daddy! Congratulations to both of you! So, you really are back from the States.
El'hadj:	Yes, a few days a week. It's been three months.	El'hadj:	Yeah. Anyway, are you looking for something?

Jason:	Actually, yes, I'd like to give several CDs to my girlfriend, Camille. Saturday is her birthday.	Jason:	Hmmm. . . . I discovered Helen Merrill not long ago. But I've never heard this particular one.
El'hadj:	Some jazz. . . . Instrumental?	El'hadj:	You can listen to it over there. It costs 15 euros.
Jason:	Yes, she listens to a lot of jazz. Or maybe a singer . . .Ella Fitzgerald or Helen Merrill. Actually I listen to them too. By the way, on Saturday, we'll probably go to a concert with some other friends. You remember Flo and Aziza?	Jason:	Well, I trust you. I'll take it and I'm going to take this CD by Ella as well. Hey! You want to come on Saturday?
		El'hadj:	Okay. And who are you going to see in concert?
El'hadj:	Yes, we talk sometimes on the phone with Aziza. Here's a very good one by Helen Merrill with the Quincy Jones orchestra.	Jason:	We won't know until Saturday. Florence and Aziza want to surprise us. Then we'll celebrate with champagne.
		El'hadj:	That's cool. Yes, that's a great idea. That way, I'll see everyone again.

HEAR . . . SAY 2

Aziza:	Here we are!	Julienne:	Yes, no doubt about it, it's worth the trip.
Florence:	They've already opened the doors.		
Julienne:	We're going to see Richard Bona? Hey, you got me, Paco! I almost bought tickets!	Paco:	We'd better to go in now, with all these people waiting.
		Florence:	Yes, the concert starts in a bit. . . . Do you see that, Ziza, everyone who's anyone is here.
Camille:	Great! Thank you!		
Paco:	From all of us, happy birthday, Camille!		

Inside the hall, the stage is ready, the audience waits impatiently for the group, then claps their hands.

Jason:	Happy birthday! And to all three of you, a big thank you.	Jason:	Hey, here comes El'hadj . . . Aziza, Flo . . .
The others:	Happy Birthday, Camille! So how old are you?	Florence:	El'hadj, it's so great to see you! You're just on time. Here they are! Bravo!
Camille:	I'm still twenty! Yes, thank you very much. It's so cool to invite us. Jason gave me the CD of this artist. I loved it!		

After a hot and moving concert, the friends go backstage to pay their regards to the musicians. Then they'll all go to Paco's, to celebrate the newly twenty-year-old Camille, the reunion with El'hadj and this great concert.

| Aziza: | Well, wait until you see him play, he's a great musician and a talented songwriter! | | |

ANSWER KEY

ACTIVITY 1

a) Non, la scène se passe pendant la semaine.
b) Jason rencontre El'hadj, un ancien copain, à la FNAC.
c) Jason cherche des CDs de jazz pour l'anniversaire de sa copine, Camille.
d) Son copain, El'hadj, lui annonce son mariage avec Audrey et la naissance de son fils.
e) Jason propose à El'hadj de venir samedi à un concert.

ACTIVITY 2

a) Ce soir, je boirai du champagne.
b) Il ne me croira pas.
c) Nous pourrons lui acheter des CDs.
d) Pour son anniversaire, tu devras aller au magasin.
e) Elles recevront bientôt nos cadeaux.
f) Vous verrez ce soir, c'est une surprise.
g) Ils ne sauront rien.

ACTIVITY 3

a) Nous t'attendrons au concert.
b) Quel plaisir, on entendra bien le son.
c) Je ne comprendrai pas ces paroles.
d) Tu me diras si tu peux venir à la répétition demain.
e) Cela te prendra du temps d'enregistrer tout ça?
f) Tu feras du bon boulot.

ACTIVITY 4

a) Je n'entends personne.
b) C'est l'anniversaire de mon ami, je dois lui trouver quelque chose.
c) Tous mes amis sont venus à mon anniversaire.
d) Elle est très difficile. Rien ne lui plaît jamais.
e) Est-ce que quelqu'un veut du champagne?
f) Chaque moment d'une vie est important.

ACTIVITY 5

tout le monde-personne / en general-en particulier / plusieurs-un / triste-joyeux *or* content / peu sympathique-sympa *or* cool / souvent-de temps en temps *or* jamais / être bien-être mal *or* souffrir / il y a peu de temps-il y a un bail *or* il y a longtemps / même-différent

ACTIVITY 6

For example:
a) J'aime la musique du monde.
a) Oui, j'ai déja vu des artistes francophones sur scène. / Non, je n'ai jamais vu d'artistes francophones sur scène.

ACTIVITY 7

a) Les amis vont au concert de Richard Bona.
b) Oui, les amis sont très contents de la surprise.
c) Non, le public est impatient.
d) Le concert est chaud et émouvant.
e) Les amis iront chez Paco célébrer l'anniversaire de Camille, les retrouvailles ave El'hadj et le concert.

ACTIVITY 8

j'ai découvert, tu as découvert, il / elle a découvert, nous avons découvert, vous avez découvert, ils / elles ont découvert

ACTIVITY 9

a) Les hommes aiment souffrir.
b) Qu'est-ce qu'on t'a offert pour ton anniversaire?
c) Il y a tant de choses à découvrir.
d) Personne n'ouvre son cadeau maintenant.

ACTIVITY 10

a) Ces coffrets de jazz valent très chers.
b) Il vaut mieux acheter les places aujourd'hui.
c) Combien valent ces CDs?
d) Rien ne vaut une chanson bien écrite.

ACTIVITY 11

a) So That You'll Still Love Me
b) L'amour

ACTIVITY 12

Je voudrais offrir plusieurs CDs à ma copine Camille. Ce sera son anniversaire samedi.—On ira probablement à un concert avec d'autres amis . . . —Florence et Aziza veulent nous faire une surprise— Après, on ira arroser ça au champagne.—De notre part à tous, joyeux anniversaire, Camille!!!—Bon anniversaire!—Joyeux anniversaire, Camille!—Alors, quel âge as-tu?—J'ai toujours vingt ans!—Oui, merci beaucoup. C'est super sympa de nous inviter. Jason m'a offert le CD de cet artiste.—Ils iront tous chez Paco célébrer les nouveaux vingt ans de Camille.

15. "THE AMERICAS" HOTEL

Hôtel des Amériques

Allow me to come up with you!

COMING UP . . .

- *Closed for vacation*: Learning the French you'll need in hotels and on vacation
- *Head and shoulders . . .* : Names for body parts
- *I scream, you scream*: The irregular verbs *paraître* (to seem), *connaître* (to know), and *mettre* (to put, to place)
- *The way we were*: A new tense to talk about how things used to be
- *To whom it may concern*: Putting sentences together using relative pronouns
- *Strut your stuff!*

Hôtel des Amériques ("*The Americas*" *Hotel*) was directed by André Téchiné in 1981. Téchiné started his career as a film critic for the famous *Cahiers du Cinéma*. Catherine Deneuve, the famous French actress, has worked several times with Téchiné. She remains at the top of the French cinema with movies like *Belle Maman*, *Place Vendôme* and, more recently, *Dancers in the Dark*.

LOOKING AHEAD

This chapters brings you *dans le sud de la France* (to the South of France), in the *région de Collioure*, where *l'air*, coming from the Mediterranean, is fresh and *salé* (salty). This will give me the opportunity to tell you about *les traditions locales* (local traditions) and more.

In the dialogues, we'll be following *l'histoire d'un couple anglais* (the story of an English couple) arriving Collioure after a long and tiring trip from Bath *en Angleterre* (in England). By the way, you've heard of the Channel Tunnel. . . . Of course! Well, Mr. and Mrs. Wilson seemingly haven't, since they opted to travel on the ferry across *La Manche* (the English Channel). It could have been nice if it weren't for the *tempête* (storm). *Enfin* (finally), when they arrive in the *adorable petit Hôtel du Soleil Couchant*, they are not exactly in the best of moods. Meanwhile, the town of Collioure is getting ready for *un festival de musique*, just when the couple is craving *le calme total* (complete quiet) and *la climatisation* (air conditioning).

HEAR...SAY 1

A Charming Hotel   (Un hôtel charmant)

Mrs. Wilson: Il n'y a personne?

Valérie, la propriétaire du petit hôtel, apparaît à la réception.

Valérie: Madame, Monsieur, bonsoir!

Mrs. Wilson: Bonsoir, ma chère dame. Je suis madame Wilson, et voici mon mari, qui ne parle pas bien le français.

Valérie: Ah oui, vous avez fait une réservation pour une chambre double depuis Bath. Comment s'est passé votre voyage?

Mrs. Wilson: Notre voyage! C'était très fatigant, il y avait une tempête et le bateau allait comme ça, ça n'en finissait pas!

Valérie: Eh bien! En tous cas, ici, vous vous reposerez bien. Le soleil brille tous les jours et c'est très calme.

Le son d'un saxophone retentit, puis celui d'un piano. Les yeux des touristes s'arrondissent.

Valérie:	Mon mari et une pianiste répètent pour le festival. Votre chambre, qui est au premier étage, est prête. Permettez-moi de vous accompagner. Vous avez une belle vue sur la mer, sur le phare.
Mr. Wilson:	*No elevators?!*
Valérie:	Ah non, Monsieur, il n'y a pas d'ascenseur ici.

En face de l'escalier se trouve la chambre. Valérie ouvre la porte. Elle allume la lumière, ouvre les rideaux de la fenêtre. Un groupe de jeunes passe dans le couloir.

Mrs. Wilson:	Hmm! . . . C'est charmant! *Look, John, isn't it lovely?*
Mr. Wilson:	*Very nice, Betty, but where's the air conditioning?*
Valérie:	Vous parlez de la climatisation? Avec l'air de la mer, ce n'est pas nécessaire ici. Eh bien, passez une bonne nuit.

Leur voisins de chambre et leurs invités arrivent bruyamment.

Mrs. Wilson:	Ah! Ne fais pas cette tête! On va enfin se reposer.
Mr. Wilson:	Pas d'ascenseur, pas de climatisation et du bruit. On rêvait d'un hôtel calme, Betty! Et si on changeait d'hôtel?

LET'S PUT IT IN WRITING

Read this tourist ad for Collioure.

"Bercée par la mer Méditerranée, sous le regard des Pyrénées, Collioure vous invite à venir vous reposer sur ses plages de sable fin ou de galets . . . Le vent y est parfumé, les étés doux et longs, les sites naturels et historiques inoubliables. N'hésitez pas plus longtemps. Contactez l'office du tourisme de la ville de Collioure ou de la région Languedoc-Roussillon."

ACTIVITY 1: HOW'S THAT AGAIN?

a) *Qui sont les personnages dans le dialogue?*

b) *Où se passe la scène?*

c) *D'où viennent Mr. et Mrs. Wilson? Ont-ils fait un bon voyage?*

d) *Comment est la chambre du couple?*

e) *Est-ce que Mr. Wilson est content de l'hôtel?*

f) *Où se trouve Collioure?*

Did You Know?

Did You Know?

WORKSHOP 1

THE NITTY-GRITTY

I SCREAM, YOU SCREAM: THE IRREGULAR VERBS *PARAÎTRE* (TO SEEM), *CONNAÎTRE* (TO KNOW), AND *METTRE* (TO PUT, TO PLACE)

1. For the present tense of verbs ending in *-aître*, such as the verb *paraître* (to seem) and the related verbs *apparaître* (to appear), *disparaître* (to disappear), *connaître* (to know), and *reconnaître* (to recognize), we use the present tense endings you are now familiar with:

   For *je, tu, il / elle* forms: **–s, –s, –t.**
   For *nous, vous, ils / elles* forms: **–ons, –ez, –ent.**

THE PRESENT TENSE OF THE IRREGULAR VERB *PARAÎTRE* (TO SEEM)			
je parais	I seem	*nous paraissons*	we seem
tu parais	you seem	*vous paraissez*	you seem
il / elle paraît	he / she seems	*ils / elles paraissent*	they seem

THE PRESENT TENSE OF THE IRREGULAR VERB *CONNAÎTRE* (TO KNOW)			
je connais	I know	*nous connaissons*	we know
tu connais	you know	*vous connaissez*	you know
il / elle connaît	he / she knows	*ils / elles connaissent*	they know

Heads Up!

The present of the verbs in –*ettre*, such as *mettre* (to put), *permettre* (to allow), *promettre* (to promise), and *admettre* (to admit) is formed by adding the same sets of endings to the stem (*per/pro/ad*) *met*–.

THE PRESENT TENSE OF THE IRREGULAR VERB *METTRE* (TO PUT, TO PLACE)			
je mets	I put	*nous mettons*	we put
tu mets	you put	*vous mettez*	you put
il / elle met	he / she puts	*ils / elles mettent*	they put

Note the double "tt" in the *nous, vous,* and *ils/elles* forms. The single "t" in *je mets, tu mets,* and *il/elle met* is not pronounced.

ACTIVITY 2: TAKE IT FOR A SPIN

Look at *paraître* and *mettre* one more time! Then write down the present tense forms of *apparaître* (to appear) and *permettre* (to allow).

2. To form the past participle of verbs ending in –*aître*, drop the ending –*aître* and add the ending –*u*.

   The verbs *paraître* and *connaître* use the verb *avoir* to form the *passé composé;* the verb *apparaître* commonly uses the auxiliary verb *être*. So:

   paraître (to seem) → **j'ai paru** (I (have) seemed), etc.
   connaître (to know) → **j'ai connu** (I knew / have known), etc.
   apparaître (to appear) → **je suis apparu** (I (have) appeared), etc.

   To form the past participle of verbs in –*ettre*, drop the ending –*ettre* and add –*is* to their stem.

   mettre (to put, to place) → **j'ai mis** (I (have) put), etc.
   permettre (to allow) → **j'ai permis** (I (have) allowed), etc.

3. The imperative of the verbs in -*aître* and -*ettre* is regular. As you know now, you need to use the *tu, nous, vous* forms of the present tense.

THE IMPERATIVE OF THE VERBS PARAÎTRE, CONNAÎTRE AND METTRE		
PARAÎTRE (TO SEEM)	CONNAÎTRE (TO KNOW)	METTRE (TO PUT)
parais	connais	mets
paraissons	connaissons	mettons
paraissez	connaissez	mettez

4. The future tense of the verbs in -aître and ettre is also regularly formed.

THE FUTURE TENSE OF THE IRREGULAR VERB PARAÎTRE (TO SEEM)			
je paraîtrai	I will seem	nous paraîtrons	we will seem
tu paraîtras	you will seem	vous paraîtrez	you will seem
il / elle paraîtra	he / she / it will seem	ils / elles paraîtront	they will seem

The future tense of the irregular verb *connaître* (to know) is *je connaîtrai, tu connaîtras*, etc. Note that all the future forms have the "î". Yes, that's because the "t" shows up in all these forms.

The future tense of *mettre* (to put, to place) is *je mettrai, tu mettras*, etc. No problem there either!

ACTIVITY 3: TAKE IT FOR A SPIN

Put the verbs in parentheses into the future tense.

    a)   *Vous (connaître) bientôt la réponse.*
    b)   *La direction ne (permettre) plus de jouer de la musique.*
    c)   *Quand est-ce qu'ils (admettre (admit)) leur mauvaise humeur?*
    d)   *Elle n'(apparaître) pas avant la fin de la semaine.*
    e)   *Ce soir, nous ne (mettre) pas la climatisation.*
    f)   *Notre quartier nous (paraître) bien calme à notre retour.*

THE WAY WE WERE: A NEW TENSE TO TALK ABOUT HOW THINGS USED TO BE

When you want to talk about things you did habitually or for long periods of time in the past, or when you want to express your past state of mind or a past state of things, you must use in French a past tense called the imperfect. When we talk about things using the imperfect, we are not interested so much in when things happened in the past, but more so, how they happened and how long they lasted.

Let's look at some examples. You'll notice that the imperfect can be translated into English in various ways.

Il buvait son café dans sa chambre.

He was drinking his coffee in his room.

Ils aimaient la mer.

They loved the sea.

Nos voisins étaient bruyants.

Our neighbors were noisy.

Ils passaient leurs vacances dans un hôtel du sud de la France.

They used to spend their vacation in a hotel in the South of France.

Ce voyage était fatigant.

This trip was tiring.

It is rather simple to form the imperfect. As with the future, we use the same set of endings with all types of verbs.

For *je, tu, il / elle* forms: **–ais, –ais, –ait.**
For *nous, vous, ils / elles* forms: **–ions, –iez, –aient.**

You add these endings to the stem, which you will get if you take the *nous* form of the present tense and take away the *–ons* ending. For example:

nous arrivons* → *arriv-* → *j'arrivais, etc.

1. The Imperfect Tense of Regular Verbs in –er

THE IMPERFECT TENSE OF THE REGULAR VERB *ARRIVER* (TO ARRIVE)			
j'arrivais	I arrived / was arriving	*nous arrivions*	we arrived / were arriving
tu arrivais	you arrived / were arriving	*vous arriviez*	you arrived / were arriving
il / elle arrivait	he / she arrived / was arriving	*ils / elles arrivaient*	they arrived / were arriving

The Fine Print

The verbs ending in -ger add an "e" between their stem and the imperfect endings starting with "a" (*–ais, –ais, –ait, –aient*) so that the "g" may still be pronounced (zh). One such verb is *voyager* (to travel).

THE IMPERFECT TENSE OF THE REGULAR VERB *VOYAGER* (TO TRAVEL)	
je voyageais	*nous voyagions*
tu voyageais	*vous voyagiez*
il / elle voyageait	*ils / elles voyageaient*

The verbs ending in *–cer* need a cedilla under the letter "c" before the endings starting with "a" (*–ais*, *–ais*, *–ait*, *–aient*) so that "c" may still be pronounced (s).

One such verb is *commencer* (to start).

THE IMPERFECT TENSE OF THE REGULAR VERB *COMMENCER* (TO START)	
je commençais	nous commencions
tu commençais	vous commenciez
il / elle commençait	ils / elles commençaient

2. The Imperfect Tense of Regular Verbs in –ir

Okay. . . . This is what we do with a verb such as *finir* (to finish):

nous finissons → finiss– → je finissais (I finished / was finishing), etc.

THE IMPERFECT TENSE OF THE REGULAR VERB *FINIR* (TO FINISH)	
je finissais	nous finissions
tu finissais	vous finissiez
il / elle finissait	ils / elles finissaient

3. The Imperfect Tense of the Auxiliary Verb Avoir (to have)

The imperfect of the auxiliary verb *avoir* is regularly formed. So:

nous avons → av– → j'avais (I had / was having), etc.

THE IMPERFECT TENSE OF THE AUXILIARY VERB *AVOIR* (TO HAVE)	
j'avais	nous avions
tu avais	vous aviez
il / elle avait	ils / elles avaient

4. The Imperfect Tense of the Auxiliary Verb Être (to be)

The imperfect of the verb *être* is irregular. That is, you can't apply the trick I taught you before. Its imperfect stem is *ét–*, to which you add the standard endings. So:

ét- → j'étais (I was / was being), etc.

THE IMPERFECT TENSE OF THE AUXILIARY VERB *ÊTRE* (TO BE)	
j'étais	nous étions
tu étais	vous étiez
il / elle était	ils / elles étaient

5. The Imperfect Tense of the Irregular Verb Aller (to go)

With *aller* (to go), we're back to the usual pattern again.

nous allons → **all-** → **j'allais** (I went / was going), etc.

THE IMPERFECT TENSE OF THE AUXILIARY VERB *ALLER* (TO GO)

j'allais	*nous allions*
tu allais	*vous alliez*
il / elle allait	*ils / elles allaient*

The Fine Print

Used with *si* (if), the imperfect doesn't refer to the past, but expresses a suggestion. This is a common use of the imperfect that I suggest you try to remember.

Et si on changeait d'hôtel?

What if we changed hotels? (*Lit.* of hotel)

Et si on prenait une autre chambre?

What about taking another room?

Et si vous alliez vous promener?

What if you took a stroll?

ACTIVITY 4: **TAKE IT FOR A SPIN**

Put the following sentences into the imperfect.

- a) *Es-tu à Collioure cet été?*
- b) *Nous aurons tout le temps de nous reposer.*
- c) *Tu choisis toujours des hôtels bruyants.*
- d) *Ils ne réserveront jamais à cet hôtel.*
- e) *Vous m'accompagnez en voyage?*
- f) *Je suis allée à la plage tous les matins.*

WORDS TO LIVE BY

CLOSED FOR VACATION: LEARNING THE FRENCH YOU'LL NEED IN HOTELS AND ON VACATION

Time for a vacation, don't you think? After some browsing on the Web, talking to your friends and a couple of agents, you finally choose your destination and your hotel, and you are ready to prepare for your trip.

préparer pour le voyage	to prepare for the trip
découvrir	to discover
faire une réservation	to make a reservation
réserver	to book, to reserve
se trouver	to be located

After *un voyage fatigant* (a tiring trip), here you are in a *charmant* (charming) little hotel. *La propriétaire*, the owner of the hotel, is here to welcome you at l'Hôtel du Soleil Couchant (Sunset Hotel).

à la réception	at the desk
accompagner	to accompany
allumer	to turn on
changer de chambre	to change rooms
la chambre double	double room
la clé	key

You should know that the French are not particularly keen on air conditioning. If you can't live without it, make sure that you ask about it when you're booking a room or renting a place to stay. And make sure that it also works!

la climatisation	air conditioning
le lit	bed
le rideau	curtain
la salle d'eau, la salle de bain	bathroom

The good thing is that most old buildings in France have *fenêtres* (windows that you can actually open wide) and sometimes, even *des balcons* (balconies). You can enjoy *la lumière naturelle* (the natural light) and *la vue* (the view).

Similarly, if you choose to stay in an old hotel, there may not be *un ascenseur* (an elevator) in it; you'll have to use *un escalier* (a staircase).

France is bordered by beautiful *mer* (sea) and varied *plages* (beaches) on the north, west and south.

le galet	pebble
la (mer) Méditerranée	Mediterranean (Sea)
le phare	lighthouse
les Pyrénées	Pyrenees
le sable fin	fine sand
la tempête	storm

Word on the Street

faire bon voyage	to have a nice trip
faire la tête	to sulk
Ne fais pas cette tête!	Don't sulk!
Ça n'en finissait pas!	It seemed to never end!
Bonne nuit!	Good night!

TAKE IT FOR A SPIN

Let's pretend! Using words from the following list, describe the room you booked in a nice, charming hotel in the South of France on your last summer vacation there. (Your tense of choice will be imperfect here.)

la fenêtre, la vue, l'ascenseur, la salle d'eau, le lit double, les rideaux, calme, le balcon, les voisins, la climatisation, bruyant, la mer

And now, let's go back to the dialogue and check on how Mr. and Mrs. Wilson are doing after a good night's sleep. Well, as a matter of fact, it seems that because of *leurs voisins bruyants*, they did not get much sleep at all.

HEAR...SAY 2

Finally, Some Quiet!   (Du calme enfin!)

Mrs. Wilson: Et si on allait s'asseoir à cette terrasse de café? Cette promenade était agréable, mais j'ai mal aux pieds!

Mr. Wilson: Si tu veux . . . Garçon, le menu, s'il vous plaît.

Mrs. Wilson: Où se trouvent les toilettes, s'il vous plaît?

Mrs. Wilson, qui est de retour à table, regarde le menu. Son mari paraît avoir déjà choisi.

Mrs. Wilson: Tu sais ce que tu veux? Je vais prendre une tasse de thé citron et deux gaufres.

Mr. Wilson: Cette mauvaise nuit que nous avons passée m'a donné mal à la tête. Si je vois ces voyous . . .

Mrs. Wilson: C'était la nuit dernière, oublions tout ça.

Le serveur vient prendre la commande.

Le serveur: Alors, un thé citron, deux gaufres, une omelette bacon et un sorbet à la fraise. Ce sera tout?

Mrs. Wilson: Et deux verres d'eau glacée. Oui, profitons du calme et du soleil. Puis, j'ai parlé à la propriétaire, qui est vraiment charmante. Elle allait leur parler et . . .

Mr. Wilson: Leur parler de quoi? Il faut les mettre dehors! Ils ne vont pas nous casser les oreilles toutes les nuits.

Le son d'une guitare électrique met fin à leur conversation. Le couple se retourne et reconnaît leurs voisins de chambre, qui répètent sur la scène derrière le café.

Mr. Wilson: Ce n'est pas possible! Betty, on retourne à Bath où on pourra se reposer. Garçon, l'addition!

Le serveur:	Vous n'aimez pas ce que vous avez commandé? Ah ça, ça change de votre nourriture.

LET'S PUT IT IN WRITING

Revue de presse

"**Le Festival Des Trois Cultures** annonce sa nouvelle saison. Le festival aura lieu dans les trois villes habituelles de Caboure au Pays Basque, Calvi en Corse, et Collioure dans le Languedoc-Roussillon aux mois de mai et juin. Plusieurs spectacles de danse et de théâtre, des concerts, des expositions et des manifestations sportives sont prévus. Ces festivités permettront aux visiteurs de découvrir ces cultures régionales . . .

Le motto du festival: *"Pour mieux s'enrichir de nos différences."*

FRENCH WITHOUT THE FUSS

ACTIVITY 6: HOW'S THAT AGAIN?

Let's check on how you're doing.

a) *Qu'est-ce que Mr. et Mrs. Wilson ont fait ce matin?*
b) *Que propose Mrs. Wilson?*
c) *Est-ce que Mr. Wilson est de bonne humeur? Pourquoi?*
d) *Qu'est-ce qui se passe?*
e) *Que décide Mr. Wilson?*
f) *Qu'est-ce que cette revue de presse (press release) annonce?*

WORKSHOP 2

THE NITTY-GRITTY

TO WHOM IT MAY CONCERN: PUTTING SENTENCES TOGETHER USING RELATIVE PRONOUNS

Let's look at a sentence from the last dialogue:

Mrs. Wilson, _qui_ est de retour à la table, regarde le menu.

Mrs. Wilson, who is back at the table, is looking at the menu.

Who (in the English translation) is a relative pronoun that refers to *Mrs. Wilson*. *Who* is used to put two sentences—*Mrs. Wilson is looking at the menu* and *She is back at the table*—together into a single sentence.

Relative pronouns normally follow the noun they refer to.

1. The three most commonly used relative pronouns are:

qui	who, which, that
que	whom, which
où	where; when

The relative pronoun *qui* (who, which, that) usually refers to the preceding noun which is a subject of the sentence. *Qui* can stand for either a thing or a person.

C'est ce voyage _qui_ m'a donné mal à la tête.

It's this trip that gave me a headache.

Voici mon mari _qui_ ne parle pas français.

This is my husband, who doesn't speak French.

J'ai parlé à la propriétaire _qui_ est vraiment charmante.

I spoke to the owner, who is really nice.

Qui (who, which, that) can also be preceded by a preposition—*avec* (with), *à* (to), *pour* (for), *sans* (without), *de* (of), or *par* (by). In this case, *qui* can only be a person.

Mon mari _avec qui_ j'ai voyagé est malade.

My husband, with whom I traveled, is sick.

Cet ami _sans qui_ je suis perdue est arrivé.

This friend without whom I'm lost has arrived.

The relative pronoun *que* "which, that" refers to a noun that is the object of the verb. It can stand for either a person or a thing.

C'est l'hôtel _que_ j'aime.

That's the hotel (that) I like.

Les voisins _que_ nous avons sont bruyants.

The neighbors (that) we have are noisy.

Cette nuit _que_ nous avons passée m'a donné mal à la tête.

The night we had gave me a headache.

Note that in French, relative pronouns cannot be dropped, unlike in English.

The relative pronoun *où* (where; when) refers to an expression of place or time.

L'hôtel <u>où</u> nous restons est charmant.

The hotel where we are staying is charming.

C'est l'heure <u>où</u> ils arrivent.

That's the hour when they arrive.

ACTIVITY 7: **TAKE IT FOR A SPIN**

Qui, que, or *où*? Choose the appropriate relative pronoun to complete the following sentences.

    a)   Les voisins _____ ont fait du bruit sont partis.

    b)   L'hôtel _____ j'ai réservé une chambre double semble bon.

    c)   La plage _____ je vois de ma chambre d'hôtel est superbe.

    d)   La région _____ nous avons passé nos vacances est touristique.

    e)   Ceux _____ ne sont pas heureux peuvent partir.

2. More on relative pronouns

While we cannot cover everything about relative pronouns in French, we'll introduce another type of relative pronoun that is quite useful and common in everyday speech.

The relative pronouns *ce qui* (that which / subject) and *ce que* (that which / object) are not preceded by a noun; instead, they refer to an "indefinite" object or situation.

<u>Ce qui</u> ne me plaît pas, c'est tout ce bruit!

What I don't like is all that noise!

Tu sais <u>ce que</u> tu veux?

You know what you want?

Vous n'aimez pas <u>ce que</u> vous avez commandé.

You don't like what you ordered.

ACTIVITY 8: **TAKE IT FOR A SPIN**

Rewrite the following sentences by putting the words in the right order.

    a)   charmant / nous / où / l'hôtel / restons / est.

    b)   du / apporté / qui / vin / sympas / amis / sont / les / ont / nous.

    c)   se / qui / passe / je / pas / ce / n'aime.

    d)   la fête / hier soir / qu' / il / était / a / bruyante / organisée / .

    e)   ne / ce / pas / disons / comprennent / nous / ils / que.

Did You Know?

LET'S PUT IT IN WRITING

Collioure, sîte remarquable du goût . . .

Si Collioure est traditionellement une ville riche en art, en artisanat (craft), elle est surnommée aussi le sîte remarquable du goût . . .

La pêche y est une tradition. Mille recettes à base de poissons et de coquillages (shellfish) peuvent être dégustées (savored); l'anchoïade, à base d'anchois (anchovies) est succulente (delicious). Si vous préférez les produits de la terre, vous pouvez toujours aller à une cargolade, une sorte de grillades d'escargots (a type of snail barbecue).

Les anciennes vignes sont de qualité. Vous pouvez goûter toutes sortes de vins; mais la spécialité est le vin doux naturel, tel le Banyuls.

WORDS TO LIVE BY

The goal of traveling is to open one's mind and heart to new people and their *cultures locales* (local cultures), to discover new places, to learn new languages, to try new scents and tastes . . .

s'enrichir	to enrich oneself; to get rich
l'artisanat	craft
le peintre	painter
la peinture	painting
le port	harbor

Take the time to relax and eat on the terrace of a café . . .

commander	to order; to lead
prendre la commande	to take the order
l'addition	check
la carte, le menu	menu
le citron	lemon
les fruits de mer	seafood
la gaufre	waffle
une omelette	omelet
le sorbet à la fraise	strawberry sorbet
le thé citron	tea with lemon

Word on the Street

Ça change de . . .	It's quite a change from . . .
casser les oreilles	to break one's ears
donner mal à la tête	to give a headache
faire du bruit	to make noise
mettre quelqu'un dehors	to kick someone out
Tchin, tchin! or **Santé!**	Cheers!

HEAD AND SHOULDERS . . . : NAMES FOR THE BODY PARTS

A vacation is also an opportunity to rest and rejuvenate your body. So here are all the pieces you'll use and want to take care of.

la tête	head
la bouche	mouth
les cheveux	hair
le cou	neck
le bras	arm
le doigt	finger
le dos	back
l'épaule (fem.)	shoulder
les fesses	buttocks
le genou, les genoux	knee(s)
la jambe	leg
la main	hand
le nez	nose
l'oeil (masc.)(uh-nuhy), **des yeux** (deh-zyuh)	eye, eyes
l'oreille (fem.)	ear
la poitrine	chest
le pied	foot
le ventre	belly

Note that in English, we use the possessive adjective in front of a body part, as in *He raises his hand*; in French, one says, *Il lève la main*, using a definitive article.

ACTIVITY 9: **TAKE IT FOR A SPIN**

Y a-t-il quelque chose qui vous plaît sur le menu? (Is there anything you like on the menu?) *Choisissez ce que vous voulez manger* (choose what you'd like to eat) by writing a list of all the food vocabulary you've learned so far and especially in this lesson.

And you've waited for this moment to . . .

STRUT YOUR STUFF!

Let's take this last chance to review some of the things you've learned since Lesson 10.

ACTIVITY 10: **TAKE IT FOR A SPIN**

Put the verbs in parentheses into the correct form of the present tense.

a)   *Elles (se promener) sous la pluie.*
b)   *Nous ne (se parler) plus.*
c)   *Vous en (se servir) tous les matins.*
d)   *Comment (s'appeler) tu?*
e)   *Vous ne pouvez pas (s'asseoir) sur ces chaises.*

ACTIVITY 11: **TAKE IT FOR A SPIN**

And now, turn the sentences written in the present tense into past tense (*passé composé*).

a)   *Elles ne se voient pas depuis longtemps.*
b)   *Ce film leur plaît beaucoup.*
c)   *Quand venez-vous à la maison?*
d)   *Vous ne me dites pas de me reposer.*
e)   *Ils se promènent à vélo tous les après-midi.*
f)   *Nous prenons le train de bonne heure à la Gare du Nord.*

ACTIVITY 12: **TAKE IT FOR A SPIN**

En or *y?* Replace the underlined phrases with the correct word.

a)   *Je vais <u>à la gare</u>.*
b)   *Vous avez pris beaucoup <u>de café</u>.*

c)   *Elles se sont promenées <u>dans le Quartier latin</u>.*
d)   *Mange <u>des crêpes</u>!*
e)   *Nos grands-parents ne se font pas <u>à l'informatique</u>.*

TAKE IT FOR A SPIN

Rewrite the following sentences in the future tense.

a)   *Vous voulez prendre un peu de café?*
b)   *On est tous fatigués après le voyage.*
c)   *À quelle heure a lieu le concert?*
d)   *Ils ne se font pas à leur nouvelle vie.*
e)   *Quand viens-tu nous voir à la campagne?*
f)   *Elle écrit sa vie dans un livre.*

TAKE IT FOR A SPIN

The ultimate test! Translate the following sentences.

a)   Can you tell us the address of this hotel?
b)   It's better to leave earlier on Saturdays!
c)   She's having a hard time focusing on her songs.
d)   C'mon! Come and sit next to me.
e)   He's a great artist, but he can't communicate.
f)   What a summer! It rained every day during the month of July.
g)   You have celebrated her birthday for a week!

Well, this is it for your French lessons. Or is it? I certainly hope not! I hope this is just the beginning of a long and lasting relationship with the French language and French-speaking cultures. Remember that regular and abundant exposure to the language is the best way to learn it. So keep using what's around you—TV, radio, newspapers, the Internet. Travel to Canada or France, make friends, write e-mails. . . . Don't get intimidated and don't be afraid to make mistakes. It's the effort that counts and most people can appreciate that! As for me, I certainly hope to meet you again. *À bientôt!*

CRIB NOTES

Mrs. Wilson: Is anyone there?

Valérie, the owner of the little hotel, appears at the desk.

Valérie: Madam, Sir, good evening!

Mrs. Wilson: Good evening, my dear. I'm Mrs. Wilson, and this is my husband, who doesn't speak French very well.

Valérie: Ah yes, you made a reservation for a double room from Bath. How was your trip?

Mrs. Wilson: Our trip! It was very tiring. There was a storm and the boat was going like this. It seemed to never end!

Valérie: Well! In any event, you will rest well here. The sun shines every day and it's very quiet.

The sound of a saxophone resonates, then of a piano. The tourists' eyes open wide.

Valérie: My husband and a pianist are rehearsing for the festival. Your room, which is on the second floor, is ready. Allow me to come up with you. You have a beautiful view of the sea and the lighthouse.

Mr. Wilson: No elevators?!

Valérie: No, Sir, there are no elevators here.

The room is across from the stairway, Valérie opens the door. She turns on the light, opens the window curtains. A group of young people walks through the hallway.

Mrs. Wilson: Oh! . . . It's lovely! Look John, isn't it lovely?

Mr. Wilson: Very nice, Betty, but where's the air conditioning?

Valérie: You're talking about the air conditioning? With the air coming from the sea, it's not necessary here. Well, good night.

Their neighbors and their guests arrive noisily.

Mrs. Wilson: Don't sulk! We're finally going to rest.

Mr. Wilson: No elevator, no air conditioning and noise. We were dreaming of a quiet hotel, Betty! How about if we change hotels?

Mrs. Wilson: How about sitting on the terrace of this café? This walk was pleasant, but my feet are hurting!

Mr. Wilson: If you like. . . . Waiter, the menu, please.

Mrs. Wilson: Where are the restrooms, please?

Mrs. Wilson, who is back at the table, looks at the menu. Her husband seems to have already chosen.

Mrs. Wilson: You know what you want? I'm having a cup of tea with lemon and two waffles.

Mr. Wilson: The bad night we had gave me a headache. If I see those hooligans . . .

Mrs. Wilson: That was last night, let's forget about it.

The waiter comes to take the order.

The waiter: So, one tea with lemon, two waffles, one bacon omelet and one strawberry sorbet. Is that all?

Mrs. Wilson: And two glasses of ice water. Yes, let's enjoy the quiet and the sun. I spoke to the owner, who is really charming. She was going to speak to them . . .

Mr. Wilson: Speak to them about what? They should throw them out! They are not going to disturb us every night.

The sound of an electric guitar puts an end to their conversation. The couple turns around and recognizes their neighbors, who are rehearsing on stage behind the café.

Mr. Wilson: This can't be! Betty, we're going back to Bath where we'll be able to rest. Waiter, the check!

The waiter: You don't like what you ordered? For sure, it's quite a change from your food up there.

ACTIVITY 1

a) Les personnages sont Mr. et Mrs. Wilson et Valérie, la propriétaire de l'hôtel.
b) La scène se passe dans un hôtel de la petite ville de Collioure dans le sud de la France.
c) Mr. et Mrs. Wilson viennent de Bath, en Angleterre. Ils n'ont pas fait un bon voyage car il y a eu une tempête.
d) C'est une chambre double avec vue sur la mer et le phare. Elle est en face de l'escalier.
e) Non, Mr. Wilson n'est pas content de l'hôtel car il n'y a pas de climatisation, pas d'ascenseur et il y a du bruit.
f) Collioure se trouve dans le sud de la France, dans la region Languedoc-Roussillon.

ACTIVITY 2

APPARAÎTRE: j'apparais, tu apparais, il / elle apparaît, nous apparaissons, vous apparaissez, ils / elles apparaissent
PERMETTRE: je permets, tu permets, il / elle permet, nous permettons, vous permettez, ils / elles permettent

ACTIVITY 3

a) Vous connaîtrez bientôt la réponse.
b) La direction ne permettra plus de jouer de la musique.
c) Quand est-ce qu'ils admettront leur mauvaise humeur?
d) Elle n'apparaîtra pas avant la fin de la semaine.
e) Ce soir, nous ne mettrons pas la climatisation.
f) Notre quartier nous paraîtra bien calme à notre retour.

ACTIVITY 4

a) Étais-tu à Collioure cet été?
b) Nous avions tout le temps de nous reposer.
c) Tu choisissais toujours des hôtels bruyants.
d) Ils ne réservaient jamais à cet hôtel.
e) Vous m'accompagniez en voyage?
f) J'allais à la plage tous les matins.

ACTIVITY 5

For example:
Dans ma chambre, il y avait un lit double, une salle d'eau, une fenêtre avec des rideaux et un balcon avec vue sur la mer. La chambre était calme mais il n'y avait pas de climatisation et j'avais des voisins bruyants.

ACTIVITY 6

a) Mr. et Mrs. Wilson se sont promenés. *or* Ils ont fait une promenade.
b) Mrs. Wilson propose de s'asseoir à une terrasse de café.
c) Non, Mr. Wilson n'est pas vraiment de bonne humeur, car il a mal à la tête et il n'a pas passé une bonne nuit.
d) Le son d'une guitare électrique met fin à leur conversation. Leurs voisins répètent sur la scène derrière le café.
e) Mr. Wilson décide de retourner à Bath et il demande l'addition.
f) Cette revue de presse annonce un festival de spectacles de danse, de théatre, des expos, et du sport qui aura lieu dans trois villes du sud de la France.

ACTIVITY 7

a) Les voisins, qui ont fait du bruit, sont partis.
b) L'hôtel, où j'ai réservé une chambre double, semble bien.
c) La plage que je vois de ma chambre d'hôtel est superbe.
d) La région où nous avons passé nos vacances est touristique.
e) Ceux qui ne sont pas heureux peuvent partir.

ACTIVITY 8

a) L'hôtel où nous restons est charmant.
b) Les amis qui nous ont apporté du vin sont sympas.
c) Je n'aime pas ce qui se passe.
d) La fête qu'il a organisée hier soir était bruyante.
e) Ils ne comprennent pas ce que nous disons.

ACTIVITY 9

Je veux / je voudrais manger / du café, du thé, des gaufres, une omelette bacon, un sorbet, de l'eau, du vin, du poisson, des fruits de mer, l'anchoïade, la cargolade, etc.

ACTIVITY 10

a) Elles se promènent sous la pluie.
b) Nous ne nous parlons plus.
c) Vous vous en servez tous les matins.
d) Comment t'appelles-tu?
e) Vous ne pouvez pas vous asseoir sur ces chaises.

ACTIVITY 11

a) Elles ne se sont pas vues depuis longtemps.
b) Ce film leur a beaucoup plu.
c) Quand êtes-vous venus à la maison?
d) Vous ne m'avez pas dit de me reposer.
e) Ils se sont promenés à vélo tous les après-midi.
f) Nous avons pris le train de bonne heure à la Gare du Nord.

ACTIVITY 12

a) J'y vais.
b) Vous en avez pris beaucoup.
c) Elles s'y sont promenées.
d) Manges-en!
e) Nos grands-parents ne s'y font pas.

ACTIVITY 13

a) Vous voudrez prendre un peu de café?
b) On sera tous fatigués après le voyage.
c) À quelle heure aura lieu le concert?
d) Ils ne se feront pas à leur nouvelle vie.
e) Quand viendras-tu nous voir à la campagne?
f) Elle écrira sa vie dans un livre.

ACTIVITY 14

a) Pouvez-vous nous dire l'adresse de cet hôtel?
b) C'est mieux de partir plus tôt le samedi! OR: Il vaut mieux partir plus tôt le samedi!
c) Elle a du mal à se concentrer sur ses chansons.
d) Allez! Viens t'asseoir près de moi.
e) C'est un grand artiste, mais il ne sait pas communiquer.
f) Quel été! Il a plu tous les jours durant le mois de juillet.
g) Vous avez célébré son anniversaire pendant une semaine!

APPENDIX A

A SHORTCUT TO FRENCH GRAMMAR

1. Words, words, words . . .

PRONOUNS							
SUBJECT PRONOUNS		**STRESSED PERSONAL PRONOUNS**		**DIRECT OBJECT PRONOUNS**		**INDIRECT OBJECT PRONOUNS**	
SINGULAR *je*	I	*moi*	me	*me / m'*	me	*me / m'*	me
tu / vous	you	*toi*	you	*te / t'*	you	*te / t'*	you
il	he, it	*lui*	him, it	*le / l'*	him, it	*lui*	him / her / it
elle	she, it	*elle*	her, it	*la / l'*	her, it		
on	one						
PLURAL *nous*	we	*nous*	us	*nous*	us	*nous*	us
vous	you	*vous*	you	*vous*	you	*vous*	you
ils	they (masc.)	*eux*	them	*les*	them	*leur*	them
elles	they (fem.)	*elles*	them	*les*	them		

DEFINITE AND INDEFINITE ARTICLES				
	SINGULAR		**PLURAL**	
	Masculine	**Feminine**	**Masculine**	**Feminine**
Indefinite Articles (a / an)	*un une*	*des des*		
Definite Articles (the)*le / l'*	*la / l' les*	*les*		

CONTRACTED ARTICLES						
Masculine Singular	*à*	*à + le = au*	at / to the	*de*	*de + le = du*	from / of the
Plural	*à*	*à + les = aux*	at / to the	*de*	*de + les = des*	from / of the

Note: There is no contraction in the feminine singular, e.g., *de la* or *à la*.

PARTITIVE ARTICLES

	SINGULAR		PLURAL	
Masculine	*du / de l'*	some / any	*des*	some / any
Feminine	*de la / de l'*	some / any	*des*	some / any

Note: In negative sentences, *du / de la / de l' / des* are replaced by *de* alone.

POSSESSIVE ADJECTIVES

SINGULAR		PLURAL	
Masculine	Feminine	Masculine & Feminine	
mon	*ma*	*mes*	my
ton	*ta*	*tes*	your
son	*sa*	*ses*	his, her, its
notre	*notre*	*nos*	our
votre	*votre*	*vos*	your
leur	*leur*	*leurs*	their

POSSESSIVE PRONOUNS

SINGULAR		PLURAL		
Masculine	Feminine	Masculine	Feminine	
le mien	*la mienne*	*les miens*	*les miennes*	mine
le tien	*la tienne*	*les tiens*	*les tiennes*	yours
le sien	*la sienne*	*les siens*	*les siennes*	his / hers / its
le nôtre	*la nôtre*	*les nôtres*	*les nôtres*	ours
le vôtre	*la vôtre*	*les vôtres*	*les vôtres*	yours
le leur	*la leur*	*les leurs*	*les leurs*	theirs

Note: Possessive pronouns replace the noun and the possessive adjective, e.g., *C'est mon livre.* (It's my book.) → *Non, c'est le mien.* (No, it's mine.)

DEMONSTRATIVE ADJECTIVES

SINGULAR			PLURAL		
Masculine	Feminine		Masculine	Feminine	
ce / cet	*cette*	this / that	*ces*	*ces*	these / those

DEMONSTRATIVE PRONOUNS

	MASCULINE	FEMININE	
SINGULAR	*celui-ci*	*celle-ci*	this one
	celui-là	*celle-là*	that one
PLURAL	*ceux-ci*	*celles-ci*	these
	ceux-là	*celles-là*	those

QUESTION WORDS

Combien?	how many / how much
Comment?	how
Où?	where
Pourquoi?	why
Quand?	when
Que?	what
Qui?	who / whom
Lequel? (masculine singular)	Which one?
Laquelle? (feminine singular)	
Lesquels? (masculine plural)	Which ones?
Lesquelles? (feminine plural)	
Quel (+ noun)? (masculine singular)	Which one? What kind?
Quelle (+ noun)? (feminine singular)	
Quels (+ noun)? (masculine plural)	Which ones? / What kind?
Quelles (+ noun)? (feminine plural)	

ADVERBS OF TIME

à présent	now
après-demain	the day after tomorrow
aujourd'hui	today
autrefois	formerly
avant-hier	the day before yesterday
bientôt	soon
demain	tomorrow
désormais	from now on
depuis	since, since then
encore	more; still; yet
hier	yesterday
jamais	never
longtemps	for a long time

parfois **(or more colloquially, *des fois*)**	sometimes		
pendant / durant	during		
maintenant	now		
ne . . . jamais	never		
ne . . . plus	no more, no longer		
rarement	rarely, seldom		
souvent	often		
tard	late		
tôt	early		
tôt ou tard	sooner or later		
toujours	always		

ADVERBS OF QUANTITY

beaucoup	a lot
ne . . . plus	no more, no longer
ne . . . rien	nothing
peu	a little
plus	more
rien	nothing
trop	too much
tout	everything

THE PRESENT TENSE OF *-ER* VERBS: *TRAVAILLER* "TO WORK"

SINGULAR		PLURAL	
je travaille	I work	*nous travaillons*	we work
tu travailles	you work	*vous travaillez*	you work
il / elle travaille	he / she works	*ils / elles travaillent*	they work

THE FUTURE TENSE OF *-ER* VERBS: *TRAVAILLER* "TO WORK"

SINGULAR		PLURAL	
je travaillerai	I will work	*nous travaillerons*	we will work
tu travailleras	you will work	*vous travaillerez*	you will work
il / elle travaillera	he / she will work	*ils / elles travailleront*	they will work

THE *PASSÉ COMPOSÉ* OF *-ER* VERBS: *TRAVAILLER* "TO WORK"

SINGULAR		PLURAL	
j'ai travaillé	I worked	*nous avons travaillé*	we worked
tu as travaillé	you worked	*vous avez travaillé*	you worked
il / elle a travaillé	he / she worked	*ils / elles ont travaillé*	they worked

THE IMPERATIVE OF *-ER* VERBS: *TRAVAILLER* "TO WORK"

	SINGULAR		PLURAL	
1st person			*travaillons!*	Let's work!
2nd person	*travaille!*	Work!	*travaillez!*	Work!

THE PRESENT TENSE OF *-IR* VERBS: *FINIR* "TO FINISH"

SINGULAR		PLURAL	
je finis	I finish	*nous finissons*	we finish
tu finis	you finish	*vous finissez*	you finish
il / elle finit	he / she finishes	*ils / elles finissent*	they finish

THE FUTURE TENSE OF *-IR* VERBS: *FINIR* "TO FINISH"

SINGULAR		PLURAL	
je finirai	I will finish	*nous finirons*	we will finish
tu finiras	you will finish	*vous finirez*	you will finish
il / elle finira	he / she will finish	*ils / elles finiront*	they will finish

THE *PASSÉ COMPOSÉ* OF *-IR* VERBS: *FINIR* "TO FINISH"

SINGULAR		PLURAL	
j'ai fini	I finished	*nous avons fini*	we finished
tu as fini	you finished	*vous avez fini*	you finished
il / elle a fini	he / she finished	*ils / elles ont fini*	they finished

THE IMPERATIVE OF *-IR* VERBS: *FINIR* "TO FINISH"

	SINGULAR		PLURAL	
1st person			*finissons!*	Let's finish!
2nd person	*finis!*	Finish	*finissez!*	Finish!

2. Putting words together

QUESTIONS		
Est-ce que **questions**	*est-ce-que* + subject + verb + . . . ?	informal
	question word + *est-ce-que* + subject + verb + . . . ?	
Inversion **questions**	verb + subject + . . . ?	formal
	question word + verb + subject + . . . ?	

NEGATIVE SENTENCES

subject + *ne* + verb / auxiliary + *pas* + . . .	not
subject + *ne* + verb / auxiliary + *plus* + . . .	no more
subject + *ne* + verb / auxiliary + *jamais* + . . .	never
subject + *ne* + verb / auxiliary + *rien* + . . .	nothing

COMPARISONS

comparative of superiority	*plus* + adjective + *que* . . .	*more* + adjective + *than* <u>OR</u> adjective ending in *–er* + than . . .
comparative of equality	*aussi* + adjective + *que* . . .	as + adjective + *as* . . .
comparative of inferiority	*moins* + adjective + *que* . . .	*less* + adjective + *than* . . .

Example: *Il est plus / aussi / moins grand que son ami.* (He is taller than / as tall as / less tall than his friend.)

THE POSITION OF ADVERBS

In the present tense	subject + verb + adverb . . .
In the *passé composé*	subject + auxiliary verb + adverb + past participle . . .

Examples: *Il parle <u>beaucoup</u>. / Il a <u>beaucoup</u> parlé.* (He speaks a lot. / He spoke a lot.)

APPENDIX B

EXCEPTIONS THAT PROVE THE RULE

IRREGULAR VERBS

INFINITIVE	PRES. & PAST PARTICIPLES	PRESENT INDICATIVE	PRESENT SUBJUNCTIVE	IMPERFECT INDICATIVE	FUTURE	CONDITIONAL	IMPERATIVE
acquérir to acquire (*avoir*)	*acquérant* *acquis*	*acquiers* *acquiers* *acquiert* *acquérons* *acquérez* *acquièrent*	*acquière* *acquières* *acquière* *acquérions* *acquériez* *acquièrent*	*acquér* + *ais* *ais* *ait* *ions* *iez* *aient*	*acquerr* + *ai* *as* *a* *ons* *ez* *ont*	*acquerr* + *ais* *ais* *ait* *ions* *iez* *aient*	 *acquiers* *acquérons* *acquérez*
aller to go (*être*)	*allant* *allé(e)(s)*	*vais* *vas* *va* *allons* *allez* *vont*	*aille* *ailles* *aille* *allions* *alliez* *aillent*	*all* + *ais* *ais* *ait* *ions* *iez* *aient*	*ir* + *ai* *as* *a* *ons* *ez* *ont*	*ir* + *ais* *ais* *ait* *ions* *iez* *aient*	*va* *allons* *allez*
(s')asseoir† to sit (down) (*être*)	*asseyant* *assis(e)(s)*	*assieds* *assieds* *assied* *asseyons* *asseyez* *asseyent*	*asseye* *asseyes* *asseye* *asseyions* *asseyiez* *asseyent*	*assey* + *ais* *ais* *ait* *ions* *iez* *aient*	*asseyer* + *ai* or *as* *assiér* *a* or *ons* *assoir* *ez* *ont*	*asseyer* + *ais* or *ais* *assiér* *ait* or *ions* *assoir* *iez* *aient*	*assieds-toi* *asseyons-nous* *asseyez-vous*

† There is a variant form of the conjugation of *s'asseoir* based on the present participle *assayant* and first person singular *assois*; see p. 133. There are also two variant forms for the future stem: *assiér-* and *assoir-*. *Assiér-* is frequently used.

INFINITIVE	PRES. & PAST PARTICIPLES	PRESENT INDICATIVE	PRESENT SUBJUNCTIVE	IMPERFECT INDICATIVE	FUTURE	CONDITIONAL	IMPERATIVE
avoir to have (*avoir*)	*ayant* *eu*	*ai* *as* *a* *avons* *avez* *ont*	*aie* *aies* *ait* *ayons* *ayez* *aient*	*av + ais* *ais* *ait* *ions* *iez* *aient*	*aur + ai* *as* *a* *ons* *ez* *ont*	*aur + ais* *ais* *ait* *ions* *iez* *aient*	*aie* *ayons* *ayez*
battre to beat (*avoir*)	*battant* *battu*	*bats* *bats* *bat* *battons* *battez* *battent*	*batte* *battes* *batte* *battions* *battiez* *battent*	*batt + ais* *ais* *ait* *ions* *iez* *aient*	*battr + ai* *as* *a* *ons* *ez* *ont*	*battr + ais* *ais* *ait* *ions* *iez* *aient*	*bats* *battons* *battez*
boire to drink (*avoir*)	*buvant* *bu*	*bois* *bois* *boit* *buvons* *buvez* *boivent*	*boive* *boives* *boive* *buvions* *buviez* *boivent*	*buv + ais* *ais* *ait* *ions* *iez* *aient*	*boir + ai* *as* *a* *ons* *ez* *ont*	*boir + ais* *ais* *ait* *ions* *iez* *aient*	*bois* *buvons* *buvez*
conclure to conclude (*avoir*)	*concluant* *conclu*	*conclus* *conclus* *conclut* *concluons* *concluez* *concluent*	*conclue* *conclues* *conclue* *concluions* *concluiez* *concluent*	*conclu + ais* *ais* *ait* *ions* *iez* *aient*	*conclur + ai* *as* *a* *ons* *ez* *ont*	*conclur + ais* *ais* *ait* *ions* *iez* *aient*	*conclus* *concluons* *concluez*

INFINITIVE	PRES. & PAST PARTICIPLES	PRESENT INDICATIVE	PRESENT SUBJUNCTIVE	IMPERFECT INDICATIVE	FUTURE	CONDITIONAL	IMPERATIVE
conduire to drive to lead *(avoir)*	*conduisant* *conduit*	*conduis* *conduis* *conduit* *conduisons* *conduisez* *conduisent*	*conduise* *conduises* *conduise* *conduisions* *conduisiez* *conduisent*	*conduis* + *ais* *ais* *ait* *ions* *iez* *aient*	*conduir* + *ai* *as* *a* *ons* *ez* *ont*	*conduir* + *ais* *ais* *ait* *ions* *iez* *aient*	*conduis* *conduisons* *conduisez*
connaître to know *(avoir)*	*connaissant* *connu*	*connais* *connais* *connaît* *connaissons* *connaissez* *connaissent*	*connaisse* *connaisses* *connaisse* *connaissions* *connaissiez* *connaissent*	*connaiss* + *ais* *ais* *ait* *ions* *iez* *aient*	*connaîtr* + *ai* *as* *a* *ons* *ez* *ont*	*connaîtr* + *ais* *ais* *ait* *ions* *iez* *aient*	*connais* *connaissons* *connaissez*
courir to run *(avoir)*	*courant* *couru*	*cours* *cours* *court* *courons* *courez* *courent*	*coure* *coures* *coure* *courions* *couriez* *courent*	*cour* + *ais* *ais* *ait* *ions* *iez* *aient*	*courr* + *ai* *as* *a* *ons* *ez* *ont*	*courr* + *ais* *ais* *ait* *ions* *iez* *aient*	*cours* *courons* *courez*

INFINITIVE	PRES. & PAST PARTICIPLES	PRESENT INDICATIVE	PRESENT SUBJUNCTIVE	IMPERFECT INDICATIVE	FUTURE	CONDITIONAL	IMPERATIVE
croire to believe (avoir)	croyant cru	crois crois croit croyons croyez croient	croie croies croie croyions croyiez croient	croy + ais ais ait ions iez aient	croir + ai as a ons ez ont	croir + ais ais ait ions iez aient	crois croyons croyez
cueillir to gather to pick (avoir)	cueillant cueilli	cueille cueilles cueille cueillons cueillez cueillent	cueille cueilles cueille cueillions cueilliez cueillent	cueill + ais ais ait ions iez aient	cueiller + ai as a ons ez ont	cueiller + ais ais ait ions iez aient	cueille cueillons cueillez
devoir to owe to ought (avoir)	devant dû	dois dois doit devons devez doivent	doive doives doive devions deviez doivent	dev + ais ais ait ions iez aient	devr + ai as a ons ez ont	devr + ais ais ait ions iez aient	not used
dire to say to tell (avoir)	disant dit	dis dis dit disons dites disent	dise dises dise disions disiez disent	dis + ais ais ait ions iez aient	dir + ai as a ons ez ont	dir + ais ais ait ions iez aient	dis disons dites

INFINITIVE	PRES. & PAST PARTICIPLES	PRESENT INDICATIVE	PRESENT SUBJUNCTIVE	IMPERFECT INDICATIVE	FUTURE	CONDITIONAL	IMPERATIVE
dormir to sleep (*avoir*)	*dormant* *dormi*	*dors* *dors* *dort* *dormons* *dormez* *dorment*	*dorme* *dormes* *dorme* *dormions* *dormiez* *dorment*	*dorm* + *ais* *ais* *ait* *ions* *iez* *aient*	*dormir* + *ai* *as* *a* *ons* *ez* *ont*	*dormir* + *ais* *ais* *ait* *ions* *iez* *aient*	*dors* *dormons* *dormez*
écrire to write (*avoir*)	*écrivant* *écrit*	*écris* *écris* *écrit* *écrivons* *écrivez* *écrivent*	*écrive* *écrives* *écrive* *écrivions* *écriviez* *écrivent*	*écriv* + *ais* *ais* *ait* *ions* *iez* *aient*	*écrir* + *ai* *as* *a* *ons* *ez* *ont*	*écrir* + *ais* *ais* *ait* *ions* *iez* *aient*	*écris* *écrivons* *écrivez*
envoyer to send (*avoir*)	*envoyant* *envoyé*	*envoie* *envoies* *envoie* *envoyons* *envoyez* *envoient*	*envoie* *envoies* *envoie* *envoyions* *envoyiez* *envoient*	*envoy* + *ais* *ais* *ait* *ions* *iez* *aient*	*enverr* + *ai* *as* *a* *ons* *ez* *ont*	*enverr* + *ais* *ais* *ait* *ions* *iez* *aient*	*envoie* *envoyons* *envoyez*
être to be (*avoir*)	*étant* *été*	*suis* *es* *est* *sommes* *êtes* *sont*	*sois* *sois* *soit* *soyons* *soyez* *soient*	*ét* + *ais* *ais* *ait* *ions* *iez* *aient*	*ser* + *ai* *as* *a* *ons* *ez* *ont*	*ser* + *ais* *ais* *ait* *ions* *iez* *aient*	*sois* *soyons* *soyez*

INFINITIVE	PRES. & PAST PARTICIPLES	PRESENT INDICATIVE	PRESENT SUBJUNCTIVE	IMPERFECT INDICATIVE	FUTURE	CONDITIONAL	IMPERATIVE
faillir† to fail (*avoir*)	*faillant* *failli*	not used	not used	not used	*faillir* + *ai* *as* *a* *ons* *ez* *ont*	*faillir* + *ais* *ais* *ait* *ions* *iez* *aient*	not used
faire to do to make (*avoir*)	*faisant* *fait*	*fais* *fais* *fait* *faisons* *faites* *font*	*fasse* *fasses* *fasse* *fassions* *fassiez* *fassent*	*fais* + *ais* *ais* *ait* *ions* *iez* *aient*	*fer* + *ai* *as* *a* *ons* *ez* *ont*	*fer* + *ais* *ais* *ait* *ions* *iez* *aient*	*fais* *faisons* *faites*
falloir to be necessary, must (used only with *il*) (*avoir*)	no pres part. *fallu*	*il faut*	*il faille*	*il fallait*	*il faudra*	*il faudrait*	not used
fuir to flee (*avoir*)	*fuyant* *fui*	*fuis* *fuis* *fuit* *fuyons* *fuyez* *fuient*	*fuie* *fuies* *fuie* *fuyions* *fuyiez* *fuient*	*fuy* + *ais* *ais* *ait* *ions* *iez* *aient*	*fuir* + *ai* *as* *a* *ons* *ez* *ont*	*fuir* + *ais* *ais* *ait* *ions* *iez* *aient*	*fuis* *fuyons* *fuyez*

† Used in expressions such as *Il a failli tomber.* He nearly fell (lit., he failed to fall).

INFINITIVE	PRES. & PAST PARTICIPLES	PRESENT INDICATIVE	PRESENT SUBJUNCTIVE	IMPERFECT INDICATIVE	FUTURE	CONDITIONAL	IMPERATIVE
haïr to hate (avoir)	*haïssant* *haï*	*hais* *hais* *hait* *haïssons* *haïssez* *haïssent*	*haïsse* *haïsses* *haïsse* *haïssions* *haïssiez* *haïssent*	*haïss + ais* *ais* *ait* *ions* *iez* *aient*	*haïr + ai* *as* *a* *ons* *ez* *ont*	*haïr + ais* *ais* *ait* *ions* *iez* *aient*	*hais* *haïssons* *haïssez*
lire to read (avoir)	*lisant* *lu*	*lis* *lis* *lit* *lisons* *lisez* *lisent*	*lise* *lises* *lise* *lisions* *lisiez* *lisent*	*lis + ais* *ais* *ait* *ions* *iez* *aient*	*lir + ai* *as* *a* *ons* *ez* *ont*	*lir + ais* *ais* *ait* *ions* *iez* *aient*	*lis* *lisons* *lisez*
mettre to put to place (avoir)	*mettant* *mis*	*mets* *mets* *met* *mettons* *mettez* *mettent*	*mette* *mettes* *mette* *mettions* *mettiez* *mettent*	*mett + ais* *ais* *ait* *ions* *iez* *aient*	*mettr + ai* *as* *a* *ons* *ez* *ont*	*mettr + ais* *ais* *ait* *ions* *iez* *aient*	*mets* *mettons* *mettez*

INFINITIVE	PRES. & PAST PARTICIPLES	PRESENT INDICATIVE	PRESENT SUBJUNCTIVE	IMPERFECT INDICATIVE	FUTURE	CONDITIONAL	IMPERATIVE
mourir to die (*être*)	*mourant* *mort(e)(s)*	*meurs* *meurs* *meurt* *mourons* *mourez* *meurent*	*meure* *meures* *meure* *mourions* *mouriez* *meurent*	*mour* + *ais* *ais* *ait* *ions* *iez* *aient*	*mourr* + *ai* *as* *a* *ons* *ez* *ont*	*mourr* + *ais* *ais* *ait* *ions* *iez* *aient*	*meurs* *mourons* *mourez*
mouvoir† to move (*avoir*)	*mouvant* *mû*	*meus* *meus* *meut* *mouvons* *mouvez* *meuvent*	*meuve* *meuves* *meuve* *mouvions* *mouviez* *meuvent*	*mouv* + *ais* *ais* *ait* *ions* *iez* *aient*	*mouvr* + *ai* *as* *a* *ons* *ez* *ont*	*mouvr* + *ais* *ais* *ait* *ions* *iez* *aient*	*meus* *mouvons* *mouvez*
naître to be born (*être*)	*naissant* *né(e)(s)*	*nais* *nais* *naît* *naissons* *naissez* *naissent*	*naisse* *naisses* *naisse* *naissions* *naissiez* *naissent*	*naiss* + *ais* *ais* *ait* *ions* *iez* *aient*	*naîtr* + *ai* *as* *a* *ons* *ez* *ont*	*naîtr* + *ais* *ais* *ait* *ions* *iez* *aient*	*nais* *naissons* *naissez*
ouvrir to open (*avoir*)	*ouvrant* *ouvert*	*ouvre* *ouvres* *ouvre* *ouvrons* *ouvrez* *ouvrent*	*ouvre* *ouvres* *ouvre* *ouvrions* *ouvriez* *ouvrent*	*ouvr* + *ais* *ais* *ait* *ions* *iez* *aient*	*ouvrir* + *ai* *as* *a* *ons* *ez* *ont*	*ouvrir* + *ais* *ais* *ait* *ions* *iez* *aient*	*ouvre* *ouvrons* *ouvrez*

† *Mouvoir* is seldom used except in compounds like *émouvoir*, to move (emotionally).

INFINITIVE	PRES. & PAST PARTICIPLES	PRESENT INDICATIVE	PRESENT SUBJUNCTIVE	IMPERFECT INDICATIVE	FUTURE	CONDITIONAL	IMPERATIVE
partir to leave to depart *(être)*	*partant* *parti(e)(s)*	*pars* *pars* *part* *partons* *partez* *partent*	*parte* *partes* *parte* *partions* *partiez* *partent*	*part* + *ais* *ais* *ait* *ions* *iez* *aient*	*partir* + *ai* *as* *a* *ons* *ez* *ont*	*partir* + *ais* *ais* *ait* *ions* *iez* *aient*	*pars* *partons* *partez*
plaire to please (to be pleasing to) *(avoir)*	*plaisant* *plu*	*plais* *plais* *plaît* *plaisons* *plaisez* *plaisent*	*plaise* *plaises* *plaise* *plaisions* *plaisiez* *plaisent*	*plais* + *ais* *ais* *ait* *ions* *iez* *aient*	*plair* + *ai* *as* *a* *ons* *ez* *ont*	*plair* + *ais* *ais* *ait* *ions* *iez* *aient*	*plais* *plaisons* *plaisez*
pleuvoir to rain (used only with *il*) *(avoir)*	*pleuvant* *plu*	*il pleut*	*il pleuve*	*il pleuvait*	*il pleuvra*	*il pleuvrait*	not used
pouvoir† to be able, can *(avoir)*	*pouvant* *pu*	*peux (puis)* † *peux* *peut* *pouvons* *pouvez* *peuvent*	*puisse* *puisses* *puisse* *puissions* *puissiez* *puissent*	*pouv* + *ais* *ais* *ait* *ions* *iez* *aient*	*pourr* + *ai* *as* *a* *ons* *ez* *ont*	*pourr* + *ais* *ais* *ait* *ions* *iez* *aient*	not used
prendre to take *(avoir)*	*prenant* *pris*	*prends* *prends* *prend* *prenons* *prenez* *prennent*	*prenne* *prennes* *prenne* *prenions* *preniez* *prennent*	*pren* + *ais* *ais* *ait* *ions* *iez* *aient*	*prendr* + *ai* *as* *a* *ons* *ez* *ont*	*prendr* + *ais* *ais* *ait* *ions* *iez* *aient*	*prends* *prenons* *prenez*

† The interrogative of *pouvoir* in the first person singular is always *Puis-je?*

INFINITIVE	PRES. & PAST PARTICIPLES	PRESENT INDICATIVE	PRESENT SUBJUNCTIVE	IMPERFECT INDICATIVE	FUTURE	CONDITIONAL	IMPERATIVE
résoudre to resolve (*avoir*)	*résolvant* *résolu*	*résous* *résous* *résout* *résolvons* *résolvez* *résolvent*	*résolve* *résolves* *résolve* *résolvions* *résolviez* *résolvent*	*résolv +* ais, ais, ait, ions, iez, aient	*résoudr +* ai, as, a, ons, ez, ont	*résoudr +* ais, ais, ait, ions, iez, aient	*résous* *résolvons* *résolvez*
rire to laugh (*avoir*)	*riant* *ri*	*ris* *ris* *rit* *rions* *riez* *rient*	*rie* *ries* *rie* *riions* *riiez* *rient*	*ri +* ais, ais, ait, ions, iez, aient	*rir +* ai, as, a, ons, ez, ont	*rir +* ais, ais, ait, ions, iez, aient	*ris* *rions* *riez*
savoir to know (*avoir*)	*sachant* *su*	*sais* *sais* *sait* *savons* *savez* *savent*	*sache* *saches* *sache* *sachions* *sachiez* *sachent*	*sav +* ais, ais, ait, ions, iez, aient	*saur +* ai, as, a, ons, ez, ont	*saur +* ais, ais, ait, ions, iez, aient	*sache* *sachons* *sachez*
suffire to be enough, to suffice (*avoir*)	*suffisant* *suffi*	*suffis* *suffis* *suffit* *suffisons* *suffisez* *suffisent*	*suffise* *suffises* *suffise* *suffisions* *suffisiez* *suffisent*	*suffis +* ais, ais, ait, ions, iez, aient	*suffir +* ai, as, a, ons, ez, ont	*suffir +* ais, ais, ait, ions, iez, aient	*suffis* *suffisons* *suffisez*

INFINITIVE	PRES. & PAST PARTICIPLES	PRESENT INDICATIVE	PRESENT SUBJUNCTIVE	IMPERFECT INDICATIVE	FUTURE	CONDITIONAL	IMPERATIVE
suivre to follow (*avoir*)	*suivant* *suivi*	*suis* *suis* *suit* *suivons* *suivez* *suivent*	*suive* *suives* *suive* *suivions* *suiviez* *suivent*	*suiv* + *ais* *ais* *ait* *ions* *iez* *aient*	*suivr* + *ai* *as* *a* *ons* *ez* *ont*	*suivr* + *ais* *ais* *ait* *ions* *iez* *aient*	*suis* *suivons* *suivez*
(se)taire to be quiet, to say nothing (*être*)	*taisant* *tu (e) (s)*	*tais* *tais* *tait* *taisons* *taisez* *taisent*	*taise* *taises* *taise* *taisions* *taisiez* *taisent*	*tais* + *ais* *ais* *ait* *ions* *iez* *aient*	*tair* + *ai* *as* *a* *ons* *ez* *ont*	*tair* + *ais* *ais* *ait* *ions* *iez* *aient*	*tais-toi* *taisons-nous* *taisez-vous*
tenir to hold, to keep (*avoir*)	*tenant* *tenu*	*tiens* *tiens* *tient* *tenons* *tenez* *tiennent*	*tienne* *tiennes* *tienne* *tenions* *teniez* *tiennent*	*ten* + *ais* *ais* *ait* *ions* *iez* *aient*	*tiendr* + *ai* *as* *a* *ons* *ez* *ont*	*tiendr* + *ais* *ais* *ait* *ions* *iez* *aient*	*tiens* *tenons* *tenez*
vaincre to conquer (*avoir*)	*vainquant* *vaincu*	*vaincs* *vaincs* *vainc* *vainquons* *vainquez* *vainquent*	*vainque* *vainques* *vainque* *vainquions* *vainquiez* *vainquent*	*vainqu* + *ais* *ais* *ait* *ions* *iez* *aient*	*vaincr* + *ai* *as* *a* *ons* *ez* *ont*	*vaincr* + *ais* *ais* *ait* *ions* *iez* *aient*	*vaincs* *vainquons* *vainquez*

INFINITIVE	PRES. & PAST PARTICIPLES	PRESENT INDICATIVE	PRESENT SUBJUNCTIVE	IMPERFECT INDICATIVE	FUTURE	CONDITIONAL	IMPERATIVE
valoir to be worth (*avoir*)	*valant* *valu*	vaux vaux vaut valons valez valent	vaille vailles vaille valions valiez vaillent	val + ais ais ait ions iez aient	vaudr + ai as a ons ez ont	vaudr + ais ais ait ions iez aient	vaux† valons valez
venir to come (*être*)	*venant* *venu(e)(s)*	viens viens vient venons venez viennent	vienne viennes vienne venions veniez viennent	ven + ais ais ait ions iez aient	viendr + ai as a ons ez ont	viendr + ais ais ait ions iez aient	viens venons venez
vivre to live (*avoir*)	*vivant* *vécu*	vis vis vit vivons vivez vivent	vive vives vive vivions viviez vivent	viv + ais ais ait ions iez aient	vivr + ai as a ons ez ont	vivr + ais ais ait ions iez aient	vis vivons vivez
voir to see (*avoir*)	*voyant* *vu*	vois vois voit voyons voyez voient	voie voies voie voyions voyiez voient	voy + ais ais ait ions iez aient	verr + ai as a ons ez ont	verr + ais ais ait ions iez aient	vois voyons voyez

† The imperative of *valoir* is not often used.

IRREGULAR COMPARATIVES: BON AND MAUVAIS

	COMPARATIVE OF SUPERIORITY	COMPARATIVE OF INFERIORITY	COMPARATIVE OF EQUALITY
bon (good)	*meilleur que . . .* (better than)	*moins bon que . . .* (less good than)	*aussi bon que . . .* (as good as)
mauvais (bad)	*pire que...* or *plus mauvais que . . .* (worse than)	*moins mauvais que . . .* (less bad than)	*aussi mauvais que . . .* (as bad as)

IRREGULAR SUPERLATIVES: BON AND MAUVAIS

	SUPERLATIVE OF SUPERIORITY	SUPERLATIVE OF INFERIORITY
bon (good)	*le / la / les meilleur(e)(s)* (the best)	*le / la / les moins bon(ne)(s)* (the least good)
mauvais (bad)	*le / la / les pire(s)* or *le / la / les plus mauvais(e)(s)* (the worst)	*le / la / les moins mauvais(e)(s)* (the least bad)

COMMON IRREGULAR ADJECTIVES

MASCULINE SINGULAR	FEMININE SINGULAR	MASCULINE/FEMININE PLURAL	
favori	*favorite*	*favoris, favorites*	favorite
frais	*fraîche*	*frais, fraîches*	fresh
doux	*douce*	*doux, douces*	gentle
long	*longue*	*longs, longues*	long
sec	*sèche*	*secs, sèches*	dry
vieux, vieil	*vieille*	*vieux, vieilles*	old

MORE IRREGULAR PATTERNS WITH ADJECTIVES

ENDING	MASCULINE SINGULAR	FEMININE SINGULAR	MASCULINE/ FEMININE PLURAL	
in -f	*neuf*	*neuve*	*neufs, neuves*	new
in -n	*bon*	*bonne*	*bons, bonnes*	good
in -l	*cruel*	*cruelle*	*cruels, cruelles*	cruel
in -s	*gris*	*grise*	*gris, grises*	gray
in -s	*bas*	*basse*	*bas, basses*	low
	épais	*épaisse*	*épais, épaisses*	thick
	gras	*grasse*	*gras, grasses*	fat
	gros	*grosse*	*gros, grosses*	big
	las	*lasse*	*las, lasses*	tired
in -et	*discret*	*discrète*	*discrets, discrètes*	discreet
	inquiet	*inquiète*	*inquiets, inquiètes*	worried
in -et	*coquet*	*coquette*	*coquets, coquettes*	flirtatious
in -er	*cher*	*chère*	*chers, chères*	dear; expensive
in -c	*blanc*	*blanche*	*blancs, blanches*	white
	public	*publique*	*publics, publiques*	public

IRREGULAR NOUN PLURALS

SINGULAR	PLURAL	
l'aïeul	*les aïeux*	ancestors
(ancestor)	*les aïeuls*	grandparents
l'oeil	*les yeux*	eyes
ciel (sky)	*cieux*	heavens
travail	*travaux*	works
bail	*baux*	leases
mal	*maux*	pains
vitrail	*vitraux*	stained-glass windows

MORE IRREGULAR NOUN PLURAL PATTERNS

ENDING	SINGULAR	PLURAL	
in -z	*le nez*	*les nez*	noses
in -s	*le bois*	*les bois*	woods
in -x	*la noix*	*les noix*	nuts
in -au	*le tuyau*	*les tuyaux*	hoses; pipes (plumbing)
in -eau	*le cadeau*	*les cadeaux*	presents
in -eu	*le jeu*	*les jeux*	games
in -al	*le cheval*	*les chevaux*	horses
in -ou	*le bijou*	*les bijoux*	jewelry

APPENDIX C

WHEN YOU'RE STUCK FOR WORDS . . .

TRAVELING	
Here is my passport.	Voici mon passeport.
May I close my luggage?	Je peux refermer ma valise?
Can I exchange dollars here?	Est-ce que je peux changer des dollars ici?
I would like a ticket for the 8:30 train.	Je voudrais acheter un billet pour le train de 8h30 (huit heures trente).
At what time does the train for . . . leave?	À quelle heure est-ce que le train pour . . . part?
How much is a ticket for . . . ?	Combien coûte un billet de train pour . . . ?
This seat is taken.	Cette place est prise.
May I smoke?	Est-ce que je peux fumer, s'il vous plaît?
These are my suitcases.	Ce sont mes valises.
At what time do we arrive?	À quelle heure est-ce qu'on arrive?
Please, fill it up.	Faites le plein, s'il vous plaît!
My car broke down.	Ma voiture est tombée en panne.
How long will it take you to repair it?	Quand est-ce qu'elle sera / va être réparée?
How far is . . . ?	Est-ce que c'est loin jusqu'à
Is this the road to . . . ?	Est-ce que c'est bien la route pour . . . ?
Can I exchange this traveler's check here?	Est-ce que je peux changer ce chèque de voyage ici, s'il vous plaît?
What's the exchange rate for a dollar?	À combien est le dollar, s'il vous plaît?

IN A RESTAURANT	
Can you recommend a good restaurant?	Est-ce que vous pouvez nous conseiller un bon restaurant?
How much do I owe you?	Combien est-ce que je vous dois, s'il vous plaît?
How much is it?	Combien ça coûte, s'il vous plaît?
At what time do you serve dinner / lunch?	À quelle heure est-ce que vous servez le dîner / le déjeuner?
Where can we sit?	Où est-ce que nous pouvons nous asseoir?
Which wine do you recommend?	Quel vin est-ce que vous recommandez?
I am on a diet. I may only eat veggies.	Je suis au régime. Je prends peut-être juste des légumes.
I want my meat very well done.	J'aime la viande très cuite.

IN THE HOTEL

Have we arrived yet?	Est-ce qu'on est enfin arrivé(e)s?
I have a reservation under the name . . .	J'ai fait une réservation au nom de . . .
Can I have the bill?	La note, s'il vous plaît?
Are there any messages?	Est-ce que j'ai eu des messages?
Do you a city map?	Est-ce que vous avez une carte de la ville, s'il vous plaît?

SHOPPING LIKE A REAL TOURIST

I want to develop this film.	J'aimerais faire développer cette pellicule.
I want to buy batteries for my camera.	J'aimerais acheter des piles pour mon appareil photo.
At what time do you close?	À quelle heure est-ce que vous fermez?

WHEN YOU WANT TO WRITE HOME

Where can I buy a postcard and a stamp?	Où est-ce que je peux acheter une carte et un timbre, s'il vous plaît?
Where can I mail these letters?	Où est-ce que je peux poster ces lettres, s'il vous plaît?

LET'S HOPE YOU WON'T NEED IT, BUT . . .

Where does it hurt?	Où est-ce que cela vous fait mal?
I have a headache / stomachache.	J'ai mal à la tête / mal à l'estomac.
We'll have to check you into the hospital.	Vous devez entrer à l'hôpital.
You'll have to stay in bed.	Vous devez rester au lit.
I need a prescription for . . .	J'ai besoin d'une ordonnance pour . . .
I'm going to take your blood pressure / your pulse.	Je vais prendre votre tension / votre pouls.
I have sprained my ankle.	Je me suis tordu la cheville.
You'll need stitches.	On doit vous faire des points.
I think I'm going faint.	Je crois que je vais m'évanouir.

BETTER SAFE THAN SORRY

Is it dangerous to swim here?	Est-ce que c'est dangereux de se baigner ici?
Is this water drinkable?	Est-ce que cette eau est potable?

APPENDIX D

A SHORTCUT TO SOUNDING FRENCH

À l'aide!	Help!
Ah! Ne commence pas!	Don't start!
Ah, je ne sais pas	I don't know
Ah, non!	No way!
Aïe aïe aïe	Ow
Et merde!	Oh, shit!
Et puis quoi encore?	What else?!
Fais gaffe!	Careful!
Fous-moi la paix! (slang)	Leave me alone!
Ils se foutent de nous? (slang)	Are they kidding?
J'en ai marre!	I'm fed up!
Jamais de la vie!	Over my dead body.
Mais je rêve . . .	What's that . . .
Ne me prends pas la tête!	Don't bug me with that!
Non, mais ça va pas?	Are you crazy?
On y va!	Let's go!
Oh là là . . .	Whoa
Punaise!	Shoot!
Que c'est cher!	How expensive!
Quel culot!	How dare he / she / they?
Quoi?	What?
Tirons-nous!	Let's get out of here!
Va te faire voir	Go to hell!
Vous avez un problème?!	You have a problem with that?
Vous n'avez pas le droit!	You have no right . . .

And more...

À mon avis . . .	In my opinion . . .
À vos souhaits!	Bless you!
Ah, mais on s'arrose!	Let's drink to it!
C'est la vie	That's life!
C'est le pied . . .	Great . . .
C'est pour aujourd'hui ou c'est pour demain?	Are you ready?
Ça vaut le coup!	It's worth it!
Fais ce que je dis, mais ne fais pas ce que je fais	Do as I say and not as I do
Fais comme chez toi!	Make yourself comfortable!
Il débloque complètement!	He totally lost it!
Il n'a pas inventé la poudre	He's not really a genius

Il ne faut pas se gêner!	Don't be embarrassed by it! / Feel free . . .
Je m'éclate!	I'm having great fun!
Je suis totalement cassé!	I'm exhausted! / I'm drunk:
Je suis totalement crevé!	I'm completely exhausted.
le téléphone arabe	by word of mouth
Mais je vous parle à vous?	Did I talk to you?
Mais où il va chercher ça?	But where does he get that from?
Mais oui, cause toujours, tu m'intéresses . . .	Keep talking . . .
N'en fais pas une montagne.	Don't exaggerate!
On s'appelle et on s'fait une bouffe?	Let's talk on the phone and have dinner
On s'fait une toile?	Feel like going to the movies?
Par ici la bonne soupe!	Send it over here.
Pour qui il se prend?	Who does he think he is?
Tu peux me filer un coup de main?	Can you give me a hand?
Un coup de maître!	Congratulations!
Un emmerdeur de première!	A pain in the ass!
Une fois n'est pas coutume.	Just this once.

WHAT DO ALL THOSE GRAMMAR TERMS REALLY MEAN?

ADJECTIVE	a word that describes a noun; e.g. *good, red, nice*. Don't forget that in French, adjectives usually come **after** the noun and they always agree with it in gender and number, e.g. *un homme fou* but *une femme folle*.
ADVERB	a word that describes an action (a verb), a quality (an adjective) or another adverb, e.g., *quickly, very*, and *often*. Adverbs never change for agreement.
AGREEMENT	changing a word to match the grammatical features of another word. In French, adjectives and articles agree with the gender and number of the nouns they describe, e.g. *un homme fou, une femme folle, des hommes fous, des femmes folles*.
ARTICLE	"a / an" or "the." Definite articles mean "the" and indefinite articles mean "a / an." In French, articles match the gender and number of the noun, e.g., *un / le jeune homme* but *une / la jeune femme*.
COMPARATIVE	"more" or "less": an expression comparing two people or things or two qualities. In French, the comparative is expressed with *plus que*, "more than," and *moins que*, "less than," e.g., *Nathalie est plus jeune que Luc*, "Nathalie is younger than Luc."
CONJUGATION	changing a verb to show who the subject is and when the action takes place (i.e., tense—past, present, future). For example, *je parle*, but *tu parles, elle parle, nous parlons*, etc.
CONJUNCTION	a word that connects other words or phrases. The most common conjunctions are *et*, "and," *mais*, "but," and *ou*, "or."
DEMONSTRATIVE	"this" and "that." In French, demonstratives match the gender and number of the nouns they describe or replace, e.g. *ce jeune homme* but *cette jeune femme*.
DIRECT OBJECT	in the sentence *J'écris une carte à Marc*, "I'm writing a postcard to Marc," the direct object is *une carte*, "a postcard."
GENDER	strictly a grammatical category. In French, nouns, adjectives, and articles have gender: they can be masculine or feminine.
IMPERSONAL VERB	a verb that is used to make a general statement, where the subject is a general "you, one," or "they," as in *on parle anglais ici*, "English is spoken here."

INDIRECT OBJECT	in the sentence *J'écris une carte à Marc,* "I'm writing a postcard to Marc," the indirect object is *à Marc,* "to Marc." Indirect objects receive the action of the verb, usually with the "help" of a preposition, like *à,* "to," or *pour,* "for."
INFINITIVE	the basic form of a verb (the one you'll find in a dictionary), before it's been changed (or conjugated) to show who the subject is or when the action takes place; most common infinitive endings in French are *–er, –ir,* and *–re.*
NOUN	a person, place, thing or idea, e.g. *sea, pizza, love.*
NUMBER	There are two numbers: "one" or "more than one," also called "singular" and "plural."
PARTITIVE	words expressing a partial quantity of an item that cannot be counted, like "water," "rice," or "pie," i.e., "some / a little / any **of**." In French, the partitive is expressed with the preposition *de* (which combines with different articles), and translates as *some (of)* in English, or the expressions *un peu de* (a little bit of) or *beaucoup de* (a lot of).
PAST PARTICIPLE	the form of a verb (usually ending in *–é, –i,* or *–u*) used to form the *passé composé* or used as an adjective, e.g., *j'ai parlé,* "I spoke" or *je suis allé(e),* "I went."
POSSESSIVE	"my / mine, your / yours," etc. A word that shows ownership. In French, possessives agree in gender and number with the object or person **possessed**, not the owner.
PREPOSITION	"to, from, on, in," etc. A connective word that shows spatial, temporal, or other relationships between other words.
PRONOUN	"I, him, mine, this one," etc. A word that takes the place of a noun.
REFLEXIVE VERB	a verb conjugated with a reflexive pronoun: *me,* "myself," *te,* "yourself," *se,* "him / herself; themselves," *nous,* "ourselves," *vous,* "yourselves."
SUBJECT	a person, place, or thing performing the action of the verb or being in the state described by it; e.g. in *Marc is jogging* or *This vase is beautiful,* "Marc" and "this vase" are subjects.
SUFFIX	an ending that is attached to a word to change its meaning, e.g., *–et / te,* meaning "small," or *–ment,* the equivalent of our "–ly" which changes an adjective to an adverb.
SUPERLATIVE	"most, least," etc. An expression indicating the highest degree and used when comparing three or more things, people or qualities, e.g., *Elle est la plus belle fille du monde,* "She's the most beautiful girl in the world."
TENSE	the time of an action or state of being, i.e. past, present, future, etc.
VERB	a word showing an action or a state of being, e.g., *parler,* "to speak," *être,* "to be."

GLOSSARY

Abbreviations

adjective	*adj*	Internet	*Int*
adverb	*adv*	Latin	*Lat*
article	*art*	literal	*lit*
colloquial	*col*	masculine	*m*
definite	*def*	noun	*n*
demonstrative	*dem*	plural	*pl*
direct object	*dir obj*	preposition	*prep*
familiar	*fam*	pronoun	*pron*
feminine	*f*	possessive	*poss*
formal	*fml*	singular	*sing*
impersonal	*imp*	someone	*so*
indefinite	*indef*	something	*sth*
invariable	*inv*	slang	*sl*

FRENCH–ENGLISH

A

à (ah) *at; to; in*
  à bientôt (byih^{n}toh) *see you soon*
  à cause de (koz duh) *because of*
  à l'air libre (lehr leebr) *in the open air*
  à l'avance (lah vah^{n}s) *in advance*
  à la fin (lah fih^n) *in the end*
  à louer (looeh) *for rent*
  à moins que (mwih^n kuh) *unless*
  à pied (pyeh) *on foot*
  à plus (tard) (plü tahr) *see you (later)*
  à la prochaine fois (prohshehn fwah) *see you (next time)*
  à reculons (ruhküloh^n) *going backwards*
  à temps (tah^n) *in time*
  à tout à l'heure (toot ah luhr) *see you in a while*
un abonnement (abohnmah^n) *membership*
aborder (ahbohrdeh) *to approach*
absolument (ahbsohloomah^n) *absolutely*
absurde (ahbsürd) *absurd*
un accident (ahkseedah^n) *accident*
accompagner (ahkoh^{m}pahnyeh) *to accompany, to go with*
un accord (ahkohr) *agreement*
un accordéon *accordion*
accorder (ahkohrdeh) *to grant*
  être d'accord *to agree*
  d'accord *OK*

des **accras** (ahkrah) *fritter*
(s') **accrocher** (ahkrohsheh) *to hang (on to)*
un achat (ahshah) *something bought / a purchase*
acheter (ahshuhteh) *to buy*
un acheteur, –euse (ahshuhtuhr; ahshuhtüz) *buyer*
acquiescer (ahkyehseh) *to nod*
un acte (ahkt) *act*
un acteur, –trice (ahktuhr, ahktrees) *actor, actress*
actif, –ive (ahkteef, -eev) *active*
une activité (ahkteeveeteh) *activity*
une addition (adeesyoh^n) *addition; bill, check*
admettre (ahdmehtr) *to admit*
admis, –e (ahdmee, -z) *admitted*
une adresse (ahdrehs) *address*
adresser (ahdrehseh) *to address*
adorable (ahdohrahbl) *adorable*
adorer (ahdohreh) *to adore*
une aération (aehrahsyoh^n) *ventilation*
aérer (aehreh) *to air*
un aéroport (aehrohpohr) *airport*
une affaire (ahfehr) *thing; case; affair; deal*
  faire des affaires *to get a good deal; to do business*
  ce sont mes affaires! *it's my business!*
une affiche (ahfeesh) *poster; notice*
afficher (ahfeesheh) *to put out; to display*

l'**Afrique** (ahfreek) *(f.) Africa*
africain, –e (ahfreekeh^n; -eh^n) *African*
un âge (ahzh) *age*
  quel âge avez-vous / as-tu? *how old are you?*
âgé, –e (ahzheh) *old; aged*
une agence (ahzhah^{n}s) *agency*
  agence pour l'emploi *employment agency*
  agence immobilière *real estate agency*
un agent (ahzhah^n) *agent*
agir (ahzheer) *to act*
  il s'agit de *it's a matter of; this is*
agréable (ahgrehahbl) *pleasant*
une aide (ehd) *help*
aider (à faire) *to help (to do)*
l'**ail** (ahy) *(m.) garlic*
une aile (ehl) *wing*
ailleurs (ahyuhr) *elsewhere*
  d'ailleurs *besides*
l'**aioli** (ahyohlee) *(m.) garlic mayonnaise*
(s') **aimer** (ehmeh) *to like; to love (each other)*
ainsi (eh^{n}see) *so; thus*
un air (ehr) *air; tune*
(à) l'**aise** (ehz) *comfortable; at ease*
ajouter (ahzhooteh) *to add*
une alarme (ahlahrm) *alarm*
un alcool (ahlkohl) *alcohol; liquor*
alcoolique *(adj / n, f. and m.) alcoholic*

(aux) **alentours** (ahlah"toor) *around; in the vicinity*

un **aliment** (ahleemahn) *food*

une **alimentation** *food; groceries*

une **allégorie** (ahlehgohree) *allegory*

l'**Allemagne** (ahluhmahny) *(f.) Germany*

allemand, –e (aluhmah"; aluhmahnd) *German*

aller (à) (ahleh) *to go (to)*
   aller chercher *to fetch*
   aller faire *to be going to do*
   allez! (ahleh) *c'mon*
   allons! (ahloh") *let's go*
   ça va barder (sahvah bahrdeh) *it's gonna get hot (col)*
   ça va mal / bien (-mahl / byeh") *it's going wrong / well*
   s'en aller (sah" ahleh) *to go away*
   y aller doucement (doosmah") *to take it easy*
   y aller fort (fohr) *to be too much*

un **aller simple** (ahleh seh"pl) *one-way ticket*

un **aller retour** (ahleh ruhtoor) *round trip ticket*

une **allergie** (ahlehrzhee) *allergy*

allô (ahloh) *hello*

(s') **allonger** (sahloh"geh) *to lie down*

allumer (ahlümeh) *to turn on; to light up*

alors (ahlohr) *so; then*
   alors que *as; when; whereas*

un **alphabet** (ahlfahbeh) *alphabet*

un **amant** (ahmah") *lover*

un **amateur** (ahmahtuhr) *amateur*

une **amatrice** (ahmahtrees) *amateur*

une **ambassade** (ah"bahsahd) *embassy*

une **ambiance** (ah"byah"s) *mood*

ambitieux, –ieuse (ah"beesyuh; -uhz) *ambitious*

une **âme** (ahm) *soul*

améliorer (ahmehlyohreh) *to improve*

aménager (ahmehnahgeh) *to arrange; to set up*

une **amende** (ahmah"d) *fine*

amener (ahmuhneh) *to bring (someone)*

amer, amère (ahmehr) *bitter*

Amérique (ahmehreek) *(f.) America*

américain, –e (ahmehreekeh"; -ehn) *American*

un **ami, une amie** (ahmee) *friend*
   se faire des amis *to make friends*

amical, –e (ahmeekahl) *friendly*

une **amitié** (ahmeetyeh) *friendship*

un **amour** (ahmoor) *love*

amoureux, –euse (ahmooruh; -z) *in love*

amusant, –e (ahmüzah"; -ahnt) *amusing*

(s') **amuser** (ahmüzeh) *to amuse (oneself); to have fun*

une **anchoïade** (ah"shohyahd) *anchovy paste*

un **anchois** (ah"shwah) *anchovy*

l'**Andalousie** (ahndahloozee) *(f.) Andalusia*

anglais, –e (ahngleh; anglehz) *English*

l'**Angleterre** (angluhtehr) *(f.) England*

un **animal** (ahneemahl) *animal*

animé, –e (ahneemeh) *animated; busy; lively*

un **an, une année** (ah", ahneh) *year*

une **année sabatique** (ahneh sahbahteek) *a year off*

un **anniversaire** (ahneevehrsehr) *birthday; anniversary*

une **annonce** (ahnoh"s) *advertisement; ad*
   passer une annonce *to put an ad*

un **annuaire** (ahnüehr) *phone book*

annuel, annuelle (ahnüehl) *yearly*

une **annulation** (ahnühlahsyoh") *cancellation*

annuler (ahnüleh) *to cancel*

antérieur, –e (ah"tehryuhr) *previous*

les **Antilles** (ah"teey) *West Indies*

un / une **antiquaire** (ah"teekehr) *antique dealer*

août (oot) *August*

(s') **apercevoir** (ahpehrsuhvwar) *to see; to notice*

un **apéritif** (ahpehreeteef) *aperitif*

une **apostrophe** (ahpohstrohf) *apostrophe*

apparaître (ahpahrehtr) *to appear*

apparemment (ahpahrahmah") *apparently*

un **appareil** (ahpahrehy) *device; appliance*

un **appareil–photo** (-fohtoh) *a camera*

une **apparition** (ahpahreesyoh") *apparition*

un **appartement** (ahpahrtuhmah") *apartment*

appartenir (ahpahrtuhneer) *(à) to belong (to)*

un **appel** (ahpehl) *call*

(s') **appeler** (ahpuhleh) *to call; to call each other; to be called*
   appeler au téléphone *to call on the phone*

appétissant, –e (ahpehteesahn; -t) *appetizing*

un **appétit** *appetite*
   bon appétit! *enjoy your meal!*

applaudir (ahplohdeer) *to applaud, to clap*

un **applaudissement** (ahplohdeesmah") *applause*

apporter (ahpohrteh) *to bring sth*

apprécier (ahprehsyeh) *to appreciate*

apprendre (ahprahndr) *to teach; to learn*

s'**apprêter** (sahprehteh) *(à) to get ready (to)*

(s') **approcher** (ahprohsheh) *(de) to approach, to come closer*

approuver (ahprooveh) *to approve*

après (ahpreh) *(que) after (that)*
   après tout (ahpreh too) *after all*

un / une **après–midi** (ahpreh meedee) *afternoon*

un **arbre** (ahrbr) *tree*

l'**argent** (ahrzhah") *(m.) money; silver*

un **arrêt** (ahreh) *stop*

(s') **arrêter** (ahrehteh) *to stop*

une **arrivée** (ahreeveh) *arrival; arriving*

arriver (ahreeveh) *to arrive; to manage*

un **arrondissement** (ahroh"deesmah") *Parisian district*

(s') **arrondir** (ahroh"deer) *to open; to become round*

arroser (ahrohzeh) *to water; to sprinkle*
   arroser la nouvelle (noovehl) *to celebrate over a drink*

un **art** (ahr) *art*
   les beaux–arts (bohzahr) *fine arts*

un **article** (ahrteekl) *article*

un **artisan** (ahrteezah") *artisan; craftsman*

un **artisanat** (ahrteezahnah) *arts and crafts*

un / une **artiste** (ahrteest) *artist*

un **ascenseur** (ahsah"suhr) *elevator*

une **assemblée** (ahsah"bleh) *assembly*

s'**asseoir** (sahswar) *to sit down*

assez (ahseh) *enough*

une **assiette** (ahsyeht) *plate*

un **assistant, –e** (ahseestah"; -ahnt) *assistant*

assister (ahseesteh) *to assist*
   assister à (ahseesteh ah) *to attend*

un **associé, –e** (ahsohsyeh) *partner*

une **assurance** (ahsrah"s) *insurance*

une **astrologie** (ahstrohlozhee) *astrology*

un **atelier** (ahtuhlyeh) *workshop*

une **atmosphère** (ahtmohsfehr) *at-mosphere*
un **atout** (ahtoo) *asset*
atteindre (ahteh^ndr) *to reach*
attendre (ahtah^ndr) *to wait for*
　attendre un enfant *to expect a baby*
　en attendant (ahn ahtah^ndah^n) *in the meantime*
une **attente** (ahtah^nt) *wait*
attentif, –tive (ahtah^nteef; -teev) *attentive*
(faire) attention (fehr ahtah^nseeah^n) *to be careful; to pay attention*
une **attestation** (ahtehstahsyoh^n) *certificate*
attirant, –e (ahteerahn; -t) *attractive; attracting*
attirer (ahteereh) *to attract*
une **attitude** (ahteetüd) *attitude*
attraper (ahtrahpeh) *to catch*
au (oh) *at the; to the*
　au bon moment (boh^n mohmah^n) *at the right time*
　au bord des larmes (bohr deh lahrm) *on the verge of tears*
　au bout de (boo duh) *at the end of*
　au contraire (koh^ntrehr) *on the contrary*
　au moins (mwih^n) *at least*
　au revoir (ruhvwar) *goodbye*
　au sujet de (süzheh duh) *regarding, about*
　au téléphone (tehlehfohn) *on the phone*
　au travail (trahvahy) *at work*
　au volant (vohlah^n) *behind the wheel*
aucun, –e (ohkuh^n; -kün) *none*
augmenter (ohgmah^nteh) *to increase*
aujourd'hui (ohzhoordwee) *today*
aussi (ohsee) *too, as well*
autant (ohtah^n), **tout autant** *as much*
un **auteur** (ohtuhr) *author*
un **auteur dramatique** (drahmahteek) *playwright*
autour (ohtoor) **(de / du)** *around*
un **autobus, bus** (ohtohbüs) *bus*
automatiquement (ohtohmahteekmah^n) *automatically*
un **automne** (ohtohn) *fall*
autoriser (ohtohreezeh) *to authorize*
autre (ohtr) *other / else*
　l'un ou l'autre (luh^n oo lohtr) *either*
autrui (ohtrwee) *other one*
un **avancement** (ahvah^nsmah^n) *promotion*
　avancer (ahvah^nseh) *to move forward*

avant (que) *before (that)*
avare (ahvahr) *avaricious; greedy*
l'**avarice** (ahvahrees) *(f.) avarice; greediness*
avec (ahvehk) *with*
une **aventure** (ahvah^ntür) *adventure*
avertir (ahvehrteer) *to warn*
un **avertissement** (ahvehrteesmah^n) *warning*
un **avion** (ahvyoh^n) *plane*
　par avion *by plane; air mail*
un **avis** (ahvee) *opinion; notice*
avoir (ahvwar) *to have*
　avoir 24 ans *to be 24*
　tu m'as eu (mah ü) *you got me*
　avoir besoin (buhzweh^n) **de** *to need*
　avoir de la chance (shah^ns) *to be lucky*
　avoir du mal à faire *to have trouble doing*
　avoir du retard (ruhtahr) *to be late*
　avoir faim (feh^n) *to be hungry*
　avoir failli *to have almost done*
　avoir froid (frwa) *to be cold*
　avoir la grippe (greep) *to have the flu*
　avoir l'habitude (ahbeetüd) **(de)** *to be used to*
　avoir mal à (mahl ah) *to hurt*
　avoir les moyens (moyeh^n) *can afford*
　avoir la paix (peh) *to be at peace*
　avoir soif (swahf) *to be thirsty*
avril (ahvreel) *April*

B

un / une **baby–sitter** *baby-sitter*
　faire du baby–sitting *to baby-sit*
un **bagage** (bahgahzh) *luggage*
　bagage à main (ah meh^n) *carry-on luggage*
une **bague** (bahg) *ring*
(se) baigner (behnyeh) *to bathe*
un **bail** (bahy) *lease*
　il y a un bail *(col) it's been a while*
un **bain** (beh^n) *bath*
　prendre un bain *to take a bath*
un **bal** (bahl) *ball (dancing)*
une **balance** (bahlah^ns) *scale; balance; Libra*
balancer (bahlah^nseh) *(col) to throw*
un **balcon** (bahlkoh^n) *balcony*
une **balle** (bahl) *ball*
un **ballon** (bahloh^n) **de foot** *soccer ball*
balnéaire (bahlneher) *(adj.) seaside, beach*
une **banane** (bahnahn) *banana*

une **bande originale** (bahnd ohrihzheenahl) *soundtrack*
une **banlieue** (bahnlyuh) *suburb*
une **banque** (bah^k) *bank*
　banque de données (duh dohneh) *databank*
un **relevé bancaire** (ruhluhveh bah^nkehr) *banking statement*
un **bar** (bahr) *bar*
un **barman** (bahrmahn) *bartender*
bas (bah), **basse** (bahs) *low*
　le bas *(n) bottom; stocking*
　en bas de *at the bottom*
le **basket** (baskeht) *basketball*
une **basse** (bahs) *bass*
un **bassiste** (bahseest) *bass player*
un **bateau** (pneumatique) (bahtoh pnuhmahteek) *(rubber) boat*
un **bâtiment** (bahtihmah^n) *(n) building*
une **batterie** (bahtree) *drum kit*
un **batteur** (bahtuhr) *drummer*
bavard, –e (bahvahr; -ahrd) *talkative*
un **bazar** (bahzahr) *(col) jumble;mess*
beau (boh), **bel, belle** (behl) *beautiful (masc / fem)*
beaucoup (bohkoo) *many, a lot, plenty*
un **beau–fils** *stepson*
un **beau–frère** *brother-in-law*
un **bébé** (behbeh) *baby*
la **Belgique** (behlzheek) *Belgium*
belge (behlzh) *Belgian*
un **bélier, Bélier** (behlyeh) *ram, Aries*
une **belle–famille** *in-laws*
une **belle–mère** *mother-in-law*
une **belle–sœur** *sister-in-law*
bercer (behseh) *to rock; to craddle*
une **bestiole** (behstyohl) *(col) bug*
une **bêtise** (behteez) *stupidity; stupid thing*
un **beurre** (buhr) *butter*
un **bibelot** (beebloh) *knick-knack*
une **bibliothèque** (beebleeyohthehk) *library*
une **bicyclette** (beeseekleht) *bicycle*
　faire de la –, aller à bicyclette *to ride the bike*
bien (byeh^n) *(n) good; property*
　faire du bien (à) *to do good (to someone)*
　c'est pour son bien *it's for his own good*
bien *(adv) well, fine; quite*
　bien que *although*
　bien sûr (byeh^n sür) *of course*
　Eh bien *well*
bientôt (byeh^ntoh) *soon*
bienvenue (byeh^nvuhnü) *welcome*
　souhaiter la bienvenue *to welcome*

une **bière** (byehr) *beer*
un **bijou** (beezhoo) *jewel; jewelry*
bilingue (beelehⁿg) *bilingual*
un **billet** (beeleh) *ticket*
une **bise** (beez), **un bisou** (beezoo) *(col) kiss*
  faire la bise *to kiss*
bizarre (beezahr) *strange, odd, weird*
une **blague** (blahg) *joke*
blanc (blahⁿ), **blanche** (blahⁿsh) *white*
  un (vin) blanc *white (wine)*
blasé (blahzeh) *blasé*
(se) **blesser** (blehseh) *to (get) hurt*
une **blessure** (blehsür) *wound*
bleu, –e (bluh) *blue*
blond, –e (blohⁿ; blohⁿd) *fair, blond*
boire (bwar) *to drink*
  aller boire un pot *to go and have a drink*
un **bois** (bwa) *wood*
  en bois *in wood*
une **boisson** (bwasohⁿ) *drink*
bon, –ne (bohⁿ; bohn) *good; right*
  bon anniversaire *happy birthday*
  bonne année *happy new year*
  bonne journée *good day*
  bonne nuit *good night*
  bon voyage *have a good trip*
un **bonheur** (bohnuhr) *happiness*
bonjour (bohⁿzhoor) *hello, good morning, good afternoon*
bonsoir (bohⁿswahr) *good evening*
(au) bord (bohr) **de** *on the edge of*
une **bouche** (boosh) *mouth*
un **bouchon** (booshohⁿ) *cork; (col) traffic jam*
une **bouffe** (boof) *(sl) food; meal*
bouffer *(sl) to eat*
bouger (boozheh) *to move*
une **bougie** (boozhee) *candle*
une **boulangerie** (boolahⁿzhree) *bakery*
un **boulot** (booloh) *(col) job, work*
un **bouquet** (bookeh) *bunch*
un **bouquin** (bookehⁿ) *(col) book*
une **bourse** (boors) *purse; stock exchange*
un **bout** (boo) *bit, tip, end*
une **bouteille** (bootehy) *bottle*
une **boutique** (booteek) *store*
une **braderie** (brahdree) *cut price market*
une **branche** (brahⁿsh) *branch*
branché, –e (brahⁿsheh) *trendy; hooked up*
un **bras** (brah) *arm*
bref (brehf), **brève** (brehv) *brief*
en bref *in short*
la **Bretagne** (bruhtahny) *Brittany*

Breton, –ne (brehtohⁿ; brehtohn) *Breton*
brillant (breeyahⁿ) *brilliant; shiny*
brillamment (breeyahmahⁿ) *brilliantly*
briller (breeyeh) *to shine*
britannique (breetahneek) *British*
un **brouillard** (brooyahr) *fog*
un **bruit** (brwee) *noise*
brûlant, –e (brülahⁿ; brülahnt) *burning*
brûler *to burn*
  faire du bruit *to be noisy*
bruyant (brweeyahⁿ) *noisy*
brun, –e (bruhⁿ; broon) *brown*
brutal, –e (brütahl) *brutal*
bûcher (büsheh) *(col) to study*
bûcheur, bûcheuse *(col) studious*
un **bureau** (büroh) *office; desk*
un **bureau de change** *change bureau*

C

ça (sah) *it, this*
une **cabine** (kahbeen) *cabin; booth*
un **cabinet** (kahbeeneh) *professional office*
  les cabinets *(col) toilets*
une **cacahuète** (kahkahweht) *peanut*
(se) **cacher** (kahsheh) *to hide (oneself)*
une **cachette** (kahsheht) *hiding place*
  en cachette *on the sly*
un **cadeau** (kahdoh) *present*
un **cadre** (kahdr) *frame; surroundings*
un **café** (kahfeh) *coffe shop; coffee*
un **cahier** (kahyeh) *notebook*
un **caillou** (kahyoo) *stone; pebble*
une **caisse** (kehs) *register; cashier*
  la caisse d'épargne (dehpahrny) *savings bank*
calculer (kahlküleh) *to calculate*
un **calendrier** (kahlahⁿdryeh) *calendar*
(se) **calmer** (kahlmeh) *to calm (down)*
une **caméra** (kahmehrah) *shooting camera*
un **caméraman** *camera operator*
le **Cameroun** (kahmroon) *Cameroon*
camerounais, –e (kahmrooneh; -ehz) *Cameroonese*
une **campagne** (kahᵐpahny) *the country; countryside*
le **Canada** (kahnahdah) *Canada*
canadien, –dienne (kahnadyehⁿ; -dyehn) *Canadian*
un **cancer** (kahⁿsehr) *cancer (disease); Cancer (sign)*

une **canne à sucre** (kahnahsükr) *sugar cane*
la **cannelle** (kahnehl) *cinnamon*
un **caprice** (kahprees) *whim; caprice*
capricorne (kahpreekohrn) *Capricorn*
car (kahr) *because*
un **caractère** (kahrahktehr) *character*
  avoir bon / mauvais caractère *to be good / ill natured*
les **Caraïbes** (kahraheeb) *Caribbean islands*
caresser (kahrehseh) *to caress*
une **cargolade** (kahrgohlahd) *snail broiling party*
un **carnet** (kahrneh) *notepad*
  carnet de timbres (tehⁿbre) *stamp booklet*
une **carotte** (kahroht) *carrot*
une **carrière** (kahryehr) *career; query*
une **carte** (kahrt) *card, map, menu*
  une carte bancaire (bahnkehr) *bank card*
  une carte de crédit (krehdiht) *credite card*
  une carte postale (pohstahl) *postcard*
  une carte de téléphone (tehlehfohn) *phone card*
un **carton** (kahrtohⁿ) *cardboard*
un **cas** (kah) *case*
  au cas où *in case*
  en aucun cas *in no account*
  en cas de *in case of*
un **casino** (kahzeenoh) *casino*
(se) **casser** (kahseh) *to break; (col) to leave*
  casser les oreilles, les pieds *(col) to bother*
un **cauchemard** (kohshmahr) *nightmare*
à cause (kos) **de** *because of*
une **cave** (kahv) *cellar; cave*
c', ce, cet, cette, ces *(dem adj) this, that, these, those*
  ça y est! (sahyeh) *this is it!*
  c'est-à-dire (sehtahdeer) *that is to say*
ce que, ce qui, ce dont *what*
ceci (suhsee), **cela** (suhlah) *this, that, it*
une **ceinture** (sihⁿtür) *belt*
célèbre (sehlehbr) *famous, well-known*
célébrer *to celebrate*
un / une **célibataire** (sehleebahtehr) *single*
celle, celui, ceux, celles *the one(s)*

celle–ci, celui–là . . . / celle–là /
celui–ci / ceux–ci /
ceux–là / celles–ci / là *this
one, that one . . . / these /
those (ones)*

cent (sah^n) *hundred (inv)*

un centre (sah^{n}tr) *center*

censé, –e (être) (sah^{n}seh) *to be supposed to*

cependant (suhpah^{n}dah^n) *however*

un cercle (sehrkl) *circle*

une cérémonie (sehrehmohnee) *ceremony*

certain, certaine (sehrteh^n) *some*
certain *very probable / certain*
certainement (sehrtehnmah^n) *certainly*

chacun, –cune (shahkuh^n; -kün)
each one

une chaîne (shehn) *channel; chain*

une chaise (shehz) *chair*

une chaleur (shahluhr) *heat*

chaleureux, –euse (shahluhruh;
-ruhz) *warm hearted*

une chambre (shah^{m}br) *room;bed-
room*
chambre d'amis *guest room*

un champagne (shah^{m}pahnyuh)
champagne

un champignon (shah^{m}peenyoh^n)
mushroom

un champion (shah^{m}pyoh^n) *champion*

une championne (shah^{m}pyohn)
champion

une chance (shah^{n}s) *luck*
avoir de la chance *to be lucky*
chanceux, –euse (shah^{n}suh; -suhz)
lucky

un change (shah^{n}zh) *(currency) exchange*

(se) changer *to change (oneself),
to exchange*
changer d'avis *to change one's
mind*
changer de place *to change seat*

un changement (shah^{n}zhmah^n)
change

une chanson (shah^{n}soh^n) *song*

un chant (shah^n) *song; singing*

chanter (shah^{n}teh) *to sing*

un chanteur, –teuse (shah^{n}tuhr;
-tuhz) *singer*

un chapeau (shahpoh) *hat*

un chapitre (shahpeetr) *chapter*

chaque (shahk) *every / each*

une charge (shahrzh) *burden; re-
sponsibility*

charger (shahrzheh) *to charge*

un chariot (shahryoh) *cart*

charmant, –e (shahrmah^n; -mah^{n}t)
charming

un charme (shahrm) *charm*

charmer *to charm*

un chat (shah), une chatte (shaht)
cat

chaud, –e (shoh; -ohd) *warm; hot*
il fait chaud *it's hot*
j'ai chaud *I'm hot*

chauffer (shohfeh) *to heat*

un chef cuisinier (shehf
kweezeenyeh) *chef*

un chef d'orchestre (ohrkehstr)
conductor

un chef d'oeuvre (shehduhvr) *masterpiece*

un chemin (shuhmeh^n) *path; way*
chemin faisant (fuhzah^n) *on the
way*
un chemin de fer (duh fehr) *railroad*

une cheminée (shuhmeeneh) *fireplace*

une chemise (shuhmeezh) *shirt*

un chèque (shehk) *check*
un compte–chèque *checking account*

un chéquier (shehkyeh) *checkbook*

cher, chère (shehr) *dear; expensive*

chercher (shehrsheh) *to look for*

chéri, –e (shehree) *darling*

un cheval, –vaux (shuhvahl; -voh)
horse (sing / pl)
faire du cheval *to go horseback
riding*

un cheveu, –x (shuhvuh) *hair*

une cheville (shuhveey) *ankle*

une chèvre (shehvr) *goat*
fromage, crottin de chèvre *goat
cheese*

chez (sheh) *at; to*
chez moi (mwah) *at home*
chez quelqu'un (kehlkuh^n) *at
someone's place*

chic (sheek) *chic, smart*

un chien, –ienne (shyeh^n; -yehn)
dog

un chiffre (sheefr) *figure; numeral*

un chocolat (shohkohlah) *chocolate*

un choeur (kuhr) *chorus; choir*

choisir (shwahzeer) *to choose*

un choix (shwah) *choice*

le chômage (shohmahzh) *unemployment*

choper (shohpeh) *(sl) to catch*

choquer (shohkeh) *to shock; to
shake up*

une chose (shohz) *thing*

un chou, choux (shoo) *cabbage
(pl)*

chuchoter (shüshohteh) *to whisper*

une chute (shüt) *fall*

ci–dessous (seeduhsoo) *as below*
ci–dessus (seeduhsü) *as above*
ci–joint (seezhweh^n) *enclosed*

un cidre (seedr) *apple cider*

un ciel (syehl) *sky*

les cieux (syuh) *heavens*

une cigarette (seegahreht) *cigarette*

un cimetière (seemtyehr) *cemetery*

un cinéma (seenehmah) *cinema;
movies / movie theater*
une salle de cinéma *movie theater*

un / une cinéphile (seenehfeel)
cinema-lover

cinq (seh^{n}k) *five*

cinquante (seh^{n}kah^{n}t) *fifty*

une circulation (seerkülahsyoh^n) *circulation; traffic*

un citadin, une citadine (see-
tahdeh^n; -deen) *city dweller*

citer (seeteh) *to quote*

un citoyen, une citoyenne (see-
toyeh^n; -yehn) *citizen*

un citron (seetroh^n) *lemon*

clair, –e (klehr) *clear*

une classe (klahs) *class; grade*

classique (klahseek) *classical; standard*

un clavier (klahvyeh) *keyboard*

une clé, clef (kleh) *key; clef*
un trousseau (troosoh) de clés
key holder

un client, –e (kleeyah^n; -yah^{n}t) *client*

un climat (kleemah) *climate*

une climatisation
(kleemahteezasyoh^n) *air-condi-
tioning*

cliquer (kleekeh) *to click*

un code (kohd); code postal
code; zip code

un coeur (kuhr) *heart*
avoir bon coeur *to be kind-
hearted*
avoir mal au coeur *to feel sick*
par coeur *by heart*

un coffret (kohfreh) de CDs / disques *a CD box*

un coiffeur, une coiffeuse (kwahfuhr; -fuhz) *hairdresser*

(se) coiffer *to do one's hair*

un coin (kweh^n) *corner*

une colère (kohlehr); en colère
anger; angry, upset

un colis (kohlee) *parcel*

collant, –e (kohlah^n; lahnt) *sticky;
(col) clinging*

une colle *glue*

coller (kohleh) *to stick up*
un pot de colle (poh duh kohl)
glue jar; (col) clinging

un collège (kohlehzh) *junior high
school*

un / une collègue (kohlehg) *colleague*

une colonie (kohlohnee) *colony;
camp*

le **colonialisme** (kohlohnyahleesm) *colonialism*

une **colonne** (kohlohn) *column*

combien (koh^mbyehⁿ) *how many*

une **comédie** (kohmehdee) *comedy*

un **comédien, –dienne** (kohmehdyehⁿ; -yehn) *a theater actor / actress*

un / une **comique** *a comedian*

comique (kohmeek) *comical*

une **commande** *order*

commander *to order*

comme (kohm) *as; like*

  comme si *as if*

  c'est comme ça *that's the way it is*

un **commencement** *(n) beginning*

commencer (kohmahⁿseh) **(à)** *to begin (to), to start*

comment (kohmahⁿ) *how*

un **commentaire** (kohmahⁿtehr) *commentary; comments*

un **commerce** (kohmehrs) *trade*

un **commissariat de police** *police precinct*

commun, –e (kohmuhⁿ; -muhn) *common*

la **Communauté Économique Européenne (CEE)** *European Economic Community (EEC)*

la **Communauté Européenne (CE)** *European Community*

une **communication** (kohmneekahsyohⁿ) *communication / phone call*

communiquer (kohmneekeh) *to communicate*

une **compagnie** (koh^mpahnee) *company*

comparer (koh^mpahreh) *to compare*

une **compétition** (koh^mpehteesyohn) *competition*

complet, –plète (koh^mpleh; -pleht) *complete*

(se) **comporter** *to behave*

composer (koh^mpohzeh) *to compose; to dial*

un **compositeur** (koh^mpohzeetuhr) *composer, songwriter*

comprendre (koh^mprahⁿdr) *to understand*

compris, –e (koh^mpree; -preez) *understood; included*

un **compte bancaire** (koh^mt) *banking account*

  un compte d'épargne *saving account*

  un compte rendu (rahⁿdü) *report; account*

un **comptoir** (koh^mtwar) *counter*

(se) **concentrer** (kohⁿsahⁿtreh) *to focus*

un **concert** (kohⁿsehr) *concert*

concret, –crète (kohⁿkreh; -reht) *concrete*

une **condition** (kohⁿdeesyohⁿ) *condition*

un / une **conducteur, conductrice** (kohndüktuhr; trees) *driver*

conduire (kohⁿdweer) *to drive*

une **confiance** (kohⁿfyahns) *confidence; trust*

  faire confiance *to trust*

connaître *to know*

connu, –e *well known*

consacré, –e à *devoted to*

content, –e *glad, happy*

un **contrat** *contract*

contrairement *unlike*

un **contrôleur (SCNF)** *(SNCF) inspector*

un / une **copain, copine** *pal*

les **coquillages** *seafood*

un **corps** *body*

la **Corse** *Corsica*

un **costume** *costume, suit*

un **côté** *side, edge*

un **cou** *neck*

couler *to sink*

les **coulisses** *backstage*

un **couloir** *aisle, hallway*

un **coup de sifflet** (koo duh seefleh) *whistle*

(se) **couper** (koopeh) *to cut (oneself)*

  se faire couper les cheveux *to get a haircut*

un **coupable** (koopahbl) *(n) guilty; culprit*

une **cour** (koor) *courtyard; court*

bon courage (bohⁿ koorahzh) *be brave*

courageux, –euse (koorahzhuh; -uhz) *brave*

couramment (koorahmahⁿ) *fluently*

  être au courant (koorahⁿ) de *to know about*

un **coureur** (kooruhr) *runner*

courir (kooreer) *to run*

un **courrier** (kooryeh) *mail*

un **courrier électronique** *e-mail*

une **course** (koors) *errand; race*

  faire les courses *to do the shopping*

court, –e (koor; koort) *short*

un **court de tennis** *tennis court*

un **court–métrage** *short film*

un **cousin, une cousine** (koozehⁿ; -zeen) *cousin*

coûter (kooteh) *to cost*

  combien ça coûte? *how much is it?*

une **coutume** (kootüm) *custom*

un **couturier, –ère** (kootüryeh; -ryehr) *sewer; taylor; designer*

couvert, –e (koovehr; -ehrt) *covered; overcast*

un **couvre–feu** (koovrfuh) *curfew*

craindre (krehⁿdr) *to fear*

un **crayon** (krehyohⁿ) *pencil*

une **création** (krehahsyohⁿ) *creation*

créer (kreheh) *to create*

une **crème** (krehm) *cream; creme*

une **crêpe** (krehp) *crepe*

une **crêperie** (krehpree) *creperie*

un **critique** (kreeteek) *critic*

une **critique** *criticiscm; review*

critiquer (kreeteekeh) *to criticize*

croire (krwahr) *to believe*

croiser (krwahzeh) *to cross; to pass*

  croisons les doigts *let's cross our fingers*

une **croisière** (krwahzyehr) *cruise*

un **croyant, –e** (krwahyahⁿ; -ahⁿt) *believer*

cruel, –elle (krüehl) *cruel*

cueillir (kuhyeer) *to pick up*

une **cuillère** (kweeyehr) **à café** *teaspoon*

  une cuillère à soupe (soop) *spoon*

cuire (kweer) *to cook; to bake*

un **cuisinier, –ère** *cook*

une **cuisse** (kwees) *thigh; leg*

culinaire (küleenehr) *culinary*

une **culpabilité** (külpahbeeleeteh) *guilt*

cultivé, –e (külteeveh) *cultured; cultivated*

une **culture** (kültür) *culture*

curieux, –euse (küryuh; -uhz) *curious*

un **curriculum vitae** (cv) *résumé*

cyclable (seeklahbl) *for bicycles*

D

le **daim** (dehⁿ) *suede*

une **dame** (dahm) *lady; queen (games)*

  jeu de dames *checkers*

un **danger** (dahⁿzheh) *danger*

dangereux, –reuse (dahⁿzhuhruh; -ruhz) *dangerous*

dans (dahⁿ) *in*

une **danse** (dahⁿs) *dance*

danser (dahⁿseh) *to dance*

un **danseur, –seuse** (dahⁿsuhr; -suhz) *dancer*

une **date** (daht) *date*

dater (dahteh) *to date*

de, du (duh, dü) *of; from*

(se) **débarasser de** *to get rid of, to rid*

un **débat** (dehbah) *debate*

debout (duhboo) **(être)** *to be up; to stand up*

(se) **débrouiller** *to handle, to manage*
un **début** (dehbü) *debut; beginning*
débuter (dehbüteh) *to start*
décéder (dehsehdeh) *to die*
décembre (dehsah^mbr) *December*
une **décennie** (dehsehnee) *decade*
déchirer (dehsheereh) *to tear down*
décidé, –e (dehseedeh) *decided; determined*
décider (dehseedeh) *to decide*
une **décision** (dehseezyoh^n) *decision*
une **déclaration** (dehklahrahsyoh^n) *declaration*
déclarer (dehklahreh) *to declare; to register*
un **déclin** (dehklih^n) *decline*
déconfit, –e (dehkoh^nfee; -feet) *not fresh; not joyful*
un **décor** (dehkohr) *setting; scenery*
décourageant, –e (dehkoorahzha^n; -zha^nt) *discouraging*
décourager (dehkoorahzheh) *to discourage*
découvert, –e (dehkoovehr; -vehrt) *discovered; exposed*
découvrir (dehkoovreer) *to discover*
décrire (dehkreer) *to describe*
déçu, –e (dehsü) *disappointed*
dedans (duhdah^n) *inside*
dédier (dehdyeh) *to dedicate*
un **défaut** (dehfoh) *fault; defect; flaw*
défendre (dehfah^ndr) *to defend*
un **degrès** (duhgreh) *degree*
dégriffé, –e (dehgreefeh) *tag-off, untagged*
déguster (dehgüsteh) *to taste; to savor*
dehors (duhohr) *out, outside*
Dehors! *Get out!*
   mettre quelqu'un dehors *to kick someone out*
déjeuner (dehzhuhneh) *to have lunch*
un **déjeuner** *lunch*
un **petit déjeuner** *breakfast*
déjà (dehzhah) *already, ever*
demain (duhmeh^n) *tomorrow*
   après–demain *day after tomorrow*
demander (duhmah^ndeh) *to ask for; to demand*
(se) **demander** *to wonder*
démarrer (dehmahreh) *to start*
un **déménagement** (dehmehnahzhmah^n) *moving*
déménager (dehmehnahzheh) *to move*

demeurant (duhmuhrah^n) *living in*
demeurer (duhmuhreh) *to remain, to live*
demi, –e (duhmee) *half*
   un **demi–tarif** (duhmee tahreef) *half-price*
une **démocratie** (dehmohkrahsee) *democracy*
démodé, –e (dehmohdeh) *out of fashion*
une **demoiselle** (duhmwazehl) *young lady*
un **démon** (dehmoh^n) *demon*
une **dent** (dah^n) *tooth*
un **dentiste** (dah^nteest) *dentist*
un **départ** (dehpahr) *departure*
se **dépêcher** (dehpehsheh) *to hurry up*
une **dépense** *expense*
déposer (dehpohseh) *to deposit*
déprimé, –e (dehpreemeh) *depressed*
depuis (duhpwee) *since; for*
un **député** (dehpüteh) *congressman*
déranger (dehrah^nzheh) *to bother; to disturb*
   en dérangement *out of order*
dernier, –nière (dehrnyeh; -nyehr) *last*
dernièrement (dehrnyehrmah^n) *recently*
derrière (dehryehr) *behind, in the back of*
des (deh) *some*
dès que (deh kuh) *as soon as*
désagréable (dehzahgrehahbl) *unpleasant*
descendre (dehsah^ndr) *to get off; to go down*
une **description** (dehskreepsyoh^n) *description*
un **désert** (dehzehr) *desert*
un **désespoir** (dehzehspwar) *despair*
(se) **déshabiller** (dehzahbeeyeh) *to undress*
un **désir** (dehzeer) *desire*
désirer (dehzeereh) *to desire*
désolé, –e (dehzohleh) *sorry; desolate*
désordonné, –e (dehzohrdohneh) *untidy; messy*
un **désordre** (dehzohrdr) *mess; disorder*
désormais (dehzohrmeh) *from now on*
un **dessert** (dehsehr) *dessert*
un **dessin** (dehseh^n) *drawing; draft*
dessiner (dehseeneh) *to draw; to design*
dessous (duhsoo) *under*
   en dessous de *underneath*
   un dessous de plat *table mat*

dessus (duhs) *over*
   au dessus de *above; over*
un **destin** (dehstih^n) *destiny; fate*
un **destinataire** (dehsteenahtehr) *addressee*
une **destination** (dehsteenahsyoh^n) *destination*
détester (dehtehsteh) *to hate*
deux (duh) *two*
   deux fois *twice*
deuxième (duhzyehm) *second*
devant (duvah^n) *in front of*
devenir (duhvuhneer) *to become*
deviner (duhveeneh) *to guess*
une **devise** (duhveez) *motto*
un **devoir** (duhvwahr) *homework, duty*
devoir *must; to have to; to owe*
dieu (dyuh) *god*
différent, –e (deefehrah^n; -rah^nt) *different*
difficile (deefeeseel) *difficult*
un **dimanche** (deemah^nsh) *Sunday*
un **dîner** (deeneh) *dinner*
dîner *to have dinner*
   faire à dîner *to cook dinner*
un **diplôme** (deeplohm) *diploma*
dire (deer) *to say; to tell*
   dire l'heure (deer lhuhr) *to tell the time*
   ça te dit de *do you feel like*
   on dit que *they say that*
   on dirait que *it looks as if*
   disons (deezohn) *let's say; well*
direct, –e (deerekt); **en direct** *direct; live*
diriger (deereezheh) *to conduct; to run; to direct*
discret, –crète (deeskreh; -kreht) *discreet*
discuter (deesküteh) *to discuss; to chat*
disparaître (deespahrehtr) *to disappear*
(se) **disputer** (deespüteh) *to quarrel; to argue*
un **disque** (deesk) *record*
un **disque compact, CD** (kohmpahkt, sehdeh) *compact disk*
divers (deevehr) *various; diverse*
(se) **divertir** (deevehrteer) *to entertain (oneself)*
un **divertissement** (deevehrteesmah^n) *entertainment*
un **divorce** (deevohrs) *divorce*
divorcé, –e (deevohrseh) *divorced*
divorcer (deevohrseh) *to divorce*
dix (dees) *ten*
dix–huit (deezweet) *eighteen*
une **dizaine** (deezehn) *ten; ten or so*
un **docteur** (dohktuhr) *doctor*
un **document** (dohkümah^n) *document*

une **documentation** (dohkümahⁿ-tahsyohⁿ) *literature*
un **doigt** (dwah) *finger*
donc (dohⁿk) *therefore; thus*
donner (dohneh) *to give*
  donner la main *to give one's hand*
dont (dohⁿ) *whose; of which*
dormir (dohrmeer) *to sleep*
un **dos** (doh) *back*
un **dossier** (dohsyeh) *file; report*
douala (dwah*lah*) *douala (fr: Cameroon)*
la **douane** (dwahnn) *customs*
doubler (doobleh) *to double; to pass; to dub*
doucement (doosmahⁿ) *softly; smoothly*
une **douche** (doosh) *shower*
se **doucher** (doosheh) *to shower*
une **douleur** (dooluhr) *pain*
un **doute** (doot) *doubt*
  (se) douter de (dooteh) *to doubt*
  sans aucun doute *undoubtedly*
doux (doo), **douce** (doos) *sweet; soft; smooth*
une **douzaine** (doozehn) *dozen*
draguer (drahgeh) *(col) to flirt*
dramatique (drahmahteek) *dramatic*
un **drame** (drahm) *drama*
un **droit** (drwah) *right*
le **droit** *law*
(à) **droite** (drwat) *(on) the right*
drôle (drohl) *funny*
du (de+ le) (dü) *some*
dû, due, dues, dus (dü) *owed*
dur, –e (dür) *hard*
durant (dürahⁿ) *during; for*
durer (düreh) *to last*

E

une **eau** (oh), **de l'eau** *water, some water*
un **échange** (ehshahⁿzh) *exchange; trade*
échanger (ehshahⁿzheh) *to exchange; to change*
s'**échauffer** (sehshohfeh) *to warm up*
un **échec** (eshehk); **les échecs** *failure; chess*
s'**éclater** (sehklahteh) *(col) to have a blast, fun*
une **école** (ehkohl) *school*
une **école maternelle; –primaire** *nursery; grammar school*
un / une **écologiste** (ehkohloh-zheest) *ecologist*
écouter (ehkooteh) *to listen to*
un **écran** (ehkrahⁿ) *screen*

écrire (ehkreer) *to write*
un **écrivain** (ehkreevehⁿ) *writer*
une **éducation** (ehdkahsyohⁿ) *education*
en effet (ahⁿ ehfeh) *indeed*
un **effort** (ehfohr) *effort*
égal, –e (ehgahl) *even, equal*
  ça m'est égal *I don't mind*
une **église** (ehgleez) *church*
égoïste (ehgoheest) *selfish*
une **élection** (ehlehksyohⁿ) *election*
électoral, –e (ehlehktohrahl) *electoral*
élire (ehleer); **élu, –e** (ehlü) *to elect; elected*
élever (ehluhveh) *to raise*
elle, elles (ehl) *she / it, they; her, them*
éloigné, –e (ehlwahnyeh) *removed;away*
éloquent, –e (ehlohkahⁿ; -kahⁿt) *eloquent*
(s') **emballer** (ah^mbahleh) *to wrap; to be thrilled*
emballé, –e *wrapped up*
embêter (ah^mbehteh) *(fam) to bother*
  s'embêter *to be bored*
(s') **embrasser** (ah^mbrahseh) *to kiss (each other)*
une **émission** (ehmeesyohⁿ) *emission; show*
emménager (ah^mmehnahzheh) *to move in, into*
une **émotion** (ehmohsyohⁿ) *emotion*
émouvant, –e (ehmoovahⁿ; -vahⁿt) *moving*
s'**emparer** (sahⁿpahreh) **de** *to seize; to grab*
un **empire** (ah^mpeer) *empire*
un **employé, –e** (ah^mplwahyeh) *employee*
emporter *to take with; to take away*
en (ahⁿ) *in; on; as; made of; to*
  en fait (ahⁿ feht) *in fact; actually*
enceinte (ahⁿsehⁿt) *pregnant*
enchanté, –e (ahⁿshanteh) *pleased (to meet you)*
encore (ahⁿkohr) *again; still; even; yet*
encourageant, –e (ahⁿkoorazhahⁿ; -zahⁿt) *encouraging*
(s') **encourager** (ahⁿkoorahzheh) *to encourage (oneself)*
un **encouragement** (ahⁿkoorahzhmahn) *encouragement*
un **endroit** (ahⁿdrwa) *place*
une **enfance** (ahⁿfahⁿs) *childhood*
un / une **enfant** (ahⁿfahⁿ) *child*
enfin (ahⁿfehⁿ) *finally; at last*
s'**enfuir** (ahⁿfweer) *to run away*

énorme (ehnohrm) *huge*
enregistrer (ahⁿruhzheestreh) *to record*
(s') **enrichir** *to enrich, to get rich*
enseigner (ahnsehnyeh) *to teach*
un **ensemble** (ahⁿsahⁿbl) *suit; outfit; ensemble*
ensemble *together*
ensuite (ahⁿsweet) *then*
entendre (ahⁿtahⁿdr) *to hear; to understand*
entier *whole*
entourer (ahⁿtooreh) *to surround; to circle*
un **entraînement** (ahⁿtrehnmahⁿ) *practice; training*
(s') **entraîner** (ahⁿtrehneh) *to train; to practice*
un **entraîneur** (ahⁿtrehnuhr) *trainer; coach*
une **entrée** (ahⁿtreh) *outset; entrance; appetizer*
entrer (ahⁿtreh) *to go in; to come in; to enter*
une **enveloppe** (ahⁿvuhlohp) *envelope*
un **envers** (ahⁿvehr) *reversal*
  l'envers *upside down*
une **envie** (ahⁿvee) *desire*
  avoir envie de *to want; to feel like*
un **envoi** (ahⁿvwah) *sent*
  un envoyé spécial *anchor; reporter*
envoyer (ahⁿvwahyeh) *to send*
épais, –aisse (ehpeh; -ehs) *thick*
une **épaule** (ehpohl) *shoulder*
une **épice** (ehpees) *spice*
épicé, –e (ehpeeseh) *spiced up; hot*
une **épicerie** (ehpeesree) *small grocery store; deli*
épouvantable (ehpoovahⁿtabl) *dreadful; horrendous*
une **équipe** (ehkeep) *team*
équipé, –e (ehkeepeh) *equipped*
une **escale** (ehskahl) *stop*
un **escalier** (ehskahlyeh) *stairway*
un **escargot** (ehskahrgoh) *snail*
un **esclavage** (ehsklahvahzh) *slavery*
un / une **esclave** (ehsklahv) *slave*
l'**Espagne** (ehspahny) *(f.) Spain*
espagnol, –e (ehspahnyohl) *Spanish*
espérer (ehspehreh) *to hope*
un **espoir** (ehspwahr) *hope*
un **esprit** (ehspree) *mind; spirit*
un **essai** (ehseh) *trying; try; essay*
essayer (ehsehyeh) *to try; to attempt*
une **essence** (ehsahⁿs) *gas; essence*
  prendre de l'essence *to get gas*
est (ehst) *east*

est-ce que . . . (ehskuh) *is it that...*
un **étage** (ehtahzh) *floor*
au premier étage *on the second floor*
une **étagère** (ehtahzhehr) *shelf*
un **état** (ehtah) *state; condition*
les **États-Unis** (ehtathz ünee) *The United States*
un **été** *summer*
éteindre (ehtehⁿdr) *to turn off; to extinguish*
éteint, -e *off*
une **étiquette** (ehteekeht) *label; etiquette*
une **étoile** *star*
étonnant (ehtohnahⁿ) *astonishing; surprising*
étonner (ehtohneh) *to surprise*
un / une **étranger, -ère** (ehtrahⁿzheh; -zhehr) *foreigner; stranger*
être (ehtr) *to be*
étroit, -e (ehtrwah; ehtrwaht) *narrow*
une **étude** (ehtd) *study*
un / une **étudiant, -e** (ehtüdyahⁿ; -dyahⁿt) *student*
étudier (ehtdyeh) *to study*
un **euro** (uhroh) (€) *euro*
eux *them*
un **évènement** (ehvehnmahⁿ) *event*
évidemment (ehveedahmahⁿ) *obviously*
évoluer (ehvohlüeh) *to evolve*
exactement *exactly*
un **examen** (ehgzahmehⁿ) *examination; exam; test*
s'**excuser** (sehksküzeh) *to apologize*
un **exemple** (ehgzah^mpl) *example*
un **exercice** (egzehrsees) *exercise*
faire de l'exercice *to exercise*
un **expéditeur** *sender*
une **exposition** *exhibition*
expliquer (ekspleekeh) *to explain*
extérieur (ekstehryuhr) *exterior; outside*
à l'extérieur *on the outside*
un **extrait** *extract*
extraordinaire *extraordinary*

F

une **fable** (fahbl) *fable*
en face de / à (ahⁿ fahs duh; -ah) *in front of; opposite*
facile (fahseel) *easy*
une **façon** (fahsohⁿ) *way*
une **facture** (fahktür) *bill*
une **faculté** (fahkülteh) *university; faculty*
faible (fehbl) *weak*
avoir failli (fahyee) *to have almost done...*

une **faim** (fehⁿ); **avoir faim** *hunger; to be hungry*
faire (fehr) *to make; to do*
faire un numéro *to dial a number*
il fait beau *it's nice weather*
cela fait $2 *it's $2*
un **faire-part** (fehr pahr) *announcement*
un **fait** (feh, feht) *fact*
au fait *by the way*
en fait *in fact; actually*
falloir (fahlwahr); **il faut** *have to; must; need*
familier, -ière (fahmeelyeh; -yehr) *familiar; informal*
une **famille** (fahmeey) *family*
une **farine** (fahreen) *flour*
favori, -ite (fahvohree; -reet) *favorite*
fatigant, -e (fahteegahⁿ) *tiring*
fatiguer (fahteegeh) *to make tired; wear out*
fatigué, -e (fahteegeh) *tired*
faux (foh), **fausse** *wrong; out of tune*
un **faux numéro** *wrong number*
félicitations (fehleeseetahsyohⁿ) *congratulations*
féliciter (fehleeseeteh) *to congratulate*
féminin, -e (fehmeenehⁿ; -neen) *feminine*
une **femme** (fahm) *woman*
une **fenêtre** (fuhnehtr) *window*
férié, -e (fehryeh), **un jour férié** *public holiday*
fermer (fehrmeh) *to close; to shut(down)*
une **fermeture** (fehrmuhtür) *closing*
les **fesses** *(f.pl.)* *buttocks*
un **festin** (fehstehⁿ) *feast*
une **fête** (feht) *feast; holiday; party*
faire la fête *to party*
un **feu** (fuh) *fire*
une **feuille** (fuhy) *leaf*
février (fehvryeh) *February*
je m'en fiche (feesh) *(col)* *I don't care*
fiche-moi la paix *(col)* *leave me alone*
une **file** *lane*
une **file d'attente** (feel dahtahⁿt) *line*
un **filet** (feeleh) *net*
une **fille** (feey) *girl; daughter*
un **film** (feelm) *movie*
un **fils** (fees) *son*
une **fin** (fehⁿ); **à la fin** *end; in the end*
final, -e (feenahl) *final*
finir (feeneer) *to finish; to end*
une **flamme** *flame*
une **fleur** (fluhr) *flower*

une **foi** *faith*
de bonne foi *in good faith*
une **fois** (fwah); **à la fois** *once; one time; at once*
fondre (fohⁿdr) *to melt; to blend*
le **football** *soccer; football*
une **force** (fors) *strength*
un **forfait** (fohrfeh) *package deal; set price*
fort, -e (fohr; fohrt) *strong, loud*
fou (foo), **folle** (fohl) *crazy, mad*
fournir *to provide*
un **fournisseur** (foorneesuhr) *provider*
(se) **foutre** (footr); **je m'en fous** *(sl)* *I don't give a damn; I don't care*
fragile (frahzheel) *fragile*
frais (freh), **fraîche** (frehsh) *fresh; cool*
les **frais** (freh) *expenses*
une **fraise** (frehz) *strawberry*
français, -e (frahⁿseh; -sehz) *French*
la **France** (frahⁿs) *France*
un **franc** (frahⁿ) *franc*
Francfort (frahⁿkfohr) *Frankfurt*
francophone (frahⁿkohfohn) *French-speaking*
la **fraternité** (frahtehrneeteh) *brotherhood*
un **frère** (frehr) *brother*
un **frigo** (freegoh) *(fam)* *fridge*
froid (frwah) *cold; cool*
j'ai froid *I'm cold*
il fait froid *it's cold*
un **fromage** (frohmahzh) *cheese*
un **front** (frohⁿ) *forehead; front*
une **frontière** (frohntyehr) *border; frontier*
un **fruit** (frwee) *fruit*
une **fumée** *smoke*
fumer (fümeh) *to smoke*
un **fumeur, -euse** (fümuhr; fümuhz) *smoker*
futé, -e (füteh) *sharp; smarty*
un **futur** (fütür) *future*
futur, -e (fütür) *(adj)* *future*

G

un **gagnant, -e** (gahnyahⁿ; -yahⁿt) *winner*
gagner (gahnyeh) *to win*
une **galerie** (gahlree) *gallery*
un **galet** (gahleh) *pebble*
un / une **gamin, -e** (gahmehⁿ; -meen) *kid*
un **garçon** (gahrsohⁿ) *boy*
Garçon! Waiter!
garder (gahdeh) *to keep*
une **garderie** (gahrduhree) *nursery*
une **gare** (gahr) *station*

(se) **garer** (gahreh) *to park (one's) car*

un **gâteau** (gahtoh) *cake*

gâter *to treat*

une **gauche** (gohsh); **à gauche** *left; on the left*

une **gaufre** (gohfr) *waffle*

un **gémeau** (zhehmoh) *Gemini*

un **gendre** *son-in-law*

la **Genèse** (zhehnehz) *Genesis*

gènial, –e *great*

un **genou** (zhuhnoo) *knee*

des **gens** (zhahⁿ) *people*

gentil, gentille (zhahⁿteey) *kind; nice*

gentiment *nicely*

une **glace** (glahs) *ice; ice cream; mirror*

glacé, –e *iced*

un **glaçon** (glahsohⁿ) *ice cube*

une **gorgée** (gohrzheh) *sip; gulp*

un **goût** (goo) *taste*

goûter (gooteh) *to taste*

une **goutte** (goot) *drop*

un **gouvernement** (goovehrnmahⁿ) *government*

grâce à (grahs ah) *thanks to*

grand (grahⁿ) *tall; big*

une **grand–mère** (grahⁿmehr) *grandmother*

un **grand–parent** *grandparent*

un **grand–père** (grahⁿpehr) *grandfather*

grandir (grahⁿdeer) *to grow up*

gras, grasse (grah; -ahs) *greasy; fat*

gratuit, –e (grahtwee, -weet) *free*

un **grenier** (gruhnyeh) *attic*

une **grève** (grehv); **en grève** *strike; on strike*

une **grippe** *flu*

gris, –ise (gree; greez) *gray*

gros, grosse (groh; -ohs) *fat; big; large*

un **groupe** *group, band*

la *Guadeloupe* (gwahduhloop) *Guadaloupe*

gueuler *(col) to get mad, to yell*

une **guerre** *war*

un **guichet** (geesheh) *window; counter*

une **guitare** (geetahhr) *guitar*

H

une **habileté** *skill*

(s') **habiller** (ahbeeyeh) *to dress (up)*

un **habitant, –e** (ahbeetahⁿ; -tahⁿt) *inhabitant; occupant*

habiter *to live; to inhabit*

une **habitude** (ahbeetüd) *habit*

habitué, –e (ahbeetüeh) *used to it; regular*

haïr (aheer) *to hate*

un **hall de gare** *station terminal*

haut, –e (oh; oht); **en haut** *high; on the top; upstairs*

là haut *up there*

hebdomadaire (ehbdohmahdehr) *weekly*

hésiter *to hesitate*

hélas (ehlahs) *alas*

une **heure** (uhr); **à l'heure** *hour; time; on time*

heure de pointe *rush hour*

un **quart, une demie heure** *quarter of, half an hour*

heureux, –euse (uhruh; -uhz) *happy; fortunate*

heureuse année *happy new year*

heureusement *happily; fortunately*

hier (eeehr) *yesterday*

avant–hier *day before yesterday*

une **histoire** (eestwahr) *story; history*

historique (eestohreek) *historical; historic*

un **hiver** (eevehr); **en hiver** *winter; in winter*

un **hommage** (ohmahzh) *tribute*

rendre un hommage à *to pay a tribute to*

un **homme** (ohm) *man*

un **honneur** (ohnuhr) *honor*

honnête (ohneht) *honest*

un **hôpital** (ohpeetahl) *hospital*

un **horaire** (ohrehr) *schedule*

hors de *out of*

un **hôte** (oht) *host*

un **hôtel** (ohtehl) *hotel*

hôtel de ville *town hall; city hall*

une **hôtesse** *hostess, female flight attendant*

une **hôtesse de l'air** (ohtehs duh lehr) *air stewardess*

une **huile** (weel) *oil*

huile d'olive *olive oil*

huit (weet) *eight*

une **humeur** (ümuhr) *mood*

de bonne / mauvaise humeur *in a good / bad mood*

humilité (ümeeleeteh) *humility; humbleness*

l'**hymne** *(m.)* **français** *French national anthem*

I

ici (eesee) *here*

un **idéal** (eedehahl) *ideal*

idéal, –e *(adj) ideal*

une **idée** (eedeh) *idea*

idiot, –e (eedyoh; -yoht) *stupid; goofy*

ignorer (eenyohreh) *to ignore*

une **ignorance** (eenyohrahⁿs) *ignorance*

il (eel) *it, he*

ils (eel) *they*

une **île** (eel) *island*

une **image** (eemahzh) *image*

imaginer (eemahzheeneh) *to imagine*

un **immeuble** (eemuhbl) *building*

immigré, –e (eemeegreh) *immigrant*

l'**immobilier** (eemohbeelyeh) *(m.) real estate*

impatient, –e (ehⁿpahsyahⁿ; -ahⁿt) *impatient*

impoli, –e (ehⁿpohlee) *impolite; rude*

impossible (ehⁿpohseebl) *impossible*

une **impression** (ehⁿprehsyohⁿ) *impression; feeling*

inconnu, –e (ehⁿkohnü) *not known; unknown*

inconscient, –e (ehⁿkohnsyahⁿ; -yahⁿt) *unconscious*

une **inconscience** *unconsciousness*

incroyable (ehⁿkrwahyahbl) *incredible*

indépendant, –e (ehⁿdehpahⁿdahⁿ; -dahⁿt) *independent*

indiquer (ehⁿdeekeh) *to point out; to tell*

indispensable (ehⁿdeespahⁿsahbl) *indispensable*

une **information; les informations** (ehⁿfohrmahsyohⁿ) *information; the news*

l'**informatique** (ehⁿfohrmahteek) *(f.) computer science*

un **ingrédient** (ehⁿgrehdyahⁿ) *ingredient*

inoubliable (eenoobleeyahbl) *unforgettable*

inquiet, –ète (ehⁿkyeh; -yeht) *anxious*

s'**inquiéter** (ehⁿkyehteh) *to worry*

insister (ehⁿseesteh) *to insist*

une **inspiration** (ehⁿspeerahsyohⁿ) *inspiration*

(s') **installer** (ehⁿstahleh) *to settle*

un **instant** (ehⁿstahⁿ) *moment*

un / une **instituteur, –trice** (ehⁿsteetütuhr; -trees) *school teacher*

insupportable (ehⁿnsüpohrtahbl) *unbearable*

interdire (ehⁿtehrdeer) *to forbid*

(s') **intéresser** (ehⁿtehrehseh) **à** *to be interested in*

intérieur, à l'intérieur *inside*

un **internaute** (ehⁿtehrnoht) *Internet user*

Internet (eh"tehrneht) *Internet*
une **interview** (eh"tehrvyoo) *inter-view*
  faire une interview *to do an in-terview*
interviewer *to interview*
un **inventeur** (eh"vah"tuhr) *inventor*
un **invité, –e** (eh"veeteh) *guest*
  inviter *to invite, to treat*

J

jamais (zhahmeh) *never*
  à jamais *forever*
une **jambe** (zhah"b) *leg*
janvier (zhah"vyeh) *January*
jaune *yellow*
je (zhuh) *I*
une **jetée** (zhuhteh) *jetty; pier*
jeter *to throw; to cast*
  jeter un sort *to cast a spell*
un **jeu** (zhuh) *game; acting*
un **jeudi** (zhuhdee) *Thursday*
jeune (zhuhn) *young*
une **jeunesse** *youth*
joindre (zhwih"dr) *to join; to en-close*
joli, –e (zhohlee) *pretty*
jouer (zhooeh) *to play; to act; to perform*
un **jour** (zhoor) *day*
un **journal** (zhoornahl) *newspaper; TV news*
un / une **journaliste** (zhoor-nahleest) *journalist*
une **journée** (zhoorneh) *day*
joyeux; –euse (zhwayuh; -uhz) *joy-ous; cheerful; happy*
juger (zhzheh) *to judge*
juillet (zhweeyeh) *July*
juin (zhüih") *June*
un **jus** (zhü) *juice*
jusqu'à (zhüskah) *until; up to*
juste (züst) *fair; just; only*

K

kaki (kahkee) *khaki*
un **kilogramme** (keelohgrahm) *kilogramme*
un **kilomètre** (keelohmehtr) *kilome-ter*
klaxonner (klahksohneh) *to beep the horn*

L

la, le , les, l' *the; her, him, it*
là, là–bas (lahbah) *there*
un **lac** (lahk) *lake*
lâcher (lahsheh) *to drop; to release*
laïc, laïque (laheek) *lay, civil*

la **laïcité** (laheeseeteh) *state of being civil*
laisser (lehseh) *to leave; to let*
  laisse–moi tranquille *(col) leave me alone*
  laisser (qn) faire (qch) *to let (so) do (sth)*
  laisser un message *to leave a message*
un **lait** (leh) *milk*
une **lampe** (lah"p) *lamp*
une **langue** (lah"g) *language; tongue*
laquelle, lequel, lesquelles *which*
large *wide*
(se) **laver** (lahveh) *to wash (up)*
une **leçon** (luhsoh") *lesson*
un **légume** (lehgüm) *vegetable*
un **lendemain** (lah"duhmih") *day after*
lentement (lah"tmah") *slowly*
une **lettre** (lehtr) *letter*
leur (luhr) *their; them*
lever (luhveh) *to raise*
  se lever *to get up; to rise*
une **liaison** (lyehzoh") *liaison*
libérer *to release*
la **liberté** (leebehrteh) *freedom*
libre (leebr) *free*
un **lien** (lyeh") *link; connection*
un **lieu** (lyuh); **avoir lieu** *place; to take place*
  au lieu de *instead, rather than*
un **lièvre** (lyehvr) *hare*
une **ligne** (leeny); **en ligne** *line; in / on line*
lire (leer) *to read*
une **liste** *list*
un **lit** (lee) *bed*
un **litre** (leetr) *liter*
une **littérature** (leetehrahtür) *litera-ture*
un **livre** (leevr) *book*
local, –e (lohkahl) *local*
un / une **locataire** (lohkatehr) *tenant*
une **location** (lohkahsyoh") *rental*
un **logement** (lohzhmah") *housing; apartment*
loger (lohzheh) *to accommodate*
un **logiciel** (lohzheesyehl) *software*
une **loi** (lwah) *law*
loin (lwih") *far; a long time ago; away*
Londres (loh"dr) *London*
long, –gue (loh"; loh"g) *long*
longtemps (loh"tah"m) *a long time*
  depuis longtemps *for a long time*
lorsque (lohrsk) *when; as*
louer (looeh) *to rent; to praise*
lourd, –e (loor; loord) *heavy*

un **loyer** (lwayeh) *rent*
lui (lwee) *him; her*
une **lumière** (lümyehr) *light*
un **lundi** (luh"dee) *Monday*
une **lune** (lün) *moon*
un **lycée** (leeseh) *senior high school*

M

ma, mes, mon *my*
Madame, Mesdames (mehdahm) *Mrs, Ms; Madam*
Mademoiselle, Mesdemoi-selles (mehduhmwahzehl) *Miss*
un **magasin** (mahgahzih") *store*
  un grand magasin *department store*
un **magnétoscope** *VCR*
mai (meh) *May*
un **mail** (mehl) *e-mail*
une **main** (meh") *hand*
maintenant (meh"tuhnah") *now*
une **mairie** (mehree) *town hall; city hall*
mais (meh) *but*
une **maison** (mehzoh") *house*
un **maître, –tresse** (mehtr; -trehs) *master, mistress*
  une maîtresse de maison *host*
une **majorité** (mahzhohreeteh) *ma-jority*
mal (mahl); **le mal** *bad; (n) evil*
  avoir mal à *to hurt*
  avoir du mal à faire *to have trou-ble doing*
  faire du mal à; se faire mal *to hurt so; -oneself*
malade (mahlahd) *sick*
malchanceux, –euse *unlucky*
malgrè (mahlgreh) *in spite of*
malheureusement (mahluhruhzmah") *unfortunately*
maman (mahmah") *mommy*
la **Manche** (mah"sh) *English Chan-nel*
un **mandat** (mah"dah) *mandate; money order*
manger (mah"zheh) *to eat*
une **manière** (mahnyehr) *way, manner*
une **manifestation** (maneefehstah-syoh") *demonstration;event*
manquer (mah"keh) *to miss; to fail*
un **manteau** (mah"toh) *coat*
un **marchand, –e** (mahrshah"; -shah"d) *stallholder*
un **marché** (mahrsheh) *market*
  un marché aux puces *flea mar-ket*
  bon marché *cheap*
marcher (mahrsheh) *to walk; to work*

un **mardi** (mahrdee) *Tuesday*
un **mari** (mahree) *husband*
un **mariage** (mahryahzh) *wedding; marriage*
un / une **marié, –e** *a groom / a bride*
marié, –e (mahryeh) *married*
  se marier *to get married*
une **marque** (mahrk) *mark; brand; score*
marrant, –e (mahrahⁿ; -rahⁿt) *(col) funny*
se **marrer** (mahreh) *(col) to laugh*
marron (mahrohⁿ) *brown*
mars (mahrs) *March*
  la *Marseillaise* (mahrsehyehz) *French anthem*
masculin, –e (mahskülehⁿ; -leen) *masculine*
un **masque** (mahsk) *mask*
un **match** (mahtsh) *game; match*
mater (mahteh) *(sl) to watch; to peep*
un **matin** (mahtehⁿ) *morning*
mauvais (mohveh) *bad*
  il fait mauvais *the weather is bad*
me (muh), **m'** *me*
une **médaille** (mehdahy) *medal*
un **médecin** (mehdsehⁿ) *doctor*
un **médicament** (mehdeekahmahⁿ) *medicine*
la **(mer) Méditerranée** (mehdeetehrahneh) *Mediterranean Sea*
meilleur (mehyuhr) *best*
un **mèl** (mehl) *e-mail*
mélanger (mehlahⁿzheh) *to mix; to blend*
même (mehm) *same; even*
mener à *to take to*
mensuel, –uelle (mahⁿsüehl) *monthly*
mentir (mahⁿteer) *to lie*
un **menu** (muhnü) *menu*
une **mer** (mehr) *sea*
merci (mehrsee) *thank you*
un **mercredi** (mehrkruhdee) *Wednesday*
merde (mehrd) *(sl) shit*
une **mère** (mehr) *mother*
merveilleux, –euse (mehrvehyuh; -yuhz) *wonderful*
un **message** (mehsahzh) *message*
une **messagerie vocale** *voice mail*
Messieurs (mehsyuh) *gentlemen*
une **météo** (mehtehoh) *weather report*
un **métier** (mehtyeh) *profession; job*
un **métro** (mehtroh) *subway*
un **mets** (meh) *dish*
un **metteur–en–scène** *director*

mettre (mehtr); **mettre** (un vête-ment) *to put; to put on*
  mettre la table *to set the table*
  y mettre du sien *to act with goodwill*
  se mettre à faire *to start doing*
un **micro** (meekroh) *microphone*
midi (meedee) *noon; midday*
un **miel** (myehl) *honey*
le **mien** (myehⁿ), **la mienne** (myehn) *mine*
mieux (myuh) *better*
  de mieux en mieux *better and better*
mijoter (meezhohteh) *to stew; (col) to plot*
un **milieu** (meelyuh) *middle; background*
mille (meel) *thousand*
milliard (meelyahr) *billion*
million (meelyohⁿ) *million*
une **mine** (meen) *face; mine*
minuit (meenwee) *midnight*
miroir (meerwahr) *mirror*
mis à jour *up to date*
une **mode** (mohd) *fashion; mode*
modéré, –e (mohdehreh) *moderate*
moderne (mohdehrn) *modern; up to date*
une **modestie** (mohdehstee) *modesty*
moi (mwah) *me*
le **moi** *the self, the ego*
moins (mwehⁿ); **le moins** *less; minus; the least*
un **mois** (mwah) *month*
une **moitié** (mwahtyeh) *half*
un **moment** (mohmahⁿ) *moment*
un **monde** (mohⁿd) *world*
  tout le monde *everybody*
une **monnaie** (mohneh) *currency; change*
Monsieur (muhsyuh) *Sir; Mister*
une **montagne** (mohⁿtahny) *mountain*
monter (mohⁿteh) *to go up; to climb*
une **montre** (mohⁿtruh) *a watch*
montrer (mohⁿtreh) *to show*
un **morceau** (mohrsoh) *piece; track*
un **mort, –e** (mohr; mohrt); **la mort** *dead person; death*
une **morue** (mohrü) *cod*
un **mot** (moh) *word; note*
un **mot de passe** *password*
mouillé, –e *wet*
mourir (mooreer) *to die*
un **mouvement** (moovmahⁿ) *movement*
moyen (mwayehⁿ); **un moyen** *average; means, way*
  avoir les moyens *to be able to afford (Lit: to have the means)*

un **mur** (mür) *wall*
mûr, –e (mür) *ripe; mature*
un **musée** (müzeh) *museum*
musical, –e *musical*
un / une **musicien, –ne** (müzeesyehⁿ) *musician*
une **musique** (mühzeek) *music, tune*

N

n'importe qui *anybody*
nager (nahzheh) *to swim*
une **naissance** (nehsahⁿs) *birth*
une **nature** (nahtür) *nature; disposition*
  être né, –e (neh) *to be born*
ne, n' . . . pas *not*
nécessaire (nehsehsehr) *necessary*
la **neige** (nehzh) *snow*
neiger (nehzheh) *to snow*
neuf *nine*
neuf (nuhf), **neuve** (nuhv) *new*
un **nez** (neh) *nose*
ni . . . ni *neither . . . nor*
une **nièce** *niece*
nocturne (nohktürn) *late at night*
un **Noël** (nohehl) *Christmas*
noir, –e (nwahr) *black*
  en noir et blanc (n&b) *in black and white (b&w)*
une **noix de coco** (nwah duh kohkoh) *coconut*
un **nom** (nohⁿ) *noun; name*
un **nombre** (nohⁿbr) *number*
nombreux, –euse (nohⁿbruh; -bruhz) *numerous*
nommer (nohmeh) *to name*
non (nohⁿ) *no*
nord (nohr) *north*
nos, notre; le nôtre (nohtr) *our; ours*
une **note** (noht) *note; mark*
une **nourriture** (nooreetür) *food*
nous (noo) *we; us*
nouveau, –velle (noovoh; -vehl) *new*
  les nouvelles (noovehl) *the news*
  à nouveau *again*
novembre (nohvahⁿbr) *November*
nu, –e (nü) *naked; bare*
nuire (nweer) *to harm*
une **nuit** (nwee) *night*
nulle part *nowhere*
un **numéro** (nümehroh) *number*

O

obéir (ohbeheer) *to obey*
un **objet** (obzheh) *object*
obtenir *to get*
une **occasion** (okahzyohⁿ) *occasion; opportunity; (col) deal*

s'**occuper** (sohküpeh) **de** to be in charge of; to take care of

occupé, –e (ohküpeh) busy

une **occupation** (ohküpahsyoh[n]) (professional) occupation

un **océan** (ohseah[n]) ocean

octobre (ohktohbr) October

une **odeur** (ohduhr) odor

un **oeil** (uhy), **des yeux** (yuh) eye, eyes

un **oeuf** (uhf), **des oeufs** (uh) egg, eggs

une **oeuvre** (uhvr) work; master work

une **offre** (ohfr) offer

offrir (ohfreer) to offer

olympique (Jeux Olympiques) olympic (games)

une **ombre** shadow

une **omelette** (ohmleht) omelet

on (oh[n]) one; we; you

un **oncle** (oh[n]kl) uncle

onirique (ohneereek) dream related

onze (oh[n]z) eleven

une **opinion** opinion

une **orange** (ohrah[n]zh) orange

un **orchestre** (ohrkehstr) orchestra

ordinaire (ohrdeenehr) ordinary

un **ordinateur** (ohrdeenahtuhr) computer

ordonné, –e (ohrdohneh) tidy; orderly; ordered

un **ordre** (ohrdr) tidiness; order

une **oreille** (ohrehy) ear

organiser (ohrgahneezeh) to organize; to set up

un **orgue** (ohrg) organ

une **origine** (ohreezheen) origin; outset

original, –e original

une **orthographe** spelling

ou (oo) or

où (oo) where

oublier (oobleeyeh) to forget

l'**ouest** (wehst) (m.) west

oui (wee) yes

un **outil** (ootee) tool

outre–mer (ootr mehr) overseas

ouvert, –e (oovehr; -ehrt) open; on

une **ouverture** (oovehrtür) opening; ouverture

ouvrir (oovreer) to open (up); to turn on

P

le **pacifique** (pahseefeek) peaceful; Pacific

une **page** (pahzh) page

un **paiement** (pehmah[n]) payment, pay

un **pain** (peh[n]) bread

paisible (pehzeebl) peaceful; quiet

une **paix** (peh) peace

un **palmarès** (pahlmahrehs) achievement list

pâné, –e breaded

un **papa** (pahpah) daddy

un **papier** (pahpyeh) paper; article

par (pahr) by; through; per

un **paradis** (pahrahdee) paradise; heaven

paraître (pahrehtr) to appear; to seem

un **parc** (pahrk) park

parce que (pahrs kuh) because

pardon (pahrdoh[n]) sorry; excuse me

pardonner (pahrdohneh) to forgive

pareil, –eille same

un **parent** (pahrah[n]) parent; male relative

une **parente** (pahrah[n]t) female relative

parfait, –e (pahrfeh; -feht) perfect

parfois (pahrfwah) at times, sometimes

un **parfum** (pahrfeh[n]) perfume; scent; flavor

parier (pahryeh) to bet

parisien, –ienne (pahreezyeh[n]; -yehn) Parisian

parler (pahrleh) **à; parler de** to speak / talk to; to speak about

les **paroles** (f. pl.) lyrics, words

une **part** (pahr) share; part; behalf

partager (pahrtahzheh) to share

un / une **partenaire** (pahrtuhnehr) partner

un **parti** (pahrtee) party

participer (pahrteeseepeh) to take part in

particulier, –ière (pahrteekülyeh; -yehr) particular; private

partir (pahrteer) to leave; to go away

partout (pahrtoo) everywhere

un **pas** (pah); **pas à pas** step; step by step

un **passager** (pahsahzheh) passenger

un **passant, –e** (pahsah[n]; -sah[n]t) passer-by

un **passé** (pahseh) past

un **passeport** (pahspohr) passport

passer (pahseh) to go by; to give; to pass

se passer to happen / to take place

une **passion** (pahsyoh[n]) passion; hobby

une **patate** (pahtaht) potato (col)

une **patate douce** (pahtaht doos) sweet potato

patiemment (pahsyahmah[n]) patiently

une **patience** (pahsyah[n]s) patience

une **pause** (pohz) break; pause

pauvre (pohvr) poor

payant; –e (pehyah[n]; -ah[n]t) paying; with a charge

payer (pehyeh) to pay; to pay for

un **pays** a country

un **paysage** (peheezahzh) landscape

une **peau** (poh) skin

une **pêche** (pehsh) fishing; peach

un **pêcheur** (pehshuhr) fisherman

peindre (peh[n]dr) to paint

une **peine** (pehn) sorrow; trouble

ce n'est pas la peine it's not necessary

faire de la peine to upset

un **peintre** (peh[n]tr) painter

une **peinture** (peh[n]tr) painting;paint

pendant (pah[n]dah[n]) for; during

pendant que while

une **pensée** thought

penser (pah[n]seh) to think of

une **percussion** (pehrküsyoh[n]) percussion

un **perdant, –e** (pehrdah[n]; -dah[n]t) loser

perdre (pehrdr) to lose

perdu, –e lost

un **père** (pehr) father

permettre (pehrmehtr) to allow; to permit

un **permis** (pehrmee) license; permit

un **personnage** (pehrsohnahzh) character; personality

une **personne; personne** (pron) person; nobody

petit (puhtee) small; little

petit à petit little by little

les **petits-enfants** grandchildren

peu (puh); **peu de** not much; few, little

un **peuple** (puhpl) people; (col) crowd

une **peur** (puhr); **avoir peur** fear; to be afraid, scared

peut–être (puht ehtr) maybe, perhaps

un **phare** (fahr) lighthouse; headlight

une **pharmacie** (fahrmahsee) pharmacy; drugstore

une **photocopie** photocopy

un / une **photographe** (fohtohgrahf) photographer

une **photographie, photo** photograph, picture

photographier to photograph

un / une **pianiste** (pyahneest) *pianist*

un **piano** (pyahnoh) *piano*

une **pièce** (pyehs) *coin; play; room*

   pièce montée *tiered cake*

   pièce d'identité *ID card*

   en pièce jointe *(int) in attachment*

un **pied** (pyeh) *foot; stem; leg*

   casser les pieds *(col) to bother*

   à pied *on foot*

un **piéton** (pyehtohⁿ) *pedestrian*

pire (peer) *worse*

   de pire en pire *worse and worse*

une **piste** (cyclable) *(bicycle) track*

une **pitié** (peetyeh) *pity*

   avoir pitié de *to pity; to feel sorry for*

un **placard** (plahkahr) *closet; cupboard*

une **place** (plahs) *spot; seat; space; ticket*

placer (une annonce) *to put (an ad)*

une **plage** (plahzh) *beach*

se **plaindre** (plehⁿdr) de *to complain of*

plaire (plehr); **ça me plaît** *to please; I like it*

   s'il te plaît / s'il vous plaît *please*

plaisanter (plehzaⁿhteh) *to joke*

un **plaisir** (plehzeer); **faire plaisir** *pleasure; to please*

un **plan** *map*

un **plat** (plah) *dish; course*

plein (plehⁿ) *full; solid*

   faire le plein *fill up (car)*

pleurer (pluhreh) *to cry*

pleuvoir (pluhwahr) *to rain*

une **plomberie** (ploh^mbree) *plumbing*

une **plume** (plüm) *feather*

   une (stylo) plume *fountain pen*

la plupart (plüpahr) *most*

plus (plü) *more*

   en plus *moreover, besides*

plusieurs (plüzyuhr) *several*

plutôt (plütoh) *rather*

un **pneu** (pnuh) *tire*

une **poche** (pohsh) *pocket*

un **poème** (poehm) *poem*

un **poète** (poeht) *poet (male)*

une **poétesse** (poehtehs) *poet (female)*

une **poésie** (poehzee) *poetry; poem*

un **poids** (pwah) *weight*

un **point** (pwehⁿ) *point; dot; period*

un **poisson** (pwahsohⁿ) *fish; Pisces*

une **poitrine** (pwahtreen) *breast; chest*

un **politicien** (pohleeteesyehⁿ) *politician*

une **politique** (pohleeteek) *policy; politics*

une **pollution** (pohlüsyohn) *pollution*

une **pomme** (pohm) *apple*

une **pomme de terre** (duh tehr) *potato*

un **pont** (pohⁿ) *bridge*

un **port** (pohr) *harbour; port; postage*

une **porte** (pohrt) *door*

un **porte-monnaie** (-mohneh) *(inv) purse, wallet*

porter (pohrteh) *to carry*

   porter un vêtement *to wear*

un **portrait** (pohrtreh) *portrait*

poser (pohzeh) *to put something down; to lay*

posséder *to possess, to own*

une **poste** (pohst) *post office*

poster *to mail, to send*

un **pote** *buddy*

un **potentiel** (pohtahⁿsyehl) *potential*

potentiel, -elle *(adj) potential*

une **potion** (pohsyohn) *potion*

un **poulet** (pooleh) *chicken; (col) cop*

pour (poor) *for; in order to*

un **pourboire** (poorbwahr) *tip*

pourquoi (poorqwah) *why*

poursuivre (poorsweevr) *to pursue; to chase*

pourtant (poortahⁿ) *however; yet*

pousser (pooseh) *to push; to grow*

un **poussin** (poosehⁿ) *duckling; chick*

un **pouvoir** (poovwahr) *power; authorities*

pouvoir (poovwahr) *can, be able to; may*

pratique (prahteek) *practical*

pratiquer (prahteekeh) *to practice; to play*

précédent, -e (prehsehdahⁿ; -ahⁿt) *preceding*

(se) **précipiter** (prehseepeeteh) *to hasten; to rush*

un **précurseur** (prehkürsuhr) *precursor*

préférable (prehfehrahbl) *preferable*

préféré, -e (prehfehreh) *favorite*

préférer *to prefer*

un **préjugé** (prehzhüzheh) *prejudice*

   avoir des préjugés *to be prejudicial*

premier, -ière (pruhmyeh; -yehr) *first*

prendre (prahⁿdr) *to take; to get; to grab*

   prendre l'air *to get some fresh air*

   prendre une commande *to take an order*

   prendre un repas *to have a meal*

un **preneur** (pruhnuhr) **de son** *soundman*

un **prénom** (prehnoh^m) *first name*

(se) **préparer** (prehpahreh) *to prepare (oneself)*

prés (preh); **prés de** *near, close; close to*

une **présentation** (prehzahⁿtahsyohⁿ) *introduction*

présenter *to featuer*

(se) **présenter** (presahⁿteh) *to introduce (oneself)*

un **président** (prehzeedahⁿ) *president*

présidentiel, -elle (prehzeedahⁿsyehl) *presidential*

presque (prehsk) *almost, quite*

une **presse** (prehs) *press*

pressé, -e (prehseh) *in a hurry*

   se presser *to hurry up; to rush*

prêt, -e (preh; -eht) *ready*

prévenir (prehvuhneer) *to warn; to inform*

prévoir (prevwahr) *to plan; to anticipate*

prier (preeyeh) *to pray; to beg*

une **princesse** (prihⁿsehs) *princess*

un **principe** (prihⁿseep) *principle*

principal, -e (prihnseepahl) *principal; main*

un **printemps** (prihⁿtah^m) *spring*

privé, -e (preeveh) *private*

un **prix** (pree) *price*

probablement (prohbahblmahⁿ) *probably*

un **problème** (prohblehm) *problem, trouble*

un **processus** *process*

prochain, -e (prohshehⁿ; -shehn) *next*

proche (prohsh) *close by*

un / une **producteur, -trice** (prohdüktuhr; -trees) *producer*

une **production** (prohdüksyohn) *production*

produire (prohdweer) *to produce*

un **professeur** (prohfehsuhr) *teacher; professor*

une **profession** *profession*

profiter (de) (prohfeeteh) *to take advantage (of), to enjoy*

un **programme** (prohgrahm) *program*

un **progrès** (progreh) *progress*

une **promenade** (prohmuhnahd) *walk; ride*

se **promener** to go for a walk
une **promesse** (prohmehs) promise
promettre (prohmehtr) to promise
 ça promet (sah prohmeh) (col) it's
 starting well
une **promotion** promotion; special offer
propre own
un / une **propriétaire** owner; landlord / landlady
prudent, –e (prüdah^n; -dah^{n}t) careful; cautious
public, –ique (pübleek) public
 un public audience
une **publicité** (pübleeseeteh), **pub** advertisement / advertising
une **puce** flea
 ma puce sweetie pie
puis (pwee) then
puisque (pweesk) since
puissant, –e (pweesah^n; -sah^{n}t) powerful
punaise (pünehz) (col) shoot; also, a bug
un **punch** (puhnsh) punch
pur, –e (pür) pure
les **Pyrénées** (peerehneh) Pyrenees

un **quai** (keh) platform
une **qualité** quality
quand (kah^n) when
une **quantité** quantity
quarante (kahrah^{n}t) forty
un **quart** (kahr) quarter
un **quartier** (kahrtyeh) neighborhood
quatorze (kahtohrz) fourteen
quatre (kahtr) four
quatre-vingts (kahtrveh^n) eighty
que (kuh) that; which
 qu'importe, quel que soit whatever (goes)
quel(s), quelle(s) (kehl) which; what
quelque (kehlkuh) some; a few
 quelque chose (kehlkuhshoz) something
 quelque part (kehlkuhpahr) somewhere
 quelquefois (kehlkuhfwah) sometimes
 quelqu'un (kehlkeh^n) someone
une **question** (kehstyoh^n) question
une **queue** (kuh) tail; rear; line (waiting); stem
 faire la queue to line up
qui (kee) who; whom; that
 à qui whose
quinze (keh^{n}z) fifteen
quitter (keeteh) to leave; to give up

quoi (kwah) what
quoique (kwahkuh) although
quotidien, –ne (kohteedyeh^n; -yehn) daily

un **rabat-joie** (rahbahjwah) party breaker
raccrocher (rahkrohsheh) to hang up
le **racisme** (rahseesm) racism
raciste (rahseest) racist
raconter (rahkoh^{n}teh) to tell
un **raisin** (rehzeh^n) grape
un **raisin sec** raisin
une **raison** (rehzoh^n) reason
 avoir raison to be right
râler (rahleh) to moan and groan
ramasser to pick up, to put in order, to put away
ranger (rah^{n}zheh) to clear up; to arrange
un **rapeur, –euse** rapper
rapide (rahpeed) fast
(se) **rappeler** (rahpuhleh) to recall; to remember
un **rapport** (rahpohr) report; relationship
une **raquette** (rahkeht) racket; bat
rarement (rahrmah^n) rarely, seldomly
rater (rahteh) (col) to fail; to miss
ravi, –e (rahvee) delighted
un **rayon** (rehyoh^n) ray; department
rayonnant, –e (rehyohnah^n; -yah^{n}t) radiant; smiling
réagir (rehahzheer) to react
un / une **réalisateur, –trice** (rehahleezahtuhr; -trees) filmmaker
réaliser (rehahleezeh) to realize; to be aware
réaliste (rehahleest) realist
rebelotte (ruhbuhloht) here it goes again (col)
récemment (rehsamah^n) recently
une **réception** (rehsehpsyoh^n) reception desk; welcome
une **recette** (ruhseht) recipe; takings
recevoir (ruhsuhvwar) to receive
une **recherche** (ruhshehrsh) search; research
rechercher to search; to research
réciter (rehseeteh) to recite; to cite
une **récolte** (rehkohlt) harvest, crop
réconforter (rehkoh^{n}fohrteh) to comfort
reconnaître (ruhkohnehtr) to recognize; to admit
un **reçu** (ruhsü) receipt
redémarrer to start again

refait, –e à neuf (ruhfeh / -feht ah nuf) redone completely
réfléchir (rehflehsheer) to reflect; to think
réflexion (rehflehksyoh^n) reflection; thought
refléter (ruhflehteh) to reflect
un **régal** (rehgahl) treat; regal
un **regard** (ruhgahr) look; glance
regarder (ruhgahrdeh) to look at; to watch
une **région** (rehzhyoh^n) region
régional, –e (rehzhyonahl) regional
(être) en règle (to be) in order
une **reine** queen
une **relation** relation
(se) **relaxer** (ruhlahkseh) to relax
une **remarque** remark, comment
remarquer (ruhmahrkeh) to notice
remercier (ruhmehrsyeh) to thank
remettre (ruhmehtr) to give
remplir (rah^{m}pleer) to fill up
une **rencontre** meeting
rencontrer (rah^{n}koh^{n}treh) to meet
un **rendez-vous** (rendeh voo) meeting; rendez-vous; appointment; date
rendre (rah^{n}dr) to give back; to return
renommé, –e (ruhnohmeh) renowned
un **renseignement** (rah^{n}sehnymah^n) information
une **rentrée** (rah^{n}treh) start of school year
rentrer (rah^{n}treh) to go in; to go home
renverser to push down; to knock down
réparer (rehpahreh) to repair; to fix
un **repas** (ruhpah) meal
répéter (rehpehteh) to repeat; to rehearse
une **répétition** (rehpehteesyoh^n) repetition; rehearsal
un **répondeur** (rehpoh^{n}duhr) answering machine
répondre (rehpoh^{n}dr) to answer; to reply
une **réponse** (rehpoh^{n}s) answer; reply
un **repos** (rupoh) rest
se **reposer** (ruhpohzeh) to rest
une **représentation** (ruhprehzah^{n}tahsyoh^n) performance
 donner un représentation to perform
une **répression** (rehprehsyoh^n) repression
reprocher (ruhprohsheh) to reproach; to blame
une **réservation** (rehzehrvahsyoh^n) booking; reservation

réserver (rehzehrveh) *to book; to reserve*

résistant, –e (rehzeestahⁿ; -ahⁿt) *robust; strong*

un **respect** (rehspeh) *respect*

respecter (rehspeh) *to respect*

respirer (rehspeereh) *to breathe*

responsable (rehspohⁿsahbl) *responsible*

ressembler (ruhsah^mbleh) *to look like*

ressentir *to feel*

un **restaurant** (rehstohrahⁿ) *restaurant*

rester (rehsteh) *to stay; to remain*

un **retard** (ruhtahr) *delay*
être en retard *to be late*

retarder (ruhtahrdeh) *to delay*

retenir (ruhtuhneer) *to hold back; to keep*

retentir (ruhtahⁿteer) *to ring out, to resonate*

retirer (ruhteereh) *to withdraw*

un **retour** (ruhtoor) *return*

retourner (ruhtoorneh) *to go back*

les **retrouvailles** *reunion, new meeting*

retrouver *to meet again (as arranged)*

réussir (rehseer) *to succeed*

un **rêve** (rehv) *dream*

se **réveiller** *to wake up*

revenir *to come back*

rêver (rehveh) *to dream*

une **révision** (rehveezyohn) *review; revision*

revoir (ruhvwahr) *to see again*

une **revue** (ruhvü) **de presse** *press release*

un **rez–de–chaussée** (rehdushoh-seh) *first floor*

un **rhum** (rom) *rum*

riche (reesh) *rich*

un **rideau** (reedoh) *curtain*

ridicule (reedeekül) *ridicule*

rien (ryehⁿ) *nothing*

rigoler (reegohleh) *(col) to laugh*

rigolo (reegohloh) *(col) funny*

rire (reer) *to laugh*

une **rivière** (reevyehr) *river*

un **riz** (ree) *rice*

un **roi** (rwah) *king*

un **rôle** (rohl) *part*

un **roman** *novel*

rompre (roh^mpr) *to break; to break up*

un **rond** (rohⁿ) *circle*

rose (rohz) *pink; rose (color)*

une **rose** *rose (flower)*

bien roulé, –e (rooleh) *(col) well built, made (almost always of women)*

rouge (roozh) *red*

une **route** (root) *road; route*

une **rubrique** (rübreek) *section*

une **rue** (rü) *street*

un **rythme** (reetm) *rhythm*

S

sa (sah), **son** (sohⁿ), **ses** (seh) *her, his, its (depending on possessor)*

un **sable** (sahbl) *sand*

un **sac** (sahk); **un sachet** (sahsheh) *bag; paper bag*

sage (sahzh) *good; wise*

une **sagesse** (sahzhehs) *wisdom*

sagittaire (sazheetehr) *Sagittarius*

sain, –e (sehⁿ;sehn) *healthy*

une **saison** (sehzohⁿ) *season*

une **salade** (sahlahd) *salad; lettuce*

un **saladier** (sahlahdyeh) *salad bowl*

un **salaire** (sahlehr) *wage; salary*

salé, –e (sahleh) *salty*

une **salle** (sahl) *room*

une **salle de bain** (behⁿ), **salle d'eau** (doh) *bathroom*

une **salle à manger** (ah mahⁿzheh) *dining room*

une **salle de concert** (kohⁿsehr) *concert hall*

une **salle de séjour** (sehzhoor) *living room*

un **salon** (sahlohn) *living room*

saluer (sahlüeh) *to greet; to pay one's regards*

salut (salü) *hi; hello*

des **salutations** (sahlütahsyohⁿ) *greetings*

un **samedi** (sahmdee) *Saturday*

sans (sahⁿ) *without*

sans fil *wireless; cordless*

une **santé** (sahⁿteh) *health*

sauf (sohf); **sauf si** *except; unless*

un **saule** (sohl) *willow*

un **saumon** (sohmohⁿ) *salmon*

un **saut** (soh) *jump; jumping*

sauter (sohteh) *to jump; to explode*

sauver (sohveh) *to save*

une **saveur** (sahvuhr) *savor; flavor*

savoir (sahvwahr) *to know*

un **savon** (sahvohⁿ) *soap*

savoureux, –euse (savooruh; -ruhz) *tasty; savory*

un **saxophone** (saksohfohn) *saxophone*

un **scénario** (sehnahryoh) *scenario; script*

un **scénariste** *scriptwriter*

une **scène** (sehn) *scene; stage*

scolaire (skohlehr) *school; schoolish*

un **scorpion** (skohrpyohn) *scorpio*

se (suh), **s'** *oneself; one another*

sec (sehk), **sèche** (sehsh) *dry*

second (suhgohⁿ), **seconde** (sukohⁿd) *second*

une **seconde** (sukohⁿd) *second*

secouer (suhkooeh) *to shake*

secoue–toi *wake up*

un **secours** (suhkoor) *help; aid; assistance*

un **secret** (suhkreh) *secret*

un / une **secrétaire** (suhkrehtehr) *secretary; assistant*

en sécurité *safe*

une **séduction** *seduction*

séduire (sehdweer) *to charm; to seduce*

séduisant, –e (sehdweezahⁿ; -ahⁿt) *attractive*

seize (sehz) *sixteen*

un **séjour** (sehzhoor) *stay*

un **sel marin** (sehl mahrihⁿ) *sea salt*

selon (suhlohⁿ) *according to*

une **semaine** (suhmehⁿ) *week*

sembler (sah^mbleh) *to seem*
faire semblant (sah^mblahⁿ) *to pretend*

semer (suhmeh) *to sow*

le **Sénégal** (sehnehgahl) *Senegal*

un **sens** (sehⁿs) *meaning; direction; sense*

une **sensibilité** *sensitivity*

un **sentiment** (sahⁿteemahⁿ) *feeling*

sentir (sahⁿteer) *to smell; to feel*
se sentir bien *to feel well*
se sentir mal *to feel sick / to not feel well*

une **séparation** (sehpahrahsyohⁿ) *separation*

séparer (sehpahreh) *to separate*

sept (seht) *seven*

septembre (sehptah^mbr) *September*

une **série** (sehree) *series; set*

sérieux, –ieuse (seryuh; -yuhz) *serious*

une **serrure** (sehrür) *lock*

un **serveur, –euse** (sehrvuhr; -uhz) *waiter, waitress; server*

servir (sehrveer) *to serve; to wait on*
cela ne sert à rien *it's no use*

un **set** (seht) *set*

seul, –e (suhl) *alone; lonely*

seulement (sulmahⁿ) *only*

sévère (sehvehr) *severe*

un **sexe** (seks) *sex*

si (see) *if; so; yes; whether*

un **siècle** (syehkl) *century*

le sien (syehⁿ), **la sienne** (syehn) *. . . his, hers, its*
faire (encore) des siennes *to play one's trick*
les siens *one's family, people*

une **sieste** (syehst); **faire une sieste** *nap; to take a nap*

un **sifflet** (seefleh) *whistle*
siffler (seefleh) *to whistle*
un **signal** (seenyahl) *signal; sign*
une **signature** (seenyahtür) *signature*
un **signe** (seeny) *sign*
signer (seenyeh) *to sign*
un **silence** (seelah^{n}s) *silence; rest*
simple (sih^{m}pl) *simple; one-way (plane / train ticket)*
sincère (sih^{n}sehr) *sincere*
sinon (seenoh^n) *otherwise*
un **sirop d'érable** (seeroh dehrahbl) *maple sirup*
un **site** (seet) *site; setting*
une **situation** (seetüahsyoh^n) *situation*
se **situer** (suh seetüeh) *to be located*
six (sees) *six*
une **société** (sohsyehteh) *company; society*
une **soeur** (suhr) *sister*
soi (swah); **soi–même** *oneself*
soif (swahf); **avoir soif** *thirsty; to be thirsty*
soigner (swahnyeh) *to treat; to nurse*
un **soin** (sweh^n) *care*
un **soir** (swahr); **une soirée** *evening*
ce soir *tonight*
une **soirée** (swahreh) *party*
passer une bonne soirée *to have a good evening*
soixante (swahsah^{n}t) *sixty*
un **sol** (sohl) *ground; soil*
un **solde** (sohld); **les soldes** *balance; sales*
en solde *on sale*
solder (sohldeh) *to put on sale*
un **soleil** (sohlehy) *sun*
la **solitude** (sohleetüd) *solitude*
sombre (soh^{m}br) *dark*
avoir sommeil (sohmehy) *to be sleepy*
un **son** (soh^n) *sound*
un **sondage** (soh^{n}dahzh) *poll*
sonner (sohneh) *to ring*
une **sonnerie** (sohnree) *ring; bell*
un **sorbet** (sohrbeh) *sherbet*
un **sort** (sohr) *spell*
une **sortie** (sohrtee) *exit; outing*
sortir (sohrteer) *to go out; to come out; to release*
sotto–voce (Lat) *in a low voice*
soudain (soodeh^n) *suddenly*
une **souffrance** (soofrah^{n}s) *suffering*
souffrir (soofreer) *to suffer*
un **souhait** (sweh) *wish*
souhaiter (swehteh) *to wish*
soulager (soolahzheh) *to relieve*
une **soupe** (soop) *soup*
sourire (sooreer) *to smile*

une **souris** (sooree) *mouse*
sous (soo) *under*
un **sous–sol** (soo sohl) *basement*
sous–titré, –e (soo teetreh) *subtitled*
un **souvenir** (soovuhneer) *memory*
se **souvenir** (soovuhneer) *to remember*
souvent (soovah^n) *often*
spacieux, –euse (spahsyüh; -syuhz) *spacious; roomy*
spécialisé, –e (spehsyahleezeh) *specialized*
une **spécialité** (spehsyahleeteh) *speciality*
un **spectacle** (spehktahkl) *show*
spirituel, –elle (speereetüehl) *spiritual; witty*
un **sport** (spohr); **faire du sport** *sport; to do sport*
un **stand** (stah^{n}d) *stall; stand*
une **station** (stahsyoh^n) **de métro** *subway station*
une **station balnéaire; –thermale** *beach resort; spa*
un **stationnement** (stahsyohnmah^n) *parking*
une **statue** (stahtü) *statue*
un **statut** (stahtü) *status*
un **steward** (steewahrd) *steward; male flight attendant*
stressé, –e (strehseh) *stressed out*
un **studio** (stüdyoh) *studio*
un **studio d'enregistrement** *recording studio*
un **stylo** *pen*
un **succès** (sükseh) *success*
avoir du succès *to be successful*
un **sucre** (sükr) *sugar*
le **sud** (süd) *south*
suffire (süfeer) *to be enough*
ça suffit (süfee) *it's enough*
suffisant, –e (süfeezah^n; -zah^{n}t) *enough; sufficient*
une **suite** (sweet) *continuation; series*
suivant, –e (sweevah^n; -ah^{n}t) *next*
suivre (sweevr) *to follow*
un **sujet** (süzheh) *subject;topic*
super (süpehr) *great*
supérieur, –e (süpehryuhr) *superior*
un **supermarché** (süpehrmahrsheh) *supermarket*
supersticieux, –euse (süpehrsteesyuh) *supersticious*
supporter (süpohrteh) *to support; to bear*
supposer (süpohzeh) *to suppose*
être supposé, –e *to be supposed to*
sur (sür) *on, over*
sûr, sûre (sür) *sure, certain; reliable, safe*

sûrement (sürmah^n) *surely, certainly, probably*
un **surgelé** (sürzhuhleh) *frozen food*
surmonter (sürmoh^{n}teh) *to overcome*
surnommé, –e (sürnoh^{n}meh) *nicknamed*
surprendre (sürprah^{n}dr) *to surprise*
une **surprise** (sürpreez) *surprise*
surtout (sürtoo) *above all; especially*
survivre (sürveevr) *to survive*
sympathique (seh^{n}pahteek) *friendly; nice*

ta (tah), **ton** (toh^n), **tes** (teh) *your*
un **tabac** (tahbah) *tobacco*
un **bureau de tabac** (büroh duh -) *tobacco store; deli*
faire un tabac (col) *to be successful*
une **table** (tahbl) *table*
un **tableau** (tahbloh) *painting*
un **tableau** (d'affichage) *(schedule) board*
un **talent** (tahlah^n) *talent*
talentueux, –euse (tahlah^{n}tüuh; -uhz) *talented*
un **tambour** (tah^{m}boor) *drum*
tandis que (tah^{n}dee) *whereas*
tant (tah^n); **tant que** *so much; as much as*
tant pis (tah^n pee) *too bad*
une **tante** (tah^{n}t) *aunt*
tata
taper (tahpeh) *to type; to hit; to bang*
tard (tahr) *late*
tarder (tahrdeh); **retarder** (ruhtahrdeh) *to be late; to delay*
un **tarif** (tahreef) *price*
une **tarte** (tahrt) *pie;tart*
une **tartine** (tahrteen) *slice of bread*
un **taureau** (tohroh) *bull; Taurus*
un **taux** (toh) *rate*
un **taxi** (tahksee) *taxi; cab*
te, t' *you (obj pron)*
tel (tehl); **tel que** *such; such as*
un **téléphone** (tehlehfohn) *telephone*
un téléphone sans fil (–sah^n feel) *cordless phone*
un téléphone portable (pohrtahbl) *cellular (phone)*
une **télévision** (tehlehveezyoh^n) *television*
tellement (tehlmah^n) *so much*
un **témoin** (tehmweh^n) *witness; best man*

une **température** (tahᵐpehrahtür) temperature

une **tempête** (tah"peht) tempest

un **temps** (tahᵐ) weather; time
  à temps in time
  avoir le temps to have time
  de temps en temps (duh tahᵐz ah"
  tahᵐ) from time to time

tendre (tah"dr) to stretch; to tighten
  tendu, –e (tah"dü) tense

tenir (tuhneer) to hold
  tenir au courant (-oh koorah") to
  keep updated

un **tennis** (tehnees) tennis
  des (chaussures de) tennis sneak-
  ers

une **tension** (tahnsyoh") tension

une **tentation** (tah"tahsyoh") temptation
  tenter (tah"teh) to tempt; to try

un **terme** (tehrm) term; end

terminer (tehrmeeneh) to finish; to
  end

une **terrasse** (tehrahs) terrace

une **terre** (tehr) earth; land; soil

un **terroir** (tehrwahr) soil; agricultural region

une **tête** (teht) head
  une tête de train beginning of
  the train
  avoir mal à la tête to have a
  headache
  faire la tête to sulk

têtu, –e (tehtü) stubborn

un **thé** (teh); **une tasse de thé**
  tea; a cup of tea

un **théâtre** (tehahtr) theater

un **ticket de métro** (teekeh)
  subway ticket

le tien (tyeh"), **la tienne** (tyehn)
  yours

tiens (tyeh") (excla) there; by the
  way

un **timbre** (tehᵐbr) stamp

timide (teemeed) shy; timid

tirer (teereh) to pull; to shoot

un **titre** (teetr) title

une **toile** (col) movie; canvas
  se faire une toile (col) to go to
  the movies

les **toilettes** (twahleht) toilets
  faire sa toilette to wash up

toi–même, vous–même (twah
  mehm; voo mehm) yourself

une **tomate** (tohmaht) tomato

tomber (toh"beh) to fall
  faire tomber to drop

avoir tort (tohr) to be wrong

tôt (toh) early

une **touche** (toosh) key; stroke;
  touch

toucher (toosheh) to touch; to move

toujours (toozhoor) always
  pour toujours forever

un **tour** (toor) turn; tower

un **tourisme** (tooreesm) tourism

une **tournée** (toorneh) tour; round

tourner to turn
  tourner (un film) to shoot (a
  film)

tous (toos), **tout** (too), **toute** (toot)
  all; every

tousser (tooseh) to cough

tracer (trahseh) to draw

une **tradition** (trahdeesyoh") tradition

une **traduction** (trahdüksyoh")
  translation

traduire (trahdweer) to translate

un **trafic** (trahfeek) traffic

une **tragédie** (trahzhehdee) tragedy

un **train** (treh") train

un **traîteur** (trehtuhr) caterer

un **trajet** (trahzheh) route; journey

tranquille (trahnkeel) quiet

un **transport** (trah"spohr) transportation

un **travail** (trahvahy) work

travailler (trahvayeh) to work

treize (trehz) thirteen

trente (trah"t) thirty

très (treh) very

trinquer to clink glasses

triste (treest) sad

trois (trwah) three

trop (de) (troh) too, too much /
  many

un **trottoir** (trohtwahr) sidewalk

trouver (trooveh) to find
  se trouver to be located

tu (tü) you

U

un (uh"), **une** (ün) a, an; one

unique (üneek) only; single;
  unique

universel, –elle (üneevehrsehl) universal

une **université** (üneevehrseeteh)
  university; college

une **urgence** (ürzhah"s) emergency

urgent, –e (ürzhah"; ürzhah"t) urgent

utiliser (üteeleezeh) to use

V

des **vacances** (vahkah"s) holidays;
  vacation

vachement (vashmah") (col) really

une **vague** (vahg) wave

vain (veh") vain
  en vain in vain

la **vaisselle** (vehsehl) the dishes
  fair la vaiselle to do the dishes

une **valeur** (vahluhr) value

une **valise** (vahleez) suitcase

valoir (vahlwahr) to be worth
  cela vaut (voh) it costs
  cela vaut le déplacement it's
  worth going

une **vanille** (vahneey) vanilla

une **variété** (vahryehteh) variety

un **vélo** (vehloh) bike

des **vendanges** (vah"dah"zh) grape
  harvest

un **vendeur, –euse** (vah"duhr;
  -duhz) salesman; saleswoman

vendre (vah"dr) to sell

un **vendredi** (vah"druhdee) Friday

venir (vuhneer) to come

un **vent** (vah") wind

une **vente** (vah"t) sale

un **ventre** (vah"tr) stomach; belly

une **vérité** (vehreeteh) truth

un **vernissage** (vehrneesahzh)
  opening

un **verre** (vehr) glass, drink

verseau (vehrsoh) Aquarius

vert, –e (vehr; vehrt) green

un **vêtement** (vehtuhmah") piece
  of clothing

vexé, –e (vehkseh) vexed; upset

vide (veed) empty

une **vie** (vee) life

vierge (vyehrzh) virgin; Virgo

vieux (vyuh), **vieille** (vyehy) old

une **vigne** (veeny) vine

un **vignoble** (veenyohbl) vineyard

une **ville** (veel) town; city

un **vin** (veh") wine

vingt (veh") twenty

une **violence** (vyohlah"s) violence

violent, –e (vyohlah"; -ah"t) violent

un **visage** (veezahzh) face

une **vision** (veezyoh") vision

une **visite** (veezeet) visit
  rendre visite à to visit so

visiter (veezeeteh) to visit (a
  place)

vite (veet) quickly

une **vitesse** (veetehs) speed

un **vitrail** (veetrahy) stained glass
  window

une **vitrine** (veetreen) store window

Vivement . . . (veevmah") I can't
  wait for . . .

vivre (veevr) to live

un **voeu, –x** (vuh) wish

voici (vwahsee) here is . . .

voilà (vwahlah) there is . . .

voir (vwahr) to see; to understand

un **voisin, –e** (vwahzeh"; -zeen)
  neighbor

une **voiture** (vwahtür) *car*
une **voix** (vwah) *voice*
  à voix basse *in a low voice*
un **vol** (vohl) *flight*
un **volant** (vohlahⁿ) *wheel (car)*
voler (vohleh) *to fly; to rob*
un **voleur** (vohluhr) *robber; thief*
une **volonté** (vohlohⁿteh) *will-power*
volontiers (vohlohⁿtyeh) *with pleasure, gladly*
vos (voh), **votre** (vohtr) *your*
  le / la vôtre / les vôtres *yours*
un **vote** (voht) *vote*

voter (vohteh) *to vote*
vouloir (voolwahr) *to want; to like*
  vouloir dire *to mean*
vous (voo) *you*
un **voyage** (vwayahzh) *trip; journey; travel*
voyager (vwayahzheh) *to travel*
un **voyageur, –euse** (vwahyah-zhuhr, –uhz) *passenger, traveler*
un **voyou** (vwayoo) *crook, bad boy*
vrai, –e (vreh) *true, real*
vraiment (vrehmahⁿ) *really, truly*
une **vue** (vü) *sight; view*

W

un **wagon** (vahgohⁿ) *wagon*
des **w.c.** (vehseh) *lavatory, toilets*
un **week–end** (weekehnd) *weekend*

Z

zéro (zehroh) *zero*
un **zeste de citron** (zehst) *lemon peel*
Zut! (züt) *(fam) Shoot!*

A

a; an *un* (uhⁿ), *une* (ün)
about *au sujet* (oh soozheh) *de*
above *au-dessus* (oh duhsü) *de*
  above all *surtout* (sürtoo)
  as above *ci-dessus*
absolutely *absolument*
absurd *absurde* (ahbsürd)
accident *un accident* (ahkseedahⁿ)
to **accommodate** *loger* (lohzheh)
according to *selon* (suhlohⁿ)
accordion *un accordéon*
achievement list *un palmarès*
  (pahlmahrehs)
to **act; an act** *agir* (ahzheer); *un
acte* (ahkt)
act with goodwill *y mettre du
sien* (mehtr dü syehⁿ)
active *actif* (ahkteef), *active*
  (ahkteev)
activity *une activité* (ahkteeveeteh)
actor, actress *un acteur* (ahktuhr);
une actrice (aktrees); *un comédien / une comédienne*
actually *en fait* (ahⁿ feht)
to **add** *ajouter* (ahzhooteh)
address *une adresse* (ahdrehs)
to **address** *adresser* (ahdrehseh);
s'adresser à
addressee *un destinataire*
  (dehsteenahtehr)
to **admit** *admettre* (ahdmehtr);
reconnaître
admitted *admis, -e* (ahdmee;
-meez)
adorable *adorable* (ahdohrahbl)
to **adore** *adorer* (ahdohreh)
adventure *une aventure*
  (ahvahⁿtür)
advertisement *une publicité*
  (pübleeseeteh), *une pub* (püb)
advertisement *une annonce*
  (ahnohⁿs)
to **afford** *avoir les moyens*
  (mwahyehⁿ)
Africa *l'Afrique* (ahfreek) *(f.)*
African *africain, -e* (ahfreekehⁿ;
-kehn)
after (that) *après* (ahpreh) *(que)*
after all *après tout* (ahpreh too)
afternoon *un / une après-midi*
  (ahpreh meedee)
again *encore* (ahⁿkohr); *à nouveau*
age *un âge* (ahzh)
aged *âgé,-e* (ahzheh)
agency *une agence* (ahzhahⁿs)
agent *un agent* (ahzhahⁿ)

to **agree** *être d'accord*
  agreement *un accord* (ahkohr)
to **air** *aérer* (ahehreh)
air–conditioning *une climatisation* (kleemahteezahsyohⁿ)
air mail *par avion* (pahr ahvyohⁿ)
air stewardess *une hôtesse de
l'air* (ohtehs duh lehr)
airport *un aéroport* (ahehrohpohr)
aisle *un couloir*
alarm *une alarme* (ahlahrm)
alas *hélas* (ehlahs)
alcohol *un alcool* (ahlkohl)
alcoholic *un / une alcoolique*
  (ahlkohleek) *(adj / n)*
all *tous* (toos), *tout* (too), *toute* (toot)
allegory *une allégorie*
  (ahlehgohree)
allergy *une allergie* (ahlehrzhee)
to **allow** *permettre* (pehrmehtr)
almost *presque* (prehsk)
alone *seul* (suhl)
alphabet *un alphabet* (ahlfahbeh)
already *déjà* (dehzhah)
although *quoique* (kwakuh); *bien
que*
always *toujours* (toozhoor)
amateur *un amateur, une amatrice*
ambitious *ambitieux, -euse*
  (ahnbeesyuh; -yuhz)
America *l'Amérique* (ahmehreek) *(f.)*
American *américain, -e*
  (ahmehreekehⁿ; -kehn)
to **amuse (oneself)** *(s')amuser*
  (ahmüzeh)
amusing *amusant* (ahmüzahⁿ)
anchor (TV) *un envoyé spécial*
  (ahⁿvwahyeh spehsyahl)
anchovy *un anchois* (ahⁿshwah)
anchovy paste *une anchoïade*
  (ahⁿshohyahd)
Andalusia *l'Andalousie*
  (ahⁿdahloozee) *(f.)*
anger *une colère* (kohlehr)
angry *en colère*
animal *un animal* (ahneemahl)
ankle *une cheville* (shuhveey)
anniversary *un anniversaire*
  (ahneevehrsehr)
announcement *un faire-part* (fehr
pahr)
answer *une réponse* (rehpohⁿs)
to **answer** *répondre* (rehpohⁿdr)
answering machine *un répondeur* (rehpohⁿduhr)
antique dealer *un / une antiquaire* (ahⁿteekehr)

anybody *n'importe qui* (nehⁿpohrt
kee)
anxious *inquiet* (ehⁿkyeh), *inquiète*
  (ehⁿkyeht)
apartment *un appartement*
  (ahpahrtuhmahⁿ)
aperitif *un apéritif* (ahpehreeteef)
to **apologize** *s'excuser* (sehksküzeh)
apostrophe *une apostrophe*
  (ahpohstrohf)
apparently *apparemment*
  (ahpahrahmahⁿ)
apparition *une apparition*
  (ahpahreesyohⁿ)
to **appear** *apparaître* (ahpahrehtr)
appetite *un appétit* (ahpehtee)
appetizer *hors d'oeuvre; une entrée*
appetizing *appétissant, -e*
  (ahpehteesahⁿ; -ahⁿt)
to **applaud** *applaudir* (ahplohdeer)
applause *un applaudissement*
  (ahplohdeesmahⁿ)
apple *une pomme* (pohm)
apple cider *un cidre* (seedr)
appointment *un rendez-vous*
  (rahⁿdehvoo)
to **appreciate** *apprécier*
  (ahprehsyeh)
to **approach** *(s') approcher*
  (ahprohsheh) *de; aborder*
  (ahbohrdeh)
to **approve** *approuver* (ahprooveh)
April *avril* (ahvreel)
Aquarius *verseau* (vehrsoh)
to **argue** *se disputer* (deespüteh)
Aries *bélier* (behlyeh)
arm *un bras* (brah)
around; in the vicinity *autour*
  (ohtoor) *(de / du / dela / des);
(aux) alentours*
to **arrange** *ranger* (rahⁿzheh)
arrival; arriving *une arrivée*
  (ahreeveh)
to **arrive** *arriver* (ahreeveh)
art *un art* (ahr)
article *un article* (ahrteekl); *un papier* (pahpyeh)
artisan *un artisan* (ahrteezahⁿ)
artist *un / une artiste* (ahrteest)
arts and crafts *un artisanat*
  (ahrteezahⁿah)
as much *autant* (ohtahⁿ); *tout autant* (too)
as soon as *dès que* (deh kuh)
as; as if *comme* (kohm); *comme si*
  as well *aussi* (ohsee)
to **ask for** *demander* (duhmahⁿdeh)

assembly *une assemblée* (ahsahⁿbleh)
asset *un atout* (ahtoo)
to assist *assister* (ahseesteh)
assistant *un assistant, -e* (ahseestahⁿ; -ahⁿt), *un / une secrétaire* (suhkrehtehr)
astonishing *étonnant* (ehtohnahⁿ)
astrology *une astrologie* (ahstrohlozhee)
at *à* (ah); *chez* (sheh)
  at the *au; à la; aux*
  at home *chez moi* (sheh mwah)
  at least *au moins* (mwehⁿ)
  at someone's place *chez quelqu'un*
  at the end of *au bout de* (boo duh)
  at the right time *au bon moment* (bohⁿ mohmahⁿ)
  at times *parfois* (pahrfwah)
  at work *au travail* (trahvahy)
atmosphere *une atmosphère* (ahtmohsfehr)
to attend *assister* (ahseesteh) *à*
attentive *attentif, -tive* (ahtahnteef; -teev)
attic *un grenier* (gruhnyeh)
attitude *une attitude* (ahteetüd)
to attract *attirer* (ahteereh)
attractive; attracting *attirant, -e* (ahteerahⁿ; -rahⁿt), *séduisant, -e* (sehdweezahⁿ; -zahⁿt)
audience *un public*
August *août* (oot)
aunt *une tante* (tahnt)
  auntie *une tata (col)* (tahtah)
author *un auteur* (ohtuhr)
to authorize *autoriser* (ohtohreezeh)
automatically *automatiquement* (ohtohmahteekmahⁿ)
average *moyen* (mwayehⁿ)
avarice *l'avarice* (ahvahrees) *(f.)*
avaricious *avare* (ahvahr)
award *un prix* (pree)
away *loin* (lwehⁿ); *éloigné, -e*

B

baby *un bébé* (behbeh)
to baby-sit *faire du baby-sitting*
baby-sitter *un / une baby-sitter*
back; in the back *un dos* (doh); *derrière* (dehryehr)
  going backwards *à reculons*
  backstage *les coulisses*
bad *mauvais* (mohveh); *mal* (mahl)
  bad boy *un voyou*
bag *un sac* (sahk)
  paper bag *un sachet* (sahsheh)
to bake *cuire* (kweer)

bakery *une boulangerie* (boolahⁿzhree)
balcony *un balcon* (bahlkohⁿ)
ball *une balle* (bahl); *un bal* (bahl)
banana *une banane* (bahnahn)
band *un groupe*
to bang *taper* (tahpeh)
bank *une banque* (bahⁿk)
  bank card *une carte bancaire* (kahrt bahⁿkehr); *une carte de crédit*
  banking account *un compte bancaire* (kohⁿt bahⁿkehr)
banking statement *un relevé bancaire* (ruhluhveh -)
bar *un bar* (bahr)
bartender *un barman* (bahrmahn)
basement *un sous-sol* (soo sohl)
basketball *le basket* (baskeht)
bass *une basse* (bahs)
bass player *un / une bassiste* (bahseest)
bath *un bain* (behⁿ)
  to take a bath *prendre un bain*
to bathe *(se) baigner* (behnyeh)
bathroom *une salle de bain, une salle d'eau*
to be *être* (ehtr)
  be 24 *avoir 24 ans*
  be afraid *avoir peur*
  be at peace *avoir la paix* (peh)
  be bored *s'embêter*
  be born *être né,-e* (neh)
  be cold *avoir froid* (frwah)
  be going to do *aller faire*
  be hungry *avoir faim* (fehⁿ)
  be in charge of / take care of *s'occuper* (sohküpeh) *de*
  be interested in *(s') intéresser* (ihⁿtehrehseh) *à*
  be kind-hearted *avoir bon coeur* (bohⁿ kuhr)
  be late *avoir du retard* (ruhtahr); *être en retard*
  be located *se situer* (seetüeh)
  be lucky *avoir de la chance* (shahⁿs)
  be noisy *faire du bruit* (brwee)
  be right *avoir raison* (rehzohⁿ)
  be sleepy *avoir sommeil* (sohmehy)
  be successful *avoir du succès* (sükseh); *faire un tabac (col)*
  be supposed to *être censé, -e* (sahnseh); *être supposé, -e*
  be thirsty *avoir soif* (swahf)
  be up *être debout* (duhboo)
  be used to *avoir l'habitude (de)*
  be worth; it costs *valoir* (vahlwahr); *cela vaut* (voh)
  It's worth going *Cela vaut le déplacement*
  be wrong *avoir tort* (tohr)

to be able to *pouvoir* (poovwahr)
beach *une plage* (plahzh); *balnéaire* (bahlnehehr) *(adj)*
beach resort *une station balnéaire* (stahsyohⁿ)
beautiful *beau* (boh), *bel, belle* (behl)
because *parce que* (pahrs kuh); *car* (cahr)
because of *à cause de* (koz duh)
to become *devenir* (duhvuhneer)
bed *un lit* (lee)
bedroom *une chambre* (shahⁿbr)
to beep the horn *klaxonner* (klahksohneh)
beer *une bière* (byehr)
before (that) *avant* (ahvahn) *(que)*
to begin *commencer* (kohmahⁿseh) *(à)*
beginning *un commencement; un début* (dehbü)
  beginning of the train *la tête du train*
to behave *se comporter* (suh kohⁿpohrteh)
behind *derrière* (dehryehr)
behind the wheel *au volant* (vohlahⁿ)
Belgian *belge* (behlzh)
Belgium *la Belgique* (behlzheek)
to believe *croire* (krwahr)
believer *un croyant* (krwahyahⁿ); *une croyante*
belly *un ventre* (vahⁿtr)
to belong (to) *appartenir* (ahpahrtuhneer) *(à)*
as below *ci-dessous*
belt *une ceinture* (sehⁿtür)
besides *d'ailleurs* (dahyuhr); *en plus* (ehⁿ ploo)
best *meilleur, -e* (mehyuhr)
best man *un témoin*
to bet *parier* (pahryeh)
better *mieux* (myuh)
better and better *de mieux en mieux* (myuhzahnmyuh)
bicycle *une bicyclette* (beeseekleht)
bike *un vélo* (vehloh)
  for bicycles *cyclable*
big *grand, -e* (grahⁿ; grahⁿd); *gros, -se* (groh; grohs)
bilingual *bilingue* (beelehⁿg)
bill *une facture* (fahktür)
billion *un milliard* (meelyahr)
birth *une naissance* (nehsahⁿs)
birthday *un anniversaire* (ahneevehrsehr)
bit *un bout* (boo)
bitter *amer, amère* (ahmehr)
black *noir, -e* (nwar)
  in black and white *en noir et blanc*

blasé *blasé, -e* (blahseh)
blue *bleu, -e* (bluh)
boat *un bateau* (bahtoh)
body *un corps* (kohr)
book *un livre* (leevr); *un bouquin (col)* (bookeh[n])
to **book** *réserver* (rehzehrveh)
booking *une réservation* (rehzehrvahsyoh[n])
booth *une cabine* (kahbeen)
border *une frontière* (frohntyehr)
to **bother** *déranger* (dehrah[n]zheh); *(col) casser les pieds, les oreilles; embêter* (ah[n]behteh)
bottle *une bouteille* (bootehy)
bottom *le bas* (bah)
  at the bottom *en bas de* (ah[n] bah duh)
boy *un garçon* (gahrsoh[n])
branch *une branche* (brah[n]sh)
brave *courageux, -euse* (koorahzhuh; -uhz)
  Be brave! *Bon courage!* (boh[n] koorahzh)
bread *un pain* (peh[n])
breaded *pâné, -e* (pahneh)
break *une pause* (pohz)
to **break; to break up** *rompre* (roh[m]pr); *(se) casser* (kahseh)
breast *une poitrine* (pwahtreen)
breakfast *un petit déjeuner* (puhtee dehjuhneh)
to **breathe** *respirer* (rehspeereh)
Breton *breton* (bruhtoh[n]); *bretonne* (bruhtohn)
bride *une mariée*
bridge *un pont* (poh[n])
brief *bref* (brehf), *brève* (brehv)
brilliantly *brillamment* (breeyahmah[n])
brilliant *brillant, -e* (breeyah[n]; -ah[n]t)
to **bring** *apporter* (ahpohrteh); *amener* (ahmuhneh)
British *britannique* (breetahneek)
Brittany *la Bretagne* (bruhtahny)
brother *un frère* (frehr)
brotherhood *la fraternité* (fratehrneeteh)
brown *brun* (bruh[n]), *brune* (broon)
brown *marron* (mahroh[n])
brutal *brutal, -e* (brootahl)
buddy *un pote*
bug *une bestiole* (behstyohl) *(col)*
building *un immeuble* (eemuhbl); *un bâtiment* (bahteemah[n])
bull *un taureau* (tohroh)
bunch *un bouquet* (bookeh)
burden *une charge* (shahrzh)
to **burn** *brûler* (brüleh)
burning *brûlant, -e* (brülah[n]; -lah[n]t)
bus *un autobus* (ohtohbüs), *un bus*
busy *occupé* (ohküpeh); *animé* (ahneemeh)

but *mais* (meh)
butter *un beurre* (buhr)
buttocks *les fesses (f.pl.)* (fehs)
to **buy** *acheter* (ahshuhteh)
buyer *un acheteur* (ahshuhtuhr); *une acheteuse* (ahshuhtuhz)
by *par* (pahr)
by heart *par coeur* (pahr kuhr)

C

cabin *une cabine* (kahbeen)
cabbage *un chou, choux* (shoo)
to **calculate** *calculer* (kahlküleh)
calendar *un calendrier* (kahlah[n]dreeyeh)
cake *un gâteau* (gahtoh)
call *un appel* (ahpehl); *une communication* (phone)
to **call** *appeler* (ahpuhleh)
  call each other *s'appeler*
  be called *s'appeler*
  call on the phone *appeler au téléphone*
to **calm (down)** *(se) calmer* (kahlmeh)
camera *un appareil-photo*
camera operator *un caméraman*
Cameroon *le Cameroun* (kahmroon)
Cameroonese *camerounais, -e* (kahmrooneh; -ehz)
camp *une colonie* (kohlohnee)
can *pouvoir* (poovwahr)
Canada *le Canada* (kahnahdah)
Canadian *canadien, -ienne* (kahnahdyeh[n]; -ehn)
to **cancel** *annuler* (ahnüleh)
cancellation *une annulation* (ahnühlahsyoh[n])
cancer; Cancer (sign) *un cancer* (kahnsehr); *Cancer*
candle *une bougie* (boozhee)
Capricorn *capricorne* (kahpreekohrn)
car *une voiture* (vwatür)
card *une carte* (kahrt)
  credit card *une carte de crédit*
cardboard *un carton* (kahrtoh[n])
care *un soin* (sweh[n])
career *une carrière* (kahryehr)
careful *prudent, -e* (prüdah[n]; -dah[n]t)
  to be careful *faire attention*
to **caress** *caresser* (kahrehseh)
Caribbean Islands *les Caraïbes* (kahraheeb)
carrot *une carotte* (kahroht)
to **carry** *porter* (pohrteh)
carry-on (luggage) *un bagage à main*
cart *un chariot* (shahryoh)
case *un cas* (kah); *une affaire* (ahfehr)

casino *un casino* (kahzeenoh)
to **cast (a spell)** *jeter (un sort)*
cat *un chat* (shah), *une chatte* (shaht)
to **catch** *choper* (shohpeh) *(sl)*; *attraper* (ahtrahpeh)
caterer *un traîteur* (trehtuhr)
cautious *prudent, -e* (prüdah[n]; -dah[n]t)
cave *une cave* (kahv)
CD box *un coffret* (kohfreh) *de disques / de CDs*
to **celebrate** *célébrer* (sehlehbreh)
  –over a drink *arroser la nouvelle* (noovehl)
cellar *une cave* (kahv)
cellular phone *un portable* (pohrtahbl)
cemetery *un cimetière* (seemtyehr)
cent (1/100 euro) *un cent*
center *un centre* (sah[n]tr)
ceremony *une cérémonie* (sehrehmohnee)
certain *certain, -e; sûr, -e*
certainly *certainement* (sehrtehnmah[n]); *sûrement*
certificate *une attestation* (ahtehstahtyoh[n])
chain *une chaîne*
chair *une chaise* (shehz)
champagne *un champagne*
champion *un champion, -ne* (shah[m]pyoh[n]; -yoh[n])
change *un changement* (shah[n]zhmah[n]); *la monnaie* (mohneh)
  to **change** *changer* (shah[n]zheh)
  to change oneself *se changer*
  to change one's mind *changer d'avis*
  to change seats *changer de place*
(TV) channel *une chaîne* (shehn) *de télé*
  English Channel *La Manche* (mah[n]sh)
chapter *un chapitre* (shahpeetr)
character *un caractère* (kahrahktehr); *un personnage* (pehrsohnahzh)
to **charge** *charger* (shahrzheh)
charm *un charme* (shahrm)
to **charm** *charmer* (shahrmeh); *séduire* (sehdweer)
charming *charmant, -e* (shahrmah[n]; -ah[n]t)
to **chat** *discuter* (deesküteh)
cheap *bon marché*
check *un chèque* (shehk); *une addition* (ahdeesyoh[n])
check book *un chéquier* (shehkyeh)

checkers un jeu de dames (zhuh duh dahm)
checking account un compte-chèque (koh^mt shehk)
cheerful joyeux, -euse (zhwahyuh; -uhz)
cheese un fromage (frohmahzh)
chef un chef cuisinier (shehf kweezeenyeh)
chess les échecs
chest une poitrine (pwahtreen)
chic chic (sheek)
chick un poussin (poosihⁿ)
chicken un poulet (pooleh)
child un enfant (ahnfahⁿ); une enfant
childhood une enfance (ahnfahⁿs)
chocolate un chocolat (shohkohlah)
choice un choix (shwah)
choir un chœur (kuhr)
to choose choisir (shwazeer)
chorus un chœur (kuhr)
Christmas le Noël (nohehl)
church une église (ehgleez)
cigarette une cigarette (seegahreht)
cinnamon la cannelle (kahnehl)
cinema le cinéma (seenehmah)
cinema–lover un / une cinéphile (seenehfeel)
circle un cercle (sehrkl); un rond
circulation une circulation (seerkülahsyohⁿ)
citizen un citoyen (seetwahyehⁿ); une citoyenne (seetwahyehn)
city une ville (veel)
city dweller un citadin (seetahdehⁿ); une citadine (seetahdeen)
class une classe (klahs)
classical classique (klahseek)
clear clair, claire (klehr)
to clear up ranger (rahⁿzheh)
to click cliquer (kleekeh)
client un client, -e (kleeyahⁿ; -ahⁿt)
climate un climat (kleemah)
to clink glasses trinquer (trihⁿkeh)
to close fermer (fehrmeh)
close (to) près (de)
close by proche (prohsh)
closet un placard (plahkahr)
closing une fermeture (fehrmuhtür)
c'mon allez (ahleh)
clothing (a piece of) un vêtement (vehtuhmahⁿ)
coach un entraîneur (ahntrehnuhr)
coat un manteau (mahⁿtoh)
coconut une noix de coco (nwah duh kohkoh)
cod une morue (mohrü)
code un code (kohd)
coffee; coffee shop un café (kahfeh)
coin une pièce (pyehs)

cold froid (frwah)
colleague un / une collègue (kohlehg)
colonialism le colonialisme (kohlohnyahleesm)
colony une colonie (kohlohnee)
column une colonne (kohlohn)
to come venir (vuhneer)
to come back revenir (ruhvuhneer)
to come in entrer (ahⁿtreh)
comedian un / une comique (kohmeek)
comedy une comédie (kohmehdee)
comical comique (kohmeek)
to comfort réconforter (rehkohnfohrteh)
comfortable à l'aise (ah lehz)
comment une remarque (ruhmahrk)
commentary un commentaire (kohmahⁿtehr)
common commun, -e (kohmuhⁿ; -mün)
to communicate communiquer (kohmüneekeh)
communication une communication (kohmüneekahsyohⁿ)
compact disk un disque compact, un CD (sehseh)
company une compagnie (koh^mpanee)
company une société (sohsyehteh)
to compare comparer (koh^mpahreh)
competition une compétition (koh^mpehteesyohⁿ)
to complain of se plaindre (plehⁿdr) de
complete complet,-ète (koh^mpleh; -pleht)
to compose composer (koh^mpohzeh)
composer un compositeur (koh^mpohzeetuhr)
computer un ordinateur (ohrdeenahtuhr)
computer science l'informatique (ehⁿfohrmahteek) (f.)
concert un concert (kohⁿsehr)
concert hall une salle de concert
concrete concret, -ète (kohⁿkreh; -kreht)
condition une condition (kohⁿdeesyohⁿ)
to conduct diriger (deereezheh)
conductor un chef d'orchestre (shehf dohrkehstr)
confidence une confiance (kohnfyahⁿs)
to congratulate féliciter (fehleeseeteh)
congratulation félicitations (fehleeseetahsyohⁿ)
congressman un député (dehpüteh)

contract un contrat
cook un cuisinier; une cuisinière
to cook cuire (kweer)
cook dinner faire à dinner (fehr ah deeneh)
cool froid (frwah); frais (freh), fraîche (frehsh)
cordless sans fil (sahⁿ feel)
cordless phone un téléphone sans fil
cork un bouchon (booshohⁿ)
corner un coin (kwehⁿ)
Corsica la Corse (kohrs)
to cost coûter (kooteh)
to cough tousser (tooseh)
counter un comptoir (koh^mtwar); un guichet
country un pays
(the) country; countryside une campagne (kah^mpahny)
court; courtyard une cour (koor)
cousin un cousin, -e (koozehⁿ; -een)
covered couvert, -e (koovehr; -ehrt)
to cradle bercer (behrseh)
craftsman un artisan (ahrteezahⁿ)
crazy fou (foo), folle(fohl)
cream une crème
to create créer (kreheh)
creation une création (krehahsyohn)
crepe une crêpe (krehp)
creperie une crêperie (krehpree)
critic un critique (kreeteek)
criticism une critique
to criticize critiquer (kreeteekeh)
crop une récolte (rehkohlt)
to cross croiser (krwahzeh)
cruel cruel, cruelle (krüehl)
cruise une croisière (krwahzyehr)
to cry pleurer (pluhreh)
culinary culinaire (küleenehr)
culprit un coupable (koopahbl)
cultivated cultivé, -e (külteeveh)
culture une culture (kültür)
cultured cultivé, -e
cupboard un placard
curfew un couvre-feu (koovruhfuh)
curious curieux, -euse (küryuh; -uhz)
currency une monnaie (mohneh)
curtain un rideau (reedoh)
custom une coutume (kootüm)
customs la douane (dwahnn)
to cut (oneself) (se) couper (koopeh)
cut price market une braderie (brahdree)

D

daddy un papa (pahpah)
daily quotidien, -enne (kohteedyehⁿ; -yehn)

to **dance** *danser* (dah*nseh)
dance *une danse* (dah*s)
dancer *un danseur* (dah*suhr); *une danseuse* (dah*suhz)
danger *un danger* (dah*zheh)
dangerous *dangereux,-euse* (dah*zhuhruh; -ruhz)
dark *sombre* (soh*br)
darling *chéri, -e* (shehree)
data bank *la banque de données*
date *une date* (daht)
to **date** *dater* (dahteh)
daughter *une fille* (feey)
day *un jour; une journée* (zhoorneh)
   day after *le lendemain* (lah*duhmeh*)
   day after tomorrow *après-demain* (ahpreh duhmeh*)
   day before yesterday *avant-hier* (ahvah* eeyehr)
dead person *un mort, une morte* (mohr; -t)
deal *une affaire* (ahfehr); *une occasion* (ohkahsyoh*)
dear *cher, chère* (shehr)
death *la mort*
debate *un débat* (dehbah)
debut *un début* (dehbü)
decade *une décennie* (dehsehnee)
December *décembre* (dehsahnbr)
   to *decide décider* (dehseedeh)
decided *décidé, -e* (dehseedeh)
decision *une décision* (dehseezyoh*)
declaration *une déclaration* (dehklahrahsyoh*)
to **declare** *déclarer* (dehklahreh)
decline *un déclin* (dehkleh*)
decor *un décor* (dehkohr)
to **dedicate** *dédier* (dehdyeh)
to **defend** *défendre* (dehfah*dr)
degree *un degrès* (duhgreh); *un diplôme* (deeplohm)
delay *un retard* (ruhtahr)
to **delay** *tarder* (tahrdeh); *retarder* (ruhtahrdeh)
deli *un bureau de tabac; une épicerie* (ehpeesree) (in France)
delighted *ravi, -e* (rahvee)
democracy *une démocratie* (dehmohkrahsee)
demon *un démon* (dehmoh*)
demonstration *une manifestation* (mahneefehstahsyoh*)
dentist *un dentiste* (dah*teest)
department *un département; un rayon*
department store *un grand magasin* (grah* mahgahzih*)
departure *un départ* (dehpahr)
to **deposit** *déposer* (dehpohseh)
depressed *déprimé, -e* (dehpreemeh)

to **describe** *décrire* (dehkreer)
description *une description* (dehskreepsyoh*)
desert *un désert* (dehzehr)
to **design** *dessiner* (dehseeneh)
to **desire** *désirer* (dehzeereh)
desire *un désir* (dehzeer); *une envie* (ah*vee)
desk *un bureau*
despair *un désespoir* (dehzehspwar)
dessert *un dessert* (dehsehr)
destination *une destination* (dehsteenahsyoh*)
destiny *un destin* (dehsteh*)
determined *décidé, -e* (dehseedeh)
device *un appareil* (ahpahrehy)
devoted (to) *consacré, -e (à)*
to **dial** *composer* (koh*pohzeh)
to **dial a number** *faire un numéro* (fehr uhn nümehroh); *composer un numéro*
to **die** *mourir* (mooreer)
different *différent, -e* (deefehrah*; -ah*t)
difficult *difficile* (deefeeseel)
dining room *une salle à manger* (sahl ahmah*zheh)
dinner *un dîner* (deeneh)
diploma *un diplôme* (deeplohm)
direct *direct, -e* (deerekt)
to **direct** *diriger* (deereezheh)
director *un metteur-en-scène* (mehtuhr ahn sehn)
to **disappear** *disparaître* (deespahrehtr)
disappointed *déçu, -e* (dehsü)
to **discourage** *décourager* (dehkoorahzheh)
discouraging *décourageant, -e* (dehkoorahzhah*; -zhah*t)
to **discover** *découvrir* (dehkoovreer)
discovered *découvert, -e*
discreet *discret, -rète* (deeskreh; -reht)
to **discuss** *discuter* (deesküteh)
dish *un mets* (meh)
   (to do) the dishes *(faire) la vaisselle*
dish (course) *un plat* (plah)
to **display** *afficher* (ahfeesheh)
to **disturb** *déranger* (dehrah*zheh)
to **divorce** *divorcer* (deevohrseh)
divorce *un divorce* (deevohrs)
divorced *divorcé, -e* (deevohrseh)
to **do** *faire* (fehr)
   do an interview *faire un interview, interviewer* (eh*tehrvyooeh)
   do one's hair *(se) coiffer* (kwahfeh)
   do you feel like . . . *ça te dit de...*

doctor *un docteur* (dohktuhr), *un médecin* (mehdsih*)
document *un document* (dohkümah*)
dog *un chien* (shyeh*), *une chienne* (shyehn)
door *une porte* (pohrt)
to **double** *doubler* (doobleh)
to **doubt** *(se) douter de* (dooteh)
doubt *un doute* (doot)
dozen *une douzaine* (doozehn)
draft *un dessin* (dehseh*)
drama *un drame* (drahm)
dramatic *dramatique* (drahmahteek)
to **draw** *dessiner* (dehseeneh); *tracer*
drawing *un dessin* (dehseh*)
dreadful *épouvantable* (ehpoovah*tahbl)
dream *un rêve* (rehv)
to **dream** *rêver* (rehveh)
dream related *onirique* (ohneereek)
to **dress (up)** *(s') habiller* (ahbeeyeh)
to **drink** *boire* (bwahr)
drink *une boisson* (bwahsoh*)
to **drive** *conduire* (kohndweer)
driver *un conducteur* (kohndüktuhr); *une conductrice*
drop *une goutte* (goot)
to **drop** *faire tomber; lâcher* (lahsheh)
drum *un tambour* (tah*boor)
drum kit *une batterie* (bahtree)
drummer *un batteur* (bahtuhr)
dry *sec* (sehk), *sèche* (sehsh)
to **dub** *doubler*
duckling *un poussin* (poosih*)
during *durant* (dürah*); *pendant*
duty *un devoir* (duhvwar)

E

e–mail *un courrier électronique; un / une mail* (mehl)
each one *chacun, -e* (shahkuh*; -kün)
each *chaque* (shahk)
ear *une oreille* (ohrehy)
early *tôt* (toh)
earth *une terre* (tehr)
(at) ease *(à) l'aise* (ah lehz)
east *est* (ehst)
easy *facile* (fahseel)
   to take it easy *y aller doucement*
to **eat** *manger* (mah*zheh); *bouffer (sl)*
ecologist *un / une écologiste* (ehkohlohzheest)
edge *un bord* (bohr); *un côté* (kohteh)
   on the edge of *au bord de*

education *une éducation* (ehdükahsyoh")
effort *un effort* (ehfohr)
egg(s) *un oeuf* (uhf), *des oeufs* (uh)
eight *huit* (weet)
eighteen *dix-huit* (deezweet)
eighty *quatre-vingts*
either *l'un ou l'autre* (luh" oo lohtr)
to elect *élire* (ehleer)
elected *élu, -e* (ehlü)
election *une élection* (ehlehksyoh")
electoral *électoral, -e* (ehlehktohrahl)
elevator *un ascenseur* (ahsah"suhr)
eleven *onze* (oh"z)
eloquent *éloquent, -e* (ehlohkah"; -kah"t)
else *autre* (ohtr)
elsewhere *ailleurs* (ahyuhr)
embassy *une ambassade* (ah"bahsahd)
emergency *une urgence* (ürzhah"s)
emotion *une émotion* (ehmohsyohn)
empire *un empire* (ahnpeer)
employee *un employé, une employée* (ah"plwahyeh)
employment agency *une agence pour l'emploi* (ahzha"s poor lah"plwah)
empty *vide* (veed)
enclosed *ci-joint* (see zhweh")
to encourage *(s') encourager* (ah"koorahzheh)
encouragement *un encouragement*
encouraging *encourageant, -e* (ah"koorazhah"; -ah"t)
end *une fin* (fih")
  in the end *à la fin*
to end *finir; terminer*
England *l'Angleterre* (lah"gluhtehr) *(f.)*
English *anglais, -e* (ah"gleh; -lehz)
enjoy your meal *bon appétit*
enough *assez* (ahseh); *suffisant* (süfeezah")
  to be enough *suffire*
  it's enough *ça suffit*
to enrich *(s')enrichir*
entertain (oneself) *(se) divertir* (deevehrteer)
entertainment *un divertissement* (deevehrteesmah")
to enter *entrer*
entrance *une entrée* (ah"treh)
envelope *une enveloppe* (ah"vuhlohp)
equal *égal, -e* (ehgahl)
equipped *équipé, -e* (ehkeepeh)
errand *une course* (koors)
euro *un euro* (uhroh) *(€)*

European Community *la Communauté Européenne* (CE)
European Economic Community *la Communauté Économique Européenne*
even *même* (mehm); *égal, -e* (ehgahl)
evening *un soir* (swahr); *une soirée* (swahreh)
event *un spectacle* (spehktahkl); *un événement; une manifestation*
every *chaque* (shahk); *tous les*
everyone *tout le monde*
everywhere *partout* (pahrtoo)
to evolve *évoluer* (ehvohleh)
exactly *exactement*
examination *un examen* (ehgzahmeh")
example *un exemple* (ehgzah"pl)
except *sauf* (sof)
to exchange *changer* (ehshah"zheh); *échanger*
exchange *un échange* (ehshah"zh)
  currency exchange *le change* (shah"zh)
  exchange office *bureau de change*
excuse me *pardon*
exercise *un exercice* (ehgzehrsees)
to exercise *faire de l'exercice*
exhibition *une exposition; une expo*
exit *une sortie* (sohrtee)
to expect a baby *attendre un enfant* (ahtah"dr uh" ah"fah")
expense *une dépense* (dehpah"s)
expenses *les frais (m.pl.)*
expensive *cher, chère* (shehr)
to explain *expliquer* (ehkspleekeh)
exterior *extérieur, -e* (ehkstehryuhr)
extract *un extrait*
extraordinary *extraordinaire* (ehkstrahohrdeenehr)
eye *un oeil* (uhy), *des yeux* (yuh)

F

fable *une fable* (fahbl)
face *un visage* (veezahzh); *une mine*
fact *un fait* (feh)
  in fact *en fait* (ah" feht)
to fail *rater* (rahteh)
failure *un échec* (ehshehk)
fair *juste* (zhüst)
fair (blonde) *blond, -e*
faith *une foi* (fwah)
  in good faith *de bonne foi*
fall *une chute* (shüt); *un automne* (ohtohn)
to fall *tomber* (toh"beh)
familiar *familier, -ière* (fahmeelyeh; -yehr)
family *une famille* (fahmeey)

famous *célèbre* (sehlehbr)
far *loin* (lweh")
fashion *une mode* (mohd)
fast *rapide* (rahpeed)
fat *gros, -sse* (groh; -ohs); *gras, -sse* (grah; -ahs)
fate *un destin* (dehsteh")
father *un père* (pehr)
fault *un défaut* (dehfoh)
favorite *favori; -rite* (fahvohree; -reet); *préféré, -e*
fear *une peur* (puhr)
to fear *craindre* (kreh"dr); *avoir peur*
feast *un festin* (fehsteh"); *une fête* (feht)
feather *une plume* (plüm)
to feature *présenter* (prehzah"teh)
February *février* (fehvryeh)
to feel *ressentir* (ruhsah"teer)
  feel well *se sentir bien*
  feel sick *avoir mal au coeur* (mahl oh kuhr); *se sentire mal*
to feel like *avoir envie de*
feeling *un sentiment* (sah"teemah")
feminine *féminin, -e* (fehmeeneh"; -neen)
to fetch *aller chercher* (ahleh shehrsheh)
few *peu de*
  a few *quelque*
fifteen *quinze* (keh"z)
fifty *cinquante* (seh"kahnt)
figure *un chiffre* (sheefr)
file *un dossier* (dohsyeh)
to fill up *remplir* (rah"pleer); *faire le plein* (d'essence)
filmmaker *un réalisateur* (rehahleezahtuhr); *une réalisatrice*
final *final, -e* (feenahl)
finally *enfin* (ahnfih")
to find *trouver* (trooveh)
fine *une amende* (ahmah"d)
fine arts *les beaux-arts* (bohz ahr)
finger *un doigt* (dwah)
to finish *finir* (feeneer); *terminer*
fire *un feu* (fuh)
fireplace *une cheminée* (shuhmeeneh)
first, 1st *premier, -ière* (pruhmyeh;yehr), *1ᵉʳ*
  first floor *un rez-de-chaussée* (reh duh shohseh)
  first name *un prénom* (prehnoh")
fish *un poisson* (pwahsoh")
fisherman *un pêcheur* (pehshuhr)
fishing *une pêche* (pehsh)
five *cinq* (seh"k)
flame *une flamme*
flaw *un défaut* (dehfoh)
flea *une puce*
flight *un vol*

flight attendant (male) *un steward*

flight attendant (female) *une hôtesse de l'air*

to **flirt** *draguer* (drahgeh) *(col)*

floor *un étage* (ehtahzh)

flour *une farine* (fahreen)

flower *une fleur* (fluhr)

flu *une grippe* (greep)
    to **have the flu** *avoir la grippe*

fluently *couramment* (koorahmah^n)

to **fly** *voler* (vohleh)

to **focus** *(se) concentrer* (koh^nsah^ntreh)

fog *un brouillard* (brooyahr)

to **follow** *suivre* (sweevr)

food *un aliment* (ahleemah^n); *une nourriture; une bouffe (sl)*

foot *un pied* (pyeh)
    on foot *à pied*

for *pour* (poor); *pendant; durant; depuis*
    for a long time *depuis longtemps* (duhpwee loh^ntah^m)

to **forbid** *interdire* (ih^ntehrdeer)

forehead *un front* (froh^n)

foreigner *un étranger; une étrangère* (ehtrahnzheh; -zehr)

forever *à jamais; pour toujours* (poor toozhoor)

to **forget** *oublier* (oobleeyeh)

to **forgive** *pardonner* (pahrdohneh)

forty *quarante* (kahrah^nt)

four *quatre* (kahtr)

fourteen *quatorze* (kahtohrz)

fragile *fragile* (frahzheel)

frame *un cadre* (kahdr)

franc *un franc* (fra^n)

France *France* (frah^s)

Frankfurt *Francfort* (frah^nkfohr)

free *gratuit, -e* (grahtwee; -weet); *libre* (leebr)

freedom *une liberté* (leebehrteh)

French *français, -e* (frahnseh; -ehz)
    French anthem *l'hymne* (eemn) *français (m.), la Marseillaise*
    French-speaking *francophone* (frahnkofohn)

fresh *frais* (freh), *fraîche* (frehsh)
    not fresh *déconfit, -e*

Friday *un vendredi* (vahndruhdee)

fridge *un frigo* (freegoh) *(col)*

friend *un ami, une amie* (ahmee)

friendly *amical, -e* (ahmeekahl); *sympathique*

friendship *une amitié* (ahmeetyeh)

from *de* (duh)
    from now on *désormais* (dehzohrmeh)
    from time to time *de temps en temps* (duh tah^m zah^n tah^m)

front *un front* (froh^n); *devant*

frontier *une frontière* (frohntyehr)

frozen food *un surgelé* (sürzhuhleh)

fruit *un fruit* (frwee)

full *plein* (pleh^n)

funny *rigolo* (reegohloh); *drôle* (drohl); *marrant, -e* (mahrah^n; -ah^t)

future *futur, -e* (fütür); *un futur*

G

gallery *une galerie* (gahlree)

game *un jeu* (zhuh)

game *un match* (mahtsh)

garlic *l'ail* (ahy) *(m.)*

garlic mayonnaise *l'aïoli (m.)*

gas *l'essence* (ehsah^s) *(f.)*

Gemini *(un) gémeau* (zhehmoh)

Genesis *la Genèse* (zhehnehz)

gentleman *Monsieur* (muhsyuh)

gentlemen *Messieurs* (mehsyuh)

German *allemand, -e* (ahluhmah^n; -ah^d)

Germany *l'Allemagne* (ahluhmahny) *(f.)*

to **get** *obtenir* (obtuhneer); *prendre* (prah^dr); *faire* (fehr)
    get up *se lever* (suh luhveh)
    get a good deal *faire des affaires* (ahfehr)
    get a haircut *se faire couper les cheveux* (shuhvuh)
    get gas *faire de l'essence* (fehr duh lehsah^s)
    get hurt *se blesser* (blehseh)
    get married *se marier* (mahryeh)
    get off *descendre* (dehsah^dr)
    get ready (to) *s'apprêter* (sahprehteh)
    get some fresh air *prendre l'air* (prah^dr lehr)
    You got me! *Tu m'as eu(e)*

gift *un cadeau* (kahdoh)

girl *une fille* (feey)

to **give** *donner* (dohneh); *passer* (pahseh); *remettre* (ruhmehtr)
    give back *rendre* (rah^dr)
    give one's hand *donner la main* (dohneh lah meh^n)

glad *content, -e* (kohntah^n, -ah^t)

glance *un regard* (ruhgahr)

glass *un verre* (vehr)

glue *une colle* (kohl)
    glue jar *un pot de colle*

to **go** *aller* (ahleh) *(à)*
    go and have a drink *aller boire un pot* (ahleh bwahr uh^n poh) *(col)*
    go away *s'en aller* (sah^n alleh); *partir*
    go back *retourner* (ruhtoorneh)
    go by *passer* (pahseh)
    go down *descendre* (dehsah^dr)

    go for a walk *se promener* (prohmuhneh)
    go home *rentrer* (rah^ntreh); *chez soi*
    go in *entrer* (ah^ntreh); *rentrer* (rah^ntreh)
    go out *sortir* (sohrteer)
    go up *monter* (moh^nteh)
    go (along) with *accompagner*

goat *une chèvre* (shehvr)

goat cheese *un crottin de chèvre*

god *un dieu* (dyuh)

good *bon, -ne* (boh^n; oh^n); *sage (adj); bien* (byeh^n) *(n)*
    good afternoon *bonjour*
    good day *bonne journée* (boh^n zhoorneh)
    good evening *bonsoir* (boh^nswahr)
    good morning *bonjour*
    good night *bonne nuit* (boh^n nwee)
    good / ill natured *(avoir) bon / mauvais caractère*
    to do good (to someone) *faire du bien* (à)

good-bye *au revoir* (oh ruhvwahr)

government *un gouvernement* (goovehrnmah^n)

grade (year) *une classe* (klahs)

grandchildren *des petits-enfants* (puhteezah^nfah^n)

grandfather *un grand-père* (grah^npehr)

grandmother *une grand-mère* (grah^nmehr)

grandparent *un grand-parent* (grah^npahrah^n)

to **grant** *accorder* (akohrdeh)

grape *un raisin* (rehzih^n)

grape harvest *les vendanges* (vah^nda^nzh)

gray *gris, -e* (gree; -eez)

greasy *gras, -se* (grah; -ahs)

great *super* (spehr); *génial, -e (col)*

greedy *avare* (ahvahr)

green *vert, -e* (vehr; vehrt)

to **greet** *saluer* (sahlüeh)

greetings *des salutations* (sahlütahsyoh^n)

groceries *une alimentation* (ahleemahntasyoh^n)

grocery store (small) *une épicerie*

groom *un marié*

ground *un sol* (sohl)

group *un groupe*

to **grow** *pousser*

to **grow up** *grandir* (grahndeer)

Guadaloupe *la Guadeloupe* (gwahduhloop)

to **guess** *deviner* (duhveeneh)

guest *un invité, une invitée* (eh^nveeteh)
    guest room *une chambre d'amis* (shah^mbr dahmee)

guilt *une culpabilité*
(külpahbeeleeteh)
guilty *coupable* (koopahbl); *un*
coupable
guitar *une guitare* (geetahhr)

H

habit *une habitude* (ahbeetüd)
hair *un cheveu, cheveux* (shuhvuh)
hairdresser *un coiffeur* (kwahfuhr);
une coiffeuse
half *demi, -e* (duhmee); *moitié*
(mwahtyeh)
    half–price *(un) demi-tarif* (duhmee
    tahreef)
hallway *un couloir*
hand *une main* (meh^n)
to **handle** *se débrouiller*
to **hang (on to)** *(s')accrocher*
(ahkrohsheh)
    hang up *raccrocher* (rahkrohsheh)
to **happen** *se passer* (suh pahseh)
happily *heureusement*
(uhruhzmah^n)
happiness *un bonheur* (bohnuhr)
happy *heureux, -euse* (uhruh; -uhz);
joyeux, -euse; content, -e
    happy birthday *bon anniver-*
    saire (boh^n ahneevehrsehr);
    joyeux anniversaire
    happy new year *bonne /*
    heureuse année (bohn / huhruhz
    ahneh)
harbour *un port* (pohr)
hard *dur, -e* (dür)
hare *un lièvre* (lyehvr)
to **harm** *nuire* (nweer)
harvest *une récolte* (rehkohlt)
to **hasten** *(se) précipiter*
(prehseepeeteh)
hat *un chapeau* (shahpoh)
to **hate** *détester* (dehtehsteh); *haïr*
(aeer)
to **have** *avoir* (ahvwahr)
    have a blast, fun *s'éclater*
    (sehklahteh) *(col)*
    have a good evening *passer une*
    bonne soirée
    have a good trip *bon voyage*
    (boh^n vwahyahzh)
    have a headache *avoir mal à la*
    tête (mahl ah lah teht)
    have lunch *déjeuner*
    (dehzhuhneh)
    have a meal *prendre un repas*
    (ruhpah)
    have almost done *avoir failli*
    (fahyee)
    have dinner *dîner* (deeneh)
    have time *avoir le temps* (tah^n)
    have trouble doing *avoir du mal*
    à faire (mahl ah fehr)

to **have to** *devoir* (duhvwahr);
falloir (fahlwahr); *(imp) il*
faut (foh)
he *il* (eel)
head *une tête* (teht)
health *une santé* (sah^nteh)
healthy *sain* (seh^n); *saine* (sehn)
to **hear** *entendre* (ah^ntah^ndr)
heart *un coeur* (kuhr)
heat *une chaleur* (shahluhr)
to **heat** *chauffer* (shohfeh)
heaven(s) *les cieux* (syeuh); *les*
paradis
heavy *lourd, -e* (loor; -rd)
hello *salut* (sahl); *allô* (ahloh); *bon-*
jour (boh^nzhoor)
help *une aide* (ehd); *secours*
(suhkoor)
to **help (to do)** *aider* (ehdeh) *(à*
faire)
her *la* (lah); *lui* (lwee)
here (is) *voici* (vwahsee); *ici*
(eesee)
    here it goes again *rebelotte*
    (ruhbuhloht) *(col)*
to **hestitate** *hésiter*
hi *salut* (sahlü)
to **hide (oneself)** *(se) cacher*
(kahsheh)
hiding place *une cachette*
(kahsheht)
high *haut* (oh); *haute* (oht)
him *le* (luh); *lui* (lwee)
his, her, its *son, sa, ses*
his, hers, its *le sien* (syeh^n), *la si-*
enne (syehn), *les siens*
historical; historic *historique*
(eestohreek)
history *l'histoire* (f.)
to **hold** *tenir* (tuhneer)
to **hold back** *retenir* (ruhtuhneer)
holidays *des vacances* (vahkahns)
homework *un devoir* (duhvwahr)
honest *honnête* (ohneht)
honey *un miel* (myehl)
honor *un honneur* (ohnuhr)
hooked up *branché, -e*
hooligan *un voyou*
to **hope** *espérer* (ehspehreh)
hope *un espoir* (ehspwah)
horrendous *épouvantable*
horse *un cheval* (shuhvahl),
chevaux (shuhvoh)
    to go horseback riding *faire du*
    cheval
hospital *un hôpital* (ohpeetahl)
host *un hôte* (oht)
hostess *une maîtresse de maison*
(mehtrehs duh mehzoh^n); *une*
hôtesse
hot *chaud, -e*
    It's gonna get hot *Ça va barder*
    (col)

hotel *un hôtel* (ohtehl)
hour *une heure* (uhr)
    quarter of an hour *un quart*
    d'heure
    half an hour *une demie heure*
house *une maison* (mehzoh^n)
housing *un logement* (lohzhmah^n)
how *comment* (kohmah^n)
    how many *combien* (kohnbyeh^n)
    how much is it? *combien ça*
    coûte? (kohnbyeh^n sah koot)
    how old are you? *quel âge avez-*
    vous / as-tu? (kehl ahzh . . .)
however *pourtant* (poortah^n);
cependant (suhpah^ndah^n)
huge *énorme* (ehnohrm)
humbleness *une humilité*
(meeleeteh)
humility *une humilité* (meeleeteh)
hundred (inv.) *cent* (sah^n)
hunger *faim* (feh^n)
    to be hungry *avoir faim*
to **hurry up** *se dépêcher*
(dehpehsheh); *se presser*
    in a hurry *pressé, -e* (prehseh)
to **hurt** *avoir mal* (mahl) *(à)*
    hurt someone / oneself *faire du*
    mal à; se faire mal
husband *un mari*

I

I *je* (zhuh)
I don't care (col) *je m'en fiche*
(zhuh mah^n feesh); *(sl) je m'en*
fous (zhuh mah^n foo)
I don't mind *ça m'est égal* (sah
mehtehgahl)
I'm hot; I'm cold *j'ai chaud*
(shoh); *j'ai froid* (frwah)
ice *une glace* (glahs)
    ice cream *une glace*
    ice cube *un glaçon* (glahsoh^n)
iced *glacé, -e*
ID card *une pièce d'identité*
(pyehs deedah^nteeteh)
idea *une idée* (eedeh)
ideal *un idéal* (eedehahl) *(n)*; *idéal,*
-e (adj)
if *si* (see)
ignorance *une ignorance*
(eenyohrah^ns)
to **ignore** *ignorer* (eenyohreh)
image *une image* (eemahzh)
to **imagine** *imaginer*
(eemahzheeneh)
immigrant *un / une immigré, -e*
(eemeegreh)
impatient *impatient, -e*
(eh^npahsyah^n; -ah^t)
impolite *impoli, -e* (eh^mpohlee)
impossible *impossible*
(eh^mpohseebl)

impression (feeling) *une impres-sion* (eh^{m}prehsyoh^n)
to **improve** *améliorer* (ahmehlyohreh)
in *à* (ah); *en* (ah^n); *dans* (dah^n)
  in a low voice *sotto-voce (Lat), à voix basse*
  in advance *à l'avance* (ah lahvah^{n}s)
  in attachment *en pièce jointe (Int)*
  in case *au cas où* (oh kah oo)
  in case of *en cas de* (ahn kah duh)
  in fact *en fait* (ahn feht)
  in front of *devant* (duhvah^n); *en face de* (ah^n fahs duh)
  in good / bad mood *de bonne / mauvaise humeur* (ümuhr)
  in love (with) *amoureux, -euse* (ahmooruh; -uhz) *(de)*
  in no account *en aucun cas* (ah^n ohkuh^n kah)
  in short *en bref* (ah^n brehf)
  in spite of *malgrè* (mahlgreh)
  in the end *à la fin* (ah lah feh^n)
  in the meantime *en attendant* (ah^n ahtah^{n}dah^n)
  in the open air *à l'air libre* (ah lehr leebr)
  in time *à temps* (ah tah^n)
  in wood *en bois* (ah^n bwah)
to **increase** *augmenter* (ohgmah^{n}teh)
incredible *incroyable* (ih^{n}krwahyahbl)
indeed *en effet* (ah^n ehfeh)
independent *indépendant, -e* (eh^{n}dehpah^{n}dah^n; -ah^{n}t)
indispensable *indispensable* (ih^{n}deespah^{n}sahbl)
information *un renseignement* (rah^{n}senyuhmah^n); *une informa-tion* (ih^{n}fohrmahsyoh^n)
informal *familier, -ière* (fahmeelyeh; -yehr)
ingredient *un ingrédient* (ihngrehdyah^n)
inhabitant *un habitant; -e* (ahbeetah^n; -ah^{n}t)
inside *dedans* (duhdah^n); *à l'in-térieur* (ah leh^{n}tehryuhr)
to **insist** *insister* (eh^{n}seesteh)
(SNCF) inspector *un contrôleur (SNCF)*
inspiration *une inspiration* (eh^{n}speerahsyoh^n)
insurance *une assurance* (ahsürah^{n}s)
Internet *Internet* (eh^{n}tehrneht)
Internet user *un Internaute* (eh^{n}tehrnoht)
interview *une interview* (eh^{n}tehrvyoo)

to **introduce (oneself)** *(se) présenter* (prezah^{n}teh)
introduction *une présentation* (prehzah^{n}tahsyoh^n)
inventor *un inventeur* (eh^{n}vah^{n}tuhr)
to **invite** *inviter* (eh^{n}veeteh)
is it that . . . *est-ce que . . .* (ehskuh)
island *une île* (eel)
it *il; elle; cela* (suhlah); *ça* (sah); *le, la, l'*
  it's – (price) *cela fait —* (prix)
  it's nice weather *il fait beau* (eel feh boh)
  it's been a while *il y a un bail (col)*
  it's enough *ça suffit* (sah süfee)
  it's for his own good *c'est pour son bien* (seh poor soh^n byeh^n)
  it's going well / wrong *ça va bien / mal* (sah vah byeh^n; -mahl)
  it's hot / cold *il fait chaud / froid* (eel feh shoh; -frwah)
  it's my business! *ce sont mes af-faires!* (suh soh^n mehz ahfehr)
  it's no use *cela ne sert à rien* (suhlah nuh sehr ah ryeh^n)
  it's not necessary *ce n'est pas la peine* (suh neh pah lah pehn)
  her *sa* (sah); *elle* (ehl); *lui* (lwee)

J

January *janvier* (zhah^{n}vyeh)
jetty *une jetée* (zhuhteh)
jewel; jewelry *un bijou* (beezhoo)
job *un métier; un travail; un boulot* (booloh) *(col)*
to **join** *joindre* (zhweh^{n}dr)
joke *une blague* (blahg)
to **joke** *plaisanter* (plehzah^{n}teh)
journalist *un / une journaliste* (zhoornahleest)
joyful; joyous *joyeux, -euse* (zhwahyuh; -uhz)
  not joyful *déconfit, -e (col)* (dehkoh^{n}fee)
to **judge** *juger* (zhüzheh)
juice *un jus* (zhü)
July *juillet* (zhweeyeh)
jumble *(col) un bazar* (bahzahr)
jump; jumping *un saut* (soh)
to **jump** *sauter* (sohteh)
June *juin* (zhüeh^n)
junior high school *un collège* (kohlehzh) *juste* (zhüst)
just *juste* (zhüst)

K

to **keep** *garder* (gahrdeh); *retenir*
  keep updated *tenir au courant* (tuhneer oh koorah^n)
  key holder *un trousseau de clés* (troosoh duh kleh)

key *une clé, clef* (kleh); *une touche* (toosh)
keyboard *un clavier* (klahvyeh)
khaki *kaki* (kahkee)
to **kick someone out** *mettre quelqu'un dehors*
kid *un gamin* (gahmeh^n); *une gamine* (gahmeen)
kilogramme *un kilogramme* (keelohgrahm)
kilometer *un kilomètre* (keelohmehtr)
kind *gentil, gentille* (zhahnteey)
king *un roi* (rwah)
kiss *une bise* (beez), *un bisou* (beezoo) *(col)*
to **kiss** *faire la bise* (fehrlah beez)
kiss (each other) *(s') embrasser* (ah^{n}brahseh)
knee *un genou* (zhuhnoo)
knick-knack *un bibelot*
to **knock down** *renverser*
to **know** *savoir* (sahvwahr); *con-naître*
  know about *être au courant* (ehtr oh koorah^n) *de*

L

label *une étiquette* (ehteekeht)
lady *une dame* (dahm)
lake *un lac* (lahk)
lamp *une lampe* (lah^{m}p)
landscape *un paysage* (peheezahzh)
lane *une file*
language *une langue* (lah^{n}g)
last *dernier, -ière* (dehrnyeh; -yehr)
  at last *enfin* (ahnfih^n)
to **last** *durer* (düreh)
late *tard* (tahr)
late at night *nocturne* (noktürn)
to **laugh** *rire* (reer); *(col) se marrer* (mahreh); *rigoler* (reegohleh) *(col)*
lavatory *des w.c.* (vehseh)
law *une loi / le droit*
to **lay down** *s'allonger* (ahlohngeh)
lay (civil) *laïc, laïque* (laheek)
leaf *une feuille* (fuhy)
  to *learn apprendre* (ahprah^{n}dr)
lease *un bail* (bahy)
least *le moins* (mweh^n)
  at least *au moins*
to **leave** *quitter* (keeteh); *partir* (pahrteer); *laisser* (lehseh)
  leave a message *laisser un mes-sage* (mehsahzh)
  leave me alone *laisse-moi tran-quille* (lehs mwah trahnkeel); *fiche-moi la paix (col)*
left *gauche* (gohsh)
  on the left *à gauche*

leg *une jambe* (zhahᵐb)
lemon *un citron* (seetrohⁿ)
lemon peel *un zeste* (zehst) *de citron*
less *moins* (mwehⁿ)
lesson *une leçon* (luhsohⁿ)
to **let** *laisser* (lehseh)
  let (someone) do (something) *laisser (quelqu'un) faire (quelque chose)*
  let's cross our fingers *croisons les doigts* (krwahzohⁿ leh dwah)
  let's go! *allons!*
  let's say *disons* (deezohⁿ)
letter *une lettre* (lehtr)
liaison *une liaison* (lyehzohⁿ)
library *une bibliothèque* (beebleeyothehk)
license *un permis* (pehrmee)
to **lie** *mentir* (mahⁿteer)
life *une vie* (vee)
light *une lumière* (lümyehr)
lighthouse *un phare* (fahr)
like *comme* (kohm)
to **like** *aimer* (ehmeh)
line *une ligne* (leeny); *une queue*; *une file d'attente* (feel dahtahⁿt)
  in / on line *en ligne* (ahⁿ leeny)
to **line up** *faire la queue* (fehr lah kuh)
link *un lien* (lyihⁿ)
list *une liste*
to **listen to** *écouter* (ehkooteh)
liter *un litre* (leetr)
literature *une littérature* (leetehrahtür); *une documentation* (dohkümahⁿtahsyohⁿ)
little by little *petit à petit* (puhtee ah puhtee)
live (adj.) *en direct*
to **live** *vivre* (veevr); *habiter* (ahbeeteh)
  living in *demeurant* (duhmuhrahⁿ) *à*
living room *une salle de séjour* (sehzhoor); *un salon* (sahlohⁿ)
local *local, -e* (lohkahl)
located *situé, -e* (seetüeh)
  to be located *se trouver*
lock *une serrure* (sehrür)
London *Londres* (lohⁿdr)
long *long* (lohⁿ), *longue* (lohⁿg)
  a long time *longtemps* (lohⁿtahⁿ)
to **look at** *regarder* (ruhgahrdeh)
  look for *chercher* (shehrsheh)
  look like *ressembler* (ruhsahmbleh)
  it looks as if . . . *on dirait que*
look *un regard* (ruhgahr)
to **lose** *perdre* (pehdr)
loser *un perdant, -e* (pehrdahⁿ; -ahⁿt)
lost *perdu, -e* (pehrdü)
(a) **lot** *beaucoup* (bohkoo)
loud *fort, -e* (fohr; fohrt)

to **love** *aimer* (ehmeh)
to **love each other** *s'aimer*
love *un amour* (ahmoor)
lover *un amant* (ahmahⁿ)
low *bas* (bah), *basse* (bahs)
  luck *une chance* (shahⁿs)
lucky *chanceux, -euse* (shahⁿsuh; -uhz)
luggage *un bagage* (bahgahzh)
lunch *un déjeuner* (dehzhuhneh)
lyrics *les paroles (f.pl.)*

M

mad *fou, folle* (foo, fohl)
  to get mad *gueuler (col)*
mail *un courrier* (kooryeh)
to **mail** *poster* (pohsteh); *envoyer* (ahⁿvwahyeh)
majority *une majorité* (mahzohreeteh)
to **make** *faire* (fehr)
  make friends *se faire des amis* (suh fehr dehz ahmee)
man *un homme* (ohm)
to **manage to** *arriver à* (ahreeveh)
mandate *un mandat* (mahⁿdah)
many *beaucoup* (bohkoo)
map *une carte* (kahrt); *un plan*
maple syrup *un sirop d'érable* (seeroh dehrahbl)
March *mars* (mahrs)
mark *une marque; une note*
market *un marché* (mahrsheh)
  flea market *un marché aux puces*
marriage *un mariage* (mahryahzh)
married *marié, -e*
masculine *masculin, -e* (mahskülehⁿ; -leen)
mask *un masque* (mahsk)
master *un maître* (mehtr)
masterpiece *un chef-d'oeuvre* (sheh duhvr)
May *mai* (meh)
may *pouvoir* (poovwahr)
maybe *peut-être* (puht ehtr)
me *moi* (mwah); *me* (muh), *m'*
meal *un repas* (ruhpah)
to **mean** *vouloir dire; signifier*
meaning *un sens* (sehⁿs)
means *un moyen* (mwahyehⁿ)
medal *une médaille* (mehdahy)
medicine *un médicament* (mehdeekahmahⁿ)
Mediterranean sea *la* (mer) *Méditerranée* (mehdeetehrahneh)
to **meet** *rencontrer* (rahⁿkohⁿtreh); *retrouver* (ruhtrooveh)
meeting *un rendez-vous* (rahⁿdehvoo); *une rencontre* (rahⁿkohⁿtr)

to **melt** *fondre* (fohⁿdr)
membership *un abonnement* (ahbohnmahⁿ)
memory *un souvenir* (soovuhneer)
menu *un menu* (muhnü); *une carte* (kahrt)
mess *un désordre* (dehzohrdr)
message *un message* (mehsahzh)
microphone *un micro* (meekroh)
midday *midi* (meedee)
middle *un milieu* (meelyuh)
midnight *minuit* (meenwee)
milk *un lait* (leh)
million *un million* (meelyhⁿ)
mind *un esprit* (ehspree)
mine *le mien* (myehⁿ), *la mienne* (myehn)
mirror *un miroir* (meerwahr); *une glace* (glahs)
Miss *Mademoiselle* (mahduhmwahzehl); *Mesdemoiselles* (mehduhmwahzehl)
to **miss** *manquer* (mahⁿkeh); *rater* (rahteh) *(col)*
mistress *une maîtresse* (mehtrehs)
to **mix** *mélanger* (mehlahⁿzheh)
to **moan and groan** *râler* (rahleh)
moderate *modéré, -e* (mohdehreh)
modern *moderne* (mohdehrn)
modesty *une modestie* (mohdehstee)
moment *un moment* (mohmahⁿ), *un instant* (ehⁿstahⁿ)
Monday *un lundi* (luhⁿdee)
money *l'argent* (ahrzhahⁿ) *(m.)*
money order *un mandat* (mahⁿdah)
month *un mois* (mwah)
monthly *mensuel, -uelle* (mahⁿsüehl)
mood *une ambiance* (ahⁿbyahⁿs); *une humeur* (ümuhr)
moon *une lune* (lün)
more *plus* (plü)
morning *un matin* (mahtehⁿ)
most *la plupart* (plüpahr)
mother *une mère* (mehr)
motto *une devise* (duhveez)
mountain *une montagne* (mohⁿtahny)
mouse *une souris* (sooree)
mouth *une bouche* (boosh)
to **move** *déménager* (dehmehnahzheh); *bouger* (boozheh); *toucher*
  move forward *avancer* (ahvahⁿseh)
  move in / into *emménager* (ahⁿmehnahzheh)
movement *un mouvement* (moovmahⁿ)
movie *un film* (feelm); *une toile (col)* (twahl)
  to go to the movies *se faire une toile (col)*

movie theatre *une salle de cinéma* (sahl duh seenehmah); *un cinéma* (seenehmah)

moving *un déménagement* (dehmehnahzhmahⁿ)

moving *émouvant, -e* (ehmoovahⁿ; -vahⁿt)

Mrs; Madam; Ms. *Madame* (mahdahm); *Mesdames* (mehdahm) *(pl.)*

mommy *maman* (mahmahⁿ)

museum *un musée* (müzeh)

mushroom *un champignon* (shahnpeenyohⁿ)

music *une musique* (müzeek)

musical *musical, -e* (müzeekahl)

musician *un musicien, -ienne* (müzeesyehⁿ; -yehn)

must *devoir* (duhvwahr); *falloir* (fahlwahr); *(imp) il faut* (foh)

my *ma* (mah), *mon* (mohⁿ), *mes* (meh)

naked *nu, -e* (nü)

name *un nom* (nohⁿ)

to **name** *nommer* (nohmeh)

nap *une sieste* (syehst)

   to take a nap *faire une sieste*

narrow *étroit, -e* (ehtrwah; -aht)

nature *une nature* (nahtür)

near *près* (preh)

necessary *nécessaire* (nehsehsehr)

neck *un cou*

to **need** *avoir besoin* (buhzwehⁿ) *de*; *falloir* (fahlwahr); *(imp) il faut* (foh)

neighbor *un voisin, une voisine* (vwahzihⁿ; -zeen)

neighborhood *un quartier* (kahrtyeh)

neither . . . nor *ni . . . ni*

net *un filet* (feeleh)

never *jamais* (zhahmeh)

new *neuf* (nuhf), *neuve* (nuhv), *nouveau* (noovoh), *nouvelle* (noovehl)

news *les informations* (ehⁿfohrmahsyohⁿ); *les nouvelles* (noovehl)

TV news *un journal*

newspaper *un journal* (zhoornahl)

next *prochain, -e* (prohshehⁿ; -shehn); *suivant, -e* (sweevahⁿ; -ahⁿt)

nice *gentil, gentille* (zhahⁿteey; -teel); *sympathique* (sehⁿpahteek)

nicely *gentiment*

nicknamed *surnommé, -e*

niece *une nièce* (nyehs)

night *une nuit* (nwee)

nightmare *un cauchemard* (kohshmahr)

nine *neuf* (nuhf)

no *non* (nohⁿ)

nobody *personne* (pehrsohn) *(pron)*

to **nod** *acquiescer* (ahkyehseh)

noise *un bruit* (brwee)

noisy *bruyant, -e* (brweeyahⁿ; -ahⁿt)

none *aucun, aucune* (ohkuhⁿ; -kün)

noon *midi* (meedee)

no one *personne* (pehrsohn) *(pron)*

north *nord* (nohr)

nose *un nez* (neh)

not *ne, n'...pas*

   not known *inconnu, -e* (ehⁿkohnü)

   not much *peu* (puh); *peu de*

note *une note* (noht); *un mot* (moh)

notebook *un cahier* (kahyeh)

notepad *un carnet* (kahrneh)

nothing *rien* (ryehⁿ)

to **notice** *(s')apercevoir* (ahpehrsuhvwahr); *remarquer* (ruhmahrkeh)

nought *un zéro* (zehroh)

noun *un nom* (nohⁿ)

novel *un roman* (rohmahⁿ)

November *novembre* (nohvahᵐbr)

now *maintenant* (mehⁿtuhnahⁿ)

nowhere *nulle part* (nül pahr)

number *un nombre* (nohⁿbr); *un numéro* (nümehroh)

numerous *nombreux, -euse* (nohᵐbruh; -uhz)

to **nurse** *soigner*

nursery *une garderie* (gahrduhree); *une école maternelle* (ehkohl mahtehrnehl)

to **obey** *obéir* (ohbeheer)

object *un objet* (obzheh)

obviously *évidemment* (ehveedahmahⁿ)

occasion *une occasion* (okahzyohⁿ)

occupation *une occupation* (ohküpahsyohⁿ)

ocean *un océan* (ohseahⁿ)

October *octobre* (ohktohbr)

odor *une odeur* (ohduhr)

of course *bien sûr* (byehⁿ sür)

of *de* (duh)

off *éteint, -e* (ehtehⁿ; -ehⁿt)

offer *une offre* (ohfr)

   special offer *la promotion*

to **offer** *offrir* (ohfreer)

office *un bureau* (büroh)

often *souvent* (soovahⁿ)

oil; olive oil *une huile* (weel); *l'huile d'olive* (~ dohleev)

okay *d'accord*

old *âgé, -e* (ahzheh); *vieux, vieille* (vyuh, vyehy)

Olympic (games) *olympique* (ohlehⁿpeek) *(Jeux Olympiques)*

omelet *une omelette* (ohmleht)

on *sur* (sür)

   on foot *à pied* (pyeh)

   on the contrary *au contraire* (oh kohⁿtrehr)

   on the edge of *au bord* (bohr) *de*

   on the phone *au téléphone* (tehlehfohn)

   on the right *à droite* (drwaht)

   on the second floor *au premier étage* (pruhmyeh ehtahzh)

   on the sly *en cachette* (ahn kahsheht)

   on the verge of tears *au bord des larmes* (bohr deh lahrm)

   on the way *chemin faisant* (shuhmehⁿ fuhzahⁿ)

once *une fois* (ün fwah)

one *un, une* (uhⁿ, ün); *on* (ohⁿ)

   one's family *les siens* (syehⁿ)

   one way *un aller simple* (ahleh sehⁿpl)

oneself *soi* (swah); *soi-même* (swahmehm); *se* (suh), *s'*

only *seulement* (suhlmahn); *juste* (zhüst); *unique* (üneek), *adj.*

to **open** *ouvrir* (oovreer)

open *ouvert, -e* (oovehr; -ehrt)

opening *un vernissage* (vehrneesahzh)

opening; ouverture *une ouverture* (oovehrtür)

opinion *une opinion* (ohpeenyohⁿ), *un avis* (ahvee)

or *ou* (oo)

orange *une orange* (ohrahⁿzh)

orchestra *un orchestre* (ohrkehstr)

order *la commande* (kohmahⁿd), *un ordre* (ohrdr)

to **order** *commander* (kohmahⁿdeh)

to **be in order** *être en règle* (rehgl)

ordinary *ordinaire* (ohrdeenehr)

organ *un orgue* (ohrg)

to **organize** *organiser* (ohrgahneezeh)

origin *une origine* (ohreezheen)

original *original, -e* (ohreezheenahl)

other *autre* (ohtr)

other one *autrui* (ohtrwee)

otherwise *sinon* (seenohⁿ)

our; ours *nos* (noh), *notre* (nohtr); *le / la nôtre*

Out! *Dehors!* (duhohr)

out of *hors de* (ohr duh)

out of fashion *démodé, -e* (dehmohdeh)

out of order *en dérangement* (ahⁿ dehrahⁿzhmahⁿ)

outfit *un ensemble* (ahⁿsahⁿbl)

outing *une sortie* (sohrtee)

outset *une entrée* (ah^ntreh); *un début* (dehbü); *une origine* (ohreezheen)
outside *extérieur, -e* (ehkstehryuhr); *dehors* (duhohr); *à l'extérieur* (sür)
over *dessus* (duhsü); *au-dessus de; sur* (sür)
to overcome *surmonter* (sürmoh^nteh)
overseas *outre-mer* (ootrmehr)
to owe *devoir* (duhwahr)
owed *dû, due, du(e)s* (dü)
own *propre* (prohpr)
to own *posséder* (pohsehdeh)
owner *un / une propriétaire* (prohpreeyehtehr)

P

Pacific *le Pacifique* (pahseefeek)
package *un forfait* (fohrfeh)
page *une page* (pahzh)
to pain *une douleur* (dooluhr)
to paint *peindre* (peh^ndr)
painter *un peintre* (peh^ntr)
painting *un tableau* (tahblo); *une peinture* (peh^ntür)
pal *un copin* (kohpeh^n), *une copine* (ün kohpeen)
paper *un papier* (pahpyeh)
paradise *un paradis* (pahrahdee)
parcel *un colis* (kohlee)
parent *un parent* (pahrah^n)
Parisian *parisien, -enne* (pahreezyeh^n; -ehn)
Parisian district *un arrondissement*
park *un parc* (pahrk)
to park (one's) a car *(se) garer* (gahreh)
parking *un stationnement* (stahsyohnmah^n)
part *un rôle* (rohl)
particular *particulier, -ière* (pahrteeklyeh; -yehr)
partner *un associé, -e* (ahsohsyeh); *un / une partenaire* (pahrtuhnehr)
to party *faire la fête* (fehr lah feht)
party *un parti* (pahrtee); *une fête* (feht); *une soirée* (swahreh)
to pass *passer* (pahseh); *doubler (car)*
passenger *un passager, une passagère* (pahsahzheh; -zhehr); *un voyageur, une voyageuse*
passer–by *un passant, une passante* (pahsah^n; pahsah^nt)
passion *une passion* (pahsyoh^n)
passport *un passeport* (pahspohr)
password *un mot de passe* (moh duh pahs)

past *un passé* (pahseh)
path; way *un chemin* (shuhmih^n)
patience *une patience* (pahsyah^s)
patiently *patiemment* (pahsyahmah^n)
pay *un paiement* (pehmah^n)
to pay (for) *payer* (pehyeh)
   pay a tribute to *rendre un hommage* (ohmahzh) *à*
   pay attention to *faire attention à*
   pay one's regards *saluer*
paying *payant, -e* (pehyah^n; -ah^t)
payment *un paiement*
peace *une paix* (peh)
peaceful *paisible* (pehzeebl); *pacifique*
peanut *une cacahuète* (kahkahweht)
pebble *un galet* (gahleh)
pedestrian *un piéton* (pyehtoh^n)
pen *un stylo*
   fountain pen *un stylo à encre*
pencil *un crayon* (krehyoh^n)
people *les gens* (zhah^n); *un peuple*
percussion *une percussion* (pehrküsyoh^n)
perfect *parfait, -e* (pahrfeh; -feht)
to perform *jouer; donner une représentation*
performance *une représentation* (ruhprehzah^ntahsyoh^n)
perfume *un parfum* (pahrfuhn)
perhaps *peut-être* (puht ehtr)
permit *un permis* (pehrmee)
person *une personne* (pehrsohn)
pharmacy *une pharmacie* (fahrmahsee)
phone book *un annuaire* (ahnüehr)
phone card *une carte de téléphone* (kahrt duh tehlehfohn)
photocopy *une photocopie; une photo*
photograph *une photographie* (fohtohgrahfee)
to photograph *photographier* (fohtohgrahfyeh)
photographer *un / une photographe* (fohtohgrahf)
piano; pianist *un piano* (pyahnoh); *un / une pianiste* (pyahneest)
to pick up *cueillir* (kuheer); *ramasser* (rahmahseh)
pie *une tarte* (tahrt)
piece *un morceau* (mohrsoh)
pink *rose* (rohz)
Pisces *poisson* (pwahsoh^n)
pity *une pitié* (peetyeh)
   to feel pity for *avoir pitié de*
place *un endroit* (ah^ndrwah); *un lieu*
   to take place *avoir lieu* (ahvwahr lyuh); *se passer* (suh pahseh)

to plan *prévoir* (prevwahr)
plane *un avion* (ahvyoh^n)
plate *une assiette* (ahsyeht)
platform *un quai* (keh)
(a) play *une pièce* (pyehs)
to play *jouer* (zhooeh); *pratiquer (sport)*
   play one's trick *faire (encore) des siennes* (syehn)
playwright *un auteur dramatique* (ohtuhr drahmahteek)
pleasant *agréable* (ahgrehahbl)
to please *plaire* (plehr)
   I like it *ça me plaît* (pleh)
   pleased to meet you *enchanté, -e* (ah^nshah^teh)
please *s'il te plaît; s'il vous plaît*
pleasure *un plaisir* (plehzeer)
plenty *beaucoup* (bohkoo)
to plot *mijoter (col)*
plumbing *une plomberie* (ploh^nbree)
pocket *une poche* (pohsh)
poem *un poème* (poehm); *une poésie* (poehzee)
poet *un poète* (poeht); *une poétesse* (poehtehs)
poetry *une poésie* (poehzee)
policy *une politique* (pohleeteek)
to point out *indiquer* (eh^ndeekeh)
point; dot *un point* (pweh^n)
police precinct *un commissariat de police* (kohmeesahryah duh pohlees)
politician *un politicien* (pohleeteesyeh^n)
politics *une politique* (pohleeteek)
poll *un sondage* (sohndahzh)
pollution *une pollution* (polüsyoh^n)
poor *pauvre* (pohvr)
portrait *un portrait* (pohrtreh)
post office *une poste* (pohst)
postage *un port* (pohr)
postcard *une carte postale* (kahrt pohstahl)
poster *une affiche* (ahfeesh)
potato *une pomme de terre* (pohm duh tehr); *une patate (col)*
potential *un potentiel* (pohtah^nsyehl), *potentiel,-le (adj)*
potion *une potion* (pohsyoh^n)
power *un pouvoir* (poovwahr)
powerful *puissant, -e* (pweesah^n; -ah^t)
practical *pratique* (prahteek)
practice *un entraînement* (ah^ntrehnmah^n)
to practice *pratiquer* (prahteekeh); *(s')entraîner* (ah^ntrehneh)
to praise *louer* (looeh)
to pray *prier* (preeyeh)

preceding *précédent, -e* (prehsehdahⁿ; -ahⁿt)

precursor *un précurseur* (prehkürsuhr)

to **prefer** *préférer* (prehfehreh)

preferable *préférable* (prehfehrahbl)

pregnant *enceinte* (ahnsehⁿt)

prejudice *un préjugé* (prehzhüzheh)
  to be prejudiced *avoir des préjugés*

to **prepare (oneself)** *(se) préparer* (prehpahreh)

present *un cadeau* (kahdoh)

president *un président* (prehzeedahⁿ)

presidential *présidentiel, -elle* (prehzeedahⁿsyehl)

press *une presse* (prehs)

press release *une revue* (ruhvü) *de presse*

to **pretend** *faire semblant* (fehr sah^mblahⁿ)

pretty *joli, -e* (zhohlee)

previous *antérieur, -e* (ahntehryuhr)

price *un prix* (pree); *un tarif* (tahreef)

princess *une princesse* (prehⁿsehs)

principal *principal, -e* (prehⁿseepahl)

principle *un principe* (prehⁿseep)

private *privé, -e* (preeveh)

probably *probablement* (prohbahblmahⁿ); *sûrement*

problem *un problème* (prohblehm)

process *un processus*

to **produce** *produire* (prohdweer)

producer *un producteur* (prohdüktuhr); *une productrice* (prohdüktrees)

production *une production* (prohdüksyohⁿ)

profession *une profession* (prohfehsyohⁿ); *un métier* (mehtyeh)

professional office *un cabinet* (kahbeeneh)

professor *un professeur* (prohfehsuhr)

program *un programme* (prohgrahm)

progress *un progrès* (progreh)

promise *un promesse* (prohmehs)

to **promise** *promettre* (prohmehtr)

promotion *un avancement* (ahvahⁿsmahⁿ); *une promotion*

to **provide** *fournir* (foorneer)

provider *un fournisseur* (foorneesuhr)

public *public, publique* (pübleek)
  public holiday *férié, -e* (fehryeh) *(adj)*; *un jour férié, une fête*

to **pull** *tirer* (teereh)

punch *un punch* (puhnsh)

purchase *un achat*

pure *pur, -e* (pür)

purse *un porte-monnaie* (pohrt mohneh) *(inv)*

to **pursue** *poursuivre* (poorsweevr)

to **push** *pousser* (pooseh)
  push down *renverser*

to **put** *mettre* (mehtr); *placer* (plahseh)
  put away *ranger*
  put an ad *placer une annonce* (ahnohⁿs)
  put on sale *solder* (sohldeh)
  put something down *poser* (pohzeh)
  put on *mettre / porter un vêtement* (vehtmahⁿ)

Pyrenees *les Pyrénées* (peerehneh)

Q

quality *une qualité* (kahleeteh)

quantity *une quantité* (kahⁿteeteh)

to **quarrel** *(se) disputer* (deespüteh)

quarter *un quart* (kahr)

queen *une reine* (rehn)

quick; quickly *rapide* (rahpeed); *vite* (veet)

quiet *tranquille* (trahⁿkeel); *paisible*

quite *presque* (prehsk)

to **quote** *citer* (seeteh)

R

race *une course* (koors)

racism *le racisme* (rahseesm)

racist *raciste* (rahseest)

racket *une raquette* (rahkeht)

radiant *rayonnant, -e* (rehyohnahⁿ; -ahⁿt)

railroad *le chemin de fer* (shuhmehⁿ duh fehr)

rain *une pluie* (plwee)

to **rain** *pleuvoir* (pluhwahr)

to **raise** *élever* (ehluhveh); *lever* (luhveh)

raisin *un raisin* (rehzihⁿ) *sec*

rapper *un rapeur; une rapeuse*

rarely *rarement* (rahrmahⁿ)

rate *taux* (toh)

rather *plutôt* (pluhtoh)
  rather than *au lieu de*

ray *un rayon* (rehyohⁿ)

to **reach** *atteindre* (ahtehⁿdr)

to **react** *réagir* (rehahzheer)

to **read** *lire* (leer)

ready *prêt, -e* (preh; preht)

real estate *l'immobilier* (eemohbeelyeh) *(m)*
  real estate agency *une agence* (ahzhahⁿs) *immobilière*

realist *réaliste* (rehahleest)

to **realize** *réaliser* (rehahleezeh)

really *vraiment* (vrehmahⁿ); *vachement (col)*

reason *une raison* (rehzohⁿ)

to **recall** *(se) rappeler* (rahpuhleh)

to **receive** *recevoir* (ruhsuhvwahr)

receipt *un reçu* (ruhsü)

recently *récemment* (rehsahmahⁿ); *dernièrement* (dehrnyehrmahⁿ)

reception desk *une réception* (rehsehpsyohⁿ)

recipe *une recette* (ruhseht)

to **recite; tocite** *réciter* (rehseeteh)

to **recognize** *reconnaître* (ruhkohnehtr)

record *un disque* (deesk)

to **record** *enregistrer* (ahⁿruhzheestreh)

recording studio *un studio d'enregistrement*

red *rouge* (roozh)

redone completely *refait(e) à neuf*

to **reflect** *refléter* (ruhflehteh); *réflecher*

reflection *une réflexion* (rehflehksyohⁿ)

regarding *au sujet de*

region; regional *une région* (rehzhyohⁿ); *régional, -e*

register *une caisse* (kehs)

rehearsal *une répétition* (rehpehteesyohⁿ)

to **rehearse** *répéter* (rehpehteh)

relationship *une relation* (ruhlahsyohⁿ)

relative *une personne de la famille; un parent / une parente*

to **relax** *(se) relaxer* (ruhlahkseh)

to **release** *libérer* (leebehreh); *sortir* (sohrteer); *relâcher*

to **relieve** *soulager* (soolahzheh)

to **remain** *rester* (rehsteh); *demeurer* (duhmuhreh)

to **remember** *se souvenir* (soovuhneer); *se rappeler*

removed *éloigné, -e* (ehlwahnyeh)

rendez–vous *un rendez-vous* (rahⁿdeh voo)

renowned *renommé, -e* (ruhnohmeh)

rent *un loyer* (lwahyeh)

to **rent** *louer* (looeh)
  for rent *à louer*

rental *une location* (lohkahsyohⁿ)

to **repair** *réparer* (rehpahreh)

to **repeat** *répéter* (rehpehteh)

repetition *une répétition* (rehpehteesyohⁿ)

report *un rapport* (rahpohr); *un dossier*

repression *une répression*
(rehprehsyoh[n])
reproach *reprocher* (ruhprohsheh)
research *un recherche*
to **research** *rechercher*
(ruhshehrsheh)
reservation *une réservation*
(rehzehrvahsyoh[n])
to **reserve** *réserver* (rehzehrveh)
to **resonate** *retentir* (ruhtah[n]teer)
respect *un respect* (rehspeh)
respect *respecter* (rehspehkteh)
responsible *responsable*
(rehspoh[n]sahbl)
rest *un repos* (ruhpoh) *(n)*
to **rest** *(se) reposer* (ruhpohzeh)
restaurant *un restaurant*
(rehstohrah[n])
résumé *un curriculum vitae (cv)*
return *un retour* (ruhtoor)
reunion *les retrouvailles*
reversal *l'envers* (m)
review; revision *une révision;*
une critique
rhythm *un rythme* (reetm)
rice *un riz* (ree)
rich *riche* (reesh)
to **rid, get rid of** *se débarrasser*
(dehbahrahseh) *de*
to **ride the bike** *faire de la bicy-*
clette (beeseekleht), *aller à bicy-*
clette; faire du vélo
ridicule *ridicule* (reedeekül)
right (legal) *un droit*
to be right *avoir raison* (ahvwahr
rehzoh[n])
right (direction) *une droite*
(drwaht)
to **ring** *sonner* (sohneh)
ring out *retentir* (ruhtahnteer)
ring *une sonnerie* (sohnree); *une*
bague
ripe *mûr, -e* (mür)
to **rise** *se lever* (luhveh)
river *une rivière* (reevyeer)
road *une route* (root)
to **rob** *voler* (vohleh)
robber *un voleur* (vohluhr)
robust *résistant, -e* (rehzeestah[n];
-ah[n]t)
to **rock** *bercer* (behrseh)
room *une salle* (sahl); *une pièce*
(pyehs)
room *une chambre* (shah[m]br)
rose *une rose* (rohz)
round-trip *un aller-retour*
to (become) *round s'arrondir*
route *un trajet* (trahzheh); *une*
route
rubber boat *un bateau pneuma-*
tique (pnuhmahteek)
rude *impoli, -e* (eh[m]pohlee)
rum *un rhum* (rohm)

to **run** *courir* (kooreer)
run away *s'enfuir* (sah[n]fweer)
runner *un coureur*
to **run (manage)** *diriger*
(deereezheh)
to **rush** *se presser* (prehseh); *se*
précipiter
rush hour *une heure de pointe*
(uhr duh pweh[n]t)

S

sad *triste* (treest)
safe *sûr, -e; en sécurité* (ah[n]
sekuhreeteh)
Sagittarius *un sagittaire*
(sahzheetehr)
salad bowl *un saladier* (sahlahdyeh)
salad *une salade* (sahlahd)
salary *un salaire* (sahlehr)
sale *un solde* (sohld); *une vente*
(vahnt)
salesman / woman *un vendeur,*
-euse (vah[n]duhr; -uhz)
salmon *un saumon* (sohmoh[n])
salt; salty *sel* (sehl); *salé* (sahleh)
same *même* (mehm); *pareil, -eille*
sand *un sable* (sahbl)
Saturday *un samedi* (sahmdee)
to **save** *sauver* (sohveh)
savings account *un compte*
d'épargne
savings bank *la caisse d'é-*
pargne (kehs dehpahrny)
savor *une saveur* (sahvuhr)
to **savor** *déguster*
savory *savoureux, -euse*
saxophone *un saxophone*
(saksohfohn)
to **say** *dire* (deer)
they say that *on dit que*
scale *une balance* (bahlah[n]s)
(to be) scared *avoir peur*
scenario; script *un scénario*
(sehnahryoh)
scene *une scène* (sehn)
schedule *un horaire* (ohrehr)
schedule board *un tableau d'af-*
fichage
school *une école* (ehkohl)
school teacher *un instituteur*
(ihnsteetütuhr); *une institutrice*
(ihnsteetütrees)
school; schoolish *scolaire*
(skohlehr)
grammar school *une école pri-*
maire
Scorpio *un scorpion* (skohrpyoh[n])
screen *un écran* (ehkrah[n])
script *un scénario*
script-writer *un scénariste*
sea *une mer* (mehr)
sea salt *un sel marin* (sehl mahreh[n])

seafood *les fruits de mer; les co-*
quillages (m.pl)
search *un recherche*
to **search** *rechercher* (ruhshehrsheh)
seaside *balnéaire* (bahlnehehr)
(adj)
season *une saison* (sehzohn)
seat *une place* (plahs)
second *second, -e* (suhgoh[n];
-oh[n]d); *une seconde (n); deux-*
ième (adj)
secret *un secret* (suhkreh)
secretary *un / une secrétaire*
(suhkrehtehr)
section *une rubrique* (rübreek)
to **seduce** *séduire* (sehdweer)
seduction *une séduction*
(sehdüksyoh[n])
to **see; to see again** *voir* (vwahr);
revoir (ruhvwahr)
see you (later) *à plus tard* (plü
tahr)
see you(next time) *à la prochaine*
(fois) (prohshehn fwah)
see you in a while *à tout à*
l'heure (toot ah luhr)
see you soon *à bientôt* (byeh[n]toh)
to **seem** *sembler* (sah[m]bleh)
to **seize** *s'emparer* (sah[m]pahreh) *de*
seldom *rarement* (rahrmah[n])
self *le / moi*
selfish *égoïste* (ehgoheest)
to **sell** *vendre* (va[n]dr)
to **send** *envoyer* (ah[n]vwahyeh)
sender *un expéditeur*
Senegal *le Sénégal* (sehnehgahl)
senior high school *un lycée*
(leeseh)
sense *un sens* (sah[ns])
sensitivity *une sensibilité*
(sah[n]seebeeleeteh)
(something) sent *un envoi*
to **separate** *séparer* (sehpahreh)
separation *une séparation*
(sehpahrahsyoh[n])
September *septembre* (sehptahnbr)
series *une série* (sehree); *une suite*
serious *sérieux* (sehryuh); *sérieuse*
(sehryuhz)
to **serve** *servir* (sehrveer)
server *un serveur*
set *un set* (seht)
to **set up** *aménager*
(ahmehnahzheh); *organiser*
set the table *mettre la table*
(mehtr lah tahbl)
setting *un décor* (dehkohr)
to **settle** *(s') installer* (ih[n]stahleh)
seven *sept* (seht)
several *plusieurs* (plüzyuhr)
severe *sévère* (sehvehr)
sewer *un couturier, -ière*
(kootüryeh; -ryehr)

sex *un sexe* (seks)
shadow *une ombre*
to **shake** *secouer* (suhkooeh)
to **share** *partager* (pahrtahzheh)
share *une part* (pahr)
sharp; smarty *futé, -e* (füteh)
she *elle* (ehl)
shelf *une étagère* (ehtahzhehr)
sherbet *un sorbet* (sohrbeh)
to **shine** *briller* (breeyeh)
shirt *une chemise* (shuhmeezh)
shit *(sl) merde* (mehrd)
to **shock** *choquer* (shohkeh)
shoot! *(col) punaise!* (pünehz); *zut!* (züt)
to **shoot** *tirer* (teereh); *tourner (un film)* (toorneh)
shooting camera *une caméra* (kahmehrah)
(to do the) **shopping** *(faire) les courses*
short *court, -e* (koor; -rt)
  short film *un court métrage* (koor mehtrahzh)
shoulder *une épaule* (ehpohl)
to **show** *montrer* (moh^ntreh)
show *un spectacle* (spehktahkl); *une émission*
shower *une douche* (doosh)
to **shower** *se doucher* (doosheh)
  to **shut** *(se) fermer*
shy *timide* (teemeed)
sick *malade* (mahlahd)
side *un bord; un côté*
sidewalk *un trottoir* (trohtwahr)
sight *une vue* (vü)
sign *un signe* (seeny)
to **sign** *signer* (seenyeh)
signal *un signal* (seenyahl)
signature *une signature* (seenyahtür)
silence *un silence* (seelah^ns)
silver *l' argent* (ahrzhah^n) *(m)*
simple *simple* (seh^mpl)
since *puisque* (pweesk); *depuis* (duhpwee)
to **sing** *chanter* (shah^nteh)
singer *un chanteur; une chanteuse* (sha^ntuhr; -euse)
singing *un chant*
sincere *sincère* (sih^nsehr)
single *un / une célibataire* (sehleebahtehr)
to **sink** *couler* (kooleh)
sip *une gorgée* (gohrzheh)
sir *Monsieur* (muhsyuh)
sister *une soeur* (suhr)
to **sit down** *s'asseoir* (sahswahr)
site *un site* (seet)
situation *une situation* (seetüahsyoh^n)
six *six* (sees)
sixteen; sixty *seize* (sehz)

sixty *soixante* (swahsah^nt)
skill *une habileté* (ahbeeluhteh)
skin *une peau* (poh)
sky *un ciel* (syehl)
slave *un / une esclave* (ehsklahv)
slavery *un esclavage* (ehsklahvahzh)
to **sleep** *dormir* (dohrmeer)
slice of bread *une tartine* (tahrteen)
slowly *lentement* (lah^ntmah^n)
small grocery store *une épicerie* (ehpeesree)
small *petit* (puhtee)
to **smell** *sentir* (sah^nteer)
to **smile** *sourire* (sooreer)
smoke *une fumée* (fümeh)
to **smoke** *fumer* (fümeh)
smoker *un fumeur; une fumeuse* (fümuhr; -uhz)
smooth *doux* (doo), *douce* (doos)
smoothly *doucement* (doosmah^n)
snail *un escargot* (ehskahrgoh)
snail broiling party *une cargolade* (kahrgohlahd)
snow *la neige* (nehzh)
to **snow** *neiger* (nehzheh)
so *alors* (ahlohr); *si* (see); *ainsi*
  so much *tellement* (tehlmah^n); *tant* (tah^n)
soap *un savon* (sahvoh^n)
soccer ball *un ballon de foot* (bahloh^n duh foot)
soccer *un football* (footbohl)
soft *doux* (doo), *douce* (doos)
softly *doucement* (doosmah^n)
software *un logiciel* (lohzheesyehl)
soil; agricult. region *un terroir* (tehrwahr); *un sol; une terre*
solitude *une solitude* (sohleetüd)
some *du* (d); *des* (deh); *certain, -e* (sehrteh^n; -eh^n); *quelque*
something *quelque chose*
  something bought *un achat* (ahshah)
sometimes *parfois; quelque-fois*
somewhere *quelque part*
son and daughter *un fils* (fees) *et une fille* (feey)
  son-in-law *un gendre; un beau-fils* (boh fees)
song *une chanson* (shahnsoh^n); *un chant*
songwriter *un compositeur*
soon *bientôt* (byeh^ntoh)
sorrow *une peine* (pehn)
sorry *pardon* (pahrdoh^n); *désolé, -e* (dezohleh)
soul *une âme* (ahm)
sound *un son* (soh^n)
  soundman *un preneur de son* (pruhnuhr du soh^n)
  soundtrack *une bande originale*

soup *une soupe* (soop)
south *le sud* (süd)
to **sow** *semer* (suhmeh)
spa *une station thermale*
spacious *spacieux, -euse* (spahsyuh; -uhz)
Spain *l'Espagne* (ehspahny) *(f)*
Spanish *espagnol, -e* (ehspahnyohl)
speak to **parler** (pahrleh) *à*
speak about *parler* (pahrleh) *de*
speciality *une spécialité* (spehsyahleeteh)
specialized *spécialisé, -e* (spehsyahleezeh)
speed *une vitesse* (veetehs)
spell *un sort*
spelling *une orthographe*
spice *une épice* (ehpees)
spicy / spiced up *épicé, -e* (ehpeeseh)
spirit *un esprit* (espree)
spiritual *spirituel, -elle* (speereetüehl)
spoon *une cuillère à soupe* (kweeyehr ah soop)
  teaspoon *une cuillère à café* (kahfeh)
sport; to do sport *un sport* (spohr); *faire du sport*
spring *un printemps* (preh^ntah^m)
stage *une scène*
stained glass window *un vitrail* (veetrahy)
stairway *un escalier* (ehskahlyeh)
stall; stand *un stand* (stah^nd)
stallholder *un marchand; une marchande* (mahrshah^n; -shah^nd)
stamp *un timbre* (teh^mbr)
  stamp booklet *un carnet* (kahrneh) *de timbres*
to **stand up** *être debout* (duhboo)
star *une étoile* (ehtwahl)
to **start** *démarrer* (dehmahreh); *débuter, commencer*
  start doing *se mettre à faire* (suh mehtr ah fehr)
  it's starting well *ça promet*
  start of school year *une rentrée* (rah^ntreh)
to **start again** *redémarrer*
state of being civil *une laïcité* (laheeseeteh)
state *un état* (ehtah)
station *une gare* (gahr)
station terminal *un hall de gare*
statue *une statue* (stahtü)
status *un statut* (stahtü)
stay *un séjour* (sehzhoor)
to **stay** *rester* (rehsteh)
stem *un pied* (pyeh); *une queue* (kuh)
step *un pas* (pah)
  step-by-step *pas à pas*

step-family *une belle-famille* (behl fahmeey)
to **stew** *mijoter* (meezhohteh)
steward *un steward* (steewahrd)
to **stick up** *coller*
sticky *collant, -e*
still *encore* (ahnkohr)
stock exchange *une bourse* (boors)
stomach *un ventre* (vah^ntr)
stone *un caillou* (kahyoo)
stop *une escale* (ehskahl)*; un arrêt* (ahreh)
to **stop** *(s')arrêter* (ahrehteh)
store *un magasin* (mahgahzeh^n)*; une boutique*
store window *une vitrine* (veetreen)
story *une histoire* (eestwahr)
strange, odd *bizarre* (beezahr)
strawberry *une fraise* (frehz)
street *une rue* (rü)
strength *une force* (fohrs)
stressed out *stressé, -e* (strehseh)
to **stretch** *tendre* (tah^ndr)
strike; on strike *une grève* (grehv)*; en grève*
strong *fort, -e* (fohr; -rt)*; résistant, -e* (rehzeestah^n; -ah^t)
stubborn *têtu, -e* (tehtü)
student *un étudiant, -e* (ehtüdyah^n; -ah^t)
studio *un studio* (stüdyoh)
studious *(col) bûcheur, -euse* (büshuhz)
to **study** *étudier* (ehtüdyeh)*; bûcher (col)*
study *une étude* (ehtüd)
stupid; goofy *idiot, -e* (eedyoh; -oht)
stupidity; stupid thing *une bêtise* (behteez)
subject *un sujet* (süzheh)
subtitled *sous-titré, -e* (sooteetreh)
suburb *une banlieue* (bah^lyuh)
subway *un métro* (mehtroh)
subway station *une station* (stahsyoh^n) *de métro*
to **succeed** *réussir* (rehüseer)
success *un succès* (sükseh)
such; such as *tel* (tehl)*; tel que*
suddenly *soudain* (soodih^n)
suede *le daim* (deh^n)
to **suffer** *souffrir* (soofreer)
suffering *une souffrance* (soofrah^s)
sugar *un sucre* (sücre)
sugar cane *une canne à sucre* (kahn ah sükr)
suit *un ensemble* (ah^sah^mbl)*; un costume*
suitcase *une valise* (vahleez)
to **sulk** *bouder*
summer *un été*
sun *un soleil* (sohlehy)

Sunday *un dimanche* (deemah^sh)
superior *supérieur, -e* (süpehryuhr)
supermarket *un supermarché* (süpehrmahrsheh)
superstitious *supersticieux, -euse* (süpehrsteesyuh; -uhz)
to **support; to bear** *supporter* (süpohrteh)
to **suppose** *supposer* (spohzeh)
sure *sûr,-e* (sür)
surely *sûrement* (sürmah^n)
surprise *une surprise* (sürpreez)
to **surprise** *surprendre* (sürprah^dr)*; étonner*
to **surround** *entourer* (ahntooreh)
to **survive** *survivre* (sürveevr)
sweet potato *une patate douce* (pahtaht doos)
sweet *doux* (doo)*, douce* (doos)
to **swim** *nager* (nahzheh)

T

table *une table* (tahbl)
  table mat *un dessous de plat* (duhsoo duh plah)
tag-off *dégriffé, -e* (dehgreefeh)
to **take** *prendre* (prah^dr)
  take advantage of *profiter de* (prohfeeteh)
  take an order *prendre une commande* (kohmah^d)
  take away / take with (you) *emporter*
  take part in *participer à* (pahrteeseepeh)
  take to *mener à*
talented *talentueux, -euse* (tahlah^tüüh; -uhz)
to **talk to** *parler* (pahrleh) *à*
talkative *bavard,-e* (bahvahr;-ahrd)
tall *grand, -e* (grah^; grah^d)
taste *un goût* (goo)
  to taste *goûter* (gooteh)*; déguster* (dehgüsteh)
tasty *savoureux, -euse* (savvooruh; -uhz)
Taurus *un taureau* (tohroh)
taxi *un taxi* (tahksee)
tea; a cup of tea *un thé* (teh)*; une tasse de thé*
to **teach** *enseigner* (ah^sehnyeh)*; apprendre* (ahprah^dr)
teacher *un professeur* (prohfehsuhr)
team *une équipe* (ehkeep)
to **tear down** *déchirer* (dehsheereh)
telephone *un téléphone* (tehlehfohn)
television *une télévision* (tehlehveezyoh^n)
to **tell** *dire* (deer) *à; raconter*
  tell the time *dire l'heure* (deer luhr)

temperature *une température* (tah^pehrahtür)
tempest *une tempête* (tah^peht)
to **tempt** *tenter* (tah^teh)
temptation *une tentation* (tahntahsyohn)
ten *dix* (dis)
  ten or so *une dizaine* (deezehn)
tenant *un / une locataire* (lohkatehr)
tennis court *un court de tennis* (koor duh tehnees)
tennis *le tennis* (tehnees)
tense *tendu, -e* (tahndü)
tension *une tension* (tah^syoh^n)
term *un terme* (tehrm)
terrace *une terrasse* (tehrahs)
test *un examen* (ehgzahmeh^n)
to **thank** *remercier* (ruhmehrsyeh)
  thank you *merci* (mehrsee)
  thanks to *grâce à* (grahs ah)
that *que, qui*
that; this *c', ce, cette, ces, cet (dem adj)*
  that, this *ceci* (suhsee), *cela* (suhlah)
  that one; this one *celle-là, celui-là, ceux-là, celles-là, celle-ci, celui-ci, ceux-ci, celles-ci*
  that is *c'est-à-dire*
  this is it *ça y est*
the *la, le , les, l'*
theater *un théâtre* (tehahtr)
their *leur* (luhr)*; leur*
them *eux* (uh)*; les* (leh)*; elles; leur*
then *puis* (pwee)*; ensuite* (ah^sweet)*; alors* (ahlohr)
there *voilà* (vwahlah)*; là; là-bas* (lah bah)
therefore *donc* (doh^k)
they *ils* (eel)*; elles* (ehl)
thick *épais, -sse* (ehpeh; -ehs)
thief *un voleur; une voleuse* (vohluhr; -luhz)
thigh *une cuisse* (kwees)
thing *une chose* (shoz)*; une affaire* (ahfehr)
to **think (of)** *penser* (pah^seh)*; réfléchir*
thirteen *treize* (trehz)
thirty *trente* (trah^t)
thirst; to be thirsty *une soif* (swahf)*; avoir soif*
thought *une pensée; une réflexion*
thousand *mille* (meel)
three *trois* (trwah)
through *par* (pahr)
throw *jeter* (zhuhteh)*; balancer (col)*
Thursday *un jeudi* (zhuhdee)
tidiness *un ordre* (ohrdr)
thus *ainsi* (eh^see)*; donc* (doh^k)

ticket *un billet* (beeyeh); *une place* (plahs); *un ticket* (teekeh) *de métro* (mehtroh)

tidy *ordonné, -e* (ohrdohneh)

tiered cake *une pièce montée*

time *une fois* (fwah); *le temps; une heure*
  on time *à l'heure* (ah luhr)
  in time *à temps*

tip *un pourboire* (poorbwahr)

tire *un pneu* (pnuh)

to **tire** *fatiguer* (fahteegeh)

tired *fatigué, -e* (fahteegeh)

tiring *fatigant, -e*

title *un titre* (teetr)

to *à* (ah); *en* (ah^n)

to the *au; à la; chez*

tobacco *un tabac* (tahbah)

today *aujourd'hui* (ohzhohrdwee)

together *ensemble* (ah^nsah^mbl)

toilets *les toilettes* (twahleht); *les w.c.*

tomato *une tomate* (tohmaht)

tomorrow *demain* (duhmeh^n)

tongue *une langue* (lah^ng)

tonight *ce soir* (suh swahr)

too *trop* (troh); *aussi* (ohsee)
  too bad *tant pis* (tah^n pee)
  too much; too many *trop; trop de*
  to be too much *y aller fort*

tool *un outil* (ootee)

tooth *une dent* (dah^n)

to **touch** *toucher* (toosheh)

tour *une tournée* (toorneh)

tourism *un tourisme* (tooreesm)

tower *une tour* (toor)

town *une ville* (veel)

town hall *une mairie* (mehree); *une hôtel de ville*

track (bicycle) *une piste (cyclable)* (peest seeklahbl)

track (music) *un morceau*

trade *un commerce*

tradition *une tradition* (trahdeesyoh^n)

traffic *un trafic* (trahfeek); *une circulation*

traffic jam *un bouchon* (col)

tragedy *une tragédie* (trahzhehdee)

train *un train* (treh^n)

to **train** *(s')entraîner* (ahntrehneh)

trainer *un entraîneur* (ahntrehnuhr)

training *un entraînement*

to **translate** *traduire* (trahdweer)

translation *une traduction* (trahdüksyoh^n)

transportation *un transport* (trah^nspohr)

to **travel** *voyager* (vwahyahzheh)
  to *treat inviter* (ihnveeteh); *gâter* (ghateh)

treat *un régal* (rehgahl)

tree *un arbre* (ahrbr)

trendy *branché, -e* (brah^nsheh)

tribute *un hommage* (ohmahzh)

trip *un voyage* (vwahyahzh)

trouble *un problème* (problehm)

true *vrai, -e* (vreh)

truly *vraiment* (vrehmah^n)

trust *une confiance* (kohnfyah^s)

to **trust** *faire confiance*

truth *une vérité* (vehreeteh)

to **try** *essayer* (ehsehyeh); *tenter*

try *un essai* (ehseh)

Tuesday *un mardi* (mahrdee)

tune *une musique* (müzeek); *un air* (ehr)

to **turn** *tourner* (toorneh)
  turn on *allumer* (ahlümeh); *ouvrir*
  turn off *éteindre* (ehteh^ndr)

twenty *vingt* (veh^n)

twice *deux fois* (duh fwah)

two *deux* (duh)

to **type** *taper* (tahpeh)

U

unbearable *insupportable* (ihnsüpohrtahbl)

uncle *un oncle* (oh^nkl)

unconscious *inconscient, -e*

unconsciousness *un inconscience*

under *dessous* (duhsoo)

under *sous* (soo)

underneath *en dessous de* (ah^n duhsoo duh)

to **understand** *comprendre* (koh^mprah^ndr)

understood *compris, -e* (koh^mpree; -prees)

undoubtedly *sans aucun doute*

to **undress** *(se) déshabiller* (dehzahbeeyeh)

unemployment *le chômage* (shohmahzh)

unforgettable *inoubliable* (eenoobleeyabl)

unfortunately *malheureusement* (maluhruhzmah^n)

the United States *les États-Unis* (ehtahz ünee)

universal *universel, -elle* (üneevehrsehl)

university; college *une université* (üneevehrseeteh); *une faculté*

unknown *inconnu, -e* (eh^nkohnü)

unless *à moins que* (ah mweh^n kuh); *sauf si*

unlike *contrairement* (koh^ntrehrmah^n)

unlucky *malchanceux, -euse* (mahlshah^suh; -uhz)

unpleasant *désagréable* (dehzahgrehahbl)

untidy; messy *désordonné, -e* (dehzohrdohneh)

until *jusqu'à* (zhüskah)

up there *là-haut* (lah oh)

up to *jusqu'à* (zhüskah)

up to date *mis à jour* (meez ah zhoor)

to **upset** *faire de la peine* (fehr duh lah pehn) *à*

upset *en colère* (ah^n kohlehr); *vexé, -e*

upside–down *à l'envers* (ah lah^nvehr)

upstairs *en haut* (ah^n oh)

urgent *urgent, -e* (ürzhah^n; -ah^t)

us *nous* (noo)

to **use** *utiliser* (üteeleezeh)
  used to *habitué, -e* (ahbeetüeh)

V

vacation *des vacances* (vahkahns)

vain; in vain *vain* (veh^n); *en vain*

value *une valeur* (vahluhr)

vanilla *une vanille* (vahneey)

variety *une variété* (vahryehteh)

various *divers* (deevehr)

vegetable *un légume* (lehgüm)

ventilation *une aération* (ahehrahsyoh^n)

very *très* (treh)

vexed *vexé, -e* (vehkseh)

VCR *un magnétoscope* (mahnyehtohskohp)

view *une vue* (vü)

vine *une vigne* (veeny)

vineyard *un vignoble* (veenyobl)

violence *une violence* (vyohlah^s)

violent *violent, -e*

virgin *vierge* (vyehrzh)

Virgo *une vierge*

vision *une vision* (veezyoh^n)

visit *une visite* (veezeet)

to **visit (a person)** *rendre visite à* (rah^ndr veezeet ah)

to **visit (a place)** *visiter* (veezeeteh)

voice *une voix* (vwah)

voice mail *une messagerie vocale* (mehsahzhree vohkahl)

to **vote; a vote** *voter* (vohteh); *un vote* (voht)

W

waffle *une gaufre* (gohfr)

wage *un salaire* (sahlehr)

wagon *un wagon* (vahgoh^n)

wait *une attente*

to **wait for** *attendre* (ahtah^ndr)
  wait on *servir* (sehrveer)
  I can't wait for . . . *Vivement . . .*

waiter, waitress *un serveur, -veuse* (sehrvuhr; -uhz)
  Waiter! *Garçon!*

to **wake up** se réveiller (rehvehyeh)
Wake up! Secoue-toi!
walk une promenade
(prohmuhnahd)
to **walk** marcher (mahrsheh)
wall un mur (mür)
wallet un porte-monnaie (pohrt
mohneh)
to **want** vouloir (voolwahr)
war une guerre (gehr)
warm chaud, -e (shoh; -ohd)
warm-hearted chaleureux, -euse
(shahluhruh; -uhz)
to **warm up** s'échauffer
(sehshohfeh)
to **warn** prévenir (prehvuhneer);
avertir
warning un avertissement
to **wash (up)** (se) laver (lahveh);
faire sa toilette
watch une montre (mohⁿtr)
to **watch** regarder (ruhgahrdeh)
water une eau (oh)
some water de l'eau
to **water** arroser (ahrohzeh)
wave une vague (vahg)
way une manière (mahnyehr); un
chemin (shuhmehⁿ); un façon;
un moyen
that's the way it is c'est comme
ça
by the way tiens; au fait
we nous (noo)
weak faible (fehbl)
to **wear** porter (pohrteh) (un vêtement)
to **wear out** fatiguer (fahteegeh)
weather un temps (tahᵐ)
the weather is bad il fait mauvais (feh mohveh)
weather report une météo
(mehtehoh)
wedding un mariage (mahryahzh)
Wednesday un mercredi
(mehrkruhdee)
week une semaine (suhmehn)
weekend un week-end
(weekehnd)
weekly hebdomadaire
(ehbdohmahdehr)
weird bizarre (beezahr)
weight un poids (pwah)
welcome (la) bienvenue
(byehⁿvuhnü)
to **welcome** souhaiter la bienvenue
well bien (adv); eh bien (eh byehⁿ)
well-built, well-made bien
roulé, -e (byehⁿrooleh) (col)

well-known connu, -e (kohnü);
célèbre
west l'ouest (wehst) (m)
West Indies les Antilles (ahⁿteey)
wet mouillé, -e (mooyeh)
what quel, quels...; ce que, ce
qui...; ce dont
what? quoi?
whatever quel que soit; qu'importe (kehⁿpohrt)
wheel (car) un volant (vohlahⁿ)
when quand (kahn), lorsque
(lohrsk)
where où (oo)
whereas tandis (tahⁿdee) que,
alors que
whether si (see)
which laquelle, lequel, lesquelles
(lehkehl); quel(s), quelles(s)
while pendant que (pahⁿdahⁿ kuh)
whim un caprice (kahprees)
to **whisper** chuchoter (shüshohteh)
whistle un (coup de) sifflet (seefleh)
to **whistle** siffler (seefleh)
white blanc (blahⁿ), blanche
(blahⁿsh)
white (wine) un (vin) blanc
who qui (kee)
whole entier (ahⁿtyeh)
whom qui (kee); que (kuh)
whose à qui (ah kee); dont (dohⁿ)
why pourquoi (poorqwah)
wide large (lahrzh)
wife une femme (fahm)
will power une volonté
(vohlohⁿteh)
willow un saule (sohl)
to **win** gagner (gahnyeh)
wind un vent (vahⁿ)
window une vitrine (veetreen); un
guichet (geesheh); une fenêtre
(fuhnehtr)
wine un vin (vihⁿ)
wing une aile (ehl)
winner un gagnant, -e (gahnyahⁿ;
-ahⁿt)
winter un hiver (eevehr)
in winter en hiver
wireless sans fil
wisdom une sagesse (sahzhehs)
wise sage (sahzh)
wish un voeu (vuh) (sing / pl); un
souhait (sweh)
to **wish** souhaiter (swehteh)
with avec (ahvehk)
with pleasure volontiers
(vohlohⁿtyeh)
to **withdraw** retirer (ruhteereh)
without sans (sahⁿ)

witty spirituel, -elle (speereetüehl)
witness un témoin (tehmweⁿ)
woman une femme (fahm)
to **wonder** se demander
wonderful merveilleux, -euse
(mehrvehyuh;-uhz)
wood un bois (bwah)
word un mot (moh)
words (lyrics) les paroles (f.pl.)
to **work** travailler (trahvahyeh);
marcher (mahrsheh)
work un travail; un boufot (col)
master work une oeuvre (uhvr)
workshop un atelier
world un monde (mohⁿd)
to **worry** s'inquiéter (sihⁿkyehteh)
worse pire (peer)
worse and worse de pire en
pire
wound une blessure (blehsür)
to **wrap** emballer (ahᵐbahleh)
wrapped-up emballé, -e
(ahᵐbahleh)
to **write** écrire (ehkreer)
writer un écrivain (ehkreeveⁿ)
wrong faux (foh), fausse (fohs)
to be wrong avoir tort (tohr)
wrong number un faux numéro
(foh nümehroh)

Y

year un an, une année (ahⁿ, ahneh)
year off une année sabatique
yearly annuel; annuelle
yellow jaune (zhohn)
yes oui (wee); si (see)
yesterday hier (eeyehr)
yet encore (ahⁿkohr); pourtant
(poortahⁿ)
you vous (voo), tu (tü); vous, te
(tuh), t' (obj. pron)
young jeune (zhuhn)
young lady une demoiselle
(duhmwahzehl)
your ta (tah), ton (tohⁿ), tes (teh);
votre (vohtr), vos (voh)
yours le tien (tyehⁿ), la tienne
(tyehn) . . . le vôtre (vohtr), les
vôtres . . .
yourself toi-même (twah mehm),
vous-même
youth une jeunesse (zhuhnehs)

Z

zero un zéro (zehroh)
zest un zeste (zehst)
Zip code code postal (pohstahl)

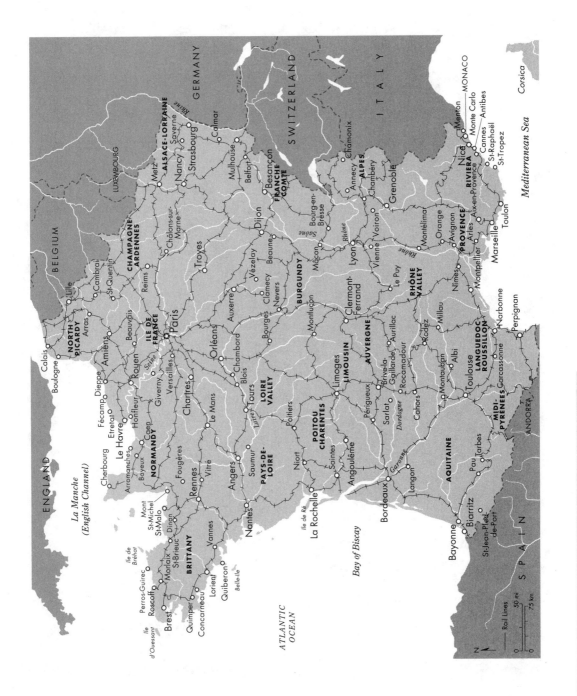

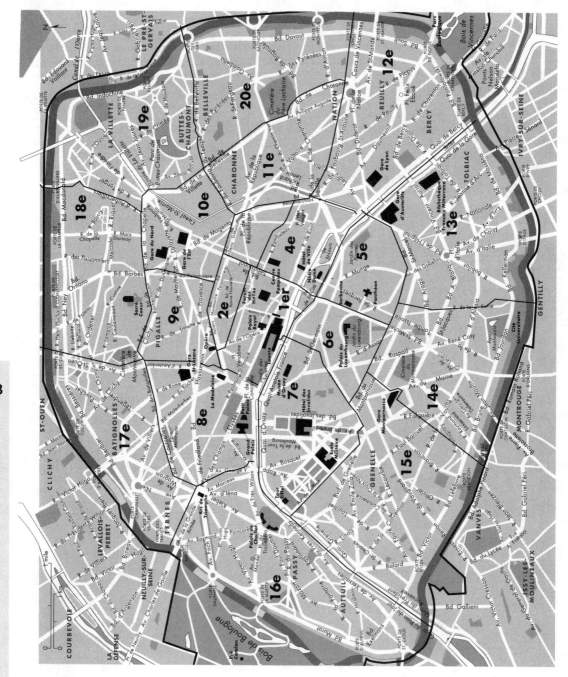

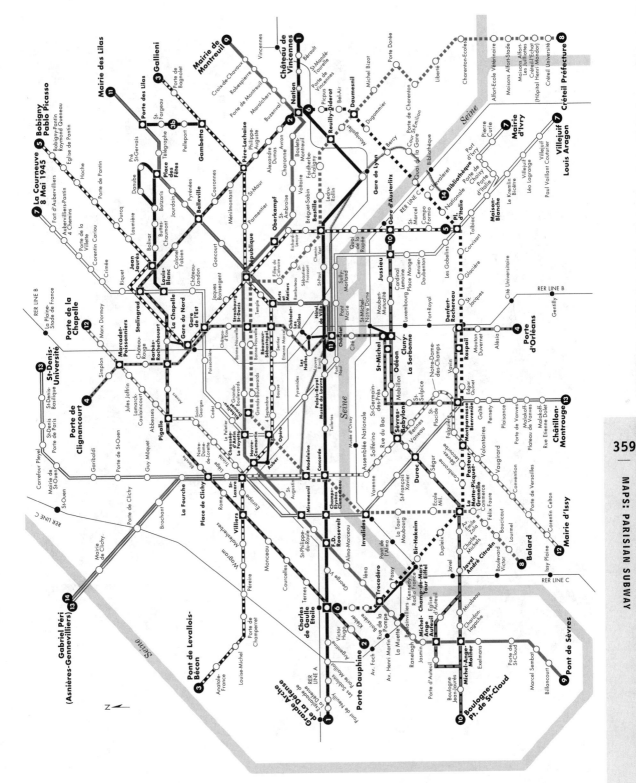

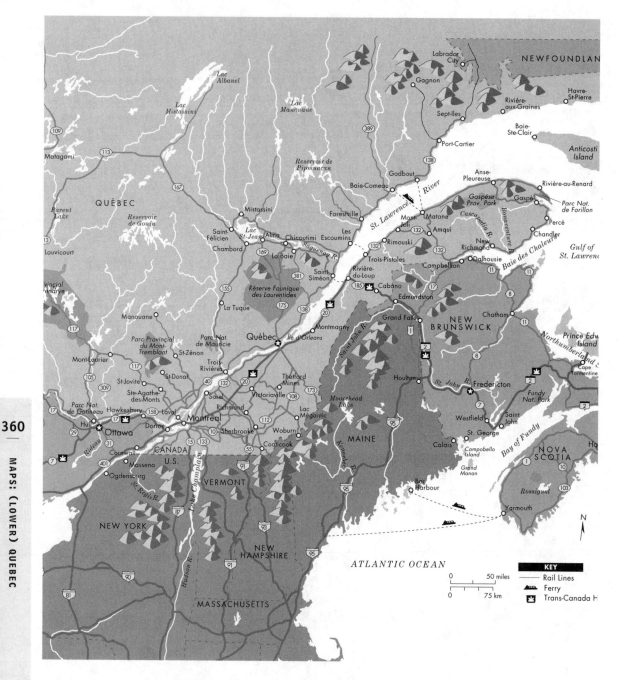

NEWFOUNDLAN

Labrador
City

Gagnon

Rivière-
aux-Graines

Havre-
St-Pierre

Sept-Iles

Baie-
Ste-Clair

Anticosti
Island

Port-Cartier

Lac
Albanel

Lac
Mistassini

Lac
Manouane

Reservoir de
Pipmuacan

138

Godbout

Anse-
Pleureuse

Rivière-au-Renard

109

Baie-Comeau

St. Lawrence

River

Gaspésie
Prov. Park

Gaspé

Parc Nat.
de Forillon

113

389

Forestville

Mont-
Joli

Matane

Percé

167

QUÉBEC

Mistassini

Les
Escoumins

132

Amqui

132

Chandler

Matagami

Parent
Lake

Reservoir
de Gouin

Saint-
Félicien

Lac
St-Jean

Alma

Chicoutimi

Rimouski

132

New
Richmond

Baie des Chaleurs

Gulf of
St. Lawrer

Chambord

169

La Baie

Saguenay R.

Trois-Pistoles

Campbellton

Dalhousie

13

381

Saint-
Siméon

Rivière-
du-Loup

17

11

8

Louvicourt

Réserve Faunique
des Laurentides

155

185

Cabano

NEW
BRUNSWICK

Chatham

11

Prince Edw
Island

'incial
'andrye

117

Manouane

La Tuque

175

138

Edmundston

Northumberland S

Mont-Laurier

Parc Provincial
du Mont-
Tremblant

Parc Nat.
de Mauricie

20

Montmagny

Grand Falls

2

Cape
Tormentine

117

St-Zénon

Québec

Ile d'Orleans

Houlton

St. John R.

Fredericton

Fundy
Nat. Park

2

105

St-Jovite

St-Donat

Trois-
Rivières

132

Thetford
Mines

173

Moosehead
Lake

95

7

309

Ste-Agathe-
des-Monts

40

20

108

8

2

17

Parc Nat.
de Gatineau

158

Laval

Richmond

112

Lac
Mégantic

MAINE

Westfield

Saint
John

Bay of Fundy

NOVA
SCOTIA

Ha

Hawkesbury

Dorion

Montréal

St. George

117

29

Hull

Ottawa

10

Sherbrooke

Woburn

Calais

Campobello
Island

1

10

Rideau

31

15

133

Coaticook

55

Grand
Manan

Rossignol

103

7

401

Cornwall

CANADA
U.S.

91

Kennebec R.

Bar
Harbour

Yarmouth

Massena

Ogdensburg

St. Regis R.

VERMONT

95

87

Lake Champlain

93

NEW YORK

NEW
HAMPSHIRE

95

ATLANTIC OCEAN

90

91

Hudson R.

81

MASSACHUSETTS

N

KEY

0   50 miles

——— Rail Lines

Ferry

0   75 km

Trans-Canada H

INDEX

smoking, 31–32

songs, 4, 24, 128, 162, 172, 250, 252, 262

sortir, 239, 240, 241

spelling-change verbs, 135, 151, 234, 277–278

stressed pronouns, 51–52, 293

subject, 6–7, 293, 318

subjunctive, 299–310

subway, 153, 156–157

suffix, 318

superlative, 230–233, 311, 318

Tati, Jacques, 40

Tavernier, Bertrand, 206

taxes, 92

Téchiné, André, 272

telephone, 128, 135, 136, 138, 141

Téléphone, 128

television, 196

tenir, 117, 186, 218–219, 255, 309

tense (verbs), 318. *See also* entries for individual tenses

theater, 228, 236–237, 239, 243

time, 78–80, 208–210, 295–296

train, 206, 214–216

travel, 29–30, 35, 206, 208, 214–216, 272–274, 279–280, 313

Truffaut, François, 58, 92

United Kingdom, 285

United States, 5

valoir, 265, 310

vendre, 95–96, 164–165

venir, 117, 122, 186, 218–219, 255, 310

verbs, 318. *See also* entries for individual verbs

  conditional, 299–310

  -er, 27–28, 132–133, 184, 233–234, 277–278, 296–297

  future, 45, 233–235, 241, 243, 253–256, 264, 276, 296, 297, 299–310

  immediate past, 122

  imperative, 184–189, 190–191, 211, 219, 241, 242, 264, 275–276, 297, 299–310

  imperfect, 276–279, 299–310

  infinitive, 299–310, 318

  -ir, 69–70, 154, 185, 234, 278, 297

  irregular, 7–8, 15, 33–34, 43–45, 67–69, 81–82, 95–96, 116–118, 122, 139–140, 147–148, 155, 164–166, 174–175, 185–188, 211, 218–219, 235, 239–243, 245, 253–254, 255–256, 263–264, 265, 274–276, 278–279, 299–310

  passé composé, 131–134, 139–140, 154–156, 164–166, 175, 191, 199, 211, 218–219, 240–241, 242, 245, 263, 265, 275, 296, 297

  past participle, 131, 134, 318

  present, 7–8, 15, 27–28, 33–34, 43–45, 67–70, 81–82, 95–96, 116–118, 135, 147–148, 151, 174–175, 211, 239–240, 242, 263–264, 265, 274–275, 296, 297, 299–310

  present participle, 299–310

  -re, 95–96, 164–165, 234–235, 254

reflexive, 196–199, 318

spelling change, 135, 151, 234, 277–278

subjunctive, 299–310

Verlaine, Paul, 222

voir, 33–34, 155, 187, 253, 310

vouloir, 43, 155, 253

vowels, xx–xxiii

weather, 213

Web sites, 167, 194, 196, 222

wine, 119, 121, 123, 124

word order, 113–114, 115–116, 131–132, 148, 150, 190–191, 198–199, 298

word stress, xxvii

work, 83

work week, 77

y, 190–191

Zola, Émile, 92

Zonka, Erik, 76